Grainger on Music

Grainger on Music

Edited by

MALCOLM GILLIES and BRUCE CLUNIES ROSS

with

Bronwen Arthur and David Pear

OXFORD

UNIVERSITY PRESS

OXFORD
UNIVERSITY PRESS

Great Clarendon Street, Oxford OX2 6DP
Oxford University Press is a department of the University of Oxford.
It furthers the University's objective of excellence in research, scholarship,
and education by publishing worldwide in
Oxford New York

Athens Auckland Bangkok Bogotá Buenos Aires Calcutta
Cape Town Chennai Dar es Salaam Delhi Florence Hong Kong Istanbul
Karachi Kuala Lumpur Madrid Melbourne Mexico City Mumbai
Nairobi Paris São Paulo Singapore Taipei Tokyo Toronto Warsaw
and associated companies in Berlin Ibadan

Published in the United States
by Oxford University Press Inc., New York

British Library Cataloguing in Publication Data
Data available

Library of Congress Cataloging in Publication Data
Grainger, Percy, 1882–1961.
[Essays. Selections]
Grainger on music / edited by Malcolm Gillies and Bruce Clunies
Ross; with Bronwen Arthur and David Pear.
p.   cm.
List of Grainger's writing: p.
Includes index.
1. Music—History and criticism. I. Gillies, Malcolm.
II. Clunies Ross, Bruce. III. Title
ML60.G74 1999 780—dc21   98-45828
ISBN 0-19-816665-6

1 3 5 7 9 10 8 6 4 2

Typeset in Adobe Stempel Garamond
by Best-set Typesetter Ltd., Hong Kong
Printed in Great Britain
on acid-free paper by
Biddles Ltd.,
Guildford & King's Lynn

Acknowledgements

For permission to reproduce Grainger's essays we acknowledge the kind agency of Stewart Manville (White Plains, New York) representing the Estate of Percy Grainger. Oxford University Press has granted permission for the reprinting of Grainger's three articles which appeared in the *Music Quarterly* (Essays 6, 29, and 37).

The texts of most essays found in this volume have been prepared from materials held in the Grainger Museum at The University of Melbourne, Australia. We are grateful to the Baillieu Librarian and successive curators at the Grainger Museum for granting us access to archival holdings. Kay Dreyfus and the late Rosemary Florrimell generously offered their advice and research support, as, at various times, did Janice Whiteside, Helen Reeves Lawrence, and Alessandro Servadei.

This project received financial assistance from the Danish Humanities Research Council, the English Department and Humanities Faculty at The University of Copenhagen and, in 1994–5, the Australian Research Council. We express our debt to Bronwen Arthur, who was employed at The University of Queensland as an ARC research assistant and greatly assisted in the preparation of texts and the compilation of information for annotations. To David Pear, we are indebted for specialist advice, assistance with the Chronology, indexing, and preparation of the Appendix, the first comprehensive List of Grainger's Writings.

We are also grateful to the following for assistance: Michael Atkinson, Teresa Balough, John Bird, Colin Brumby, Sidsel Brun (granddaughter of Grainger's agent in Trondheim), the late Burnett Cross, Jennifer Hill, Paul Kildea, Neil Lovett, Sandra McColl, Andrew McCredie, Margit Müller, Kathleen Nelson, the late K. K. Nygaard, Simon Perry, Svend Ravnkilde (Danish Music Information Centre), Ronald Stevenson, the late Johannes Tang Kristensen, Penelope Thwaites, David Walker, and colleagues from The University of Copenhagen, including Ilda Hallas-Møller (Finnish Library), Lene Østermark-Johansen, Dennis Omø (English Department Library), Chris. Sanders (Arnemagnaean Institute) and Gunnar Syréhn (Institute for Nordic Philology).

M. G.
B. C. R.

Contents

Chronology

MALCOLM GILLIES AND DAVID PEAR

1882   Born George Percy Grainger in Brighton (near Melbourne), Australia, 8 July.

c.1886   Starts formal education, at home.

c.1888   Commences piano lessons with his mother.

1890   His parents separate.

c.1891   Starts to study acting, painting, and drawing.

c.1892   Commences piano study with Louis Pabst in Melbourne (to 1894); first reads Icelandic sagas.

1894   First appears in public as a pianist. His parents seek support for him to study abroad.

1895   Commences studies at the Hoch Conservatory in Frankfurt-am-Main, with James Kwast (piano) and Iwan Knorr (composition, theory); studies composition informally with Karl Klimsch; develops over following years deep friendships with British students Henry Balfour Gardiner, Roger Quilter, and Cyril Scott, and the Dane Herman Sandby.

1897   First reads Kipling works.

1898   Begins his Kipling settings (on which he continued to work until 1958).

1899   First reads Whitman's poems; starts to teach piano. His mother's health declines.

1900   Visits France, Britain, and Holland with his parents; presents first public solo recital in Frankfurt.

1901   Moves with his mother to London, where he appears in many 'society' concerts as accompanist or assistant artist; commences his *Marching Song of Democracy*, inspired by Whitman.

1902   Undertakes first regional tours in Britain; gains his first concerto appearances, in Bath; makes initial arrangement of *Irish Tune from County Derry*; completes first setting of *Hill-Song* No. 1.

1903   Studies with Busoni in Berlin; undertakes extended concert tour of Australasia and South Africa with the contralto Ada Crossley (to May 1904).

1904   Tours Denmark with Sandby; meets Karen Holten (later Kellermann), his girlfriend until 1913.

1905   Starts serious collection and arrangement of English folk music; gains more concerto engagements, but most concert appearances are still as associate artist.

1906   Forges friendship with Grieg; first uses the phonograph to record folk-songs; composes *Brigg Fair* setting.

1907   First meets Delius; visits the Griegs in Norway; presents memorial performances of Grieg's piano concerto in Britain and Denmark; first sets *Molly on the Shore.*

1908   Publishes major article about the use of the phonograph in folk-music collection; makes first gramophone records; departs on second Australasian tour with Crossley (to May 1909).

1909   Is greatly influenced by Polynesian and Maori culture while in New Zealand; begins to present his compositions in public; completes *Father and Daughter* setting of Faeroe Islanders' music.

1910   Establishes himself as a solo recitalist and orchestral soloist, averaging about one hundred concerts per year, to 1914, the majority in continental Europe. *Mock Morris* and *Molly on the Shore* are premièred, in Copenhagen.

1911   Changes his professional name to Percy Aldridge Grainger. Schott (London) starts to publish his compositions.

1912   Hears many of his works performed at the first Balfour Gardiner concert series, in London; holds first public concert solely of his own works; starts regularly to write articles for publication; suffers minor nervous breakdown during German concert tour; completes *Handel in the Strand.*

1913   Participates in second Gardiner series; is briefly engaged to his piano student Margot Harrison; starts to compose his 'imaginary ballet' music, *The Warriors.*

1914   Postpones or cancels concert engagements when war is declared, August; soon sails to the United States, ostensibly out of regard for his mother's health; contracts with New York music publisher G. Schirmer; first appears in New York, playing the piano part in *Shepherd's Hey.*

1915   Scores a stunning success with his début recital and concerto performance in New York; contracts with Duo-Art Company to make piano rolls (to 1933); undertakes first American tour.

1916   Collaborates with Melba in recitals in support of the Allied war effort; completes *The Warriors*, dedicated to Delius. Première of *In a Nutshell* suite.

1917   Enlists in a US Army band playing oboe and soprano saxophone; makes first gramophone recordings with Columbia (to 1931); starts relationship with Mrs Lotta Mills Hough (to 1922). *The Warriors* and *Marching Song of Democracy* are premièred. Grainger's father dies, in Melbourne.

1918   Expects to be sent with the band to France and makes many recordings of unfinished works; is, instead, appointed an Army band music instructor and remains in America; assumes US citizenship; completes his most famous piece, *Country Gardens*.

1919   Is discharged from the US Army; first teaches at the Chicago Musical College (intermittently, in summers, to 1931); completes *Children's March*, for band.

1920   Undertakes long concert tours of the American Far West and Cuba; makes first attempts at 'elastic scoring' with an arrangement of his *Irish Tune*; increasing interest in questions of racial identity.

1921   Moves with his mother to their final home, 7 Cromwell Place, White Plains, New York; rescores a number of his early works.

1922   His mother's mental state deteriorates, and she commits suicide in April; he cancels most performing engagements, and sails for Europe, where he collects folk music with Evald Tang Kristensen in Jutland.

1923   Lives for six months in Frankfurt, where he assists Delius; arranges production of a memorial volume to his mother; collects folk music again in Jutland. Publication of his *Guide to Virtuosity*.

1924   Arranges concerts in Carnegie Hall, New York, in memory of his mother and in honour of Delius; sails via Polynesia to Australia, where he visits relatives and presents recitals; adopts vegetarianism.

1925   Arranges New York concerts devoted to his own and other recent chamber music; undertakes another expedition to collect folk music in Jutland.

1926   Travels to Australia for a concert tour; in Hobart meets the linguist Robert Atkinson, who revitalizes his interest in 'Nordic' (or 'Blue-eyed') English; comes to know the Swede Ella Ström, his future wife, while returning to America.

1927   Undertakes final folk-music expedition in Jutland; proposes to Ella Ström; begins the autobiographical narrative 'The Love-Life of Helen and Paris', his first major essay in 'Nordic' English (to 1928).

1928   Marries Ella Ström in the Hollywood Bowl, Los Angeles. *To a Nordic Princess* is premièred at his wedding.

1929   Visits Europe with his wife; organizes performances of 'Frankfurt Group' compositions at a festival in Harrogate; outlines his views on 'elastic scoring' and orchestration in preface to *Spoon River*.

1930   First association with the National Music Camp, Interlochen, Michigan. Orchestral première of *Spoon River*.

1931   Attends Haslemere Festival in Surrey, organized by Arnold Dolmetsch, rekindling his interest in early music; starts to adopt a more promotional approach (such as reduction in his fee) to encourage performances of his own compositions. Première of *Tribute to Foster*.

1932   Takes first steps towards building a museum at The University of Melbourne; accepts a year-long appointment as associate professor and music departmental head at New York University, where he delivers a series of twenty-nine lectures entitled 'A General Study of the Manifold Nature of Music'.

1933   Travels from Copenhagen to Australia with his wife aboard the sailing ship *L'Avenir*; writes 'The Aldridge–Grainger–Ström Saga' while on board.

1934   Undertakes his most comprehensive tour of Australia and New Zealand (to late 1935), presenting many concerts and broadcasts; writes a long article in memory of Delius; presents twelve lectures (to February 1935) entitled 'Music: A Commonsense View of All Types' for the Australian Broadcasting Commission, including the première of his first 'Free Music' work.

1935   Supervises building of the first stage of Grainger Museum in Melbourne; concert and lecture engagements in Australia and New Zealand.

1936   Returns to the United States; travels to Britain, where he attends Haslemere Festival and undertakes first BBC broadcast, conducting his own works.

1937   Writes most famous band work, *Lincolnshire Posy*, for immediate premièring in Milwaukee; begins annual teaching at Interlochen summer camp (to 1944).

1938   Revisits Australia to supervise building (with Gardiner's financial assistance) of Museum's second stage and to arrange its exhibits; clarifies his ideas about 'Free Music'.

1939   Visits Europe, returning just before outbreak of war; completes *The Immovable Do* and arrangement of 'The Duke of Marlborough' Fanfare; begins glossary of his 'Nordic' English.

1940   Employs Henry Cowell as his 'musical secretary' for one year; copies and disperses his correspondence and important musical items, fearing invasion of America; moves to Springfield, Missouri (to 1945).

1941   Travels widely, giving many concerts for the Red Cross and troops (to 1945).

1942   Attends a Grainger festival in Madison, Wisconsin. Première of *Kipling 'Jungle Book' Cycle*.

1943   Completes *The Power of Rome and the Christian Heart*; underwrites costs of production of *False Foundations of British History* by James Mackinnon Fowler; writes essay 'The Specialist and the All-Round Man'.

1944   Commences a series of recordings with Decca; starts the slow reduction in his concert commitments (to 1960). His favourite aunt, Clara Aldridge, dies in Adelaide.

1945   Comes to know the scientist Burnett Cross, with whom he soon starts to work on his 'Free Music' ideas; collaborates with Stokowski in Hollywood Bowl concerts.

1946   Undertakes first post-war visit to Scandinavia. Première of *Youthful Suite*.

1947   Hears brilliant performance of his *Hill-Song* No. 1 from West Point Band; writes his 'Bird's-Eye View of the Together-Life of Rose Grainger and Percy Grainger'; presents his first piano recitals in Britain since 1914.

1948   Embarks upon his last formal concert tour in America, although continues to perform frequently for many years, mainly for educational institutions; writes his 'Notes on Whip-Lust'.

1949   Commences his collection of 'Anecdotes' (to 1954); starts to make new arrangements of several of his popular pieces for a Stokowski recording.

1950   Starts to experience problems with his hearing. Henry Balfour Gardiner dies.

1951   Constructs the 'Estey-reed Tone-tool', with Cross, for playing 'Free Music'.

1952   Invents, with Cross, the 'Kangaroo-pouch' machine.

1953   Undergoes operation for prostate cancer in Aarhus, Denmark, recovering only slowly. Roger Quilter and Karen Kellermann die.

1954   Undergoes further operations for cancer; is awarded St Olav medal for services to Norwegian music.

1955   Travels to Australia, for the last time, to work on exhibits at his Museum in Melbourne.

1956   Returns mid-year from Melbourne to New York.

1957   Presents one of his last major performances, in Aarhus; gives only television appearance, with the BBC in London; starts to suffer from occasional mental disorders affecting speech and co-ordination; undergoes a further cancer operation.

1958   Visits Britain where he meets many folk-music acquaintances, including Benjamin Britten.

1959   Travels to Britain, for the last time; considers adding another storey to his Melbourne Museum; draws up his final will leaving the bulk of his artistic legacy to his Museum.

1960   Undertakes final work on 'Free Music' machines; gives last concert, in Hanover, New Hampshire; further deteriorates mentally and physically; writes his last essay, on *Hill-Song* No. 2.

1961   Dies of cancer in White Plains Hospital, 20 February.

Introduction

Percy Grainger's career fulfilled the ideal celebrated in his essay in praise of the 'all-round man'.[1] He was, indeed, famous as an all-round musician—composer, pianist, musicologist, inventor—but also cultivated broader talents for painting, languages, and writing. Grainger wrote prolifically;[2] the careful datings of his manuscripts indicate that he was a rapid and spontaneous writer, little inclined to revision or correction. This fluency enabled him to maintain an incredibly extensive correspondence—he wrote over two thousand letters to his wife alone—as well as to produce, in the intervals of an active career as concert pianist and composer, a large body of autobiographical writings, memoirs, and essays. Only some of Grainger's essays were published during his lifetime and most of these appeared in periodicals or newspapers which are no longer easily accessible.

Although the published essays are among Grainger's more formal writings, and were subject to editorial revision, they still show traces of the idiosyncratic, polyglot style which he used with less inhibition in his notebooks, personal writings, and letters. Grainger's multilingualism, combined with his philosophical ideals and love of all things Nordic, led him from an early age to disregard the English literary-stylistic tradition and its associated rhetoric. Even when not deliberately using 'Blue-eyed' English—the language he devised to counteract what he saw as the pernicious linguistic effects of the Norman Conquest—he still wrote English as if it were a Nordic language.

Grainger's artistic model was the Icelandic saga of 'Grettir the Strong', which he admired, among many other reasons, because it was 'rambling' and 'multitudinous', qualities which he deliberately cultivated in his own prose. In one of numerous passages where he sought to relate music and language, he suggested that 'music, when it is natural, functions very much like natural speech' and 'as regards natural speech, when we have anything to say, we just say it, without any sense that speech is grammatical or literary or mysterious in any way'.[3] His typical prose reflects this 'natural speech', unconstrained by rhetorical or grammatical *finesses*; its

---

[1] See Essay 38.   [2] See Appendix.
[3] 'Can Music be Debunked?' (1933/4), Essay 33.

predominant figure is hyperbole, achieved through superlatives, incantatory lists of names and chains of adjectives in occasionally surprising collocations. This style is well adapted to expressing enthusiasm—an impulse which Grainger shared in abundance with another favourite author, Walt Whitman—but it is smoothly neutralized in his more technical and explanatory essays.

The discursive writings of Grainger are first found in the notebooks which he kept as a student while attending the Hoch Conservatory in Frankfurt-am-Main during the late 1890s and continue in a variety of media until his penultimate year, 1960. Although relatively little appeared in print during the years he spent in London, 1901–14, it was in that period that he published his first important essays, on collecting folk music and on the music of his Frankfurt colleague, Cyril Scott. Another important early essay, on 'unwritten' music, appeared in mid-1915 and seems to have been completed just after his arrival in America. In his earliest years in America Grainger penned essays regularly, often on fairly technical pianistic issues for such music journals as the *Etude*.

The move to America also provided him with many opportunities to publish his broader ideas, and in the subsequent two decades he pursued particular themes with some concentration: racial musical characteristics in the early 1920s, jazz and use of percussion in the mid-1920s, ensemble music in the late 1920s, democracy and musical freedom in the early-mid-1930s, leading to the range of deeper philosophical questions addressed in a long series of essays of the mid-1930s. The writings of his final two decades show a continuing development of most of his passions of earlier decades and demonstrate the musical and cultural all-roundedness to which Grainger aspired. What is surprising in Grainger's six decades of writings is the degree to which his central preoccupations can be traced back to ideas expressed in the notebooks of his teenage years. In a late essay he claimed, with only slight exaggeration, that his main work as a composer was achieved between the ages of 16 and 20;[4] his main ideas appear to have been formed concurrently, even if, as with the compositions, there was a long period of incubation before they were publicly unveiled.

In 1922 the suicide of his mother motivated an autobiographical impulse which resulted in a series of voluminous, unpublished essays and anecdotes running parallel to his published writings for the next three decades. They touch on a huge variety of topics and sometimes carry his

---

[4] 'About Delius' (1950–52), Essay **44**.

idiosyncratic verbal style to its limits, through the use of 'Blue-eyed' English modulating to Danish or Swedish laced with occasional Polynesian words. The underlying motives of these essays changed little over the years. They are recurrently concerned with recording and analysing the relationship with his mother and her family in a search for personal understanding, with revising the history of twentieth-century music so as to acknowledge the primacy of his own experiments and to promote the achievements of such composers of his artistic circle as Cyril Scott and Herman Sandby, and with candidly describing his own sexuality and particularly his flagellantic predilections.

Altogether, Grainger's writings reflect a dilemma shared by all artists whose livelihood depends on appearing in public. While he was personally disposed to absolute candour about his private life (and that candidness became a cardinal principle in founding his own Museum), he was, none the less, aware that the revelation of intimate obsessions and fascinations could ruin his career. These contradictory impulses complicated the boundary between private and public in his case, yet he did manage to keep a fairly rigid line between the personal writings—almost all of which are still unpublished—and the essays which he wrote for more immediate public consumption. In fact, those essays were important vehicles for the creation and maintenance of his public image, even if for every time he adopted the role of publicist he more frequently took on the role of pedagogue or prophet. With a few exceptions, such as 'How I Became a Meat-Shunner', contributed to the *American Vegetarian*,[5] his public essays aim to enlighten readers on a wide range of musical and artistic topics, revealing Grainger as everything from a great cosmopolitan herald of the 'music of the future' to an occasionally biased crank.

The selection in this volume is drawn from Grainger's writings on music, including his essays about composition, folk music, notation, music technology, instrumentation, piano technique, performance, music history, early music, national, political, and racial musical characteristics, and about the work of the composers whom he particularly admired: Edvard Grieg, Frederick Delius, and Cyril Scott. From these essays Grainger emerges as a fearless, innovative thinker, whether or not he was fully versed in the intricacies of the many topics he addressed. In his comparative interest in music from many parts of the world and his unabashed enthusiasm for art, folk, and popular musics he stands as a man ahead of his time, concerned to knock down the fixed, preconceived notions of

---

[5] 5/4 (Dec. 1946), 4, not included in this volume.

much of his musical world just as he sought, through his Free Music, to remove the fixed steps and angularities of music itself.

Autobiographical writings, with their variety of frequently non-musical topics, have not been included in this volume; nor have any of Grainger's Museum legends, except for his short explanation of 'Free Music' (1938). Likewise, score introductions have not been included in the selection, except for the extended 'Guide to Virtuosity: Foreword to Students' (1923). Our aim has been to present essays which are intrinsically important while at the same time to represent the broadest possible range of Grainger's musical thought. We have been mindful, too, of not overlapping too extensively with the volume *A Musical Genius from Australia: Selected Writings by and about Percy Grainger*, edited by Teresa Balough,[6] nor with the synopses of lectures found in John Blacking's '*A Commonsense View of All Music': Reflections on Percy Grainger's Contribution to Ethnomusicology and Music Education*.[7] On some topics, such as universal impulses in music and recollections of Grieg and Delius, where Grainger was decidedly repetitious, we have included only his most comprehensive essay on the subject, occasionally supplemented in the footnotes with variants found elsewhere.

The mixture of published and unpublished sources for the essays in this volume has called for flexible editorial procedures. For published essays we have decided, wherever possible, to present Grainger's writings as they first appeared in print, so that readers can form an impression of the context in which his ideas were mediated and of how his literary publications were immediately related to his public career as pianist and composer. Where there are substantial differences between manuscript and printed versions we have included variants in footnotes. Occasionally, we have also introduced into the annotations comparative passages from essays not included in this volume. However, despite minor editorial revisions, introductory 'Editor's Notes', headlines, and subheadings, Grainger's printed versions accord fairly closely with the manuscript versions of his essays. Our collection retains a mixture of British, American, Australian, and Graingeresque English, according to where essays were

---

[6] (Perth: University of Western Australia, 1982). Fortunately Balough's selection contains the most significant parts of the long essay and series of transcriptions 'Collecting with the Phonograph' (1908) which, had it been included in our selection, would have severely distorted the possible balance of topics and denied space to several less accessible essays of later date.

[7] (Cambridge: Cambridge University Press, 1987), Appendix A, pp. 151–80. The present volume does, however, include some similar earlier materials from Grainger's summary of his New York University lecture series, 'A General Study of the Manifold Nature of Music' (1932), as Essay **28**.

first published and how particular editors chose to interfere with Grainger's style. Hence, conflicts of idiom and spelling variants (color/colour, single and double 'l' in past tenses) are reasonably common among the texts of already published essays collected here.

This volume's previously unpublished materials, in particular Grainger's early writings, lectures, and radio-broadcast scripts of mid-life, and late retrospective writings, have been treated variously. As far as possible, his own usage and spelling have been maintained, although where he has adopted phonetic spellings, has clearly made mistakes, or has written confusingly because of want of grammar, we have made amendments in the interest of clarifying meaning and not unduly deflecting the reader's attention from Grainger's discussion of the matter in hand. Such a procedure was particularly necessary in editing Grainger's seminal Yale lecture of 1921, 'Nordic Characteristics in Music',[8] where, apparently because of shortage of time in preparation, his script alternates between a fully written-out form and a series of undeveloped cues to ideas, associated with increasingly haphazard capitalization, punctuation, and marks of emphasis. Some standardization of titles and names has also silently been introduced into the unpublished essays, lest the reader be confused as to which works or individuals Grainger was referring.

Only three of the volume's essays first appeared in languages other than English: 'The Value of Icelandic to an Anglo-Saxon' (1920), in Icelandic; 'The Completion of the Percussion Family in the Orchestra' (1926), in German; 'Questionnaire' (1955), in Norwegian.[9] While Grainger's English-language originals exist for the Icelandic and Norwegian essays, and have been used in this volume, no English original was found for Grainger's essay about the percussion family, hence Bruce Clunies Ross's translation from the German.

A comprehensive annotation of the texts has not been attempted; we have, none the less, provided occasional footnotes to clarify ambiguities, to translate foreign words and phrases, to identify references, and to supply supplementary information about less well-known persons, works, or issues. Cross-references have sometimes been used to refer the reader to terms and issues dealt with elsewhere in the volume. Recognizing that many readers will consult the volume for individual essays rather than undertake its sequential reading, we have introduced some repetition of key points in the annotations.

[8] Essay 17.   [9] Essays 16, 21, and 46, respectively.

Part I

TO 1914

I *A Recognition*

(c.1898–1900)

Above all I recognise the ungraspable irresistibility, which is God, love, power, truth, the instincts (the only origin of so-called good) which I recognise to influence the invisible & visible system, to what quantity I cannot determine.

I recognise limitation (which is weakness, fear, selfishness, the only origin of so-called bad) as the inevitable outcome of all expression.

I recognise the irresistibility as eternal (& ungraspable) all expression as subject to limitation (& graspable) as temporal, quality eternal, quantity temporal.

I recognise life as an expression of eternity & rhythmical repetition as the expression of movement, & that the inevitable pulsation of life's expression, which is temporal, does not disturb the ungraspable life which is eternal. (The waves balance up & down yet the surface of water is smooth.) This is the condition of the relation of the eternal to its limited expression.

I recognise the irresistibility as expressed to humanity in an unembodied ecstasy (called religion) as in all other embodied ecstasies.

I recognise love to be expressed to humanity, bodiless & bodily.

I recognise no love that is not perfectly returned by equal love, no love that necessitates obligation, requires thankfulness, no love that demands the renunciation of one particle of instinctive self.

I recognise no sacrifices of instincts, for the irresistibility, which is love & all instincts, is all recognisable to humanity & all related to it.

I recognise an elementary limitation in the forming of man's reckonings & conceptions of the No 2.

I recognise sex as the expression of an elementary limitation to the No 2, & sexual love as the bodily & mental reunion & balance of opposites & the greatest possible completion of self.[1]

Source: Undated manuscript notebook, containing initial draft and final copy. Grainger Museum, Melbourne.

[1] Grainger's initial draft reads: I recognised sex as the expression of the opposites of man['s] existence & sexual love as the loving mental balance of opposites, & the greatest possible completion of self.

I recognise self, which is the individual, as the summing-up of the relation of the quantities of the instincts, as a temporal move out of the eternal.

I recognise selfishness as insufficiency of self, arising from mental limitation, when occurring [as] contact lacking balance of self to self.[2]

I recognise egotism (which is not selfishness) as the culmination of the ideal in self.

I recognise the ideal as the bodiless truth translated to the material truth by the brain.

I recognise truth as the irresistibility as recognised by the brain.

I recognise the brain as the consciousness of self & all related to self, the balance of abstracts, & recognise will as the embodiment of the instincts, brain & will as the seeds of the abstract that create the deed.

I recognise disharmony & harmony as the outcome of contact, War as the will of differences of expressions (of the one irresistibility), agreement as the similarity of expression (of the one irresistibility).

---

[2] Grainger's initial draft reads: when meeting contact, lack balance of self to self.

2   *Theme as Related to Form in Music*
(1901)

A Few Formal Conceptions (sketches for an article, 'Theme as Related to Form in Music')

I consider a perfect theme[1] in almost all cases absolutely, in very rare cases scarcely, capable of *any* development. Thus, it will be seen that our 'themes' are not what they are called. There may have been a theme written at one time or another, but I can recall none. It stands to reason that a real theme must be something fundamental, merely a germ, a pervading idea which can *only* justify itself in its subsequent development. But when we say *theme* we mean the germ, the original idea already developed to its *fullest* capabilities, already in its most intense, concentrated, & compact embodiment, so that in the direction of clearness, terseness, directness, compression, & general *maturity* of expression, nothing remains to be done.

Thus, the person gives himself away who first hatches a general misty idea, then fossilizes it into what we call a 'theme', & *then* starts to develop further. His only possible standpoint would be: To open with his 'theme', as the title-page, the conviction to be justified in the coming bars, *then* start with his germ, his undeveloped conceptions, & gradually step by step clear & concentrate, & give form, & definiteness, & dramatic distinctness till he, at the end, raises his summit, his situation with the 'Überblick'[2] gloriously tempered, the waste omitted, the inconsistencies over-gone, the whole worthy & challengeable.

Also relative to certain forms of national folklore, which, starting the climax of a story (so & so is dead, etc.), then start off at the proper place, the beginning, & lead you to the event again, & end again dwelling upon it (so & so is dead, etc.).[3]

This is relative to a lecturer who beginning states his theories, his goal, his point, then starts at the undeveloped end, & leads his listeners to the

---

Source: Manuscript notebook entitled 'Methods of Teaching and Other Things', pp. 29–39. Grainger Museum, Melbourne.

[1] Grainger's note: I here use the term as in general.
[2] Comprehensive view (Germ.).
[3] This paragraph was a later insertion.

point already started, convinces *why* he proclaimed so & so. But to start at the most difficult, advanced, at the point 'farthest north' of any subject (stating clearly that it is 'farthest north possible'), & then pretend to advance still further, would be tolerated in nothing, I believe, except in musical form.

This, of course, must not be confounded with the standpoint of him who starts from 'farthest n[orth] as yet' that he go beyond. With him, 'F.N.' is not the goal, merely the undeveloped end leading to 'further North.'

. . . based on Russian folk tunes, of melancholy character as a rule, the over-ture, although not lacking in striking and effective passages, leaves, on the whole, an unfavourable impression, little attempt being made to arouse inter-est by the development of the thematic material, while . . .[4]

This is the point where misunderstandings arise. Thus, it is not uncom-mon to refer to the so-called *theme* as the reason of existence for the coming var[iation]s. This, of course, is impossible with present *themes*. With a *real* theme, a thing unknown to us yet, it would be possible &, of course, the most ideal form of vars. No, our present themes are the ultim-ate result of a cause, the effect, never the cause itself.

But could we rear a genuine theme, a raison d'être, how lovely to grope from chaos to light, to gradually arrive at the result, the deed, the fact, so dear to us humans.

Thus, we could start with glorious nature & a solitary man felling a tree, ('The grey-haired enemy of the wood', said Cynewulf[5]) & rear it into a loathsome, fetid, smelly city, full of 'deeds' (that are crimes) & 'facts' (which tell of them). No fear of indefiniteness when you've once got the city.

I should like to prove that no school has found it possible to develop the kind of idea termed by us 'theme', not Bach his fugue-theme, Beethoven his subjects, Wagner his motives. However, other elements other than themes have been distinctly of value in certain elementary forms of development, such as rhythmical pulses & tags, harmonic germs, &, very rarely, melodic lines. But all these things have nothing to do with our meaning of the word 'theme' & 'subject'. I own that the term 'motiv' is sometimes a correct appelation, but mostly the most useful germs are too indefinite (or, if definite, too tiny) to adhere, to be classed as any par-

---

[4] Grainger inserted part of an unattributed newspaper article here.
[5] An ambiguous quotation from the Old English riddle on the plough, no longer attributed to the late 8th- or early 9th-cent. poet Cynewulf.

ticular kind of thing. Thus, a piece will start with a certain rhythmical pulse (say, triplets) so marked that the balance of the piece would be entirely upset if it ceased before a certain time had elapsed, whereas the theme built on, or containing (whichever term you please), these rhythms might fade out of creation unmourned, as long as the rhythmical pulse continued to satisfy the desire for flow.

Such a rhythmical tag is, for instance, the following, used by Bach in things uncountable. This is the only element of the 'theme' of 1st movement of G maj. Conc. (for strings)[6] that is developed *with* (it is not developed *upon*), & so also in the C min. Fugue 'Das W. T. Klavier' 1st book[7] (the recurrence of the 'theme' of the fugue being no development, merely repetition); also, it forms part of the fugue beginning:[8] . Now, taking for granted that twenty compositions of Bach are findable (the finding would be a matter of time only) in which this small rhythmical atom is the only germ developed, we are forced to the conclusion either that in these twenty pieces Bach does not develop his 'themes' properly *at all*, or that the thematic essence in all these twenty pieces is one & the same. As the unlikeness of the themes will make the latter possibility ridiculous, we must therefore submit to the former, taking the view that the piece had underlying it a certain rhythmical tag (or perhaps only *germinal rhythmical type*), forming part of the theme as well as the parts nonthematic, being no more a part of the themes than of any bar taken at random—say no 66—this is, in no way, 'a thematic working-out'. This conception is strengthened by the fact that Bach (as well as many others) will often develop such a trifle when it is not contained in the 'theme' at all, being after it, or coming anywhere at random, thus proving that he attached no importance to it whatever, proving it to be pure chance. To the best of my remembrance, a striking example of this is in [the] 1st ch[orus] of the *St Matthew Passion*, where such a rhythmical pulse *etc.* etc.[9] dominates a central portion of the movement, having no connection (to my present knowledge) with anything else in the piece, & receiving no further attention when its moment is past.

Bach has two conceptions of 'themes' & 'motivs', & these conceptions

---

[6] Brandenburg Concerto No. 3. [7] No. 2.
[8] A minor Fugue, Book I No. 20. [9] Bars 57–8 onwards.

show greater insight than many succeeding notions. *Firstly*: as a crystallized idea, something fixed, something to be left as it is, something final, thus almost something of a *refrain*. *Secondly*: as a tag (harmonic, rhythmic, or melodic) to be repeated. This clearly built for contrapuntal use.[10]

It is through the blending & combining of these conceptions that the many formal misunderstandings have risen. However, considering how rarely perhaps the greatest of formists is quoted when formal doctrines are laid down, explained & instances of their adoption given, I infer that even hard & fast formists must feel that here they are dealing with a matter not *altogether* coercible to their doctrines of thematic workings, & feel that he as often as not is contradictory to the methods they ascribe to him.

Of his first conc[eption] of 'theme' he will often use numbers in one movement, thus clearly proving that he does *not* consider the 'themes' to be the 'underlying' energy of the composition, but rather as prominent moments arrived *at* (thus being more developed out of the general idea & style of the movement, than the general style and idea of movement developed out of the 'theme') in the course of the work. Neither does he treat them as dramatic or formal climaxes, a point on which the formal future will most likely differ from his.

Of this type interesting examples occur in 1st ch. *St Matthew Passion*.

In this ch. we meet with a kind of theme (in my sense) that is, an idea of ceaseful[11] flow inside of which the contrasts are so slight as to be hardly noticeable. Then we meet with a harmonic germ which is the most influential inventiveness of the piece. (It is interesting to note how with greater definiteness of idea goes less influence over work at large, thus: The idea of flow holds most sway, next in importance *harmonic germ*, still something far from definiteness, then as we approach the definite 'thematic' points we find them centred in themselves only, developing nowhere, merely isolated, self-contained, tangible, hard & fast of beginnings & endings. This fact proves to me the unrivalled depth of his insight into formal consistency.)

Built on this is the first 'theme' proper, an indefinite melodic line, to be recognised as such where it reoccurs.

Very important is the '*choral*' which equally remains in a self-sufficient, final state, in fact almost unreconcilable in its attitude towards the movement all through. Then perhaps next in importance is the bit first appear-

---

[10] Grainger's footnote: In both cases something absolutely incapable of development, having reached final state.

[11] Probably 'ceaseless' was intended.

ing after the ascending bass[12] (which might itself almost be called a 'theme', for it reoccurs often & is as important a factor of the whole as any of those 'subjects' above mentioned & is of perhaps like importance as the melodic tag:[13] 𝄞 [musical notation] . This latter might be taken as the most important melodic-line influence in the whole movement, its ceaseless repetition might justifiably be treated as an accident, as any other embellishment that gave flow to the harmonic underwork would be equally satisfying) which is a most prominent impression, distinctly impressing the mind as a vital type.

The melody developed from [musical notation] [musical notation] is also quite thematic melodically. It repeats, is characteristic, & centres all interest on itself for the time being.

Noteworthy is the sincerity of Bach forms. If he knows that he will need material for contrapuntal polyphony he builds himself such, merely for that end. Nor does he then disguise this fact. We look in vain in his works for sentimental types amid an heroic environment, homophonic types turned to the use of counterpoint, counterpoint types assuming individual (i.e., self-sufficient, homophonic) rôles, the inconsistencies with which modern works bristle. Thus, [musical notation] never receives more notability than it starts out with; it is used throughout as a means of Steigerung[14] only. How easy for one of less insight to have raised it to a really effective but false importance. I can quite imagine the *style* most moderns would have invested it with, the blare of brass & general upheaval that would have shamed it. This, then, is a convincing example of Bach's conception of 'theme', these individual gentlemen he gives full importance to (yet through having a number does away with the very great conspicuousness that two themes only are bound to assume in a work of large proportions), rightly leaving them undeveloped, they being already the most advanced possibilities (that is, if good themes) of their type; & for working up he has the separate contrapuntal atoms, for his endings (the type first appearing in bar[15]) he has his extra coda-type, & so on all through, each thing taking the place it is ordaining for, & over all the unbroken broad, religious flow. ('Grandeur of the perfect sphere, thanks to the atoms that cohere.')

Also, the G min. Organ Fantasia & Fugue[16] are interesting in the

---

[12] Bar 6.   [13] Bar 1.   [14] Scaffolding (Germ.).
[15] Grainger perhaps refers to bars 79–80.   [16] BWV 542.

application of thematic matter, or rather in the *non*-application of thematic matter. There is nothing in the Fantasia which we could rightly
call a 'theme', yet it is one of the sublimest & most perfect bits of
form the biggest formist wrote. The only thing that might be termed
an 'idea' are two little tags for intertwining & echoing. These are

 —rather meagre

from a thematic standpoint.[17]

But this Fantasia stands quite among the first for power of invention.
Two other bits repeat, marked by A & B,[18] both grand yet in *no way
thematic*—one three bars, the other two bars, long. The remaining thirty
bars are just free ahead. The following shows the regions of influence
of the fixtures.

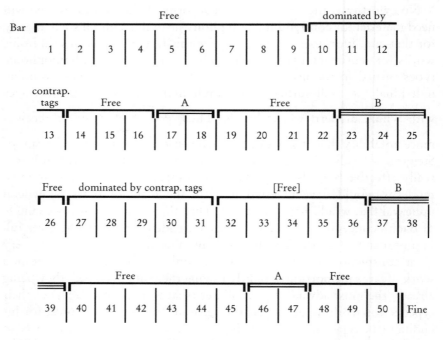

Then, one hears a lot of rot about fugues being developed from the thematic matter of a subject in counterpoint only. In most cases, it is a rhythmical unity, in which cases it is more correct to regard the fugue as a whole

---

[17] These examples first appear at bar 9 (but up a fifth) and at bars 9–10 (but down a fourth),
respectively.
[18] See the figure, below.

as dominated by a certain rhythmic continuance of which the subject partakes along with the rest. Thus, the Fugue following the Fantasia is throughout a jogging up & down in ♫ accompanied by pulsey ♩♩. It seems to me that there is nothing to choose between the conceptions (a) of the theme obeying the general law of the whole, (b) of the whole obeying the general law of the theme. I incline towards the former conception, for, while the rhythmic pulse is throughout maintained both of the ♫ &

♩♩, the form in which these rhythms appear in the theme is entirely disregarded in many cases, the melodic lines having nothing in common.

Thus, the only part of the theme ever rigidly adhered to,[19] very often turns up as , or the like.[20] If we consider the theme & its satellites merely as the prominent idea, the conspicuous part, in short, a kind of refrain—as something that keeps to itself, yet obeying with the rest the larger dominating idea of the piece (the hustling, rollicking, clanging, singing whole) beside which it is of very minor importance—we shall find the whole work more consistent than if we consider it the raison d'être, in which case we shall have to call certain parts neither flesh nor fish, but which are still most true to the dominating idea of the whole. For instance, bars 58 to 61. Take again the bass bars 63–65, a strong development of the up & down jogging idea, but not very distinctly related to his idea as it appears in theme

( ). Then again treble at bar 58 is quite consistent to the pulsey rôle of eighth notes[21] but hard to reconcile with their represen-

tation in theme .

Aug. 31. 1901

Thus, we find Bach's developmental matter to be something distantly related to the modern 'motiv', only that with him it never assumed a false guise.

But when we view the larger forms of what may rightly be called the 'German-Austrian national style' (Haydn, Beethoven, etc.) we meet with

---

[19] As at the opening of the fugue.
[20] Grainger's given example is first found at bar 21.   [21] Quavers.

appalling inconsistencies, false pretences, & unconscious insincerity in the methods employed. It will be noticed that I have not dwelt at all on Bach's small-form work, because in this department he has less excelled in method & type, the small form of the period immediately following his being as successful an intensification of small form as it was a huge deterioration in larger work. The idea of Bach as first & foremost a counter-pointist & altogether 'brainy' half scientist, is the best thing distorted brains will ever do. Bach is predominantly an emotionalist & a formist. It is in the power of imagination, intensity of feeling, even presence of soul, & the breadth, direction, & unbrokenness of expression that he excelled all others.

Some Scraps for Working up Later

We like themes for we feel we are getting as much to the square inch as possible. Themes are more beautiful to us than the germs from which they spring because we have more time to take them in; they are more opened out, more full & blooming. If, however, the atoms of which a theme is formed, are dissected & torn one from another, it can only (& rightly) awaken our pity, as strewn flower-petals do, & in this state the themal atoms represent *in no sense* the quality, type, or emotion of the original theme. It is only with the present application of thematicism that I war, with motivs used to clothe long, bleak uninventivenesses, with themal shreds stuffed into formal cracks (Lücken).[22]

The *good* quality of thematicism (as much as possible to the square inch) would be preserved in music of irregular bars & irregular phrases, for I have found the tendency to compress *very strong* in large form.

Aug. 31. 1901

[22] Gaps (Germ.).

My Musical Outlook

(1902–4)

First of all, my musical outlook:[1]

Music appeals to me merely as an expression of emotion, emotion in its broadest sense. Form, instrumentation, composition-technique generally, are to me satisfying in so far as they succeed in exploiting the underlying emotion of a composition to its fullest possible extent, & are to me unsatisfying in so far as they introduce elements which are nonconducive to the fullest possible exploitation of the underlying emotion of a composition. Other standards than this I have no use for. (Needless to say that it needs no end more technique to create form & style, so as to realize such an ideal of emotional expression, than to accomplish pretty devices of contrapuntal cleverness, thematic complexities, & trickinesses, generally.)[2]

This creed of emotional consistency gives rise to great purity of style. In one & the same composition I never introduce two contrasting styles or elements, as this would break the continuity throughout of the same emotion which is to me imperative. (Contrasts of type are admissible to me in compositions of a light & frivolous nature, dances, marches, & such, & also in the case of compositions of which the emotional type is capricious, or rhapsodical; but, in this latter case, it will be seen that the contrasts are part of the requirements of the type-as-a-whole, & do no violation to its consistency.)

Very various and contrasting emotions (such as are of necessity forced upon a New-Worlder) have given rise to equally various & contrasting styles which I shall next catalogue. The chief promptings will be found to be *nature* & *raciality* (the sea & its sailors, the grand large differences between continent & continent, & the equally grand large differences between race & race that people the same, the smaller natural divisions & their human counterparts, hills & their hillmen, plains & their teeming

Source: Extended letter to Karl Klimsch, written between 10 Sept. 1902 and Feb. 1904, in manuscript notebook entitled 'Methods of Teaching and Other Things', pp. 50–65 and various, in the hands of both Rose Grainger and Percy Grainger, and attached typewritten sections. Grainger Museum, Melbourne.

[1] This essay was written in the form of an extended letter to Karl Klimsch (1841–1926), German lithographer and Grainger's mentor, particularly in composition, during his Frankfurt years (1895–1901), but apparently never sent to him.

[2] Grainger's footnote at this point suggests he intended further elaboration here.

progressive populaces, such revelations most inspiring of all). Art appeals to me more as an expression of nature & life in broad & general (impersonal) lines, than as a depiction of the dramatic (personal) strivings of individuals. The following is the creative programme of my whole life, ideas for many of the works originating in Australia, others in the Frankfurt days, fairly all reaching back a year or so.

(Styles I have made sketches for will be prefixed with *; styles I have already completed works in will be prefixed with **)

Catalogue of Styles, Works

Title (*Collective works*)	mode of setting, instrumentation, etc.
SEA-SONGS	large string orch., in some cases supplemented by sliding-woodwind (which will be found mentioned below)
PAGAN HYMNS	some orchestral, others chorus & orch.
*SONGS OF THE GREAT PLAIN-COUNTRY (Australian bush-songs)	for large chamber-music combinations, chiefly muted strings
*OLD TESTAMENT SETTINGS (Song of Solomon, Psalms, etc.)	chorus alone, & chorus & orch.
KIPLING SETTINGS	
*Large works such as 'The Rhyme of the Three Sealers'	for male voices & orch.
Smaller works from 'Seven Seas' etc.	for male voices only
***Very small works*	some for male voices only some for mixed voices only
***Some songs* (one or two)	for solo voice accompanied
*MARCHING-SONGS	men's and boys' voices & whistlers (vocalism without text)
LONGFELLOW SETTINGS 'The Saga of King Olaf' (large); small poems 'Seaweed' etc.	for chorus, solo-voices, & orch. for mixed chorus
BRITISH MUSICAL FOLK-LORE **Arrangements of songs & dances of the British on both Sides of the Water, embracing all that is most representative	ever-changing mode of setting voices alone, voices accomp. by chamber music-combinations, chorus alone, chorus accomp. by orch., solo-instrum.

Title (*Collective works*)	mode of setting, instrumentation, etc.
from earliest Celtic remains down to latest London music-hall songs, or States' Nigger-tunes.	combination, orch. alone, etc., etc.
**HILL-SONGS	woodwind

Smaller, lighter works

**ENGLISH DANCES *and other dances, & such	for orch., & chamber music-combinations
(SINGLE WORKS) *Car-jolts (Railroad Ditty)	for orch.
*Charging Irishry etc. etc.	for orch.

Such titles as *Sea-songs, Hill-songs, Charging Irishry*, etc., might lead one to imagine these works to be created on a basis similar to that of 'program music', whereas I am *most heartily* opposed to anything in the shape of a 'program', regarding it as the outcome of a decadent conception of the reason-of-existence of music. I take it (perhaps erroneously) that the 'program musician' desires to reproduce in composition sensations resulting from phenomena & events, that he frequently seeks to imitate natural noises, & that he further believes such reproductions & imitations to be capable of intimating to the hearer the exact phenomena, events, & noises which he regards them as standing for.

The basis of my works bearing the above-mentioned titles has nothing in common with this. In a SEA-SONG I do not in the least wish to imitate the sound of the sea, nor to reproduce musically *sensations* connected with the sea, but only to give expression to *emotions resultant* on sensations & impressions having for cause THE SEA. This same applies to: *Songs of the great Plain-country; Hill-songs; Car-jolts; Charging Irishry.*[3]

Before entering upon a more detailed account of the above works, I wish to touch upon some particulars of my handling of general musical construction, form, instrumentation, & such matters of craft, a setting forth of which will make clearer what is to follow.

General Construction

(*a*) Rhythmical Structure. I use three distinct kinds of rhythmical structure:

[3] The last two paragraphs were inserted on additional slips of paper, and dated 28 Sept. 1902.

The 1st, consisting of beats occurring at regular intervals, regular groups of which are enclosed in bars. This (the usual) form of rhythmical structure I shall refer to as of *regular beats & regular bars*.

The 2nd, consisting of beats occurring at regular intervals, irregular groups of which are enclosed in bars. This form of rhythmical structure (of which I here append an example[4]) I shall refer to as of *regular beats & irregular bars*.

The 3rd, devoid of beats, or any regular pulse whatsoever. Music of this kind [is] to be written in a new notation, the practicability & manner of printing of which will be later discussed. This form of rhythmical structure I shall refer to as of *no rhythmical regularity*.

(*b*) Phrasing. In the setting of words to music my phrasing & rhythmical structure are the exact counterpart of the text I am setting, in the case of prose partaking of its irregular rhythms & phrases (sentences), in the case of poetry partaking of its regular rhythms & metre. Otherwise (than textal settings), I hardly ever make use of regular phrasing (periods, & such) holding that irregular divisions are less noticeable (& therefore do less violation to flow) than regular divisions, on account of their being unexpected.

In my most polyphonic & advanced styles (*Sea-songs*, etc.) I intend to do away with groupal phrases (phrases occurring in all, or most, parts simultaneously)[5] altogether, inside of the general formal outlines of the piece, there to be constant overlapping of free parts, free from both rhythmical & phrasal restrictions. (Restricted only in that they needs must harmonically cooperate; to each part its own rhythms, phrases.)

(*c*) Form. Through your[6] kind teachings (for which I am ever more grateful) I learnt the value of *inventive strength* (*Erfindungskraft*) & have made it a chief formal requirement. I demand *equal* inventive strength (at very high pressure) throughout each piece, & very rarely (then only in light compositions, dances, etc.) repeat any part. (There I must except settings of words, when it is my custom to conform entirely to the structural make of the text, to repeat in my setting where the text repeats, to make refrains where refrains occur in the text.) Thus, thematic material & its usual uses do not exist for me. Thematic material for melodic ideas, rhythmical motivs, choral programs would be further irreconcilable to most of my styles on account of their extremely polyphonic basis, each part (*Stimme*),

---

[4] Example not found.   [5] Added as a footnote.   [6] Karl Klimsch's.

although guided so as to form a harmonic sum-total, being of equal melodic-rhythmical importance, & free from melodic or rhythmical restrictions.[7] Theme, in our present sense, could not be co-existent with these conditions; a melodic idea would, by laying greatest stress on the part it was allotted to, do away with the equal importance of each part, a rhythmical motiv would interfere with the rhythmical part-freedom etc., etc. The only unifying, binding factor is, therefore, *style*. Each composition is in a certain style, & must meet the requirements of this same in every particular. These requirements are naturally very contrasting: *Hill-song* style is rugged, rhapsodical, homophonic, whereas *Sea-song* style (although wild) is smooth, flowing, & extremely polyphonic. My task has not been to conform to existing formal conventionalities—still less to create new ones—but rather to clear away all structural & formal limitations (regularity of bars, beats & phrases, themes, motivs, sections) barring the way to the realization of my style-ideals.
Sept. 24. 1902

The chief tendency of my form, as a whole, is towards greater breadth, compositions of ten minutes' duration, stretching unbroken, without sections, without contrasts, without change of type, being usual. I do not allow of the possibility of 'dullness'; when the underlying emotional urge is played out I close my piece. (Surely there can be no need to resort to make-believe 'interestingness' in our soulful, strenuous times; surely there cannot but be an absolute *overflow* of emotional energy.)

Another particular that I ought to mention, is that I do not recognise connection between different movements, as has been customary in symphonies, sonatas, suites, operas (acts), & other forms of the past.

My *collective works* (see style catalogue), with the exception of the Longfellow *Saga of King Olaf*,[8] & Kipling *Song of the Engl.*[9] (both composed of a number of short poems) consist of separate, single pieces, alike in style, but otherwise having no connection each with the other, no consecutiveness of performance being intended.

---

[7] This last phrase was added as a footnote.

[8] *The Song of King Olaf*, including such poems as 'The Crew of the Long Serpent', 'Thora von Rimol', and 'The Wraith of Odin'. Elsewhere in his notebooks at this time Grainger wrote several paragraphs about his intentions (largely unrealized) for the Longfellow settings, and commented: 'Often I'm drawn to these poems by their powerful metres, asking often [for] regular beats & irregular bars, but oftener just by their smack & smell.'

[9] A set of seven poems written in 1893 and collected in *The Seven Seas* (1896) by Rudyard Kipling (1865–1936), Indian-born English writer; the set includes such poems set by Grainger as 'We were Dreamers' and 'We have Fed our Sea'.

Instrumentation, etc.

Surely instrumentation (vocalism, etc.) is only in the advent. Whatever sound-producer[10] we turn to, we find none fully exploited, developed, with the exception perhaps of some solo-instruments. (Bach's organ writing, Chopin's piano writing, for instances.) But we look in vain for the welding of all the glorious sounding propensities of the individual sound-producers into a balanced whole. Great technical difficulties have been written by composers & overcome by performers, but little attention seems to have been paid to either *beauty* or *balance* of sound. It seems the past has been so busy mastering those things which *do not lie* for voice & instrument, that it has overlooked those things which *do lie*.

My vocalism & instrumentation (at least, I hope so) consist *only* of such things as are the inevitable outcome of the physical nature of the sound-producers I am writing for.

(*a*) Sound-Producers Treated Separately

Vocalism

One of the loveliest qualities of the human voice seems to me its power to sustain, the unbroken evenness of its tone, its rich continuity—especially so in chorus, where the individual singer's breathing-break is imperceivable. The ideal of vocalism is, therefore, *melodic* rather than rhythmical. But this beautiful sustaining quality disappears when words are sung. The charm (& also intelligibility) of words lies so greatly in their rhythms & in their hard, sharp, strong consonant combinations, (ch, dg, dw, wh, hv, gn, kn, th, thr, hl, hr, etc., so delightful in our Germanic tongues) which naturally are destructive to the above-mentioned tone-continuity.

Mindful of this, one of my two chief modes of writing for the voice (the one I regard as doing greatest justice to the most *beautiful* possibilities of vocalism) is non-textal, simply vowel-singing.

On the other hand, when entering upon textal settings my first care is to assure of easy intelligibility of the words. (Personally, I derive little pleasure from lengthy listenings to operas, oratorios, songs, when all catchable of the text are random consonant splutterings.)

Being of an undramatic turn of mind (& therefore not drawn towards poems interesting on account of the action they contain), the texts I

---

[10] Grainger's footnote: I use this term as embracing instruments, voices, whistling.

choose for setting appeal to me chiefly because of their *purely phonetic charm*, Kipling's staunch-sounding, unmistakably Germanic (he uses few French-derived words) rhymes, Longfellow's Norse-like lilt, the Old Testament's quaint English version of Eastern listless drowse.

Very careful to choose only such poems as *fairly cry* for the greater intensity of a musical setting, when once my text is decided upon I give myself up blindly to its dictations. My striving is not only to build form & structure entirely on the text's lines (as already stated), but further to respond to its littlest rhythmic promptings, to follow in minutest detail the rise & fall of its intensity in my melodic lines, & to match its passages of characteristic-sounding words (such as 'rough she rode on the rude tide-rip'—or: — 'Ever drifting, ˙/., ˙/., On the shifting currents of the restless heart') with passages of harmonies of a like *phonetic* type.

All my textal settings are rhythmically homophonic, the same word being sung simultaneously in all parts. This is to ensure easy intelligibility. Melodically, however, the part-writing is free & polyphonic. I also am careful to set words in that region of the voice where they are easiest to pronounce, throaty ('gaumig'[11]) sounds, such as 'fall', being set low, etc., etc.

What is particularly sympathetic to me is that the human voice (like whistling, & stringed instruments) has all possibilities of pitch, is not bound to certain notes only (like woodwind, piano, organ) but can (at least, theoretically) make twenty & more divisions to the half-tone, & can *slide at will from note to note*. This sliding-*portamento* (although condemned by singing teachers as 'bad style', which it undoubtedly is when only the result of faulty technique & uncertainty of pitch) I much desire in the performance of my vocal works (especially those non-textal) & wish the notes of melodies to glide one into the other in curving lines. The sign for this mode of performance (sl = slide) occurs with great frequency in my scores.[12]

Whistling

What more lovely quality of sound is there than whistling? To me it seems the most intense of all sounds, the most coldly passionate. Florid whistling (trills, runs, arpeggios) finds no part in my scheme, but melodic whistling (especially polyphonic) I make much use of. What has been said of *sliding* with reference to singing pertains equally to whistling. The

---

[11] Lit. palatal (Germ.).   [12] This paragraph was added as a footnote.

whistling range 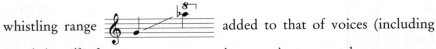 added to that of voices (including 'Stroh-bass'[13]) forms a very extensive non-instrumental compass, as follows:

'Stroh-bass'

Stringed Instruments

I took advantage of the opportunity afforded me by Sandby[14] & his cello staying with us this year, to glean practical experience of a stringed instrument from personal experiment.

This, together with some practising upon a violin, soon convinced me

(*a*) that only strictly melodic styles called forth the best attributes of strings, in fact that anything purely rhythmic proved wholly unsuitable

(*b*) that double-stopping was peculiarly well fitted to the nature of these instruments, its resources being as yet undeveloped

(*c*) that a more or less continuous sliding (glissando) up & down the strings was both an easy & beautiful manner of playing

(*d*) that the very high notes of the three lower strings have not received the exploitation they deserve

(*e*) that definite notes (as opposed to indefinite sliding) must follow each other in very slow succession if richness of tone is to accompany their execution, in fact that *beauty* of *tone* was not possible in quick passages, runs, arpeggios, etc., etc.

(*f*) that to get the rich tone, easy vibration, & continuous sliding imperative to many of my styles, it will be necessary, in the case of both the violin & viola, to stand the bottom of the belly of the instrument downward in playing as is already customary with the cello.

The peculiar prejudices of string players seem to me responsible for the backward state of string style (*Streich-satz*). By adopting new modes of

---

[13] The deep tone of the lower chest register of the bass voice (Germ.).

[14] Herman Sandby (1881–1965), Danish cellist and composer; fellow student in Frankfurt. Sandby became a lifelong friend and often stayed with the Graingers in London during 1902–3.

fingering I have been able to widely extend the possibilities of double-stopping & high playing on the lower strings. I use double-stopping *only* when I require the particular effect which only this manner of playing can produce, *never* as mere 'filling-out'. Besides double-stopping inside the octave, I frequently write unison melodies

over-the-octave

& other up-to-now rare combinations. I write a range of two octaves & over for the lower strings, finding even the very high notes of this compass quite suitable for sliding melodies of slow-succeeding notes. The uncertain speaking of these notes explains their rare occurrence in solo music, but should not exclude them from ensemble application. I owe much of my knowledge of what lies for strings to Sandby, who himself writes a string style to my mind superior to any heretofore.

I hope to shortly have an occasion of becoming acquainted with the manipulation of the double bass, which instrument ought, with proper attention to fingering (or rather handing) & bowing, be a most expressive medium for melodic basses, & even for higher middle-voices.

Much remains to be done with double-stop pizzicato, especially orchestrally. Out of a host of effective possibilities I here append two: (1) sliding of the finger after the strings have been plucked

(2) octave pizz.

Woodwind Instruments

Musically-cultivated Europe, although strong in strings, seems to me weak in woodwind, that is, as regards tone color. Strong, rich colors in landscape seem to produce like qualities of tone quality; crude & striking optical impressions create a taste for corresponding phonetic effects; the lovely tone of our strings we owe to colorful Italy.

The glorious timbre (coarse, nasal, passionately vibrating) of Egyptian & Indian wind instruments I have chanced to hear, convinces me that it is in the East (in hot climates generally) we may look for perfectly-toned woodwind.

The Australian in me requires more full-blooded, nasal, virulent sound than is to be had of these instruments in Europe; accordingly, at my earliest opportunity, I will undertake exhaustive experiments with the woodwind of All-the-World, finally perhaps to build me quite new sound-producers, perhaps merely to remodel our existing flutes, oboes, bassoons, clarinets, etc.

Another departure I intend making: while fully appreciating the very noticeable jerk which accompanies the speaking ('aussprechen') of each fresh note (resultant on our mode of pitch-making, i.e. through holes in the tubes) as a characteristic crudity admirably adapted to music of a barbaric & primitive type (such as, for instance, a *Hill-song*), I find it very ill-suited to compositions essentially expressive & melodic. For such styles I much covet the warmth & throbbing nasality of woodwind, were these qualities only combinable with a legato & sliding execution. To attain this combination I intend constructing woodwind instruments with sliding tubes, the lengthening & shortening of which will produce lowness & highness of pitch, respectively.

By this means it is possible to procure for these instruments the unlimited pitch possibilities & sliding unbroken-toned expressiveness of the human voice, whistling, strings, etc.

Other Instruments

Brass: I use very sparingly for reasons given in 'Sound-producers treated collectively.'[15]

Percussion instruments: practically not at all, occasionally a kettle-drum for a bar or so, but very rarely.[16]

Banjos, guitars, etc. occasionally find a place in my British-folk-lore settings; *harps* I never use.

(*b*) Sound-Producers Treated Collectively

I cannot but regard the conventionalising of the practically unlimited possibilities of sound mixing into a few set, stock combinations as narrowing to style versatility. Roughly speaking (excluding solo music, which I class as solo-voice, with piano, orchestral or other instrumental accompaniment, and solo instrumental, with piano, orchestral or other instrumental accompaniment), the following combinations comprise the resources in vogue at present:

chamber music, usually for from two to six, rarely for more than eight, instruments, generally strings, or strings & piano, very occasionally solo woodwind (seldom more than one of any family at a time); also pianoforte duet.

string orchestra, usual order of which is 1st violins, 2nd violins, violas, cellos, double basses.

small orchestra strings in usual order, weak woodwind & horns (one or two of each family).

large orchestra strings in usual order (occasionally more freely divided) about two (very occasionally as many as four) of each family of woodwind, strong brass (two to three trumpets, three or four trombones, tuba, four or more horns), kettle-drums, & frequently other percussion (bigdrum, cymbals, triangle, etc.).

vocal ensemble (two to four, & more voices) textal, with or without piano or other accompaniment.

---

[15] See below.

[16] Grainger did, especially in his American years, become an advocate for extensive use of percussion. See e.g. Essay **21**.

chorus (male & female, very occasionally boys' voices, separate & mixed) textal, with & without orchestral or piano accompaniment.[17]

The facility of performing music written within these narrow limits (set combinations of executants—choral, orchestral, chamber music & other societies, both professional & amateur—being prepared for the performances of works scored for their particular set combinations) is no doubt of commercial, though not of artistic, advantage. Nor are these few set combinations so satisfactory as to justify their exclusive use.

The five fat lines of sound we get from a usual string orchestra (resultant on the order of division given on the last page) are exceedingly clumsy & elementary. To say the very least, this inflexible manner of dividing does away with the practically endless number of beautiful & contrasting possibilities of tone coloring presented by a body of, say, sixty to eighty strings. To get the most perfect sound blending we often need divisions of the same instrument playing simultaneously at different altitudes, as for instance: some of the violins to be humming on the rich, soft G string while other violin divisions are soaring polyphonically at their utmost heights; or again: we want the full bass of the cello's C string, rich middle voices on the G & D strings (high up in their second octave), while the strong, piercing timbre of the A string is cutting through the dull thick tone of the violas & the low strings of the violins; so too: we desire at the same moment to hear the double bass's woolly legato bass, its pulseful, booming pizzicato, & its very high notes *arco* in a passionate lower-middle voice.

Further: Two-part passages are well scored as single-parts & double-stopping for the same instruments simultaneously. Whereas: for coarse, or very rhythmic, or heavy effects as little dividing as possible is often advisable.

To realize these, & such-like, contrasts & characteristicnesses we require flexible (by which I mean *constantly changing*) divisions.[18]

An absolute lack of balance of sound results from usual modern small & large orchestral scorings, composers having considerably augmented the number of their string, brass & percussion instruments, but neglected to place their woodwind on an equal footing of strength, with the result that these latter instruments are frequently obliged to force their tone. In

---

[17] Grainger intended to insert a passage about brass and military bands at this point in the text.

[18] The continuation of Grainger's text from this point is not clearly indicated in the manuscript. It appears, however, that he intended to continue with the discussion, given below, of tone quality and balance, and then to proceed to an apparently incomplete section 'Concerning Works Done & Styles to Come', which is not reproduced below.

order to make themselves audible above the greater volume of the rest of the orchestra, they are often heard at a disadvantage. Then again, the brass is invariably apt, even in orchestras where the strings are very numerous, to swamp the latter, with balance being only arrived at by crampedly holding back the naturally robuster tone of the brass; while the percussion (say, a pair of kettle-drums, big drum, triangle, pair of cymbals) can with ease so thoroughly overdin all else as to make it at times veritably impossible to make sure of what the other instruments are playing. In other words, the modern large orchestra consists of four large sound-bodies of very contrasting degree of strength (I might say, four 'dynamic terraces') with large gaps between the average strength of sound. With such materials how can we look for balance?

The disadvantage of having such a small number of woodwind instruments makes itself felt in that—with the exception of two or three oboes & two or three bassoons (together forming a quartet or sextet, respectively)—it is impossible to write more than two- or three-part without having to mix different woodwind families, which mixing produces muddy tone quality. Thus, no chordal effects of any volume (such as are obtainable from a. four horns, b. three trumpets, three trombones & tuba, c. string orchestra) are possible if purity of timbre (getable only by using one woodwind family only at a time) is conditional.

Further, our chamber music is on such a small scale as to render it incapable of supplying the polyphony needful to embody our modern harmonic promptings: we need a greater number than from four to eight singing melodious strings to tally the intensity of emotion befitting our fervent era. As to piano & strings together (perhaps on this point I am narrow-minded), to me they sound just *the worst* when cooperating (the piano with its florid arabesques so necessary to its effectiveness, its fogging pedal, its unsustained unmelodiousness; strings with their untechnical leanings, their transparent clearness of timbre, their sustained melodiousness).

The same applies to pianoforte accompaniment to voice or voices (be it solo song, soli ensemble, or chorus). The tone quality of the piano strikes me as colorless, or at the best, as imitatory of the effects of other instruments (harp, brass, woodwind, etc.) with the exception of some few effects (on which Chopin's, Liszt's, & the modern Slavonic piano styles are based) native to the instrument, the outcome of its physical nature, &, to my mind, the only excuse for its existence. These effects, roughly speaking, range between clanging, bell-like passages (octaves, chunking chords, ping-chingy sounds—of which two instances are the second

movement of Tchaikovsky's Piano Concerto No. 1, & Chopin's A flat
Etude[19]) & rippling wavy effects (arpeggios of the most varied kinds—to
quote a curious instance, Chopin's Prelude in E flat[20]—pedalled harp-
like cadenzas, etc.) forcibly calling to mind the double origin of the
modern pianoforte, from the plucked harp, on the one hand, & from
the Eastern European hammered string instrument, on the other. These
above-mentioned truly pianistic effects, & the styles thereon built, seem
to me to tend unmistakably solo-wards, rather than ensemble-wards. At
any rate, they are diametrically opposed to the broad expressiveness of
strings & voices, &, on that ground, seem to me unfitted to cooperate with
these in a style specializing, to such an extent as does mine, in sound
purity.

Besides the undeveloped state of vocalism generally (dealt with in
'Sound-producers treated separately' under 'Vocalism'[21]) it is remarkable
how very few examples there are of choral polyphony—*real polyphony*.

What glorious 'colouring'—unexplored country, too—remains to be
done with voices, both solo voices, combinations & choral! But to get the
richest results vocalism must be handled with sweep, breadth & audac-
ity—in large masses, twelve- to sixteen-part, if need be (six divisions of
boys' or women's voices, & three, or more, each of tenors, baritones,
basses). Flexible, too, so that the sodden thickness of, say, five-part
writing could change straight into, say, twelve, float-somer parts, soaring
& luscious.

All through I am keen for endless mutability, both as regards *a.* scoring
each piece for fresh combinations of sound-producers, & *b.* keeping the
strength, & number of divisions, of my large sound bodies flexible.

Regarding ever-changefulness of setting: each separate composition
starts, to my mind, from a slightly different prompting, each prompting
requiring something peculiar to itself in the embodiment it is to receive
(some delicately differentiated ownness to the emotional cause of each
portioning it off from all others). This individuality so never-absent
from the smallest atom of a man's work should, to my mind, not be
stifled by commercial or conventional considerations (whether a work
be easily performable, or suit the previous usuality), or attempts after
mechanical duplicatory regularity, but should rather be allowed free
scope to impress man's art works with the everlasting mutability &

---

[19] Probably Op. 25 No. 1, although conceivably Op. posth. No. 2.
[20] Op. 28 No. 19.   [21] Section (*a*), above.

never-twice-occurring-ness of the *universal scheme's way*. Personally, I find that each new idea needs its own particular selection of sound-producer combinations.

Regarding flexibility of handling large sound bodies: suppose a piece (an Australian bush-song, for instance), commencing softly, delicately, swelling gradually up to an intense pitch of breadth & force, at length again sinking down into a vague & gliding *pianissimo* ending—how fitting to open & close with the veiled, thin delicacy of solo instruments, up towards the central climax to continually introduce fresh solo instruments, then, little by little, to bring these together into the fewer, fatter sound-lines of the orchestra (each part fully-voiced, 'stark besetzt'), and reversing the process down off the climax.

Of course, compositions built on these lines—each scored for fresh combinations, inside of which the parts are flexible—in themselves are most expensive (at the present, *utterly impossible*) to print & perform, but I hold that no trouble or expense is too great if it effects only the *very least little* improvement, in any way.

So as not to destroy the balance so imperative to me, I use very little brass (with the exception of horns, which I have much liking for, particularly in conjunction with strings), & that very sparingly; indeed, it is my intention, in the future, only extremely rarely to make use of brass (horns always excepted) in conjunction with the strings & woodwinds, whereas, on the other hand, I can quite imagine a style of composition for brass & gongs & bells by themselves, that would be quite glorious in its richness & boom. Purity of woodwind timbre is a great feature in my orchestration, thus in a *Hill-song*[22] I score for six oboes, six English horns, six bassoons & one contrabassoon, while in my usual orchestral scores a band of four fl., four ob., two Engl. horns, four cl., two bass cl., four fag., one contra-fag., as against four horns, two trumpets, three trombones. In the future, I look forward to doing much with my sliding woodwind, to let them *slide* passionately together with the strings, for instance, in my *Sea-songs*.[23] Strings *espress.*[23] & gliding lack the nasal bitterness of woodwind, while woodwind *espress.* lack the legato of strings. This departure (introduction of slides) opens up a new world to woodwind, permits them to take part not only in what is plaintive & pastoral, but also in what is soulful & profound.

[22] No. 1 (1901–2). Its original instrumentation also included two piccolos.
[23] Presumably *espressivo*.

Before leaving 'Sound-producers collectively' I wish to give a few examples of some combinations typical of unrestricted use of fresh combinations to each composition. The following are some 'possibilities':

(*a*) Men's chorus, textal unison, accompanied by whistlers, strings in fourteen divisions, four horns, two bassoons.

(*b*) Four violins, three violas, three cellos, one double bass (voices, textless, two tenors, two baritones, one bass).

(*c*) Mixed chorus (textal), accompanied by twelve nasal woodwinds.

(*d*) (Folksong setting) Melody in women's chorus, unison, textal, accompanied by whistlers (divided in four parts), and four men's solo voices (textless).

(*e*) Pieces for six cellos and one double bass.

(*f*) Men's chorus (textless), in seven parts, & brass (four horns, four trombones) & contra-fag.

(*g*) (Folksong setting) Melody in men's chorus unison (textal), accompanied by three horns, four clarinets, three bassoons, cellos & double basses *pizz*.

(*h*) (A Hill-song score) Three piccolos, four oboes, four Engl. horns, four bassoons, six clarinets, four bass clarinets, two contra-bassoons.

(*i*) Whistlers in five parts, boys' voices in four parts, men's voices divided (three tenors, four baritones, three basses).

(*j*) Orchestra—violins in six divisions, violas in four divisions, cellos in five divisions, double basses in three divisions, four sliding horns, six sliding clarinets, three sliding bass clarinets, two sliding deep woodwind instruments.[24]

---

[24] Here followed Grainger's section 'Concerning Works Done & Styles to Come'. This section, apparently still incomplete, contained detailed commentary on most of the works listed in Grainger's 'Catalogue of Styles, Works' (above).

4   *Beatless-Notation Machine*
(1902/3)

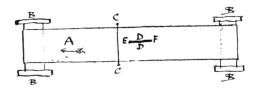

The notation will be on thin paper (A) run slowly *always at the same speed* from right to left upon electrically-rotating wheels (B), the reading to be from left to right; notes are indicated by lines, the length of which stand for the length of time they are to be held-out for, thus: when the left end (E) of a note (D) reaches a thin wire thread (C) strung right near *on the reader's side* of the passing paper, it—the note—is to be sounded & kept until its right end (F) leaves the said wire thread.[1]

The notation is so put together that the (*a*) length of duration, & (*b*) height of pitch, of each note as it is indicated on the paper, strikes the reader's eye at once, & in exact proportion to how it is to be sounded.

(*a*) The going-over from sight to sound is immediate & at first-hand, getting rid of the between-stage of oversetting[2] in the player's mind, & haphazard reliance upon the accuracy—*mostly inaccuracy*—of his individual sense of relative duration, involved by the present system. In the put-forward scheme the reader will guess the duration of each note before it reaches the wire thread, by how the length of the line indicating it strikes his eye, as he would sum up the size of a pencil, or match, not by what division—$\frac{1}{2}$, or 8th, or 32th, a.s.o.[3]—it forms of a preconceived standard of duration. This impression will be finally tested, & if need be set right, by the time taken by the said line in passing *that time between reaching & leaving* the wire thread. With oftenness of reading these two

Source: Undated manuscript sheets of 'Inventions and Technical Sundries' on headed paper of Palace Hotel Aberdeen (where Grainger stayed in Oct. 1902) and of the RMS *Omrah* (on which Grainger and his mother sailed from England to Australia in July–Sept. 1903). Grainger Museum, Melbourne.

[1] During Mar.–Apr. 1904, while aboard ship returning from South Africa to England, Grainger elaborated the design of his 'Beatless Music Typer'.

[2] Translating *Übersetzung* (Germ.).   [3] And so on.

processes of guessing in advance & testing afterward will jointly work together till as if one action.

The wheels [are] to be started all-together from a button; in the case of orchestral works, from the bandmaster's desk. The starting-off-pat & equal running *of all the wheels turning the different parts* needful to exact playing-together, will likely prove one of the things of this scheme hardest to put through.

(*b*) the farness on paper between halftones is always the same (otherwise than present notation where the space between D & E—three halftones—is greater than that between E♭ & F—three halftones)[4] as a writing-down of a chromatic scale from F to F will show:-

Thus, the same row of intervals would offer the same picture to the eye, however transposed.

Two clefs only will be used, corresponding to treble and bass, for all 8ths,[5] & all sound-producers, instead of the muddling four clefs, four 8th transpositions, & five key transpositions usual in a big orchestral score of today. The following set of staves hold all the notes of the piano:

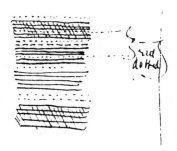

---

[4] Grainger's point here is clear, but his example is obscure. From his diagram he appears to be referring to such differences in representation as D–F (three half-tones) which is represented by the full distance between adjacent staff lines while G♯–B♮ (also three half-tones) is represented by only three-quarters of the distance between adjacent staff lines.

[5] Octaves.

I have to pay for this greater simplicity, uniformity & easier reading by the more room that my system takes, and also greater bulkiness of copies, for double-staving will be the rule for pretty well all sound-producers, as clef-changing on the same stave is not to be thought of, for [reason] that the entry of a new clef upon the stave might get in the road of the length *tokening duration* of a note-indicating line.[6] The machine will bring this notation to paper as follows: playing on a piano keyboard hung together or not at will with the sounding parts of the instrument will (*a*) in the case of a sketch-proof type straight onto paper, (*b*) in the case of ended stuff to be lastingly taken down, cut hole-lines into a thin metal sheet, by wrist-action (much on same lines as the air-driven playing of the 'Pianola'), through the slits of which the final printing will work.

As long as a note of the said keyboard be held down, so long will (*a*) in the case of a sketchproof, the line standing for it show on paper; (*b*) in the case of final-printing, the slit be cut in the metal sheet, & thence onto the ended copy.

Of any ensemble compositions the score alone will need to come onto the metal sheet, off which, while the score is being taken down in smallish type, the full number of—twenty of each, if need be—all the parts it holds will simultaneously be reeled off in double-sized type; which printing of score & parts, to the second together, will ensure the oneness of line-lengths between all voices needful towards pat rhythmic playing.

Thus, by merely playing on a keyboard—far easier & incalculably quicker than handwriting—I have all the needful same paper, & power for the machine to turn out thousands of copies, can, in short, print my own things; be my own publisher.

As bearing on performance, the notation will do away with the following evils of the present system—player's having to shift his eyes off what he is reading to follow bandmaster's beat, count rests, turn over; player's risk of losing his place on paper, risk of copy not keeping open properly, or falling off desk, wearing-out & dirtying, & unreadableness therefrom, of the copy through being fingered at turning over—& will hold out the great advantage of the bandmaster no longer needing to wave his arms about to hold things together, [but] being able to rivet his whole mind onto sound-balance & points of expression, & the bringing out of the

---

[6] Grainger provided an example of a bass clef being introduced midway through a (previously) treble stave.

finer shadings of sound-strength than before possible, & being free to get
way back to all parts of the hall to better test there at some farness.

But the biggest pull will lie in the simplicity with which now
complicated-seeming rhythmic phrases will strike the player. Thus,

will show merely as ≥_____ ≥_ ᴧ_ ᴧ_ ᴧ_ ᴧ_ ᴧ. In the most
irregular, off-beat passages the player will not need to bring to bear any
preconceived standard of regular relative duration, but will merely follow
the *rhythmic picture before his eyes at the moment*, & will feel his part
rhythmically *positively*, not *negatively*, in contrasting it with the general-
ity—the beats as now. This difference ought to make for greater rhythmic
genuineness & singleheartedness of attack in his playing.

One possibility under the old system is here done away with: that of the
difference, for instance, between

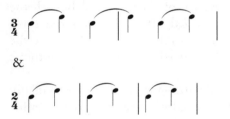

&

& all such so charmfully used by Brahms. But this is not shut out by the
notation more wholly than by the fundamental nature of the kind of
music the notation is built to set down. For the *exceptionalness* of an
irregular passage, such as

is surest proof of how, altogether, regularity is the general *rule*.

A strong point of the put-forward notation seems to me to be that,
though fundamentally other in the possibilities & rhythmic thought it
opens up than the present system, it could be easily & speedily—if not at
once—read by anyone knowing the latter.

The limitlessly narrow divisions that it would allow of would come in
handy should it ever need to do duty:

firstly, as a chart of scale-of-vibrations—should we choose to imagine at 820 vibrs (worse luck, I have no idea of the right no.)[7] at 825, at 830, at 835, the whole sum of 15 vibrations could be tucked away between the next-topmost & topmost lines of what amounts to the treble clef, thus:

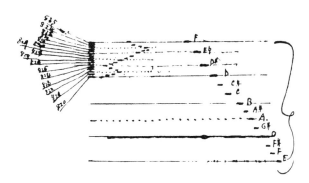

It seems to me highly wishable that the science—the *real* science, such as Helmhol[t]z's,[8] not the mockery of harmony books—& practice of the art be bridged by a notation usable for both, as this would be. Along such a common highway the two lines of thought might meet oftener than they now do, & their intercourse breed much good.

secondly, in connection with *absolute tuning* (should that question come up again). Though at first sight the notation seems to fit tempered-tuning alone, making, as it does, no difference between D♯ & E♭, & such enharmonic changes, yet in reality only such a flexible recorder as this is could cope with the nice distinctions between G×, A♮, B♭♭, C♭♭♭, a.s.o., & such, that absolute tuning leads to if driven to full lengths.

thirdly, in connection with *pitch emancipation* (relative to the *rhythmic emancipation* I have already in part, & will, I trust, one day wholly, put through) should that movement—a very likely one—once get going. It is just as much on the cards that *regular pitch divisions* should be broken down as *regular rhythmic divisions*.

The one fundamental law of sound harmonics would not stand in the road of such a movement any [more]. In it, the law applies upwards, from

---

[7] With A = 440 Hz, correctly D = 587.4 Hz.
[8] Hermann von Helmholtz (1821–94), German doctor and acoustician, author of *On the Sensations of Tone* (1863; Eng. trans., 1875).

the bottom to the top of chords & not sidelong, from one chord to another.

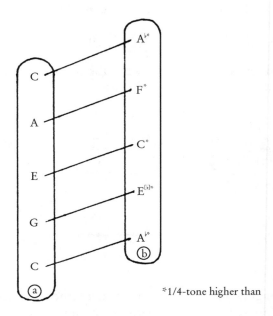

*1/4-tone higher than

Thus, a chord (side (*a*)) slid up to a height ((*b*)), lying halfway between the half-tones of the chromatic scale its starting-place lay within, would all along its upward journey between (*a*) & (*b*), as also in its final resting-place ((*b*)), be obeying the laws of harmonics as wholly as in its first position ((*a*)). In other words, harmonics have to do with chords *singly*, & not with their *shifting*, or *order-of-following*.

I touch upon pitch emancipation not as a fad, or thing I look to ever aim at—my life will have no room for it—but merely as a physical possibility, which as such is pretty sure to be worked for all it is worth, sooner or later.

fourthly, in taking down Eastern, native, or any music run on another scale than our European.

5   *The Music of Cyril Scott*
(1912)

In Cyril Scott's[1] music I see marked national characteristics as well as strong personal ones. Apart from the more obviously English note of energetic athletic gaiety that balances the dreamy and the lyrical elements in his work, I find his creative habits typical of his country. He is instinctive and wayward rather than mental and painstaking in his compositional methods, an attitude I meet with remarkably often among English composers.

Cyril Scott composes rather like a bird sings, with a full positive soul behind him, drawing greater inspiration from the physical charm of actual sound than from any impetus from philosophical preoccupations or the dramatic emotions of objective life. Thus, while Strauss is largely concerned with philosophical themes, and Debussy apparently often full of pictorial suggestions and influences, it is mainly the pure delight of the ear in musical sounds (how they sound rather than what they express) that coaxes utterance from Cyril Scott's touching and poetical emotional self. This preponderance of the purely musical elements in his art strikes me as a result that might almost be expected of the conditions of music in England.

In a country where, until recently, musical expression was not a widely cultivated or coveted accomplishment, we may expect to find those chiefly resorting to it who are primarily attracted to music for music's sake—those on whom the charm of euphony as such exerts a strong hold; just as in a country surfeited with musical experiences like Germany, where musical expression has long been a habit even of comparatively unmusical individuals (or at least of many in whom other instincts than musical ones preponderate), we are not surprised to find music often tending to become a more or less 'applied art' and a vehicle for ideas not constitutionally inclined to manifest themselves in sound, and purely acoustic sensations coveted less and less merely for the peculiar satisfaction felt in experiencing them.

No doubt the German-speaking people (open-hearted and generous

Source: Music Student, 5/2 (Oct. 1912), 31–3.
[1] (1879–1970), English pianist and composer.

towards foreign art and artists as they are) find Scott's very Englishness and the sharp contrast his methods bear to their own contemporary ones, refreshing and attractive. Certainly his fame is growing very rapidly in Germanic lands, and it was delightful to hear of the warm enthusiasm aroused by the recent performance of his orchestral *Princess Maleine Overture* in Vienna.[2]

'The' Musical Emotion

Amongst the many diverse states of feeling bound up with music, there is one I am almost tempted to call '*the* musical emotion' so universally does it underlie the musics of various races (wild and tame), the singing of birds and even the calls of beasts. I refer to that instinct for giving forth soaring, seething, throbbing sounds in a sort of rapt continuous ecstasy, a kind of half religious, half sensuous, thankful joy overflowing into sound that is suggested by Milton's *At a Solemn Music*, and is present equally in Bach (think of the opening chorus of the *Matthew Passion*) and in the chanting of savages and the sounds of the forest. This wildly dreamy elation is a dominant note in Cyril Scott's compositions. Out of countless instances I may cite the glowing euphony of the opening of the soulful slow movement of his sextet (now re-worked into a quintet) for piano and strings, the victorious sweep of the last two pages of the Finale of his quartet for piano and strings, Op. 16[3] (a highly effective printed work that we hear far too seldom), and the rich polyphonic melodic flow of high passages for strings that is such a frequent and beautiful feature of his orchestral scoring (for instance, in the *Aubade* for orchestra recently published by Schott).[4]

The Improvising Instinct

It would be hard to exaggerate the extent to which Cyril Scott is instinctive, natural and effortless as a composer. He has a natural gift for conducting, and could have been a remarkable and fascinating piano virtuoso had he chosen. The range of his musical appreciation is enormous; no

---

[2] Scott was dissatisfied with the work, however, and in the late 1920s reworked it, with help from Grainger, into *A Festival Overture*.
[3] Piano Quartet in E minor (1903).   [4] Op. 77, for large orchestra (1911).

style seems too far removed from his own personal emotional type to appeal to him, suddenly and sometimes inexplicably. The very possibility of jealous or partisan feelings about art is utterly foreign to him. A born enthusiast rather than a critic, his admiration is easily fanned into a generous and benevolent flame, and his music is for me the facile expression of a soul so noble, so poised, so delicately tuned and so void of all negative disturbing phases that it can afford to don freedom and waywardness as its most becoming garments. He is a throw-back to a type seemingly rare amongst musicians of to-day—*the improvising composer*. A large portion of his music is crystallised improvisation, or reflects the rambling flow of extemporising rather than the built-up construction of the so-called 'architectural' school of composition. He has an unusually accurate ear and can enjoy minute details in blurred and intertwined sounds and can consequently effortlessly improvise what to less naturally highly organised musicians might easily appear to be involved complexities.

Thus, in his teens in Frankfurt he often dashed off extemporised quasi-fugues similar to the Fugue in his second pianoforte Suite (Op. 75),[5] though he would probably not have been able then to bring them to paper without sophisticating them somewhat in the process.

To the delicate accuracy of his hearing he very likely, to some extent, owes the superlative charm, originality and refinement of his harmonic 'texture', by which I mean effects of chord-colour arising out of a very critical sense for the distribution of the component parts of chords. Not only are his chords delicious in the sequences in which they occur, but taken singly almost each one forms a gem of euphony in itself. In no particular does his genius seem to me more transcendental than in this matter of texture. A glance at the 'Solemn Dance' from his Op. 75 will explain anything I have failed to make clear.

Scott and Debussy

It is not unusual to hear Cyril Scott's name coupled with Debussy's, and indeed these two have many affinities. Both compose with their ears rather than with their brains, both vibrate with the wistful poetry of fleeting things, and both are above all harmonic path-breakers along the lines opened up by Grieg's great harmonic emancipations and innovations. These traits of likeness are partly fundamental ones of

[5] 1910.

temperament, partly merely the simultaneous development of similar technical resources.

But in neither case should it be assumed that the younger composer copied the elder because he resembles him. The points of likeness are much older than Cyril Scott's first contact with Debussy's music. When I heard the latter for the first time (*and before Scott did*) in 1902, passage after passage awoke the thought: 'How like Cyril Scott'. Certain Debussy-ish elements in Scott's work have no doubt intensified since that date, for such additions to the common stock of means of musical expression, such technical advances applicable to the most varied personalities as Debussy's could surely only be passed by by those too ungifted to be healthily tempted by such generous opportunities. Similarly, there is scarcely one of us composers who were thrown together with Cyril Scott early in our compositional activities whose work does not reveal frequent traces of his inspiration and influence. But the Englishness and the strong personal note in Scott's work has never been impaired by contact with Debussy's exquisite art, and the two geniuses still continue to form delightfully sharp contrasts to each other despite certain welcome affinities and mutual admiration.

A Writer of 'Singable' Songs

Cyril Scott's preoccupation with the sensations of actual sound has stood him in good stead as a song writer. It would be hard to find songs more palpably singable than his. The curves of the vocal phrases 'feel well in the mouth', and owe a great measure of their originality to the resemblance they bear to the sort of thing anybody would naturally feel inclined to sing rather than to the half-instrumental passages many modern song composers seem unnaturally inclined to write.

Perhaps his combination of singableness with wealth of harmonic invention and emotional depth has reached one of its furthest points in his wonderfully poetical and imaginative Chinese Songs, Op. 46 ('Waiting' and 'A Picnic'),[6] while one of his very most touching creations is his recent setting of Rossetti's lovely poem 'An Old Song Ended'.[7] Here the blending of simple diatonic melody with 'far-fetched' subtle and wholly Scottian harmonisation is wondrously telling, and appeals as naturally to the listener as it came to the composer.

---

[6] 1906, to texts by Giles.   [7] 1911.

The Piano Music

Nor is his piano writing one whit less pianistic than his songs are vocal. Not only has he tapped the mellow wealth of the instrument's harmonic resources to the full in pieces of a lyric, dreamy and tender nature, but has further created a clattering scintillating type of 'Klavier-satz' all his own and thereby added a whole batch of irresistibly 'taking' items to the concert repertory. The fast-growing international popularity of such varied pieces as *Lotus Land*, *Sphinx*, the two *Etudes* (Op. 64), the two *Pierrot Pieces* (Op. 35), *Danse Nègre*,[8] etc., need not surprise us.

A Man of Many Styles

The range of his contrasts and the number of his widely divergent styles are immense, but all are vividly coloured by his intense personality.

It is a far cry from the tender flower-like sensitiveness of his enchanting setting for violin and piano of 'Cherry Ripe'[9] to the rollicking 'ragtime' rhythms and 'Darky' flavour of his *Tallahassee* Suite (for violin and piano),[10] and again from the drowsy exotic lilt of the 'Danse Orientale', Op. 74,[11] to the highly Western manly energy of his vital Piano Sonata, Op. 66,[12] and the bracing vigour and thematic pregnance of his *Handelian Rhapsody*, Op. 17.[13]

But even Elkin's delightfully voluminous list of his piano pieces and songs, and Schott's publications of orchestral, chamber, and larger piano works, do not yet cover the whole field of his astonishing versatility. It is a pleasure to recall the electrically spontaneous success of his irresistible orchestral *English Dance*, No. 2,[14] at Balfour Gardiner's series of concerts last spring,[15] and again of his two orchestral Dances at Birmingham a short time back, and to see several orchestral works by him figuring in Sir Henry Wood's 'Promenade' programmes. For, poet and master as he is in dealing with small forms and the lesser sound-bodies, we shall not know Cyril Scott to the full until performances of his large orchestral and choral

---

[8] Respectively: Op. 47 No. 1 (1905), Op. 63 (1908), Op. 64 (1908), Op. 35 (1904), and (1908).

[9] 1911, No. 1 of *Two Old Airs Transcribed*.

[10] Op. 73 (1910).

[11] 1910, No. 2 of *Trois Danses Tristes*.

[12] 1909.

[13] 1901, edited by Grainger (1909), from Scott's early piano Sonata.

[14] The third of *Three Symphonic Dances*, originally Scott's Second Symphony (1903).

[15] 1 May 1912, conducted by Grainger. The concerts were financially underwritten by Henry Balfour Gardiner. See Essay **45**.

works become more frequent and representative of his great achievements in these branches. It is in handling the long lines of big musical forms and the richest and most varied blends of orchestral colour that Cyril Scott will most conclusively manifest the advantages of the free fluidity of his peculiar methods of composing, and reveal the most subtle depths of his artistic soul to those musical publics in various countries that have already acclaimed the genius of his smaller works.

Part II

1915–1921

Part II

1919-1921

6

*The Impress of Personality in
Unwritten Music*
(1915)

Extremes Attract

It seems to me a very hopeful sign that the present widespread interest
in unwritten music (be it European or Afro-American folk-songs and
dances or native music from any quarter of the globe) apparently does not
emanate from any reaction against the latest iconoclastic developments of
our written art music, but that, on the contrary, it is mainly in the ranks of
the most highly cultured musicians (men whose depth of heart and brain
makes them equally capable of appreciating the glorious creations of the
great classics and the no less thrilling achievements of the most extreme
modernists of to-day) that we meet with the keenest interest in this 'back
to the land' movement. Among those who have recently devoted themselves most ardently to the labor of actually collecting so-called 'primitive' music of various kinds or in whose creative work direct or indirect
contact with it has proven the most fruitful we find the names of such
advanced composers as Stravinsky, Debussy, Ravel, Albéniz, Granados,
Cyril Scott, Vaughan Williams, Balfour Gardiner[1] and Ferruccio Busoni,[2]
while the great Frederick Delius[3] (to my mind perhaps *the* rarest and most
precious musical genius of our age) owes the fact of his becoming a composer at all to the inspiration he received from hearing Negro workers
sing on his father's plantation in Florida, which determined him to give up
a commercial career in order to study music in Leipzig; a debt to unwritten music that he has fittingly repaid by basing three of his loveliest works
on themes of 'primitive' origin: *Appalachia*, on a Negro-American tune,
Brigg Fair on the English peasant song of that name from my collection,
and his recent *On Hearing the First Cuckoo in Spring* on the Norwegian
'I Ola Dalom' (published in Grieg's Op. 66).[4]

Source: Musical Quarterly, 1 (1915), 416–35.

[1] (1877–1950), English composer and fellow student of Grainger in Frankfurt.
[2] (1866–1924), Italian-born pianist and composer, with whom Grainger had briefly studied in
Berlin during 1903.
[3] (1862–1934), English composer, long resident in France, whose works Grainger had fiercely
championed since their first meeting in 1907.
[4] All for orchestra, 1896, 1907, and 1912, respectively.

In an essay in *The North American Review* for February, 1913,[5] full of insight and rare understanding, by that champion of Russian and other modern music, Mr. Kurt Schindler,[6] on 'Boris Godounoff, and the life of Moussorgsky,' we read how incalculably much the inspired art of that composer owed to the close contact with both the life and the music of Russian peasants.

Primitive Music is Too Complex for Untrained Modern Ears

While so many of the greatest musical geniuses listen spellbound to the unconscious, effortless musical utterances of primitive man, the general educated public, on the other hand, though willing enough to applaud adaptations of folk-songs by popular composers, show little or no appreciation of such art in its unembellished original state, when, indeed, it generally is far too complex (as regards rhythm, dynamics, and scales) to appeal to listeners whose ears have not been subjected to the ultra-refining influence of close association with the subtle developments of our latest Western art music.

The case of Grieg is typical. For over thirty years his popularity has been almost universally accredited to 'national' traits supposed to have been drawn by him from Norwegian folk-songs; but few indeed, at home or abroad, can have taken the trouble to study these elements in their native purity, or they would have discovered for themselves what has been left to Grieg's greatest and most sympathetic biographer, Mr. Henry T. Finck,[7] to point out often and ably: how much more the Norwegian genius owed the unique originality of his music to the strength of his own purely personal inventiveness than to any particular external or 'national' source whatever. They would also have been in a position to more fully realize the generosity with which Grieg threw the richness of his strong personality into the task of making the wonders of the peasant music accessible in such avowed 'arrangements' as Opp. 30, 66, and 72. In these volumes (still strangely little known) we find some of the most inspired examples of his harmonic daring, the more extreme methods of to-day being foreshadowed, again and again, some twenty years ago, with the prophetic quality of true genius.

---

[5] 1 (1913), 256.

[6] (1882–1935), German-born American composer and conductor, and editor for G. Schirmer.

[7] (1854–1926), American critic, author of *Edvard Grieg* (1906) and *Grieg and his Music* (1909).

Well-Diluted Folk Music

As a rule folk music finds its way to the hearts of the general public and of the less erudite musicians only after it has been 'simplified' (generally in the process of notation by well-meaning collectors ignorant of those more ornate subtleties of our notation alone fitted for the task) out of all resemblance to its original self. Nor is this altogether surprising when we come to compare town populations with the country-side or 'savage' folk to whom we go for the unwritten material.

Uncivilized Lives Abound in Music

With regard to music, our modern Western civilization produces, broadly speaking, two main types of educated men. On the one hand the professional musician or leisured amateur-enthusiast who spends the bulk of his waking hours making music, and on the other hand all those many millions of men and women whose lives are far too overworked and arduous, or too completely immersed in the ambitions and labyrinths of our material civilization, to be able to devote any reasonable proportion of their time to music or artistic expression of any kind at all. How different from either of these types is the bulk of uneducated and 'uncivilized' humanity of every race and color, with whom natural musical expression may be said to be a universal, highly prized habit that seldom, if ever, degenerates into the drudgery of a mere means of livelihood.

Mental Leisure and Art

Mental leisure and ample opportunity for indulging in the natural instinct for untrammelled and uncriticised and untaught artistic self-expression; these are the conditions imperative for the production and continuance of all unwritten music. Now primitive modes of living, however terrible some of them may appear to some educated and refined people, are seldom so barren of 'mental leisure' as the bulk of our civilized careers. The old ignorant, unambitious English yokel, for instance, had plenty of opportunities for giving way to his passion for singing. He sang at his work (plough songs are very general) just as the women folk sang when 'waulking' wool.[8] I need hardly mention that 'work-songs' of every

---

[8] i.e. finishing hand-woven tweed.

description form a very considerable part of the music of primitive races the world over.

Life Encroaching upon Art

Not only does the commercial slavery of our civilization hold out to the average man insufficient leisure for the normal growth of the habit of artistic expression (unless he shows talents *exceptional* enough to warrant his becoming a professional artist) but the many decorums of modern society deny to most of us any very generous opportunities for using even our various (unartistic) life-instincts to the full; 'sich ausleben', as the Germans so well put it. It is, therefore, not surprising that with us art frequently becomes the vehicle of expression for accumulated forces, thoughts and desires, which, under less civilized conditions, more often find their normal outlet in actions. This state of things no doubt in part accounts for the desire of the composers of programme music to cram their scores with passages reflecting psychological conflicts or depicting Fate or windmills or critics (I am not cavilling at this, for I adore Strauss's symphonic poems) and also accounts for the everlasting presence of erotic problems (of which Bernard Shaw has written so deliciously in his Prelude to *Plays for Puritans*[9]) in most modern literature.

Art Encroaching upon Life

In short, with us moderns life is apt to encroach upon art, whereas with uneducated or primitive folk the reverse seems more often to be the case. Their lives, their speech, their manners, even their clothes all show the indelible impress of a superabundance of artistic impulses and interests. A modern Scandinavian has said of the old Norseman: 'They were always ready to throw away their lives for a witty saying'; and much the same literary attitude towards every-day speech may be observed in the queer old illiterate cronies from whom we get the English peasant songs or sea chanties. They show little or no keenness about money or desire to 'better' themselves, but they love to be 'wags', and crowd every moment

---

[9] *Three Plays for Puritans* (1900), containing *The Devil's Disciple, Caesar and Cleopatra*, and *Captain Brassbound's Conversion*. In his Preface Shaw decried the way in which theatre had settled on 'the instinct of sex as the avenue to all hearts'.

of the day with quaint and humorous sayings and antics. When finishing a song they will add: 'No harm done', or some equally abstract remark.

One of the best folk-singers I ever knew, who had the varied career of ship's cook, brick-maker and coal merchant, won a prize ('a fine silver pencil') for dancing at the age of fifty-four, performing to the playing of his brother, who was a 'left-handed fiddler', i. e., bowed with his left hand, and fingered with his right. There is a ballad called 'Bold William Taylor', found all over Great Britain, that tells how Sally Gray, abandoned by her faithless lover, William Taylor, dons 'man's apparel' and follows him to the wars, where she is informed that 'he's got married to an Irish lady', whereupon the two concluding verses run:

> And then she called for a brace of pistols,
> A brace of pistols at her command;
> And there she shot bold William Taylor
> With his bride at his right hand.
>
> And then the Captain was well pleased,
> Was well pleased what she had done;
> And then he made her a great commander
> Aboard of a ship, over all his men.[10]

One of the best songsters I ever met, whose name happened to be Joseph Taylor (of Saxby-All-Saints, Lincolnshire) had picked up this ditty on a short absence from home when a young man. On his return he found his mother in bed and her new-born baby beside her. 'What shall we call him?' he was asked, and being just then full of the newest addition to his repertoire of 'ballets' (as they are called by the rural singers) he replied: 'Christen him Bold William Taylor', and his advice was followed. I wonder how many babies of the educated classes have been named after a song?

H. G. Wells, the novelist, who was with me during a 'folk-song hunt' in Gloucestershire,[11] on noticing that I noted down not merely the music and dialect details of the songs, but also many characteristic scraps of banter that passed between the old agriculturalists around us, once said to me: 'You are trying to do a more difficult thing than record folk-songs; you are trying to record life'; and I remember the whimsical, almost wistful, look which accompanied the remark.

But I felt then, as I feel now, that it was the superabundance of art in

---

[10] See Grainger's 'Collecting with the Phonograph', *Journal of the Folk-Song Society*, 3 (1908), 147–242 (p. 217). Grainger set the song in 1908–9.

[11] In Apr. 1908.

these men's lives, rather than any superabundance of life in their art, that made me so anxious to preserve their old saws and note their littlest habits; for I realized that the every-day events of their lives appealed to these dirty and magnificently ignorant rustics chiefly in so far as they offered them opportunities for displaying the abstract qualities of their inner natures (indeed, they showed comparatively small interest in the actual material results involved), and that their placid comments upon men and things so often preferred to adopt the unpassionate *formal* and *patterned* habits of 'art' (so familiar to us in rural proverbs) rather than resemble the more passionate unordered behaviour of inartistic 'life'.

Personal Ownership of Songs

I need hardly say that natural artists of this order sing or play without self-consciousness of any kind, and anything resembling 'stage-fright' seems unknown to them. When such a one refuses to let himself be heard, it is, more often than not, because he regards his tunes as purely *personal property*, and does not wish to part with them to others any more than he would with his pipe or his hat. I recall the case of a rustic singer, who, in his anxiety to acquire a song from a fellow-folksinger of this sort, had to hide himself in a cupboard in order to learn it, as its owner would never have consented to sing it if he had dreamt his performance were being listened to by a rival; and I have myself had to get under a bed in order to note down the singing of an old woman equally chary of passing on her accomplishments to any 'Tom, Dick or Harry'.

   This feeling of personal ownership of songs is still more strongly shown by many primitive non-European races, notably by the North American Indians. That inspired and inspiring collector of their music and devoted champion of their cause, Miss Natalie Curtis,[12] wrote in an article, 'The Perpetuating of Indian Art', in the *Outlook* of November 22, 1913: 'Some songs are owned by families, even by individuals, and so highly do the Indians hold them that a man in dying may bequeath his own personal song to another, even as we bestow tangible possessions.' Striking individual instances of this attitude on the part of the Indians will be found in the same author's touching and impressive tribute to aboriginal American life and art, *The Indians' Book* (Harper & Bros., New York).[13]

---

[12] Natalie Curtis-Burlin (1875–1921), American ethnologist and ethnomusicologist. See Essay 12.

[13] (1907), containing over two hundred songs of eighteen different tribes.

The Impress of Personality: Unwritten Music is not Standardized[14]

The primitive musician unhesitatingly alters the traditional material he has inherited from thousands of unknown talents and geniuses before him to suit his own voice or instruments, or to make it conform to his purely personal taste for rhythm and general style. There is no written original to confront him with, no universally accepted standard to criticize him by. He is at once an executive and creative artist, for he not only remoulds old ditties, but also weaves together fresh combinations of more or less familiar phrases, which he calls 'making new songs'. His product is local and does not have to bear comparison with similar efforts imported from elsewhere.

I once let an old Lincolnshire man (a perfect artist in his way) hear in my phonograph a variant of one of the songs he had sung to me as sung by another equally splendid folk-singer, and asked him if he didn't think it fine. His answer was typical: 'I don't know about it's being fine or not; I only know it's *wrong*.' To each singer his own versions of songs are the only correct ones.

It would be difficult to exaggerate the extent to which such traditional singers embellish so-called 'simple melodies' with a regular riot of individualistic excrescences and idiosyncrasies of every kind, each detail of which, in the case of the most gifted songsters at any rate, is a precious manifestation of real artistic personality, so much so that a skilled notator will often have to repeat a phonographic record of such a performance some hundreds of times before he will have succeeded in extracting from it a representative picture on paper of its baffling, profuse characteristics.

What Seems Vocal to Folk-Singers

Many of these singers retain the ringing freshness of their voices until such advanced ages as seventy years and over, when they still enjoy a command of certain phases of vocal technique which even our greatest art-singers might try (as they certainly will not do) in vain to imitate, notably an enormous range of staccato and pianissimo effects. They seldom aim at attempting anything resembling a genuine legato style, but use their breath, more as do some birds and animals, in short stabs and

---

[14] For further discussion of issues and examples raised in this and following sections, see 'Impress of Personality in Traditional Singing', in Grainger, 'Collecting with the Phonograph', 163–9.

gushes of quickly contrasted, twittering, pattering and coughing sounds
which (to my ears, at least) are as beautiful as they are amusing. Somewhat
similar non-legato tendencies may be noted in the fiddling of British and
Scandinavian peasants, who are as fond of twiddles and quirks as are the
old singers, and do not try to exchange the 'up and down' physical nature
of the bow for the attainment of a continuous tone.

The Complexity of Folk Music

Returning to the folk-singers: rhythmical irregularities of every kind are
everywhere in evidence, and the folk scales in which their so-called
'modal' melodies move are not finally fixed as are our art scales, but
abound with quickly alternating major and minor thirds, sharp and flat
sevenths, and (more rarely) major and minor sixths, and whereas the sixth
of the scale occurs usually merely as a passing note all the other intervals
are attacked freely, either jumpingly from one to the other, or as initial
notes in phrases.

At least, this is my experience after an exhaustive examination of my
collection of close on 400 phonograph records of such tunes. Some
singers evinced a rooted objection to singing more notes than syllables,
and to avoid this add 'nonsense syllables' to and in between their words
(according to a definite system that seems to obtain throughout Great
Britain) rather than 'slur' two or more notes, occasioning such sentences
as: 'For to cree-oose (cruise) id-den (in) the chad-der-niddel (channel) of
old Engger-land's (England's) fame'. The following scrap from one of the
'Marlborough' songs is typical of the ornate style of many English traditional singers:

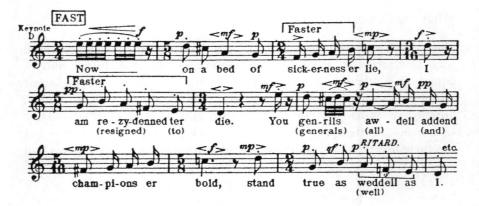

All Unwritten Music Exhibits Certain Common Traits

The whole art is in a constant state of flux, new details being continually added while old ones are abandoned. These general conditions prevail wherever unwritten music is found, and though I may never have heard Greenland or Red Indian music I feel pretty confident that as long as it is not too strongly influenced by the written music of our Western civilization it will evince on inspection much the same general symptoms as those displayed by the folk music of British, Russian or Scandinavian peasants, or by natives of the South Seas, and we may always be sure that the singing of (let us say) an unsophisticated Lincolnshire agriculturalist of the old school will in essentials approximate more closely to that of Hottentots or other savages than it will to the art music of an educated member of his own race living in a neighboring town.

Communal Polyphonic Improvisation

Even when natives have been exposed to the influence of European music long enough to have acquired from it the habit of singing in parts, sometimes the unmistakable characteristics of unwritten music will survive to a surprising extent and color all their harmonic habits. This has been brought home to me very forcibly by five phonograph records of the improvised part-singing of Polynesian natives from Rarotonga in the South Seas, which have come into my possession through the warm generosity of a very remarkable collector, Mr. A. J. Knocks, of Otaki, North Island, New Zealand.[15]

Description of Rarotongan Part-Singing

These choral songs, which were sung as thank-offerings by the Rarotongans in return for gifts they received from the Maoris of Otaki, are more full of the joy of life than any other music (art or native) it has yet been my good fortune to hear, though they also abound in touching and wistful elements. The polyphony displayed by the four to eight singers was prodigious, and as the whole thing went prestissimo (Polynesian

---

[15] (1849–1925). Grainger had visited Knocks in Otaki in 1909, and would see him again in 1925.

languages lend themselves very readily to speed) it reminded me of nothing so much as of a seething, squirming musical ant-hill, bursting into furious song for sheer joy and high spirits. No doubt the habit of harmony here displayed had been caught long ago from missionary hymns (Rarotonga was 'converted' before many of the other islands of the South Seas), yet the use made by these brilliant musicians of their foreign accomplishment was completely native in its application and was throughout governed by the individualistic dictates of Unwritten Music. Their procedure followed habits rather than laws.

Each part-song consisted of a succession of small sections, each lasting some fifteen to twenty seconds, and separated one from the other by a brief moment of silence.

A short solo began each section, consisting of a curving, descending phrase, starting off on the fourth, fifth or sixth of the diatonic major scale and ending on the tonic below. As soon as the first singer reached the keynote the other voices would chime in, one after the other or in a bunch, according to the free choice of each individual concerned, while the first singer kept up a stirring hammering and highly rhythmic patter (which in the phonograph closely resembles the twang of banjos or rattle of small drums, though actually no instruments at all were used) on the tonic until the end of the section.

These other voices also sang curving, descending diatonic phrases (never twice quite alike, but always bearing a sort of family likeness to those of the first singer), which were repeated by each singer several times before the end of the section, which was heralded by a growing lassitude in all the voices—often fading away in an indolent sort of 'dying duck' wail—whereas each new section was attacked in the most vigorous manner.

The various melodic lines as well as the whole character of the performance showed great variety during the course of a longish chain of such sections, while the harmonic and polyphonic happenings were kaleidoscopic in their everchanging aspects.

It will be seen that a great range of personal choice was left to all the members of this Rarotongan choir, in each of whom a highly complex, delicate and critical sense for ensemble was imperative. Each of these natives had to be a kind of improvising communal composer, and to a far greater degree simultaneously creative and executive than is the case with peasant songsters in Great Britain or Scandinavia, though a somewhat similar gift for complex improvised part-singing is displayed in the wonderful Russian choral folk music so admirably collected and noted by Madame Lineff.[16]

The Lack of Harmonic Consciousness

Attractive as are the passionate warmth of vocal color, the savage exhilarating rattle of the rhythms, and the often almost wistful sweetness of the melodic phrases heard in this Rarotongan music, most fascinating of all to a modern composer are the Bach-like gems of everchanging, euphoniously discordant polyphonic harmony which throughout surprise, baffle and soothe the ear, patches of concords alternating with whole successions of discords—mainly seconds.

To us moderns the results of this free polyphony makes a seductive *complex harmonic appeal*, but I doubt very much if the Rarotongans themselves hear their own music in this way, and I am more inclined to believe that they attain their unique results precisely because their exceptionally developed individualistic polyphonic instincts are still free from the kind of harmonic consciousness which art musicians have gradually built up through the centuries.

Quarter-Tones and Inexact Unison

It is, of course, widely known that many races use quarter-tones and other divisions of the scale smaller than those hitherto in vogue in Europe, and Ferruccio Busoni's illuminating pamphlet 'A New Esthetic of Music'[17] contains some very clear-sighted suggestions for the use of third-tones and other close intervals—suggestions which I fondly hope the near future may see carried into practice.

My own experience with such small intervals has been in the 'waiatas' and chants of the Maoris of New Zealand. Here all sorts of very close intervals are used in an indefinite, gliding sort of singing, which is very effective; but it is not my impression that these intervals are fixed as are those of our art scales. When several Maoris sing such chants together, great variations of intervals occur in the different voices, constituting a

---

[16] Eugenia Lineva (1854–1919), collector of songs of the Volga region, whose two-volume study appeared in 1904.

[17] 1907; Eng. trans. 1911.

kind of 'careless' or 'inexact' unison also noticeable in Egyptian singing and pipe-playing and in much Eastern music, which has a charm all its own and might with great advantage be used in our art music. In this sort of ensemble the musicians do not seem to make any attempt to attain an exact unison, and here also one is inclined to imagine that the ear of the native listener follows the path of each performer separately, and is not conscious of the discords that result from this 'loose fit' in a harmonical or 'horizontal' way, as we would be.

Musical 'Treasure Islands' in the Pacific and the Richness of African Rhythms

The South Sea Islands must simply teem with complex improvised choral music, which, according to R. L. Stevenson, Pierre Loti,[18] and many other sojourners in the 'Gentle Isles', accompanies both their ceremonies and their most ordinary actions, and makes their every-day existence constantly melodious.

Africa appears to be the home of the richest developments of what may be termed 'rhythmic polyphony', in which players upon every variety of drums and percussion instruments display in their treatment of intricately contrasted and independent rhythms a gift for communal improvisation comparable with that of Polynesian singers. Mr. H. E. Krehbiel,[19] in his valuable and engrossing book on *Afro-American Folksongs* says of the war-dances of the Dahomans (pp. 64, 65): 'Berlioz in his supremest effort with his army of drummers produced nothing to compare in artistic interest with the harmonious drumming of these savages.' Mr. Krehbiel's description of their music is exciting to a degree, and should be consulted in its entirety.

The Electrifying 'Clef Club of the City of New York'

A distant echo of the habits of unwritten music can be traced in the marvellous accomplishments of the colored instrumentalists and singers who make up the New York 'Clef Club',[20] an organization which could not fail to electrify Europe if presented there, and to hear which it is more than

---

[18] Julien Viaud (1850–1923), French naval officer; author of *The Marriage of Loti* (1880).
[19] (1854–1923), American critic and author; his *Afro-American Folksongs* dates from 1913.
[20] A club, founded in Manhattan in 1910, which also served as a union for black musicians.

worth one's while to travel across the Atlantic. The compositions they interpret are art music, and reveal the strict harmonic habits of the written art, but the ease with which those members of the Club who cannot read musical notation learn and remember intricate band and choral parts by heart (often singing tenor and playing bass) and many individualistic and rhapsodical traits in their performances suggest the presence of instincts inherited from the days of communal improvisation. These qualities are nowhere more in evidence than in their exhilarating renderings of two fascinating choral numbers by that strangely gifted American composer, Will Marion Cook[21]—'Rain-song' and 'Exhortation'—in themselves works of real genius and originality that deserve a worldwide reputation.

Musicians who have been thrilled by the passionate but always artistically refined percussion playing of the 'Clef Club' can the more easily picture to themselves the overwhelming effect of the Dahoman drumming described by Mr. Krehbiel.

The Possibilities of Massed Declamation

The war-dances of the Maoris of New Zealand strike a certain note of savage, elemental force and passion which, it seems to me, is foreign to most European music with the exception of certain heroic and violent outbursts in Beethoven.[22] These 'hakas', as they are called, consist solely of spoken declamations of highly rhythmic poems for solo and chorus, accompanied by handclapping, weird quiverings of the body and threatening gestures and grimaces.

It is hard to realize that such simple means as these can be responsible for an impression so musically pregnant and emotionally overwhelming as that produced by these graceful ex-cannibals.

Some of the Lessons of Unwritten Music

What life is to the writer, and nature to the painter, unwritten music is to many a composer: a kind of mirror of genuineness and naturalness. Through it alone can we come to know something of the incalculable

---

[21] (1869–1944), black American composer and conductor, student of Joachim, producer in 1899 of the first black musical-comedy on Broadway.

[22] Grainger is probably thinking of Beethoven's *Battle Symphony* or the Finale of the Ninth Symphony.

variety of man's instincts for musical expression. From it alone can we glean some insight into what suggests itself as being 'vocal' to natural singers whose technique has never been exposed to the influence of arbitrary 'methods'. In the reiterated physical actions of marching, rowing, reaping, dancing, cradle-rocking, etc., that called its work-songs, dance music, ballads and lullabies into life, we see before our very eyes the origin of the regular rhythms of our art music and of poetic meters, and are also able to note how quickly these once so rigid rhythms give place to rich and wayward irregularities of every kind as soon as these bodily movements and gestures are abandoned and the music which originally existed but as an accompaniment to them continues independently as art for art's sake. In such examples as the Polynesian part-songs we can trace the early promptings of polyphony and the habits of concerted improvisation to their very source, and, since all composing is little else than 'frozen inspiration', surely this latter experience is of supreme importance; the more so, if there again should dawn an age in which the bulk of civilized men and women will come to again possess sufficient mental leisure in their lives to enable them to devote themselves to artistic pleasures on so large a scale as do the members of uncivilized communities.

Then the spectacle of one composer producing music for thousands of musical drones (totally uncreative themselves, and hence comparatively out of touch with the whole phenomenon of artistic creation) will no longer seem normal or desirable, and then the present gulf between the mentality of composers and performers will be bridged.

The Tyranny of the Composer

The fact that art music has been written down instead of improvised has divided musical creators and executants into two quite separate classes; the former autocratic and the latter comparatively slavish. It has grown to be an important part of the office of the modern composer to leave as few loopholes as possible in his works for the idiosyncrasies of the performer. The considerable increase of exactness in our modes of notation and tempo and expression marks has all been directed toward this end, and though the state of things obtaining among trained musicians for several centuries has been productive of isolated geniuses of an exceptional greatness unthinkable under primitive conditions, it seems to me that it has done so at the expense of the artistry of millions of performers, and to the destruction of natural sympathy and understanding between them and the creative giants.

The Price of Harmony

Perhaps it would not be amiss to examine the possible reason for the ancient tendency of cultured musicians gradually to discontinue improvisation, and seek some explanation for the lack of variety with regard to scales, rhythms and dynamics displayed by our Western art music when compared with the resources of more primitive men in these directions. I believe the birth of harmony in Europe to have been accountable for much; and truly, the acquisition of this most transcendental and soul-reaching of all our means of musical expression has been worth *any* and *every* sacrifice. We know how few combinations of intervals sounded euphonious to the pioneers of harmonic consciousness, and can imagine what concentration they must have brought to bear upon accuracies of notation and reliability of matters of pitch in ensemble, possibly to the exclusion of any very vital interest in individualistic traits in performance or in the more subtle possibilities of dynamics, color and irregular rhythms.

The Possibilities of 'Pure Line'

With the gradual growth of the all-engrossing chord-sense the power of deep emotional expression through the medium of an unaccompanied single melodic line would likewise tend to atrophy, which perhaps explains why many of those conversant with the strictly solo performances of some branches of unwritten music miss in the melodic invention of the greatest classical geniuses—passionately as they may adore their masterliness in other directions—the presence of a certain satisfying completeness (from the standpoint of pure line) that may often be noticed in the humblest folk-song.

It always seems to me strange that modern composers, with the example of Bach's Chaconne and Violin and 'Cello Sonatas as well as of much primitive music before them, do not more often feel tempted to express themselves extensively in single line or unison without harmonic accompaniment of any kind. I have found this a particularly delightful and inspiring medium to work in, and very refreshing after much preoccupation with richly polyphonic styles. Now that we have grown so skilful in our treatment of harmony that this side of our art often tends to outweigh all our other creative accomplishments, some of us feel the need of replenishing our somewhat impoverished resources of melody, rhythm and color, and accordingly turn, and seldom in vain, for inspiration and guidance to those untutored branches of our art that have never ceased to place their chief reliance in these elements. I have already referred to the possibilities of 'inexact unison' evinced by Maori and Egyptian music. Similar rich and varied lessons might be learned from Red Indian, East Indian, Javanese, Burmese, and many other Far Eastern musics.

Our Sprouting Powers of Appreciation

Being, moreover, the fortunate heirs to the results of those centuries of harmonic experiment in which ever more and more discordant combinations of intervals came to be regarded as concordant, we are now at last in a position from which we can approach such music as the Rarotongan part-songs and similar music of a highly complex discordant nature with that broad-minded toleration and enthusiastic appreciation which our painters and writers brought to bear on the arts of non-Europeans so many generations before our musicians could boast of an equally humble, cultured and detached attitude.

The Modern Tendency to Take 'Hints'

Out in nature, however, men have long known how to enjoy discordant combinations. A telegraph wire humming B flat, a bird piping a flat B natural and factory whistles chiming in with notes resembling D and F sharp; the mournful appeal of such accidental ensembles has frequently awakened emotional response. But a musician in 1890 would have been inclined to enjoy such sounds as merely part of 'nature' and with no bearing upon his 'art', whereas we to-day are more apt to find compositional hints in such occurrences, not, I most sincerely hope, because we have any desire to 'copy nature', or because we could willingly contemplate exchanging, for however brief a moment, the precise choice and formal arrangement of artistic procedure for the choicelessness of 'life', but simply because a greater number of discordant harmonic combinations happen to charm our ears to-day than they did in 1890.

Probably Beethoven was one of the first of the 'moderns' to find such suggestions in every-day sounds. The trumpet behind the stage in the third *Leonore* seems an instance of this, while the premature entry of the horn in the first movement of the *Eroica* and the belated notes of the bassoon in the Scherzo of the *Pastoral* show his generous readiness to per-petuate in his scores hints derived from the mistakes of the rehearsal room and the happy-go-lucky ensemble of tavern 'Musikanten'.

Harmonic Emancipations

Nowadays we not only hear whole sequences of what would formerly have been considered impossibly harsh discords with rare delight, espe-cially when they are poetically treated and as delicately scored as they are in Schönberg's Five Orchestral Pieces,[23] but we are able to listen to two pianists simultaneously improvising passages of chords in different keys on two pianos, each quite independently of the other and to enjoy the crossing paths of these chord-groups in much the same way as we appre-ciate the intertwining of single parts in older music. Here is an instance of such freely moving chord-groups:[24]

Excerpt from a March for Piano and Orchestra by Percy Grainger

[23] Op. 16 (1909). Grainger had heard their first London performance on 3 Sept. 1912. Two days later he wrote of Schoenberg as 'the greatest revolution I have witnessed'.
[24] From '*The Gum-suckers' March* (1905–11), the final movement of the suite *In a Nutshell* (1916).

Two entrancing examples of this pleasure in 'double-chording' may be studied in Ravel's 'Le Gibet'[25] (in which passages in A major and modulations bristling with G sharps, A naturals, B naturals and C naturals pass over and under and through a continuous bell-like organ-point on B flat (A sharp) in the middle of the keyboard which is heard chiming from the beginning to the end of this pianistic gem) and in that famous passage in Strauss' *Rosenkavalier*[26] which accompanies the entry of the silver rose and occurs again at the close of the final duet, in which strings and voices sustain the tonic and major third while a slow cascade of foreign and remote chords of every degree of concordance and discordance are given out by flutes, harp and celesta, constituting, to my mind, a stroke of the highest genius and accounting for one of the tenderest and most touching effects ever conceived.

The 'Wrong-Note Craze' Succeeds the 'Right-Note Craze'

Modern geniuses and primitive music unite in teaching us the charm of 'wrong notes that sound right'. Indeed, Frederick Delius has aptly referred to the wave of discord that is at present sweeping over the world of civilized music as 'the wrong-note craze'. The innovations of such pioneers as Debussy, Ravel, Strauss, Schönberg, Stravinsky, Cyril Scott and Ornstein[27] open up the possibility of modern musicians being capable of combining the communal improvisation of South Sea Islanders with the harmonic consciousness of our written art music.

An Experiment in Concerted Partial Improvisation

Realizing this, I set out, some three years ago, to embody some of the experience I had gleaned from familiarity with the primitive polyphony of the Rarotongan part-songs in a composition entitled 'Random Round', which was planned for a few voices, guitars and mandolins, to which could be added (if available) mandola, piano, xylophone, celesta, glockenspiel, resonaphone or marimbaphone, strings and wind instruments. It consisted of sections (A, B, C, etc.), each of which was again divided into as many as 10 to 20 variants (A1, A2, etc.), some quiet, some noisy, some

---

[25] No. 2 of *Gaspard de la nuit* (1908).
[26] Grainger had twice seen Strauss's opera in London during Feb. 1913.
[27] Leo Ornstein (b. 1892), American composer and pianist, who had performed widely in Britain and continental Europe during 1913–14.

simple, some complex, each bar of each variant being composed in such a manner that it would form some sort of a harmonic whole when performed together with any bar of any or all of the other variants of the same section.

The guitars formed the background for all the rest, and as soon as they got going with section A any or all of the other players and singers could fall in, when and how they pleased, with any of their variants of section A, provided their beats corresponded to those of the guitars. For instance, one voice might be heard singing the second measure of its A3 while another voice was engaged on the seventh measure of its A9. Before section B was to begin, a Javanese gong would be beaten, whereupon the same sort of canonical intermingling of the different variants of B would be undertaken that had just occurred with the A variants; and so on with C, D, etc., to the end.

It will be seen that a fairly large range of personal choice was allowed to every one taking part, and that the effectiveness of the whole thing would depend primarily on the natural sense for contrasts of form, color and dynamics displayed by the various performers, and their judgment in entering and leaving the general ensemble at suitable moments.

Thus one player, by intruding carelessly and noisily at a moment when all the rest were playing softly, would wreck that particular effect, though, on the other hand, such an act, if undertaken intentionally in order to provide dynamic variety, might be very welcome. Last summer in London some fifteen of us experimented with this 'Random Round', and the results obtained were very instructive to me personally.[28] Several of those taking part quickly developed the power of merging themselves into the artistic whole, and whereas at the outset the monotonous babel produced somewhat 'resembled a day at the Dogs' Home, Battersea' (as a leading critic once described Albéniz's marvelous and touching piano piece 'Jerez'[29] when I first introduced it to London audiences some years ago), after a little practice together the whole thing took on form, color and clarity, and sounded harmonious enough, though a frequent swash of passing discords was noticeable also. I look forward to some day presenting to English and American audiences a performance of this blend of modern harmonic tendencies with experiences drawn from the

[28] Earlier, on 14 Nov. 1912, Grainger had reported to his mother that, while in Amsterdam, he had 'played thro a bit of the new silly piece, & it seems to sound quite hopeful when one hears the various parts joining in at random like that. I'll call it "Random Round" or some like name.' (*The Farthest North of Humanness: Letters of Percy Grainger, 1901–14*, ed. Kay Dreyfus (Melbourne: Macmillan, 1985), 476.)

[29] From *Iberia*, Book 4 (1908).

improvised polyphony of primitive music, although, of course, my piece represents only the veriest beginnings of what may ultimately be evolved in the realms of concerted improvisation.

In the meantime I cannot refrain from giving a tiny example of the sort of combinations that resulted from the individualistic use on the part of the various performers of the somewhat elastic material I had provided them with, remarking, however, that the effect of the actual performance was far warmer and less harsh than it appears on paper, largely owing to the transparent quality of the plucked sounds of the guitars, mandolins and mandolas, and the illusive and 'non-adhesive' tone of the brighter percussion instruments.

Primitive Music is a Closed Book to Most Musicians

When we consider how meagre the generally available records of un-written music are, it is surprising that it should have already exerted so noticeable an influence upon contemporaneous composers.

Experience of primitive music is not in any way thrust upon the budding musician. When I was a boy in Frankfurt my teacher wanted me to enter for (I think it was) the Mendelssohn Prize for piano playing, and I remember asking him: 'If I should win, would they let me study Chinese music in China with the money?' And his reply: 'No, they don't give prizes to idiots'. No doubt many a young musician is feeling to-day what I felt then—a longing to escape from the inefficiencies of theoretic teaching and to know something about the myriad musics of the various races, and to be able to track some of the creative impulses to their sources. But he will not find much exhaustive material accessible. For instance, though it may be already widely appreciated how much such delicious pieces as Debussy's 'Pagodes' and 'Reflets dans l'eau'[30] (and indeed, the whole modern French school) owe to some acquaintance with Javanese music yet we still have to journey to the Dutch Indies if we wish to hear the 'gamelan'.

Let All the World Hear All the World's Music

But I believe the time will soon be ripe for the formation of a world-wide International Musical Society for the purpose of making all the world's music known to all the world by means of imported performances, phonograph and gramophone records and adequate notations. Quite small but representative troupes of peasant and native musicians, dancers, etc., could be set in motion on 'world tours' to perform in the subscription concerts of such a society in the art centres of all lands. One program might consist of Norwegian fiddling, pipe-playing, cattle-calls, peasant dances and ballad singing, another of various types of African drumming, marimba and *zanze*[31] playing, choral songs and war dances, and yet another evening filled out with the teeming varieties of modes of singing and playing upon plucked string instruments indigenous to British India; and so on, until music-lovers everywhere could form some accurate conception of the as yet but dimly guessed multitudinous beauties of the world's contemporaneous total output of music.

Our Debt to the Past and Our Duty to the Future

Quite apart from the pleasure and veneration such exotic arts inspire purely for their own sake, those of us who are genuinely convinced that

---

[30] From *Estampes* (1903) and *Images*, Book I (1905), respectively. See, further, Essay 7.
[31] *Sanza*, an African thumb piano. Grainger discussed and demonstrated the playing of this instrument during one of his lectures at New York University in 1932–3.

many of the greatest modern composers (by no means all, however—not
Schönberg or Strauss or Fauré, for instance) owe much to their contact
with one kind or other of unwritten music, must, if we wish to behave
with any generosity toward the future, face the fact that coming generations will not enjoy a first-hand experience of primitive music such as
those amongst us can still obtain who are gifted with means, leisure, or
fighting enthusiasm. Let us, therefore, not neglect to provide composers
and students to come with the best *second-hand* material we can.
Fortunes might be spent, and well spent, in having good gramophone and
phonograph records taken of music from everywhere, and in having the
contents of these records noted down by brilliant yet painstaking musicians; men capable of responding to unexpected novelties and eager to
seize upon and preserve *in their full strangeness and otherness* just those
elements that have least in common with our own music. We see on all
hands the victorious on-march of our ruthless Western civilization (so
destructively intolerant in its colonial phase) and the distressing spectacle
of the gentle but complex native arts wilting before its irresistible
simplicity.

Everywhere men and women whose forebears were untaught individualistic musicians are inevitably finding their own expression (or not
finding any at all) along the more precise and sometimes narrow paths of
the written art. Soon, or comparatively soon, folk music on Southern
plantations, or in Scandinavia, Great Britain, Russia and Spain will be as
dead as it already is in Holland and Germany, and many native races will
have exchanged their song-lit 'savage' modes of living for the (musically
speaking) comparatively silent early stages of 'commercial prosperity'
or commercial want. Against that day—which, however, we may
confidently expect to find compensatingly more gloriously rich in art
music than any previous age—let us make noble efforts to preserve, for
the affectionate gaze of future eclectics, above all adequate printed records
of what now still remains of a phase of music which, in the nature of
things, can never be reborn again, and which comes down to us so fragrant with the sweet impress of the personality of many millions of
unknown departed artists, men and women.

7

Modernism in Pianoforte Study

(1915)

An Interview with the Distinguished Australian Pianist
and Composer, Percy Grainger[1]

Editor's Note.—Mr. Percy Grainger came to the United States last Fall by no
means unknown to the elect, but comparatively little known to the public. It
was his intention to live quietly in this country and complete several large
unfinished orchestral and choral compositions. However, the exceptionally
enthusiastic reception accorded to his orchestral compositions by press
and public alike when performed by Walter Damrosch of the New York
Symphony Orchestra in New York and other leading cities last winter
induced him to appear as a piano virtuoso, and the result was numerous
engagements to appear at more and more concerts. Thus, his successful début
to America has been accomplished quite without the usual fanfare of trumpets which we are accustomed to expect from the visiting virtuoso. Mr.
Grainger was born at Brighton, Melbourne, Australia, July 8th, 1882. His
mother was his first teacher. Thereafter he studied with Louis Pabst of
Melbourne. He then set out to earn the means to travel to Germany and after
several highly successful recitals and a large benefit concert organized by
Australia's greatest musician and composer, Professor Marshall-Hall, had his
wish gratified. In Germany he studied for six years with Professor James
Kwast and finally with the great Busoni. In 1900 he appeared in London as
a virtuoso and at once scored great successes. Thereafter he toured Great
Britain, Australia, New Zealand, South Africa, and more recently Germany,
Holland, Norway, Denmark, Finland, Russia, Bohemia and Switzerland.
His fondness for things Scandinavian began as a child and was beautifully
rewarded by Grieg's admiration for the young Australian, about whom he
wrote enthusiastically and prophetically in the European press, and whom he
chose to play his Pianoforte Concerto at the great Leeds Musical Festival.
After Grieg's death the widow of the Norwegian genius sent his watch and
chain to Mr. Grainger as a souvenir of Grieg's affectionate friendship for him.
Mr. Grainger's reverent admiration for Grieg's adaptations of Norwegian
folk music, prompted him to explore the beauties of British folksongs as

Source: *Etude*, 33/9 (Sept. 1915), 631–2.

  [1] The second part of this interview was reported in 'A Blossom Time in Pianoforte Literature',
Essay **8**. Both essays were reproduced in *Great Pianists on Piano Playing*, ed. James Francis
Cooke (Philadelphia: Theo. Presser, [1917]), 364–81.

Grieg had done those of Norway. The result has been that Mr. Grainger has made vocal and pianoforte arrangements of many of these pieces—arrangements altogether unique in their charm and appropriateness.

New Efforts with Old Means

Just at the moment when the musical pessimists were declaring that pianistic resources were coming to an end, we find ourselves on the doorstep of new forms of pianism, which, while they in no sense do away with the old means of interpretation, aid the pianist in bringing new effects even to the masterpieces of yesterday. It is interesting to think that with the advance of the art one's resources become more and more refined. Twenty years ago the whole aim of many pianoforte students seemed to be speed or the art of getting just as many notes as possible in a given space of time. With the coming of such composers as Debussy, Cyril Scott, Ravel and others, we find a grateful return of the delicate and refined in piano playing. There is a coming up again of the pianissimo. More and more artists are beginning to realize the potency of soft notes rightly shaded and delivered artistically.

The modern composer has a new reverence for the piano as an instrument. The great composers, such as Bach and Beethoven, thought of the piano as a medium for all-round expression, but perhaps they did not so often feel inspired by its specifically pianistic attributes as do several of the moderns. Many of the Beethoven Sonatas could be orchestrated and a symphonic effect produced. In other words, the magnificent thoughts of most of the great masters of the past were rarely peculiarly pianistic, though Scarlatti, Chopin and Liszt in their day (just as Debussy, Albéniz, Ravel and Cyril Scott to-day) divined the soul of the piano and made the instrument speak its own native tongue.

The Modern Piano a Percussion Instrument

Indeed the real nature of the modern piano as an instrument is in itself more or less of a modern discovery. No one would be altogether satisfied by trumpet passages played upon a violin, because the violin and the trumpet have characteristics which individualize them. In precisely the same fashion the piano has individual characteristics. The piano is distinctly an instrument of percussion—a beating of felt-covered hammers upon tightened wires. Once we realize this, a great deal may be learned. Debussy has retained in his pianistic vocabulary many of the beautiful kaleidoscopic effects a gifted child strumming upon the piano would produce, but which our over-trained ears might have rejected in the past. Thus, his methods have implied a study of the problem of just how much dissonance can be artistically applied and yet keep his work within the bounds of the beautiful. It has been said that Debussy learned much from a Javanese instrument called a gamelan. This instrument is a kind of orchestra of gongs. I have been told that when the players from the far East performed at one of the Paris expositions Debussy was greatly attracted by their music, and lingered long near them to note the enchanting effect of the harmonics from the bells. There can be no doubt that he sought to reproduce such an effect on that other instrument of percussion, the piano, when he wrote his exquisite 'Reflets dans l'eau' and the following significant measures in 'Pagodes' [No. 1]:

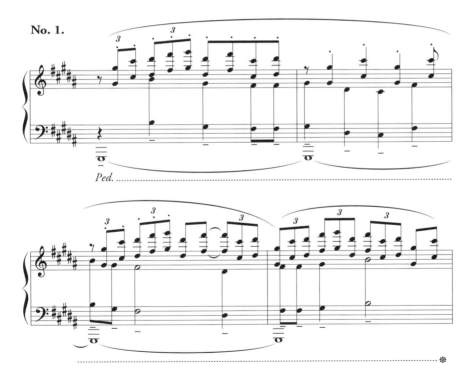

In all gong effects we hear one note louder than the surrounding 'aura' of ethereal harmonies. This suggests many new and delightful effects upon the piano, for all the past pianists have been accustomed to playing all the notes of a chord, for instance, with more or less the same degree of force. It seldom seemed to occur to the average piano student that it is possible to play chords in succession and at the same time bring out some inner voice so that the whole effect is delightfully altered.

Indeed, we are coming to a day when the pianist will more and more be expected to play melodies concealed in masses of chords. Busoni in his edition of the Bach Chorales (Breitkopf & Härtel, *Volksausgabe*, No. 1916) gives us a splendid instance of an inner voice carrying the melody in the 'Nun freut euch, lieben Christen' (No. 4). The following measures serve to illustrate this [No. 2]. Any one who has heard Mr. Busoni play this will find it difficult to forget the clear sonority with which he plays the melody and how delicate and exquisitely subdued is the lace-like embroidery which surrounds the melody.

No. 2.

In playing chords so that one note may stand out above the others we confront what many seem to think is a really difficult task, but as a matter of fact it is not. It is a habit easily acquired.

Whatever is the need for ever making a note in a chord stand out above its fellows? In all good part-writing, whether for the piano or other instruments or for voices, each voice in a sequence of chords has some melodic value. Many voices have a distinctive melodic value. In the orchestra or in a quartet of strings or of human voices each part has a certain tone color which gives it individuality and distinguishes it from the other parts. But on the piano we have no such contrasting tone colors or tone qualities to work with. What in the orchestra, for instance, is accomplished largely by contrasts of *quality* we on the piano must accomplish by contrasts of *quantity*, or different sound strengths. Don't you see that the only recourse is to individualize the melody in an internal voice by making that melody louder, or by subduing the other notes in the chords? It is quite possible to play a chord in the following fashion [No. 3]:[2]

No. 3.

That is, the E flat is loud and the D flat and B flat are soft. Nothing is simpler. My own method is to hold my fingers rigidly; with the second finger, which would play the E flat, protruding downwards, while the thumb and fifth finger, which are to play the D flat and B flat, are kept high, so that the force of the blow descends on to the E flat key (which is pressed down as far as it will go), while the other two keys are only lightly struck (and pressed down only one-third or one-half of the total distance they could descend.)

This opens up interesting vistas even yet not fully explored. It would be more profitable for many of our students to spend a little more time upon the quality of effects and a little less time in trying to clamber over an immense amount of technic work. Playing two such chords as the following in the manner indicated [No. 4] requires an amount of thought, hand control, far in excess of that demanded by many supposedly difficult technical exercises.

No. 4.

[2] The original typography of this example in the *Etude* emphasized the Eflat–Bflat fifth; the D♭ seventh was placed awkwardly to the side.

An Interesting Artistic Application

It is possible to show how this plan of bringing out the middle voice may be employed by quoting my pianistic setting of the lovely *Irish Tune from County Derry*.[3] The melody is believed to be very old and was collected by Miss J. Ross, of Limavady, County Derry, and the melody was first published in the *Petrie Collection of the Ancient Music of Ireland*.[4] It is a tune very susceptible to modern harmonic treatment, and if the student will play the first measures with the method of bringing out the melody notes in the inner part as we have described it, he will see that very rare effects may be produced [No. 5].

No. 5.   Slowish, but not dragged, and wayward in time.
M. M. ♪ = between 72 and 104.
Rubato il tempo, e non troppo lento.

[3] 1902–11.
[4] George Petrie's complete collection was edited by Charles Villiers Stanford and published during 1902–5.

New Effects with the Pedal

Modern pianism has brought into vogue certain pedal effects which were only employed by the most iconoclastic a few decades ago. A very striking effect of diminuendo, for instance, can be produced by what I call 'half-pedaling'. The problem is to melt from forte to pianissimo through the use of the pedal. By 'half-pedaling' I mean repeatedly lifting up the damper pedal just so high that the dampers only partially arrest the vibrations of the strings, thereby accomplishing a gradual diminuendo. In the following three last measures of my *Colonial Song* for piano[5] [No. 6] the notes marked with stars are gradually melted away by this process in the second bar of the example, though this is not the case with the other six notes, the keys of which are pressed down silently before the half-pedaling begins, so their dampers are not affected by the movements of the damper pedal. These six notes are thus heard vibrating on to the very end of the piece.

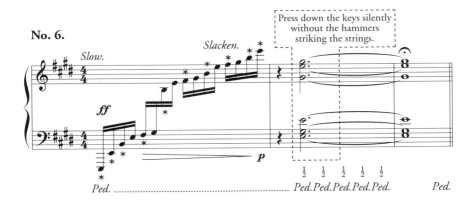

---

[5] 1914.

8   A Blossom Time in Pianoforte Literature
(1915)

From an Interview with the Distinguished Australian Pianist and Composer, Percy Grainger

Editor's Note.—It is fortunate that the *Etude* may present the second section of Mr. Percy Grainger's notable interview upon Modernism in Piano Playing in the present issue. Mr. Grainger is an intimate friend of many Scandinavian artists. Grieg was a kind of musical foster-father to him. He has toured repeatedly with great success in Scandinavian countries.

It seems to me that we live in an age in which the piano has again come very much into its own. The developments of the last fifteen or twenty years seem to me enormous. Again let me say that this is a period in which the piano is not merely a practical and serviceable medium for expressing noble and touching musical feelings of a nature not especially limited or adapted to the piano or any other particular instrument, but in which the very soul and body of the instrument, all its most individual peculiarities and idiosyncrasies, are especially catered for, and in which the technical aspects of the piano are developed to a degree and in a manner so that they are able to play an emotional and highly soulful rôle.

An Inspired Period

Composers such as Scarlatti, Couperin, Chopin and Liszt at once leap to one's mind as creative geniuses of this particularly high pianistic type. They have not only written great music for the piano, such as the giants like Bach, Beethoven, Brahms, etc., but the greatness of their achievement lies in the peculiarly pianistic note of their style and of the elements contained in their works that prove unusually stimulating and developing to pianists playing their works. Though personally I feel perhaps the deepest attraction in the works of men such as Bach, Wagner, Grieg and Frederick Delius, in whose creations the inventive germ and the inner musical idea and emotion come always first, and the instrument or instruments

Source: Etude, 33/10 (Oct. 1915), 709–10.

employed are comparatively secondary considerations (men who compose much the same *kind* of music whether they write it for organ or chorus or piano), still I feel we can hardly ever value the refreshing stimulating incentive (especially for the executive artist performing such works) found in the work of men whose gifts lie to a great extent in the power to concentrate on the physical nature of the particular instrument employed and who are capable of quaffing technical and color resources to the very dregs as it were.

It seems to me we live in a period in which such technically inspired composers for the piano abound, and I think the results to pianists of all the new and fresh and lovely and startling piano creations that have appeared in print since, let us say, about 1900, have been extremely rich and their importance and benefit impossible to exaggerate. Pianistically speaking, it seems as if there never had existed a more prolific period than the present. What diversity! What contrasts between the work of Albéniz and Cyril Scott, Debussy, Ravel, Schönberg and Ornstein.

Pioneers in a New Field

At the risk of mentioning a very incomplete list, I wish to specialize on those composers whose pianoforte works I have had the pleasure of being the first to introduce into many different countries on my tours in various parts of the world, as follows: Debussy, Ravel, Cyril Scott, Frederick Delius, Albéniz. At various times I have had the joy of introducing these men for the first time to audiences in England, Holland, Germany, Scandinavia, Australia, New Zealand, and I know no privilege more enticing and no event connected with a performer's career more satisfying and exciting and worthwhile than being able to introduce the torch-bearing works of new iconoclasts to broad-minded audiences all over the world, hungry and eager for beautiful new things.

The soulfully sensuous and wistfully tender and pathetic creations of the modern French composers have occasioned a reaction against 'banging' and over-energetic virtuoso playing in general for which we can never be too thankful. They have reintroduced certain types of charmful pianism that had been neglected since the days of Couperin and Scarlatti. They have also opened our eyes to the entrancing beauties of certain long pedal effects, which are particularly convincing in Debussy's 'Reflets dans l'eau', 'Pagodes', and in Ravel's *Jeux d'eau*[1] and 'Ondine'.[2] There are, after

---

[1] 1901.   [2] No. 1 of *Gaspard de la nuit* (1908).

all, many very purely percussive and bell-like and gong-like effects peculiarly native to the nature of the metallic modern piano which lay dormant until so wonderfully developed by Ravel and Debussy, which no doubt they owe in part, if not chiefly to their contact with gamelans and other Eastern instruments and musics.

Cyril Scott's Unique Achievements

There are certain possibilities of the modern pianoforte that it seems to me only Cyril Scott has known how to utilize to their fullest extent. Modern musicians have long been profoundly attracted to irregular rhythms of every kind. As early as 1899 I was myself busy evolving a style of rhythmically irregular music in which every bar-length, every beat-length, could have a duration that had no regular relation whatever to those preceding or following it. If our present system can be described as 'meter in music', then what I was attempting might be termed 'prose in music'. These experiments of mine led Cyril Scott to pursue highly original developments of his own.

It is one thing to write highly irregular rhythms for chorus or orchestra or chamber combinations; it is another thing to get such rhythms accurately performed, with complete unanimity between the different performers! Cyril Scott realized that the absolute solo nature of the piano offered unique opportunities. It is far easier for a single performer to reproduce complex rhythms than for several musicians playing or singing together to do so. Therefore the most successful and revolutionary developments of irregular rhythms yet in print can be studied in Cyril Scott's piano works, such as his great Sonata, Op. 66, his Suite, Op. 75, and such entrancing and highly original and significant smaller numbers as the following from his *Poems* for piano: 'The Garden of Soul-sympathy', 'Bells', 'The Twilight of the Year', 'Paradise Birds', etc.[3]

As a pianistic colorist he has exploited the metallic, bell-like, clanging upper octaves of the piano in ways no other composer has, producing brittle iridescent cascades of chord-sounds that have a captivating charm wholly their own.

Apart from all this Cyril Scott's music most soulfully expresses one of the most interesting, noble and poetic artistic personalities of our age.

---

[3] Nos. 2–5 of *Poems* (pub. 1912).

The Influence of Spanish Gipsy Music

It is highly interesting to trace the influence of guitars, mandolins, etc., in such pieces as Debussy's 'La Soirée dans Grenade' and 'Minstrels',[4] Ravel's 'Alborada del Gracioso',[5] and Albéniz's *Iberia*.[6] Albéniz developed the 'two-hand' technique perhaps more than anyone else. His piano style might also be nicknamed a 'concertina' style, so much does it consist of 'right, left, right, left' devices. Albéniz seems to me to give us a volume of sonority, a dashing intensity and glowing brilliancy that have been lacking in composers for the piano since Liszt and Balakirev, and without which we should be very much the poorer. At other times the vibrating gloom of his music suggests old Spanish pictures. But in all his phases he appears to me a real genius, occupying a wholly unique and precious niche amongst the greatest pianistic composers of all time.

A Notable Concerto

Frederick Delius' Pianoforte Concerto in C Minor[7] is to my mind the most important, the most deeply musical and emotionally significant concerto produced for several decades. This is not merely a fine pianistic concerto, but apart from all that a glowing representative work by one of the greatest creators of all time. To many keen observers of modern compositional developments the great Frederick Delius seems to tower above most or all of his contemporaries because of the irresistible emotional power, passion, and inner sincerity of his creations. A wizard in orchestration, a harmonist second to none, it is the human soul behind all his other marvelous qualities that marks him out as a genius among geniuses, and makes him so particularly touching and endearing, and accounts for the unique position among modern composers held by Delius in England, Germany, Holland and elsewhere, and the extraordinary international vogue of such complex creations as *Brigg Fair, Paris, Dance Rhapsody, Sea-drift, Appalachia, Mass of Life, On Hearing the First Cuckoo in Spring*, etc.

His polyphony is marvelous and has an indefinable Bach-like quality that is no less noticeable in his emotional make-up, and in the non-effect-

[4] No. 2 of *Estampes* (1903) and No. 12 of *Préludes* Book I (1910), respectively.
[5] No. 4 of *Miroirs* (1904–5).   [6] 1906–8.
[7] 1897. Grainger would perform this work with the New York Philharmonic Orchestra on 26 Nov. 1915.

seeking sincerity and depth of his whole being and utterance. His artistic soul is akin to great cosmic men such as Bach, Wagner, Goethe, Walt Whitman, Milton—he is most at home in great broad lines, and his work glows with a great lovingness, almost religious, in its all-embracing and cosmic breadth.[8]

[8] At the end of the reprint of this essay, in *Great Pianists on Piano Playing*, ed. James Francis Cooke (Philadelphia: Theo. Presser, [1917]), 381, the following section was added:

Questions in Style, Interpretation, Expression and Technic of Pianoforte Playing— Series XXVI—Percy Grainger

1. Give some of the chief differences between piano playing of twenty years ago and the piano playing of today.
2. Give the names of some composers whose compositions are peculiarly pianistic.
3. In what class of instruments does the piano properly belong?
4. From what oriental instrument did Debussy learn much?
5. Why is it desirable to emphasize certain notes in chords?
6. What have been some of the chief innovations of Cyril Scott?
7. Tell something of the pianistic accomplishments of Albéniz.

9 Modern and Universal Impulses in Music
(1916)

Especially Written for the Etude by the Eminent Australian Pianist-Composer, Percy Grainger[1]

> Whoever walks a furlong without sympathy walks to his own funeral dressed in his shroud. (Walt Whitman[2])

When asked whether I consider the most recent developments of European musical composition to be of permanent or merely passing importance I can only reply that to my mind the best efforts of Delius, Debussy, Ravel, Richard Strauss, Cyril Scott, Schönberg, Stravinsky, Scriabin, Albéniz, constitute deathless music of unchangeable value, and that I regard the gospel of novelty and experiment which they contain in the light of an incalculable boon to living and future composers. At the same time I cannot refrain from adding that, attracted though I am to 'modernism' in music, I am still more compellingly attracted towards 'universalism' in music. Just as I revere European art music, not as the music of all humanity, but as a highly interesting and instructive expression of merely a portion of humanity, so I revere 'modern' music, 'futurist' music, not necessarily as a competitor with the music of past and future ages, but primarily as a momentary manifestation, offering quite sufficient justification for its existence, now and in the future, in the fact that it is truly vocal of our particular age and place. In my case, the appeal of all new music is very greatly further enhanced by my consciousness of its close blood-relationship with all the achievements of the past, and of the portent it holds for as yet unimagined styles to come.

Some people are rather fond of talking about 'hyper-modern' or 'futurist' music as if it were some kind of new animal, only very distantly, if at all, related to former types. This seems to me an unduly romantic and imaginative view to take of the matter, though no doubt one that will not

Source: *Etude*, 34/5 (May 1916), 343–4.

[1] The second section of this essay appears as 'The World Music of To-morrow', Essay 10.
[2] From 'Song of Myself' No. 48, in *Leaves of Grass* (1891–2 edn.) by Walt Whitman (1819–92), American poet. All references to Whitman's poems refer to the culminating edition of 1891–2, not to dates of composition, revision, or initial publication.

be without its appeal to some of the futurists, who, apparently, delight in magnifying differences rather than in discovering artistic kinships. It is, no doubt, chiefly as regards its harmony that the most 'advanced' music differs from its forebears; through the inclusion of more and yet more sharp discords into the normal language of compositional expression. But surely this very process has been in steady and historically traceable operation since the days of Monteverdi, if not long before!

The most drastic developments of Schönberg, Cyril Scott, Ornstein and Stravinsky appear to me just as logically and inevitably the outcome of the strivings of the creative generations before them as were Bach, Beethoven or Berlioz in their day. What is novel to-day becomes normal to-morrow through familiarity, and immediately some new twist, some fresh distortion is instinctively desired, since it is always some divergence from the normal that fascinates in art. This is clearly seen in our pleasure in modulations. No sooner is any key really firmly established in our ears than a yearning is born to stray away from it. As with modulation, so with musical style in general. At any given moment certain things seem permissible and desirable to a composer in his own compositions, others not. Yet with each new work he will probably find himself drifting farther and farther away from his original premises, until, in the fullness of time, he finds himself including in his habits of composition tricks and attributes that once would have shocked him and seemed to him utterly foreign to his artistic personality. And the more naturally gifted the man, the greater the likelihood that he will say with Walt Whitman: 'I resist anything better than my own diversity.'[3] The whole course of so-called 'musical progress' is along such paths, is not an amelioration from worse to better or a deterioration from better to worse, but simply a continual and restless spirit of change guaranteeing that life itself is behind the processes of art.

Richard Strauss and Cyril Scott are two geniuses interesting to observe upon their style-wanderings. The 'silver rose' passage in *Rosenkavalier* and a succession of somewhat Debussy-ish dissonant chords during the 'golden rain' episode towards the end of *Ariadne auf Naxos*[4] are instances of the way the great-hearted Bavarian has of late branched out into harmonic subtleties but little to be expected from the general trend of his younger methods. And I can remember when Cyril Scott composed almost exclusively in perfect concords. The results he then obtained were beautiful and surprisingly original, yet unknowingly and unintentionally

---

[3] From 'Song of Myself' No. 16, in *Leaves of Grass* (1891–2 edn.).
[4] Grainger had heard Strauss's opera (1911–12) in London during May–June 1913.

he got swept into the discordant vortex like all the rest of us, and was soon foreshadowing many of Debussy's most novel harmonic innovations some years before he first came in contact with any of the works of that transcendental iconoclast.

Speaking of musical modernism in general, what amazes me is not that it is with us now, but rather that it has been so slow in coming. If anything of this nature is surprising it is surely that stagnant last quarter of the last century when we compare it with the prodigious changes brought about in fifty years by Beethoven, Chopin, Wagner, and their contemporaries, and with the not inconsiderable pathbreaking activities manifested since about 1900. In that stagnant period Grieg stands out almost alone as a real iconoclastic harmonic innovator; perhaps the only man offering real revolutionary nourishment to men of go-ahead harmonic tendencies who had already digested Wagner's amazing contributions to compositional progress, and it is no doubt very largely on account of his isolated position as a pioneer of discord and 'consecutive fifths' that his influence is so unmistakably apparent in the work of composers of such otherwise divergent tastes and tendencies as Delius, Debussy, Ravel, MacDowell,[5] Cyril Scott, Herman Sandby, Albéniz, Puccini, Sibelius, Sinding,[6] etc.

Since 1900, certainly, a good deal has happened in the realms of musical composition, but I shall be greatly surprised, and I may add deeply disappointed, if the near future does not bring with it a goodly store of even more striking innovations. 'So little done, so much to do.'

Cyril Scott and Schönberg have liberated us from the *inevitability* of 'harmony', and I feel that we can never be too thankful to them for that. Not that I dislike 'harmony'. I adore it. But I am thankful to have a modern substitute to contrast it with, just as I am also thankful to have unaccompanied unison, for instance. We need not fear that Schönberg's, or Cyril Scott's, or Ornstein's influence will tend to destroy our appreciation of 'harmony' any more than the chromaticists destroyed our pleasure in diatonicness.

If I may be permitted to allude to my own creative work I should like to point out that the chords of my *Mock Morris*[7] are at least as diatonic and unmodulating as Handel's, if not more so, in spite of the fact that I had for years before its conception steeped myself in chromatic, whole-tone, discordant and every other to me available form of harmonic 'decadence' (so-called).

[5] Edward MacDowell (1860–1908), American composer and pianist.
[6] Christian Sinding (1856–1941), Norwegian composer.
[7] (Pub. 1911), originally for string sextet or string band.

Various compositional styles, vogues, tendencies and methods should give place to one another like the different seasons of the year—each excellent in its own time and place and implying no reproach to the others that go before and after it. To return to the question of Schönbergism: I firmly believe that the style of almost any composer cannot fail to gain something in the direction of greater freedom and naturalness through contact with the work of the much discussed Austrian, and independently of whether the composer happens to like or dislike Schönberg's actual compositions. Such contact can hardly fail to infect us all with a beneficial impulse towards greater artistic self-indulgence, greater unrestraint. Emboldened by Schönberg's plucky example, we unconsciously feel ourselves freer than before to indulge in part-writing that 'makes harmony' or in part-writing that neglects to 'make harmony' at will; and surely this is an incalculable advantage to certain phases of European emotionalism—if, indeed, in the deeper sense, *any* influence outside of himself can be rightly termed an advantage or disadvantage to a creative artist.

But we still await 'liberation' from rhythmical regularity. Why should the rhythms of our music be everlastingly limited to halves, half-halves, sixteenths, thirds, sixths, twelfths, etc., of regular beats, *i.e.*, beats of a standard value of duration? Stimulated by some experiments I made in irregular rhythms as a boy of sixteen, Cyril Scott has, it is true, made splendid use of what can be done with irregular barrings, by constant changes from measure to measure such as 6/8 9/16 2/4 7/16 3/8 2/4 7/16 13/16, producing fascinating and pregnant results that can nowhere be studied in fuller perfection than in his exquisite volume of piano pieces entitled *Poems*, and in his magnificent Piano Sonata, Op. 66. I ask: Is there anything in the whole literature of music more impulsively inspired, more deliciously wayward, more complexly 'natural' than pages 5, 6, 7, 8, 10, 11, 26 and 27 of this Sonata? In some of these passages Scott, in an always wholly original way, has united the lyric ecstasy of Chopin with the rippling polyphonic 'flow' of Bach. But even in Cyril Scott's rhythmically most advanced music the *underlying beat values* remain regular (though he subdivides them irregularly) and in each phrase the various parts that make up his polyphony obey rhythmic impulses in common; that is to say, a definite 'beat feeling' is still present in each phrase and *is shared by the various polyphonic parts at the same moment.*

We cannot admire too much the artistic beauty of Cyril Scott's irregular barrings; with them he has evolved a new rhythmic language of the most elastic eloquence—a language which will soon form part of every composer's every-day stock in trade; but these irregular barrings do not constitute complete liberation from rhythmical regularity. Ever since a young child I have heard in my head a polyphonic sort of music in which no kind of rhythmical regularity whatever obtains, in which not only no regular standard duration of beat is either stated or felt, but in which the various polyphonic parts *do not obey rhythmic impulses in common*. On the contrary, each part will, as a general rule, feel its beat impulse at a different moment, thus producing a rhythmic clash of a basically different nature from the mere syncopations possible under our present system.

Practical difficulties of notation and performance still bar the way to complete realization of my boyhood's dream, but I hope, nevertheless, to bring my 'beatless music' before the musical world fairly soon.[8] Should I not succeed in doing so, somebody else will, I feel sure, succeed in solving my problem, for compositional progress (I hasten to add that by 'progress' I do not mean 'improvement', but simply the path of the spirit of change and the instinct for ever wider universality) imperiously demands in its scheme the inclusion of the liberation inherent in 'beatless music', which will be to the whole art of music much what 'prose' is to literature, while our present-day music on a rhythmically regular basis can be compared with 'poetry'. Incidentally, are there any rhythms in the world more enthrallingly subtle and complex than the always utterly irregular rhythms of ordinary everyday speech?

While I have never happened to encounter any demand for beatless music outside of my own imagination, several voices have, at various times, urged the need for smaller intervallic divisions of the scale (quarter-tones, third-tones, etc.), if for no other reason so that various native musics, such as that of the Maoris of New Zealand, employing closer intervals than our own, can be more efficiently studied and recorded. I do not doubt that the introduction and use of such closer intervals will, when they come, prove as beneficial and fructifying as does Schönbergism at present. Those who oppose or dislike these various innovations (which might almost be called musical 'constitutional amendments') often seem to regard them as substitutes threatening the established forms and habits of music with extinction. If I believed for one moment that musical modernism harbored such destructive propensities I, too, would promptly become its bitter opponent. If to appreciate the lovely creations of, let us say, Debussy, Cyril Scott and Stravinsky we had to lose any of our capacity to enjoy to the full the warm glories of Brahms, I would reckon our

[8] See Essay 32.

newer tastes dearly bought indeed. Under such circumstances the path of art would be as needlessly and revoltingly tragic as the feuds of the Scottish border or the Kentucky mountains.

Is it not, however, the peculiar nature of art that nothing within its province is ever superseded, but that, on the contrary, every genuinely artistic creation *forever* (as long as its physical manifestation is spared from destruction) retains its original lustre, at least to discerning eyes?

In literature, prose has not ousted poetry, or *vice versa*, and I see no reason why 'beatless' music and our present metrical music should not prosper side by side on equally fraternal terms. As a rule the genuine innovator is seldom blind to the charm of older forms, nor even to their possibilities in his own art works. Who has expressed himself oftener or more trenchantly in diatonic and even triadic mediums than that chromatic giant Wagner? Grieg, the most chromatic Scandinavian of his generation, was also the one to whom the totally non-chromatic folk-scales of Norway provided the most inspiration. In the present-day popular music of various countries we note a preference for pentatonic melody side by side with an equally marked liking for certain chromatic chord-progressions in the accompaniment.

The fact can hardly be too often emphasized that it is largely the 'hyper-modern' men who prove the most susceptible to the lure of 'primitive' music, which not only confronts them with a simplicity (in certain directions) refreshing to them by reason of the sharp contrast it affords to art music, but which also contains certain elements of extreme complexity, particularly as regards rhythms and dynamics, to which the modernist may turn to *increase* the range of his ornate compositional resources; the artist with the healthiest appetite for complexity can generally be relied upon to possess the strongest craving for simplicity also. The last time I met Dr. Richard Strauss I enjoyed witnessing his unfeigned appreciation of a band of Catalonian street-musicians who were performing thrillingly at Lady Speyer's in London.[9]

It took a man of Sir Charles Villiers Stanford's[10] international culture, complex personality, creative originality (is not his touching and ethereal *The Fairy Lough*[11] one of the master-songs of all time?) and 'symphonic' erudition to exploit the full compositional possibilities of Irish country-side ditties and to achieve in his arrangements of them a monument to

[9] Probably in May 1910.

[10] (1852–1924), Irish-born composer, conductor, and Cambridge University professor, who had helped to foster Grainger's career in London.

[11] From Op. 77 (pub. 1901).

autochthonous song ranking right alongside Brahms' immortal *Deutsche Volkslieder*.[12]

It need not surprise us to find a daring modernist like Herman Sandby (whose strangely lovely 'Cello Concerto,[13] so entrancingly Danish in its dreamy idyllic moodfulness, so full of pregnant melodic and harmonic inventiveness, so weirdly individual in its veiled shimmering color scheme, has been one of the most deeply significant novelties of the present season) able to appreciate the simplest Scandinavian peasant song or herdsman's cattle-call, nor that so 'advanced' and subtle a stylist as John Alden Carpenter[14] responds as sensitively to the tender warmth of Negro music and the exhilaration of ragtime as he does to the most intricate sophistications of the latest Debussy, Ravel, or Stravinsky. After all, Bach, Haydn, Beethoven, Brahms, Balakirev were not so different in their day.

---

[12] *Twenty-Eight German Folksongs* (1858) and *Forty-Nine German Folksongs* (1894).

[13] Pub. 1933.

[14] (1876–1951), American composer, student of Amy Fay and Edward Elgar.

The World Music of To-morrow

(1916)

A Prospect of the Nature of our Musical Progress based upon the Musical Tendencies of To-day

Editor's Note: Have you given thought of what kind of music your children or your grandchildren may demand fifty years hence? Mr. Percy Grainger has for years been ranked among the most progressive musical thinkers of the day. In Europe, where he is as widely acclaimed as a pianist and composer as he has been in America, he was among the first to introduce the works of the modernists at public concerts. Grieg admired his work so much that he became a kind of musical foster-father to Mr. Grainger. Few musicians of to-day could therefore assume the rôle of prophet with less presumption. This article is the second and concluding section of Mr. Grainger's 'Modern and Universal Impulses in Music', which appeared in the May special issue devoted to the 'Futurists and Modernists in Music'. All music lovers who aspire to keep in touch with the progress of their art will profit by securing the first section and reflecting upon Mr. Grainger's observations.

A great deal has been written lately about the 'externality' of modern art, premising that the artist of to-day is primarily concerned with the objective observation and statement of 'things' rather than with the subjective voicing of more purely personal states of feeling. Whether this tendency be so exclusively modern or not as is claimed for it in certain quarters (are not the Icelandic sagas of the thirteenth and fourteenth centuries 'external'?), there is no doubt that its presence in contemporaneous music can be plentifully observed.

Musical Portraits

It is noticeable how many recent compositions are, as it were, musical portraits of *other types of music*. Debussy's touching 'Hommage à Rameau'[1] is a sort of (highly unphotographic!) portrait of Rameau's muse;

Source: Etude, 34/6 (June 1916), 412.

[1] No. 2 of *Images,* Set I (1905).

Debussy's exquisite 'Pagodes' a sort of (more photographic) portrait of the sounds of an Eastern orchestra of gongs. Now when Chopin penned a Nocturne we are inclined to feel that his own inner momentary feelings provided the 'Nocturne mood' of which his composition was a first-hand expression, but when Debussy gives us 'Minstrels' we are more apt to scent in it some elaboration of (or reaction from) some actual minstrels heard or objectively imagined by him than to regard it as a direct emanation of his more subjective emotionality. Of course, we are merely considering the *source* of the inspiration, not the results, which latter seem to me equally satisfying in both cases.

No doubt we can likewise, if we so will, attribute to a phase of this same 'externality' much of the attraction which folk music exerts upon noticeably many of us modern composers. When Delius, Stravinsky, Herman Sandby or I use folksong material in our works, I am convinced we do so, not so much because of our close affinity with primitive music, but, on the contrary, because we relish enormously the dramatic clash of the archaic non-harmonic folk tune with our own overflowing harmonic exuberance. The unbridgeable gulf between the two styles proves an inspiring compositional irritant, just as, similarly, we discover Bach in his chorale Vorspiele[2] spurred on to his most lavish arabesques by the most staid and unbending of hymn tunes. Perhaps Stravinsky is, however, the most obviously 'external' of all the moderns. The first of his most recent *Three Grotesques* for string quartet[3] (superbly introduced to America by the Flonzaleys[4] this season) is his impression, *not of the Russian Steppes*, but his impression *of a bagpipe playing in the Russian Steppes*.

Stravinsky's Individuality

In his masterly ballet-music *Petrouchka*[5] and in his stirringly experimental opera *Rossignol*[6] we see him responding obediently to the stimulus of divers musics not of his own 'art' line: barrel organs (two simultaneously), circus trumpetings, peasant songs and dances, Japanese music (or his imagination of it), mechanical music (the clock-work nightingale), etc. These things are not introduced into his scores merely because the plots demand them; the plots are deliberately chosen to contain such

[2] Preludes.
[3] *Three Pieces* for string quartet (1914).
[4] Leading American string quartet, *fl.* 1902–28.
[5] Burlesque for orchestra (1910–11).
[6] Musical fairy-tale (1908–9, 1913–14).

opportunities because they happen to prove peculiarly fertilizing to Stravinsky's creativity. Nor, to my mind, is his music one whit less 'original' (not that mere 'originality' matters: Does it lessen the value of Ravel's rare genius that he is so reflective of Debussy?) because so much of it originates in extraneous sources. The significant fact remains that he is so supremely capable of such genuine inspiration *from whatever source*, and that the final result is so unmistakably individual.

In a somewhat lesser degree similar things are true of several other modern composers. Albéniz was never so original as when he was typifying the local musics of various Spanish towns in his captivating collection *Iberia*; Grieg was nowhere else more amazingly his own weird, partly selfish, partly heroic self, than in his settings for piano of *Norwegian Folksongs*, Op. 66, and of *Peasant Dances* (Slaatter), Op. 72. Has Cyril Scott's muse ever been more lavishly 'Scottian' than in his entrancing treatment of 'Cherry Ripe' for violin and piano?

Early in this article I have alluded to 'universality' in music, meaning thereby a big-souled interest in the music of all ages, races, classes and places. Such an all-embracing attitude seems to me to be increasingly thriving everywhere to-day, and I see in it the loveliest and most hopeful showing of our era. No doubt some large measure of this generous open-heartedness has generally been an accompanying attribute of genius in all ages; but I am inclined to think that the special circumstances of to-day— world-wide travel and democratic fostering of music—favor a more effortlessly prolific blossoming of this blessed quality than heretofore. How otherwise shall we explain the neglect of so much of Bach's music after his death—the *Matthew Passion* unperformed for generations—and hundreds of dainty Scarlatti pieces lying unpublished until their quite recent availability under Alessandro Longo's editorship.[7]

Shall we Adopt the Music of the East?

It was on a par with the good folks who covered up carved oak with stucco in English country houses. Yet we are still only too parochial, even to-day. Are there not 'modernists' to be found (though they are fast becoming only funny) who deny themselves all pleasure in the music of the past, and seem to feel no thrill in recognizing the close affinity between all art of all ages? What do our average musicians yet know, or

---

[7] The 11-vol. Domenico Scarlatti collection, ed. Longo (1864–1945), appeared between 1906 and 1910.

care to know, of Asiatic musics, African musics, South Sea Island musics?
Certainly less than our decorators, painters and writers know of non-
European decorative arts, paintings, literature. In most houses of taste we
find Oriental art-objects, but no records of Oriental music, in spite of the
fact that talking machine companies do an enormous trade in the East
with records of Eastern musics, which could easily be available anywhere
if there were a demand for them. In most large cities examples of African
bead-work can be bought, but where is African music upon the market?
Is it, perhaps, because the music of non-European races is inferior to their
other arts? Fortunately the presence in America of Ratan Devî, the much-
revealing singer of East Indian music,[8] gives the lie to any such suggestion
in the most convincing possible manner. Those who cry out for 'beauty'
in music will surely find their cravings stilled by Ratan Devî's performances, or be hard to satisfy indeed.

Here is a consummate artist rendering consummate music—and
'absolute' music. Here are delicacies and refinements of vocal technic
utterly undreamt of by European art-singers, though not equally
unknown to European folk-singers. Our art-singers should go and listen.
Our composers will hardly need telling. Those of us who love subtle
harmonic effects find them in plenty in the blend of her wondrously
controlled voice with the vibrant buzzing drone of the 'tambura', the
indescribably satisfying native plucked instrument with which she
accompanies her Indian 'professional' songs. Those of us who are especially responsive to the fragrant freshness of unaccompanied unison are
ravished by her Kashmiri folksongs. How can it be that such pure and
irresistible artistic delights as these have been withheld from us for so
long? Perhaps the difficulties and limitations of musical notations and
the lack of familiarity with them on the part of our traveling classes is
accountable for much of our amazing ignorance of exotic musics, and
apathy towards them.

But all this parochialism will have to go, and go soon, and it is largely
the pioneer work of geniuses such as Frederick Delius (whose *Appalachia*
advertised the charm of Negro music to European musicians), Debussy,
Ravel (which twain opened our eyes to Javanese and Spanish music),
Balakirev, Stravinsky (both inspired exploiters of the Oriental musics
easily available to Russians), and Cyril Scott (whose art is redolent of an
Orientalism not limited to his music) that is coaxing out of us all the
inborn desire for more cosmic musical experiences.

---

[8] Compiler of *Thirty Indian Songs from the Punjab and Kashmir* (London, 1913).

Increasingly there is no quarter of the globe towards which our brotherly musical yearnings do not go out; no popular music in our own local communities from which we are not discovering ourselves able to cull some precious hints; no music of the past so foreign to our own methods and feelings to which we fail to thrill; no disused instruments of former days which we are not grateful to hear once more, and to welcomingly include in the permanent palette of available sound-colors; no singing of birds or braying of animals in which we do not recognize, awestruck, the touching efforts of somewhat remote brother artists. The whole world, human and animal, is ringing with strange and significant music, and we are just beginning to scent the full magnitude and generosity of it all.

Our Glorious To-morrow

It will be glorious to be a musician when scientific accuracies of notation are so far developed and so generally practised that a really representative share of the world's continual output of lovely and expressive sounds will be before us all in available forms, and when to speak of 'music' will not merely mean the work of a few 'classical' and 'popular' composers in a very few countries, but will imply as far as possible the entire musical creativity of all races (and even perhaps some study of bird and animal musics), and when a sort of soulful great-hearted musical theosophy will be rampant over all the earth.

11   *Richard Strauss: Seer and Idealist*
(1917)

Among the great composers of our era, Richard Strauss seems to me to stand forth as a type of the *gemütlich* family man in music: normal, kindly, well-balanced; a genius by reason of attributes of the soul and heart rather than of the head; a seer rather than a pure artist, an emotionalist rather than a craftsman; above all, an inveterate idealist, seeking always heroic nobility and spiritual exaltation, and able to find them in what may seem unexpected places and subjects.

The generous magnitude of his soul leads him to desire to inclose and depict, as far as possible, all phases of existence, not only those universally considered worthy of artistic presentation, but also many that appear merely gruesome, sordid, and 'unpleasant' to a less cosmic vision than his own.

I see permeating his music (the songs no less than the tone poems and operas) a humane soul overflowing with the milk of human kindness, a lackadaisically robust personality replete with tender affection and fatherly insight.

Wondrously Bavarian, is he not perhaps the most supremely *gemütlich* of all composers, past and present?

Brusque and roughshod on the surface at times; careless, uncritical and unfastidious at all times; not, perhaps, a craftsman of the highest degree; but a *man*, a *human being* of the great order, supremely possessed of the ability to soar above the petty affairs of everyday existence into the eternal realms of cosmic contemplation and religious ecstasy.

No doubt he has an almost childish weakness for tinsel and tricks, and is no eschewer of storms, turmoils, and the vagaries of passion.

But it seems to me that it is essentially as a portrayer of 'the calm that follows the storm', as a prophet of eternal values, that Strauss reigns supreme among contemporaneous composers. He loves to render the human soul ensconced in the serenity of philosophic calm, looking back over the struggles of life or across the strokes of fate in a mood of benign forgiveness and understanding.

Source: Henry T. Finck, *Richard Strauss: The Man and his Works* (Boston: Little, Brown & Co., 1917), pp. xvii–xxv.

Battles and the myriad manifestations of energy merely serve to usher in this final state of lofty repose, out of which Strauss himself seems to speak in the telling accents of the first person singular.

This Nirvana, liberally tinged, it is true, with the aforesaid typical South German *Gemütlichkeit*, is the very essence of the composer's own lovable temperament, and it is to this goal, therefore, that he loves to lead his heroes toilsomely, precariously, outrageously, but inevitably.

It is hard to conceive of any other composer possessing to a greater degree the peculiar qualities that go to make for a perfect exposition of this particular soul-state.

Constraining considerations of 'style' (such as inclose a Debussy, a Ravel, a Cyril Scott, within the narrow bands of exquisite choice) exist no more for Strauss than for Frederick Delius. Uncritical and unselfconscious in the extreme, and chastened by no strict standards of artistic morality, Strauss is singularly able to give his inner nature free rein in an ingenious musical language of sweeping breadth. Somewhat commonplace, somewhat sentimental phrases flow forth with a ring of perfect truth and conviction (for they are really typical of the man), and are handled with a sense of bigness that always seems inspirational rather than premeditated. The greater the moment, the more truly does Strauss appear to be himself, and himself only.

His inherent propensity for rising above all worldly deterrents to final glory is shown no less strikingly in the last act of *Salome* than it is in the trio in *Rosenkavalier* or in the great spiritual climaxes of *Tod und Verklärung, Ein Heldenleben, Also sprach Zarathustra, Don Quixote* and *The Legend of Joseph*,[1] though it is shown in a different way. Here, again, we note Strauss's idealism. *Salome* might have been many things in many men's hands. Through Strauss's vision, we see the purifying white heat of self-effacing passion resulting in a rapt trance of world-forgetting ecstasy, in which are drowned all puny personal considerations of life.

This sublime tragedy of the senses seems to have awakened in Strauss's philosophic intuitions the same universally religious note that it equally would in the mind of an Oriental mystic, and were Salome's swansong put before us as religious music, I feel sure it would not seem to us incongruous in that character, so noble, so cosmically devout is its whole tenor.

---

[1] For Grainger's initial reactions to various of these works, see *The Farthest North of Humanness: Letters of Percy Grainger, 1901–14*, ed. Kay Dreyfus (Melbourne: Macmillan, 1985), 161, 164, 362, 488–9. It is unlikely that he had seen Strauss's ballet *Josephs-Legende*, Op. 63 (1912–14).

No less perfect than Strauss' exponence of the calmly sublime appears to me his ability to voice a certain warm and gentle phase of modern affection, a comradely emotionalism well watered with sentiment but deliciously free from mawkishness. We find lovely instances of what I mean in his song, 'Mit deinen blauen Augen',[2] in the ingratiating ariette 'Du, Venus' Sohn, gibst süssen Lohn' in *Der Bürger als Edelmann*,[3] in the breakfast scene in the first act of *Rosenkavalier*, and in the final duet of the same opera.

It is as if the whole world melts in a motherly mood of gentle lovingkindness and graceful generosity.

It seems to me that in estimating Strauss, too little is usually said of the balmy, sentimental, affectionate, and idealistic side of his nature, while an altogether disproportionate emphasis is laid upon his 'diabolical cleverness' as a technician, the daring of his originality, his skill as an orchestrator, and his wizardry as a descriptive programist.

In all modesty I must confess that it is not where technical deftness or abstract musical mastery is concerned that I find Strauss preëminent.

Strauss is not an intrinsically exquisite composer like Delius, the complex beauties of whose scores baffle full realization at first acquaintance, but which yield up new and ever new secrets of delicate intimacy at each fresh hearing.

Nor is Strauss a born innovator like Debussy, changing the face of contemporaneous music with one sweep, nor a prolific iconoclast like Cyril Scott, Scriabin or Stravinsky, bringing new impulses and interests to the brotherhood of fellow composers by a thousand versatile experiments.

Strauss is no dream-inspired colorist like Debussy or Ravel, weaving round his musical ideas veil upon veil of subtle tonal enchantment. Though capable of wonderful momentary inspirations as a colorist, I cannot deny that his *average* orchestration seems to me afflicted with a certain dull, flat, stodgy quality that for want of a better term, I venture to call 'middle class'. Practical it is, and safe; it never sounds thin, but it is often 'muddy' in the extreme, and though it covers large surfaces with a magnificent stride, it does so at the expense of charm of details, and evinces but little sensitiveness with regard to the harmonious balance of sound proportions.

Nevertheless, Strauss's every score is lit up by occasional flashes of orchestral imaginativeness of a transcendingly original quality, and the more daring these moments are—the more they emerge from the pure

[2] Op. 56 No. 4 (1903–6).   [3] Op. 60 (1912), incidental music.

flame of Strauss's own whimsical imagination rather than from the nucleus of previous orchestral experiences—the more bewitchingly lovely they are.

Is this not yet another proof of the inborn effortless greatness of the man: a token that his genius is, at its best, at least, of the purely inspirational order; not a built-up laborious product, sullied with 'cleverness' and trickery, but a spirit utterance, welling forth in native and unconsidered purity from the soul within?

The imitations of sheep-bleatings in *Don Quixote* appeal to most people's sense of the comical for non-musical reasons, no doubt. But let us set these considerations aside for a moment and listen to the orchestral bleatings as pure sound; and I ask: Is not this one of the most soothing, mesmeric, opalescent acoustical achievements in musical history?

Here again we see the soaring idealist, the inveterate beautifier in Strauss revealed.

As a mere programist, his purpose would have been amply fulfilled by making the sheep in *Don Quixote* merely sheeplike and comic, by making the chorus of carping critics (high chromatic polyphonic woodwind passage) in *Heldenleben* merely ludicrous and cacophonous.

But in both these cases, as in a myriad others I might name, the instinctive (though possibly unconscious) aesthete in Strauss was not to be denied. In the place of what might have been two emotionally barren descriptive passages we have a precious pair of tonal creations of the most sensitive abstract beauty.

I am myself too little in sympathy with the artistic viewpoint that leads a musician to write program music—I see too little connection between literary plots and music, between everyday events and music—to be in a position to judge fairly of Strauss's 'descriptive' powers. Certainly it is not on account of these that I consider him a great genius.

Strauss grew up in a would-be 'brainy' age, an irreligious and emotionally impoverished age, curiously susceptible to the cheapest fripperies of intellectualism; and it is just possible that what seems to some of us the somewhat shallow descriptive tendencies of some of his tonepoems are the toll he had to pay to that environment. In the later Strauss, however, I seem to note an ever-increasing development of the pure musician at the expense of all side issues, and for that reason the *Rosenkavalier* and *Ariadne* (particularly the latter)[4] kindle, in my case, a still warmer glow of

---

[4] On 11 June 1913 Grainger had written of *Ariadne*'s overture as 'Strauss's most moving work' (*Farthest North*, 494).

sympathy, strike a still deeper note of reverence than even the most splendid and brilliant of his earlier compositions. Strauss appears to me to become more mellow, more genuine, more effortlessly himself with each successive work—another sign, for me, of the depth and truth of his genius, and of the abiding value of his muse.

With the exception of certain exquisite but very rare moments, his resources as a harmonist strike me as lagging sadly behind those of most other great living composers.

Whether as regards harmonic originality or a refined sense for the euphonious and expressive distribution of the component parts in chords, one could not for one moment dream of comparing him with such harmonic giants as Debussy, Ravel, Delius, or Cyril Scott.

But here, again, the later Strauss by far outstrips the younger, and the harmonic beauties of the *Ariadne* overture denote, to my mind, a, for him, quite new sensitiveness in respect to harmonic possibilities, possibly derived from contact with the remarkable life-giving innovations of French and English composers in this field, or, equally likely, evolved by himself independently straight out of his own evergreen imagination, now, for the first time, focussed upon a more purely 'chordy' style. Perhaps, however, his supreme harmonic achievement is the cascade of wondrously unrelated triads associated with the silver rose in *Rosenkavalier*, constituting one of the most ravishing chord passages in modern music and certainly something entirely unprecedented in Strauss's own compositional career.

It is interesting to compare with this the no less lovely and epoch-making chord progressions in the middle of Ravel's incomparable 'Le Gibet', published in 1909. Whether or not both of these emanations of the highest harmonic originality came into being without influence on either side, of one thing we can be certain: that Strauss in his 'silver rose' music no less than Ravel in 'Le Gibet' has given the world of harmony a new inspiration and impetus from which discerning composers can, if they will, drink a profitable draught of freshness.

To my mind, however, the greatest purely musical quality of Strauss's genius is manifested in the pith and pregnance of his musical ideas, which, though frankly and bravely commonplace at times, burst forth with an almost Beethoven-like explosive inevitability and naturalness that disarm criticism, and bear upon the face of them the stamp of the great personality from which they spring.

His themes and motives make their appeal chiefly through their sharply chiselled intervallic and rhythmic physiognomy, and not by reason of their adaptability to sophisticated color treatment. They create almost the same vital impression when played on a piano, a harmonium, or a penny whistle that they do in their original orchestration, and this seems to me a conclusive proof of the initial inventive vigor that gave them birth.

On the whole, Strauss does not seem to appeal to the younger generation of composers as much as he, perhaps, deserves to do, and this, I imagine, is largely due to the somewhat coarse, careless, and uncritical methods of his compositional workmanship.

The general public seems capable of continuing to love a genius chiefly because of his emotional type, but fellow composers have to be able to *admire qualities of craftsmanship* as well, if they are not to weary of an art product.

Strauss is not a musician's musician like Bach, Mozart, Schubert, Grieg or Debussy, capable of turning out flawless gems of artistic subtlety and perfection, but rather is he a great cosmic soul of the Goethe, Milton, Nietzsche, Walt Whitman, Edgar Lee Masters[5] calibre: full of dross, but equally full of godhead; lacking refinement, but not the supremer attributes; and uniquely able to roll forth some great uplifting message after gigantic preliminaries of boredom and inconsequentialness.

And is not the general public fundamentally right (as usual) in its instinctive response to Strauss? For is not, at least from the non-musician's standpoint, grandeur and purity of soul of more account than the most exquisite gifts of musical sensitiveness, originality, and culture? Is not, therefore, Strauss's hold upon the general public a good omen? For does not his personal message, like that of George Moore's indescribably significant *The Brook Kerith*,[6] contain the exact reaction most needed from the present world-wide immersion in strife and commercial enslavement and competition; the message that the seer, however, at all times has to proclaim to the empirical world; that the real gold dwells in the heart within, and is not to be captured in any other place, and that the real hero is he, who, turning dissatisfied away from the outer world's illusionary shows of victory and defeat, finds contentment finally within himself in viewing in the mirror of his own contemplative soul the whole universe suffused in a glory of love and understanding?

April 26, 1917.

[5] (1868–1950), American poet; Grainger collected his books and was greatly influenced by his *Spoon River Anthology* (1915).
[6] (1916), retelling the Gospel story, by the Irish writer George Moore (1852–1933).

12   *The Unique Value of Natalie Curtis'*
Notations of American Negro Folksongs
(1917/18)

What is musical composition but improvisation frozen into a permanent form by the action of the critical aesthetic faculties?

The improvisational or inspirational impulse in musical composition probably does not vary so much, at different stages of musical culture, as do the selective and critical factors that mold the original fluid idea into its ultimate shape. For instance, the intervallic, rhythmic, and harmonic consciousness that comes with the knowledge and practice of musical notation introduces quite a new element into the critical aesthetic activities—so much so that the whole world of music that knows nothing of musical notation (folk music and primitive music the world over) is thereby absolutely cut off from that other world of music that has thriven on the results of the consciousness born of musical notation (European classical and popular music of every grade and age).

The unmistakable hallmark of unwritten music (that produced and remembered without the help of musical notation) unites, in certain very outstanding characteristics, 'primitive' music of such otherwise divergent types and origin as Russian, British, Scandinavian, Kashmiri folksongs, native Australian, Greenlandic, Rarotongan (Polynesian), and American Negro musics. On the other hand, however unlike, on the surface, American ragtime may seem to the Bach *Matthew Passion*, to Wagner's *Tristan*, and to Schoenberg's orchestral pieces, yet all these four bear the unmistakable traces of that compositional consciousness that comes solely through a familiarity with musical notation, and which, in all their cases, is the first condition inseparable from their existence. For the purpose of these remarks, let us term all the music fostered by the process of musical notation *conscious* music, and call all the rest *unconscious* music. Both types have their supreme advantages, and also their inevitable limitations. It would probably be safe to assert that no composer of conscious music seems, or has ever seemed, capable of creating tunes of a certain indescribable melodic fragrance that abounds in almost every branch of unconscious music! On the other hand, unconscious music

Source: *New York Times Book Review*, 14 Apr. 1918.

(very naturally) rarely, if ever, rises to the heights of harmonic and poly-phonic intricacy and subtlety native to conscious music.

It is readily seen, as soon as we examine these two kinds of music, that one of them can never satisfactorily figure as a substitute for the other. Nor can we simply regard conscious music as a more advanced and con-sistently ameliorated form of unconscious music, for what is gained on the one hand is lost on the other—what is gained in harmonic expressibil-ity, for instance, is lost in melodic inventiveness, and what is gained in rhythmic definiteness is lost in rhythmic subtlety and variety (for art music is far 'simpler' than so-called primitive music in these latter respects).

We might compare unconscious music with the manifold dialects of a language, and conscious music with the standardized form of the same tongue; for the study of spelling and grammar does very much for speech what the practice of musical notation does for music—it makes possible the scientific preservation of already existent varieties, while it tends to prevent and stultify the growth of new varieties by the setting up of men-tally controlled permanent habits. But for the unifying bond of a (com-paratively) standard English spelling and grammar, would we not have to-day myriads of forms of widely divergent and scarcely inter-understandable English spoken throughout Great Britain, America, and the British Empire? Similarly, the habit of musical notation is a great uni-fying, a great internationalizing, force; but it is also, it goes without saying, a dangerously deindividualizing influence. It discourages the effortlessly prolific native growths, and spreads abroad, in their stead, a few musical attitudes and forms of musical speech momentarily peculiarly favored by opportunity.

The worldwide victorious path of musical education will, in time, destroy the very existence of unconscious music. Before very long, no doubt, the music of the American Negroes of the Southern States, of the Polynesians of Samoa, Hawaii, and New Zealand, of the agricultural populations of Russia, will be as obviously a product of the influence set up by a familiarity with musical notation as is to-day the art music of Paris or Berlin, as is to-day the popular music of London, Vienna, or New York. Therefore, it seems to me, it is the duty of those of us peculiarly versed in the intricacies of musical notation to see to it that a generous preservation is now made of all truly representative extant examples of unconscious music, so that when the composers and musical students of the future ask themselves the question, 'What would the musical art of unsophisticated folk be like?' there shall be adequate records for them to turn to—records that will prove inspirational as well as illuminating, records that will carry with them the irresistible appeal of unconscious, unpremeditated emotional self-expression. Such records are these of American Negro folk music by Natalie Curtis-Burlin.[1] Of all the various kinds of beautiful and thrilling music, classical or popular, primitive or cultured, that it has been my good fortune to hear in the United States, this Negro folk music easily occupies the first place in my mind, as regards its sheer acoustical beauty, its emotional depth, and by reason of its musico-historical import. This is the most truly vocal of music, ideally adapted for singing by choirs and solo organizations. It is the most American music imaginable, breathing the spiritual fervor and abandonment and the fragrance of sentiment so strangely typical of this wondrous, this generous-souled continent; yet worldwide in its applicability—as is all truly great emotional music. But the unique instructional message of Natalie Curtis' work lies in the fact that it is a record of unconscious harmony. Most of the unconscious music of the world (such as the British, Scandinavian, Greenlandic, American Indian, Kashmiri, African, Australian folk music), consists of 'single line', i.e., unaccompanied melody with no undercurrent of harmonic thought. Only rarely (as in the case of Russian peasant, Polynesian and American Negro part-singing), do we find harmonic habits associated with a complete lack of knowledge of musical notation. This makes the few available examples all the more precious and worthy of the most careful investigation and preservation, especially when the purely aesthetic results, when viewed from the angle of a modern composer, are as ravishing as they are in the case of these Negro part-songs now before us. But the task of noting down accurately such improvisational part-singing is the very hardest of musical undertakings; solely by ear it is impossible to reach the needful degree of detail-accuracy, and even with the help of the phonograph the problem is one calling for the sharpest of ears, the most alert of musical mentalities, the warmest and most expansive of racial sympathies. But Natalie Curtis-Burlin has all these qualifications in a superlative degree, as she has amply shown in her previous remarkable musical and literary accomplishment, *The Indians' Book* (Harper and Brothers). She possesses a splendidly acute hearing, accompanied by a unique realization of just what she heard and how to write it down, while her depth of artistic feeling and breadth of culture enable her to enter into the soul life of an alien race, of an alien class, as not one in many millions can. When I peruse these, her strangely perfect and satisfying recordings of these superb American

---

[1] *Negro Folksongs* (1918–19), in *The Hampton Series of Negro Folksongs*.

Negro part-songs, I cannot refrain from exclaiming: How lucky she
to have found such noble material, and it such an inspired
transcriber.

Percy Grainger, Nov. 26, 1917.

Possibilities of the Concert Wind Band from the Standpoint of a Modern Composer

(1918)

Modern Wind Band a Product of Recent Musical Thought—Reed and Brass Sections as They Should Exist—Finer Possibilities of Arranging for the Modern Wind Band—Adaptability of Classic and Modern Music to the Needs of a Complete Wind Band—Suggestions for Strengthening the Double-reed Sections—The Percussion Section as It Should Be Perfected.

When we consider the latent possibilities of a modern concert wind band[1] it seems almost incomprehensible that the leading composers of our era do not write as extensively for it as they do for the symphony orchestra. No doubt there are many phases of musical emotion that the wind band is not so fitted to portray as is the symphony orchestra, but on the other hand it is quite evident that in certain realms of musical expressiveness the wind band (not of course the usual band of small dimensions as we most often encounter it, but an ideal band of some fifty or more pieces) has no rival. It is not so much the wind band as it *already is*, in the various countries, that should engage the creative attentions of contemporaneous composers of genius, as the band as it *should be* and *will be*; for it is still in a pliable state as regards its make-up as compared with the more settled form of the sound-ingredients of the symphony orchestra. Those who are interested in exploring the full latent possibilities of the modern concert wind band should consult Arthur A. Clappé's *The Wind Band and its Instruments*,[2] an epoch-making work which is to the band of today what Berlioz's *Treatise on Instrumentation* was to the orchestra of his time—a standard work that no composer, musician, bandmaster or bandsman should fail to know and absorb.

Source: *Metronome Orchestra Monthly*, 34/11 (Nov. 1918), 22–3.

[1] In his initial draft Grainger referred throughout to 'military band'. He had been a US Army bandsman since June 1917, and was during 1918 a band-music instructor at Governor's Island.

[2] (New York: Henry Holt, 1911). Clappé (1850–1920) had been director of the US Military Academy Band at West Point until 1895. In 1911 the US Army Music School was established under his leadership.

On page 46 of Mr. Clappé's work the reader will find outlined an ideal concert wind band of sixty-four performers, which as a medium of expression peculiarly adapted to certain phases of the modern and ultra-modern composer outrivals any symphony orchestra in existence.

Modern Wind Band a Product of Recent Musical Thought

The wind band, as we know it today, is a later growth than the symphony orchestra, and is, therefore, the product of recent musical thought, just as the music of Delius, Richard Strauss, Debussy, Cyril Scott, John Alden Carpenter is the product of recent musical thought. It is, therefore, not so surprising that the wind band should prove a more satisfying means of expression to the kind of music written by the geniuses of our own day than it does to the works of the older classics, which are naturally more at home in the symphony orchestra which grew out of their activities and was influenced (in its make-up) by their musical viewpoints.

The wind band is peculiarly effective in music of a predominantly harmonic nature and, as we all know, harmony (rather than melody or even rhythm) is the principal means of expression with the most modern composers. The rich emotional harmonic languages of Delius and Cyril Scott, for instance, would sound magnificent for the wind band, and so would a large proportion of the music of the other moderns, particularly if composed directly for the wind band by the composers themselves, and not merely adapted and arranged for it from their orchestral scores.

Reed and Brass Sections as they should Exist

It is, of course, the reed sections of the ideal wind band (such as given in Mr. Clappé's above-mentioned book) that prove so very inspiring to the modern composer. The brass section, lovely, noble and heroic as its sound colors are, has not the great variety and expressibility of a fully-equipped reed section, comprising *complete families* of each of the following groups: Clarinets, saxophones, oboe-bassoon group and sarrusophones.[3] It is only when *family grouping* of reed instruments (a complete oboe-bassoon family consisting of oboes, English horn, bass oboe, bassoons and contrabassoon; a complete clarinet family consisting of E flat and B

---

[3] A double-reeded brass instrument of conical bore, designed by Sarrus, a French bandmaster, in the 1850s.

flat clarinets, alto clarinet, bass clarinet and contrabass clarinet; a complete quintet of saxophones; a complete sextet of sarrusophones) is insisted upon by composers and carried out by performers that the present, often monotonous tone color of wind bands will give place to a kaleidoscopic variety of tone colors comparable to those in the orchestration of Wagner, Stravinsky, or Delius.

Mr. Clappé lays great stress upon these facts in his above-mentioned book, *The Wind Band and its Instruments*, and he has furthermore demonstrated in practice the truth and practicability of his theories in the beautifully balanced 'Institute of Musical Art' Band that he has built up at the Army Music Training School at Governor's Island of which he is principal. When I first heard this band, at a concert at Washington Irving High School, with its quintet of saxophones, its quartet of alto and bass clarinets, its quartet of oboes, bass oboe and bassoon, with the tone of its well-rounded brass section so proportioned and controlled so as never to (except for quite special intentional effects) obscure or over-blare the more subtly expressive sound colors of its unusually complete woodwind sections, I realized, more than ever before, the truly immense potentialities of the concert wind band as an emotional musical medium.

Finer Possibilities of Arranging for the Modern Wind Band

There is *plenty of variety* of tone color in ordinary wind bands even as at present constituted, but this variety is not utilized in the average arrangements for band because the arranger has to adapt his instrumentation to the haphazard make-up of most of the bands that will perform his adaptations. Thus there is great tonal contrast between the same note played upon the bassoon, bass clarinet or baritone saxophone. But the arranger cannot often utilize these contrasts to the full as he cannot be sure that all three instruments will be present in the bands that will play his arrangements. Consequently a great deal of doubling occurs in most publications, and we find parts published for 'Alto Clarinet or Alto Saxophone', although the tone quality of the former is strikingly different from that of the latter. And the same thing holds good all along the line. Such delicious contrasts as those between the French horns and E flat altos, between the brass basses and the deep reed basses (contrabassoon, double sarrusophone, contrabass clarinet, bass saxophone) are seldom, if ever heard at present, but we can be sure that they will form part of the normal stock-in-trade of contrast in the scores for wind bands of the near future—when once the band has assumed a *definite form* through the *uncompromising demands of composers* (think what has accrued to the richness of symphony orchestras through the insistent demands of such men as Wagner, Richard Strauss and Delius!) and the gradual realization of the utter necessity of providing *complete families* of each type of reed instrument, as before alluded to.

Adaptability of Classic and Modern Music to the Needs of a Complete Wind Band

In much of the older music, such as that by Mozart, Beethoven, Rossini, Weber, etc., the chief expressibility will frequently be found to lie above middle C (*c′*) owing to the strong melodic interest of such music and the comparatively weaker interest of its harmonic or polyphonic sides. It is undoubtedly the influence (direct and indirect) of such music that has developed the higher-voiced reed instruments at the expense of those of lower compass in wind bands; as it is equally obviously the result of the greater harmonic richness (with consequently greater concentration upon the lower-toned members of reed groups) of such more modern composers as Wagner, Tchaikovsky, Grieg, Dvořák, Puccini, etc., that we have to thank for the gradual (though still irregular and incomplete) appearance of a few of the lower reeds such as the bassoon, baritone saxophone and bass clarinet, in the average band of today.

A large part of the expressiveness of the most modern music (say, that of Delius and Cyril Scott) lies below, rather than above, middle C (*c′*) owing to the fact (before mentioned) that modern music is more harmonic than melodic or rhythmic. This makes the presence of a variety of deep and moderately deep reed instruments an absolute necessity to the modern composer. An oboe is of but little use to him unless he can be sure of being able to continue the oboe color downwards by means of the English horn and the bass oboe (the latter peculiarly well-fitted for use in wind bands), just as alto and tenor saxophones do not provide him with a sufficiency of saxophone color unless supplemented by baritone and bass saxophones. If the necessity of such demands are insisted upon by composers with sufficient tenacity we will soon meet wind bands able to carry out such contrasts of reed family groupings as the four following examples show, and when this happens the wind band will constitute a medium for emotional musical expression second to nothing that has ever existed in musical history. See music examples Nos 1, 2, 3 and 4.

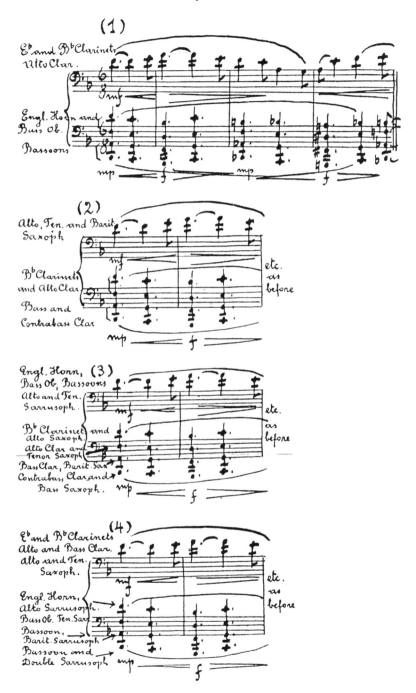

Suggestions for Strengthening the Double-Reed Sections

A word should be said as to the particular need (from the viewpoint of the ultramodern composer) for strengthening the *double-reed* sections of the wind band, by providing a complete family of sarrusophones (forming a sextet), as well as adding a bass oboe and English horn to the oboe-bassoon family. This is particularly desirable as the double reeds are able to add a quality of 'fierceness' and intensity to the band that no other instruments, reed or brass, can boast. It is this fierce, primitive, 'wild-man' note that stirs us in the shrill strident tones of the Scotch or Italian bagpipes and in Egyptian or East Indian double-reed pipes, and which most modern composers (with their tendency to 'throw-back' to primitive emotions and impressions—so noticeable in Stravinsky and Delius, for instance) keenly desire to incorporate in their instrumentations. The brass can be heroic and magnificent, the piccolos shrilly whistling, the clarinets brilliant and 'reedy', but none of the instruments of the band except the double reeds can reproduce the snarling, skirling, nasal wildness of the bagpipe and similar primitive pipes—yet combining this quality with the accuracy of intonation needful to modern music.

The Percussion as it should be Perfected

The percussion section must be completed in its family groupings if it is to be of real musical value to contemporary composers; that is to say, the xylophone should be extended several octaves downwards by the wooden marimba and the Deagan[4] nabimba (a glorious instrument)[5] and the bells (Glockenspiel) should likewise be completed downwards by steel marimbas, reveille tubes, etc., reaching as far as possible in the bass clef. All that has been said of the modern composer's need of low and medium low reed instruments applies with equal force to all the lower members of the various metal and wooden bell, bar and tube percussion instruments. When these instruments are employed in complete families they will form an adjunct as desirable to the full concert wind band as is (in a different way) the reed section or brass section today, and particularly if equipped with a piano keyboard (with octave couplers and an electric tremolo action like Deagan's 'Una-fon')[6] their usefulness will be incalculable. But

---

[4] A Chicago firm of instrument makers, founded by John Deagan in 1880.
[5] A five-octave marimba-like instrument sounding something like a clarinet.
[6] A small, but powerful electric organ, suitable for outdoor performances.

at present, a single glockenspiel and single xylophone is hardly more useful to the modern composer than a single trombone or single trumpet would have been to Wagner. When we recall the effects produced by Wagner in the 'Ring' (in the Valhalla motiv music) by using tubas plenteously in groups, and by his whole system of group orchestration, we can imagine the equally magnificent (though wholly different) gamut of group contrasts that the military band will offer to composers who will possess the insight, enthusiasm and tenacity to bring about the completion in the instrumentation of concert wind bands of those manifold (but as yet mostly fragmentary) elements that even now prove so strangely fascinating and attractive to onward-looking creative musicians.

14   *Let Us Sit in Wait No Longer for the Advent of Great American Composers—They are with Us Already*
(1919)

We read in George Moore's 'Ave' (one of the volumes of his entrancing trilogy *Hail and Farewell*)[1] of the author speaking these pregnant words at a literary dinner in Dublin: 'We must not be afraid of praising Mr. Yeats' poetry too much.' I often think of that sentence in connection with the American composers of our day and the duties that artistic justice lays upon us. Many people are instinctively inclined to fear bestowing too glowing a praise upon the artistic output of their contemporary fellow countrymen; yet, if we are dealing with the work of geniuses or men of great talent, the probabilities more often lie in the exactly opposite direction; more often our danger lies *in refraining from exceeding praise*, in refraining from what at the time may seem *excessive praise*; for a remarkable accomplishment deserves a remarkable acclaim, and in underrating a work of art we are showing no sounder a lack of judgment than in overrating the same—with this difference; that undervaluation is a meaner error than overvaluation, and one more enervating to the artistic atmosphere of the land we live in; since it is sympathy and not fault-finding that spurs creative artists to worthiest goals.

I think it would be utterly inaccurate and ungrateful to pretend that the gifted American composer of today walks a thorny and unholpen[2] path. There are probably few, if any, lands where deserving composers are more likely to find their works more worthily published, more satisfactorily performed (and this whether their works be easy or exacting, severe or popular in style) and more humanly and sincerely received. All these things are splendidly fortunate, and no composer who loves the welfare of his fellow composers could fail to feel warmth and gratitude and happiness for such generous and favorable and constructive conditions.

Source: *Quarter-notes of the Brooklyn Music School Settlement*, 10 Dec. 1919, pp. 1–3.

[1] 'Ave' is the first essay in *Hail and Farewell* (New York: D. Appleton, 1917).
[2] Unhelped.

But in spite of all this I oftenest feel that the best native-born American composers are still decidedly underrated by the average American musician and music-lover. In both England and America musical composition along large and complex and highly cultured lines is still so comparatively new an advent in the life of the nation that the average Englishman and American still feels somewhat diffident of the achievements of their native-born composers, and are slightly reluctant of believing that among their contemporary fellow-countrymen are composers as great as the greatest contemporary composers of any land. Americans are not yet as confident of their own composers as they are of their own athletes, soldiers or business men, nor do they, in the bulk, realize that their own country has already produced musical creators as great in the world of music as Whistler and Sargent[3] in the pictorial world. Yet such is undoubtedly the case, or I am blind to the true facts of the artistic history we are living in and making.

It is true that several native composers are known widely as significantly gifted men—but not as such *extremely gifted* men as they are in reality. They are acclaimed as fine talents when in reality they are true geniuses. Their brilliance as local composers is often sensed while their fitness to rank as leading world-composers is, not unnaturally, overlooked. I say 'not unnaturally' since all public appreciation of any art requires the passage of time, and many of the finest examples of American musical creativity are too recent to have been able to permeate all sections of musical life of the nation as yet. Thus, though Rubin Goldmark's orchestral *Requiem*[4] is deeply appreciated by many, some years will have to pass ere the average American concert-goer regards it with the reverent awe with which he views an equally fine work by Strauss or Elgar or D'Indy. Personally, I consider Goldmark's *Requiem* one of the most touching and expressive orchestral pieces of our era.

When John Alden Carpenter's *Concertino* for piano and orchestra had its first performance in Chicago it was welcomed as a spirited work of talent.[5] While I believe that it is all this, I am equally confident that it is very much more: I am sure that it is a work of singular perfection of form and color, one of the most pianistic and 'becoming' of modern piano concertos, and standing absolutely alone in the manner in which it presents

---

[3] See Essay **22**.

[4] *Requiem suggested by Lincoln's Gettysburg Address* (1919), by Rubin Goldmark (1872–1936), composer and teacher of Gershwin and Copland.

[5] Carpenter's jazz-influenced Concertino had been premièred by Grainger in Chicago in 1916.

the solo instrument and the orchestra in a delicately balanced relation, one to the other, that recalls the intimacy of chamber music rather than the swash-bucklering externality of most piano concertos. In short, I see in it a 'classic' that will soon, by reason of its intrinsic beauties and effortless charm, find its way into the permanent repertory of pianists, the world over. Howard Brockway's *Lonesome Tunes* (settings of Kentucky folk-songs for voice and piano)[6] seem universally appreciated, but are they appreciated at their immense *full* value? Are they ranked, in contemporary judgment, alongside the finest folk music settings of all time, all countries? For this they fully deserve to be, as I see it. To my mind, Brockway, in his new collection, *Kentucky Mountain Tunes*,[7] no less than in his earlier collection, *Lonesome Tunes*, has accomplished the finest voice-and-piano settings of folksongs in the English language yet given to the world. The subtle poetry, the sensitive emotionality, the expressive harmonies and fragrant originality and 'raciness' of Brockway's piano accompaniments to these splendid old airs place them, to my mind, directly alongside the Bach organ *Choralvorspiele*,[8] the Brahms *Deutsche Volkslieder*, the Grieg *Slaatter* and *Folkeviser* (Opus 66),[9] the Eduard Moulet *Chansons populaires de Haute Normandie*[10]—and higher honor than that I cannot conceive.

Realizing how recent has been the appearance of most of the American compositions that I admire most—and the fact that these works cannot yet, on account of their youth, have found their way to the majority of American modernity-loving musicians and amateurs, I am adding a little list of some of the works of native-born American composers for piano, for voice and piano, and for chorus, that have stirred and thrilled me the most deeply within the past year or so—in the hopes that these gems of native creativity will bring to some of my fellow musicians (who are not yet familiar with them) the same delight and inspiration that they have brought to me. The following list is not pretended to be comprehensive or complete, in any way, and merely presents a purely personal choice of such American compositions of rare talent and genius that I happen to have been lucky enough to have come in contact with during a brief period.

---

[6] (Pub. 1916). Howard Brockway (1870–1951) was a New York composer and pianist.
[7] Pub. 1920.
[8] Chorale preludes.
[9] Norwegian Peasant Dances, Op. 72, and Norwegian Folksongs, Op. 66.
[10] Édouard Moullé, turn-of-the-century French arranger. His arrangement of fifty-two songs from Normandy was published in 1913.

Piano Solo

J. A. CARPENTER, *Impromptu* and *Polonaise Americaine*. (Publisher, G. Schirmer, Inc.)

J. A. CARPENTER, *Concertino* for piano and orchestra. (In the press, G. Schirmer, Inc.)

R. NATHANIEL DETT, 'Juba' Dance, from Suite *In the Bottoms*. (Publisher, Clayton, Summy Co.)

DANIEL GREGORY MASON, 'The Whippoorwill' and 'Cloud Pageant' from *Country Pictures*. (Publisher, Breitkopf und Härtel.)

HOWARD BROCKWAY, 'Wedding March' from *Three Armenian Folktunes*. (Publisher, G. Schirmer, Inc.)

FANNIE DILLON, 'Birds at Dawn', from Opus 20. (Publisher, The John Church Co.)

LEO SOWERBY, *The Irish Washerwoman*. (Publisher, The Music Press, Chicago.)

RUBIN GOLDMARK, 'From the Old Mission', No. 3 of *Prairie Idylls*. (Publisher, G. Schirmer, Inc.)

DAVID W. GUION, *Turkey in the Straw*. (Publisher, G. Schirmer, Inc.)

Voice and Piano

HOWARD BROCKWAY, *Lonesome Tunes*, folksongs from the Kentucky Mountains. (Publisher, H.W. Gray Co.)

HOWARD BROCKWAY, *Kentucky Mountain Tunes*. (In the press, Oliver Ditson Co.)

J. A. CARPENTER, *The Player Queen*. (Publisher, G. Schirmer, Inc.)

J. A. CARPENTER, 'Spring' from *Improving Songs for Anxious Children*. (Publisher, G. Schirmer, Inc.)

Chorus

NATALIE CURTIS-BURLIN, *Negro Folksongs*, four books now reprinted in one volume. (Publisher, G. Schirmer, Inc.)

NATALIE CURTIS-BURLIN, *Two Old Negro Christmas Songs*. (Publisher, Huntzinger & Dilworth.)

R. NATHANIEL DETT, *The Chariot Jubilee*, Motet. (Publisher, The John Church Co.)

R. NATHANIEL DETT, 'Listen to the Lambs', 'Music in the Mine', 'O Holy Lord'. (Publisher, G. Schirmer, Inc.)

Often in selecting modern piano solos for programs we encounter a strange dearth of quiet, melodious poetical numbers—items that could fill somewhat the same role that do the piano poems of Chopin and Schumann, for instance. But I venture to claim that in the *Impromptu*, 'The Whippoorwill', 'Birds at Dawn', 'From the Old Mission', of the above list, we have four touching, telling, gentle pieces, each one of them rich in personality and tender appeal. 'Birds at Dawn', despite its modernity, is like some old exotic, ornate embroidery, wafting to us the fragrance of a past delicacy and exquisiteness. 'The Whippoorwill' has the wistful poignancy of the little poem that heads the music. About Daniel Gregory Mason's[11] 'Cloud Pageant' is the spacious grandeur suggested by its title. It breathes a lofty calm, a gold warmth, and in its splendidly flowing form, its natural manly delivery, it has a certain kinship with the Brahms piano Rhapsodies. Brockway's 'Armenian Wedding March' is a miniature of completest perfection. In addition to being a characteristic concert number full of local color, it is a useful study in simultaneous *staccato* and *legato* playing.

American piano music is particularly rich in 'bring-down-the-house' pieces of a rollicking nature, and anything more inevitably effective and exhilarating to hear and more entertaining to play and practice than the above-listed *Polonaise Americaine*, 'Juba' Dance, *The Irish Washerwoman* and *Turkey in the Straw* are hard to imagine. These things are as striking as skyscrapers, as nationally typical as baseball. It would be impossible to find anywhere in piano literature four numbers more suitable to the concert platform, more irresistible to each and every kind of audience, simple or sophisticated.

Most of John Alden Carpenter's songs (such as his 'Gitanjali', 'Don't Ceare', The Home Road', 'Wull Ye Come') are already too well known to need my mention here.[12] But I would like to single out two, not yet so widely heard, that are among his very loveliest. *The Player Queen* is, to my ears, one of the most distinctive songs of all time—a perfect setting of a bewitching poem.[13] Very exquisite in its graceful yet austere simplicity is the same composer's 'Spring', with delicious words by Carpenter himself.[14] The negro traditions of unlettered part-singing are providing

---

[11] (1873–1953), American composer and MacDowell Professor at Columbia University, 1929–42.

[12] Respectively: *Song Offerings* (1913), *Don't Ceáre* (1911), *The Home Road* (1917), *Wull Ye Come in Early Spring* (1914).

[13] W. B. Yeats's 'A Song from *The Player Queen*' appeared in *Responsibilities* (1914). Carpenter's setting dates from the same year.

[14] One of Carpenter's *Improving Songs for Anxious Children* (1901–2).

American musical culture with a choral style that, on its own ground, it were hard to equal in any other country. Nothing could possibly be more absolutely suitable for choral singing, all over the musical world, than the Southern spirituals, play-songs and dance-songs so excellently and faithfully recorded by that inspired artist-soul, Natalie Curtis-Burlin.[15] Such music is born of the musically sacred gift of polyphonic improvisation and carries upon its face the hallmark of its instinctive and untrammelled origin. Similarly effective and chorally adroit are the choruses of Nathaniel Dett;[16] as full of popular appeal as they are of sterling artistic workmanship and unfailing euphony. If choral societies wish to 'sound their best' I would advise them to sing these pieces of Curtis-Burlin's and Dett's. Such works are to the choral world what Wagner is to the orchestra and Chopin to the piano; the fullest normal exploitation of the medium employed. They recall Walt Whitman's meaningful line: 'This is the meal equally set, this the meat for natural hunger'.[17]

To students training for the concert platform and intending to embark upon international careers as interpretative artists, I would like to suggest that they may fit themselves the better for such a task by specializing, in greater or lesser degree, in the compositional output of their own country's best composers. All over the world the musical public, rightly enough, likes to hear an artist render the art of his own race. We do not go to German singers for ideal renderings of Italian opera. Likewise we do not go to Italian singers for ideal performances of German music-drama. We naturally prefer to hear both Germans and Italians in their own racial spheres. And so it is with the concert platform, to a not inconsiderable extent; we like a performer to bring us, in his artistry, a breath of his own native heath, hills, plains, woods, deserts and waters.

My advice to American students would be: Immerse yourselves without delay in the splendid world of music that is flowing from the pens of your own native-born musicians. Let us sit in wait no longer for the advent of great American composers; they are with us already. Let us hasten to capitulate to them, respond to them and enjoy them and make part of ourselves the beauties and expressivenesses they are furnishing us with. Let us, as performers, quickly and eagerly do our patriotic part as they, as creators, are doing, have done, theirs already. For this kind of patriotism is free of all chauvinism, defeats nobody and enriches the rest

---

[15] See Essay 12.

[16] (1882–1943), Canadian-born American composer, conductor, and pianist. During 1913–31 he was music director at the Hampton Institute in Virginia.

[17] 'Song of Myself' No. 19, in *Leaves of Grass* (1891–2 edn.).

of the world while it enriches us. Moreover, the patriotism that finds its
vent in racial self-expression through the medium of art does not wilt and
die as empires and supremacies wilt and die, but lives on through the ages,
a 'carte de visite' to future humanity, engendering cosmic love.

New York City, November 21, 1919.

15 The Influence of Anglo-Saxon Folk Music
(1920)

Nothing could be more obvious than the fact that the musical tendencies of a people or community are determined by the economic conditions under which it lives. In agricultural or grazing districts where acres are wide, where farms or ranches or stations or saeters[1] are far apart, where men and women work singly in lonely occupations we find that individualistically melodious folksongs flourish and the playing of instruments, such as the fiddle, the bagpipes, and the accordion, in a distinctly soloistic manner.

In village and town life, wherever factories abound and wherever massed labor in any form is the order of the day, whether in rural or urban surroundings, there we may expect to find choral singing, saenger-fests,[2] brass bands, and, finally, symphony orchestras and opera.

Where humanity is herded together in groups we find a widespread growth of the sense of harmony, as in most countries of Continental Europe, among American negroes, Polynesians, or we find the habit of inexact massed unison prevalent, as in China, Java, Egypt, etc. On the other hand, where more individualistic, more lonely lives are led we find the fullest fruition of the art of individualistic melody, as among Scandinavian peasants, Eskimos, shepherds or agriculturalists in the British Isles, and in this country among the mountaineers of the South and the cowboys of the Southwest.

By individualistic melody I mean an unaccompanied single stream of vocal or instrumental sound in which the emotional message of the composer is conveyed chiefly by means of the expressiveness of linear curves of sound (intervallic relationships) and in a lesser degree by rhythmic and dynamic contrasts and impressions. The appeal of such a melody does not depend upon any potential added harmonic accompaniment or upon any effects of timbre (tonal color) other than those of the single voice or instrument carrying the melody.

Source: 'Music Number', *Evening Post* (New York), 30 Oct. 1920, pp. 1–2, a condensed version of Grainger's longer lecture entitled 'The Potential Influence of Anglo-Saxon Folk Music upon Art Music', which he had presented in Portland, Maine, on 4 Oct. 1920.

[1] Summer pastures in the Norwegian mountains.
[2] Choral festivals (Germ.).

I have already remarked that the art of individualistic melody is generally found carried to greater heights of beauty by men engaged in lonely
pursuits (the lone shepherd, the farmer who ploughs alone, the cowboy
who rides alone, the boatman who rows alone), than by men who live,
work, and sing in groups, such as villagers, tribesmen, mass workers on
plantations, sailors on sailing ships and the like. Nor is the cause far to
seek. Where men sing in groups (as in the case of American negroes, for
instance), and the musical expression takes the form of harmonic part-
singing (different singers singing different musical parts), the addition of
the harmonic interest soon weans the creative concentration away from
melodic inventivity in the direction of a more harmonic expression, with
the result that an inferior standard of melodic vigor is set and tolerated—
and rightly so, since the melodic loss is oftenest offset by a corresponding
harmonic gain. That is why we find the greatest geniuses among classical
composers, such as Bach, Beethoven, Wagner, and Delius, incapable of
creating melodies that, viewed solely as melodies, can compare with such
pinnacles of folksong melodiousness as the Swedish 'Värmlandsvisan',[3]
the Norwegian 'Fraanar Ormen',[4] the Irish 'Tune from County Derry',[5]
the English 'Green Bushes' (Cecil Sharp's collection),[6] the American
'Little Sparrow' (Brockway's *Lonesome Tunes*).[7]

Again the habit of group unison singing stunts the intervallic range of
melodies, which, if they are to be well adapted to unison performance by a
group of voices, must not soar above the compass of the lower voices of
the group, nor descend below the effective range of the group's higher
voices. As a result of this limitation we get stunted melodies spread over
a range of four, five, or six notes. Often enough these small-range melodies have considerable charm (for instance, many of the Scandinavian
Faeroe Island dance-songs so ideally collected by Hjalmar Thuren[8])
though they inevitably lack the free expansiveness and untrammelled
sweep of songs fostered by the individualistic vocalism born of lonely
pursuits, which frequently show such wide intervallic ranges as one
octave and a sixth (nearly two octaves) in the 'Irish Tune from County

---

[3] Grainger had set this national song as the second movement of his *La Scandinavie* Suite
(1902–4).
[4] Norwegian heroic song, found in M. B. Landstad's 1853 collection of Norwegian folksongs,
which Grieg had used as a source for folksongs. See, further, Essay **31**.
[5] Set by Grainger in many different arrangements (first pub. 1911).
[6] Set variously by Grainger as a 'passacaglia on an English folksong' (first pub. 1921).
[7] Grainger frequently played Brockway's 'Little Sparrow' (1916) in concerts.
[8] (1873–1912), Danish folklorist, whose collection of Faeroese songs appeared in 1908.

Derry', one octave and a fifth in the Swedish 'Värmlandsvisan', one octave and a fourth in the Lincolnshire (England) folksong 'The Pretty Maid milking the Cow'.[9]

In addition to exploiting the obvious melodic advantages arising out of a more generous choice of intervals the singer singing entirely alone can indulge in a freer self-abandonment of emotional expression, a greater variety of personal artistic idiosyncrasies than can a singer forming part of a singing group and having to preserve a due regard for the tonality and the harmonic, rhythmic, and dynamic trend of his neighbors.

Thus many influences unite to make the lonely singer the melodist par excellence, and it is, therefore, not surprising, in viewing the musical achievements of the Caucasian races, to find that the most beautiful, the most complex, the most highly organised and sensitized melodies are to be found in the greatest profusion in those lands where economic conditions favor the largest percentage of lonely pursuits, of pioneer lives: in such countries as Norway, Sweden, Russia, Great Britain, Ireland, and North America.[10]

Compared with the more southerly European races (such as Germans, French, Austrians), a large proportion of the Scandinavian and English-speaking people have craved, above all things, plenty of elbow room for themselves and their offspring and the opportunity to carve their own careers without too much interference from their fellow men.

Musically speaking, this preference for rough and lonely and independent ways of living over smooth and crowded and more communal ways of living on the part of a large proportion of the northern races has not only resulted in a profusion and variety of complex and highly organized melodies, such as no other racial group could hope to equal at present, but in addition it has induced a racial standard of melodiousness, a racial demand for melodic achievement that, in various ways, now permeates the popular musical life of the cities no less than that of the rural districts. The average Anglo-Saxon, townsman no less than countryman, expects 'music with a tune in it', something that he can readily whistle or hum, and I do not doubt it is this nation-wide insistence upon melodic vigor and inventivity (in itself a survival of the musical tastes of pioneer days)

---

[9] Collected by Grainger himself in Aug. 1906, and set by him for voice and piano (pub. 1921).

[10] Grainger's lecture typescript contained a further paragraph here: The history of the Northern races (Scandinavians, British, Americans) is largely one of wave upon wave of adventurous colonization born of a racial preference for the discomforts and freedom of pioneer life (the exploring of oceans, the felling of forests, the fording of rivers, the crossing of deserts) over the comforts and enslaving trammels of crowded village and town living.

that is responsible for the outstanding excellence of so much of American and British contemporary popular music (music hall ditties, Sousa marches, ragtime, and jazz)—music that, in the course of a few years, has taken the international world by storm.

In the meantime, what have the less adventurous, less independent, more docile, more closely herded peoples of Europe contributed to the art of music? To my mind a gift at least as golden as that of the noblest achievements of individualistic melody. I am alluding to the birth of the habit of harmony, started somewhere (in England or the Netherlands, or wherever it was) during the Middle Ages and gradually developed and extended by the compositional schools of Italy, France, Austria, and Germany until, to-day, harmony is, without doubt, the most deeply moving of all our present modes of musical expression.

The crowded village and city life of Continental European countries favored the formation of choirs, orchestras, and chamber music combinations, as well as the construction of complicated keyboard instruments, such as the organ, harpsichord, and piano, invaluable to the growth of the harmonic sense.

The results of these newly invented and developed musical habits (polyphony and harmony) gradually turned the popular ear of Continental Europe away from the melodic and narrative appeal of folk songs in the direction of an absorbing interest in those massed musical effects and complex harmonic lines of thought and perception that have culminated in the oratorios, fugues, symphonies, sonatas, operas, music dramas, concertos, symphonic poems, chamber and virtuoso music of the last three or four hundred years, representing a general musical advance the like of which the world has probably never seen and to the true magnitude of which it is difficult to do full mental justice, so iconoclastic have been the changes effected, so seemingly limitless the new æsthetic realms opened up. But we shall be doing no injustice to the great musical geniuses of Continental Europe if we assert that their great progress in emotional expressibility by means of an ever more and more subtle use of harmony, dynamics, and orchestral tone color was accompanied by a comparative atrophy of melodic and rhythmic inventivity.[11]

Despite the achievements of the English composers of the sixteenth and seventeenth centuries and the occasional advent of a Scandinavian such as Buxtehude, it is not until comparatively recently that our northern races

---

[11] Grainger's typescript added: What was more natural than that they should temporarily overlook the fullest possibilities of rhythm and melody, absorbed as they were in the engrossing potentialities of harmony and the rich palette of orchestral combinations?

can be said to have taken a vital and national interest in the art music evolved in Continental Europe.[12]

But during the last half century all this has changed dramatically. Under the stress of international commercialism the Anglo-Saxon of to-day has abandoned much of the freedom-loving outdoor adventurousness of former days and seems now to value less the independence offered by rough and ready pioneer careers than the greater security and softer inducements of city life and to secure these latter he is not averse to entering the semi-slavery and art-destroying drudgery of factory life and the effeminate employments of offices and large stores. There are those who find the Anglo-Saxon of to-day less jealous of his rights of free speech than of yore, and discover him less and less characterized by his one-time individualistic independence and more and more prone to think in droves.

Be that as it may, the steady influx of the rural population into the cities over most parts of the English-speaking world has resulted in herded habits of living that foster no inconsiderable taste for those more complex, more communistic, less individualistic forms of musical utterance that we call 'classical' music, or art music. And though a large proportion of typical Anglo-Saxons still turn unadmiringly away from the music performed by symphony orchestras, choirs, chamber-music organizations and virtuosi because they 'can discover no tune in it', an ever increasing minority have abandoned the old-fashioned racial craving for melody and are quite content with cosmopolitan music fare. Out of this growing taste for art music have emerged quite a few English-speaking composers who must be reckoned among the greatest musical creators of their own age, if not of all time.

Personally, I doubt if a greater tonal poet and more intrinsic musician has ever put pen to paper than Frederick Delius, the English composer. The American Howard Brockway has made exquisite arrangements of Kentuckian folksongs that, for soulfulness of vision and perfection of workmanship, may justly be ranked alongside the choral-preludes of Bach and the folksong settings of Grieg and Brahms. Cyril Scott is one of the most inspired and significant harmonic and rhythmic experimentalists of our era, as well as an artistic mystic of compelling spiritual force.

John Alden Carpenter has struck a truly American as well as a truly

---

[12] Grainger's typescript added: Whatever interest was present was evidently not racial enough, did not permeate all classes sufficiently, to produce a northern creative musical output along 'classical' (i.e. harmonic, polyphonic and symphonic) lines that could compare in volume or distinctiveness or fragrance with the racial output in the domain of folk music.

personal note in contemporary music, backed by a Mozartian suavity and perfection of style and form. Roger Quilter's[13] lovely songs deserve a place beside the immortal songs of Schubert, Schumann, Brahms, Grieg, and Fauré, while large symphonic works of genuine greatness and depth have come from Elgar, Rubin Goldmark, Ralph Vaughan Williams, Charles Griffes,[14] and others. And the above list of notable Anglo-Saxon composers is far from complete.

As might be expected, in fundamentals the art of these men stands much closer to that of the classical music of Continental Europe than it does to the folk music of the English-speaking world. Yet during the last twenty years or more most of our composers have begun to be more or less imbued with a musical 'back to the land' movement, a desire for 'local color' and 'racial feeling' in their work—a tendency which, no doubt, consciously or unconsciously, is part of that worldwide stir of racial self-assertiveness that has made itself so much felt in the World War and in the settlements ensuing upon the same.[15]

Most musicians know nowadays how rich is almost every section of the British Isles in some form or other of folk music. But the average American musician does not yet fully realize how wondrously rich his own country is in similar resources. Leaving aside the wonderful music of the Indians and confining ourselves solely to strictly English-speaking folk music and its derivatives (such as the American Negro folk music) we find both in the South (among Kentuckian, Appalachian and Blue-Ridge mountaineers) and in the North (Maine and elsewhere) a profusion of British ballads and folk songs in an unusually archaic stage of development. In the fiddle tunes of the Middle West, South, etc., we find instru-

[13] (1877–1953), English composer, especially of songs; a fellow student of Grainger in Frankfurt. See Essay **35**.

[14] (1884–1920), progressive American composer and educator, who had died the previous Apr.

[15] Grainger's typescript added: and which, in widely different ways, has inspired the artistic and linguistic activities of such movements as the Peasant Language Party of Norway, the Frisian Society of Holland, the Gaelic League of Ireland and the Flemish Movement in Belgium.

Quite independently of this peasant art influence, however, leading composers in several lands have come to realize the melodic impoverishment that has resulted to so much modern music through too one-sided a concentration upon harmonic means of expression, too consistent an indifference to the more subtle aspects of melody and rhythm. While Scandinavian, Slavonic and Spanish composers turned to their native folk music as the most natural antidote, French musicians (first St.-Saëns, later Debussy and others) sought vitalization in Oriental music—all of them with refreshing results that the oncoming wave of Anglo-Saxon composers could not fail to be impressed by.

Thus our creative musicians entered the list of cosmopolitan musical life only to find themselves impelled by the cosmopolitan creeds of their age to seek a large proportion of their inspiration in the primitive folk music stored up among the most rural and most uneducated populations of their own races.

mental dance music very closely allied to that of the British Isles, yet with an unmistakable local American tang to it. The American Negro is responsible for a great variety of folk music, ranging from individualistic melodies of great linear beauty to such gems of improvised harmonic part-singing as those so perfectly recorded by Natalie Curtis-Burlin in her four volumes of *Negro Folk-songs.*

No stone should be left unturned in the task of handing down to future generations this great heritage of traditional music in as complete and intact a preservation as possible.

But the fact that stamps our present musical era with particular meaning, the fact that may have a very determining influence on Anglo-Saxon musical life to come, is the fact that our folk music is still with us as a living art at a time when English-speaking composers of cosmopolitan qualifications have already made their appearance.

In this respect—in possessing simultaneously out-standing composers of 'classical' music and a living (even though a dying) folk music—we must consider ourselves classed with such countries as Russia, Scandinavia, Finland, Spain, etc., in contrast to such countries as Germany, France, Holland, Belgium, Italy, and Austria, where a high degree of art-music development is accompanied by a total, or almost complete, dearth of living folk music.[16]

Those Anglo-Saxon composers that are recognized as great today had for the most part already formed their habits of composing before the inwardness of their native folk music became revealed to them. It is for younger men whose tastes are forming, and will form, under the dual stimulus of native folk music and cosmopolitan art music simultaneously imbibed, that the fuller or fullest fruition of our present folk music consciousness may be expected.

I think it is not unreasonable to look for a vigorous and refreshing amalgamation from the clash of such vital contrasts as those presented by our folk music and our art music. In particular, I think we may hope that early contact with the exquisite linear achievements of our individualistic folk melodies will imbue our art-music composers of the future with a craving for essentially melodic expression similar to that craving which, in a somewhat different manner, informs the popular music (ragtime, jazz)

---

[16] Grainger's typescript added: A noteworthy feature of our musical condition is that while our modern composers (such as Scott, Delius, Brockway, and Carpenter) are more exaggeratedly harmonic in their compositional methods than the composers of most other countries, our folk music, on the other hand, is more exaggeratedly melodic than that of almost any other peoples. These two violent extremes have but recently been introduced to each other and it is still too early to predict what the reaction from this clash will mean to our future music.

of the race today. Our best art-music composers already shine as great harmonists. Let us hope that ensuing generations of English-speaking composers may shine as great melodists also, and will bequeath to the cosmopolitan world of art music a new degree and standard of melodic vigor and beauty, interwoven with the marvellous harmonic expressiveness of modern music. Such a result would infuse into the sometimes somewhat stuffy and namby-pamby art music of our time a kind of lithe Grecian beauty of line and form, a breath of out-door fragrance and freshness, and would be a fitting artistic monument to our athletic, independent, freedom-loving, adventurous pioneer past.

16   *The Value of Icelandic to an Anglo-Saxon*
(1920/1)

I would like to see the study of the Icelandic tongue and literature have a place in every educational curriculum throughout the English-speaking world, and I would like to see such study take precedence over the learning of such 'dead' languages as Greek and Latin, and over such living languages as German, French, Italian, Spanish, etc.

I am moved towards this desire by both personal and impersonal considerations. My personal reasons are rooted in the fact that the most inspiring, life-giving and satisfying artistic adventure of my life, the one wielding the most determining sway upon my work and standards as a creative artist, as well as upon my actions and character as a man, has been the gradual unfolding before me of the Icelandic racial spirit, as revealed to me through my growing familiarity with the Icelandic language. The effortlessly heroic keynote struck alike by the best and the worst of the personages of the sagas has always seemed to me to sound a bugle-call to soldierly endeavour, in work or in life, to which it is impossible to turn a deaf ear. The metallic vividness of life, as depicted in the old tales, has brought to me always a wind-swept invigoration more refreshing even than that to be had from contact with the very wilds of virgin nature herself. The very essence of great mountains, austere deserts and briny oceans seems concentrated down to the most intense point in the old Norse humanity, in which these elements of inanimate nature seem to move in spiritualized forms.

Amidst the mawkish pettiness and grovelling slavishness of so much of modern life, the thought of those bounding men and those self-sufficient women, truly supermen and superwomen in many respects, brings to one a chuckle of stoical contentment, as it were a kind of cheery handshake with eternal values. Life in the Viking Age reads as if based upon a serious and profound application of one of the greatest of our modern proverbs: 'It's a great life if you don't weaken' (which, typically enough, modern

Source: 'þýðing íslenzkrar tungu fyrir Engil-Saxa', *Timarit* (Winnipeg) 2 (1920), 60–8, repr. Grainger's original English-language typescript dated Dec. 1920–Jan. 1921 (Grainger Museum, Melbourne) as pub. in *From a Southern Shore* (Melbourne), 1 (1985), 30–8.

humanity regards as a joke!), and in the face of the lofty examples of unswerving determination that crowd the old sagas and modern Icelandic stories alike, it seems unseemly not to do one's keenest best at all times.

The age we live in is a great one for an English-speaking musician of creative activities, for our Anglo-Saxon race, whether in the various parts of the British Empire, or in the United States, is, musically speaking, emerging from the local and parochial stage of culture, and our leaders of musical thought are already measuring their artistic stature alongside the great creative musicians of all times and all races, not, of course, in competitive rivalry, but in soulful realization of the cosmic unity of the art of music—anxious to add their quota to the whole. Such a moment is always an enviable one in the artistic history of any race, and I have had the awestruck pleasure of realizing the solemnity of this moment since a boy. And continually in my efforts (such as they are) to assist in leaving Anglo-Saxon music, at my life's end, in a different place from where I found it at my manhood's beginning, I ask myself the question, 'Am I prosecuting my goal with the tireless tenacity of an Icelander? Is my artistic craftsmanship worthy of one conversant with the literary technique of Icelandic literature, ancient and modern? Is my artistic morality, my behaviour towards my fellow composers, such as might be expected of one enjoying the influence of old Norse aristocratic codes of warrior-conduct?' For (let me repeat) Icelandic standards of behaviour, Icelandic examples of character, Icelandic achievements of artistic expression, are the loftiest, the noblest, the most intense, the most uplifting that I know.

So much for my purely personal impulses. My impersonal reasons for considering a knowledge of Icelandic to be more valuable to an Anglo-Saxon than knowledge derived from most other studies are swayed by a number of considerations (racial, political, linguistic, cultural and artistic), some of which I shall try to set forth in the remainder of this article.

I cannot count myself among those who consider strong racial characteristics to be decreasingly valuable and desirable. I can appreciate that the distant goal of humanity will probably prove to be a cosmopolitan one, but it seems to me that the qualities most needed in the path towards that goal will remain, for a long time at least, mainly racial ones. An exquisite variety of needs, throughout the world, calls for an exquisite variety of racial aptitudes, tendencies, preferences, born of age-long specialization in certain areas, climates, occupations. I feel that we need an intensification of characteristics rather than an effacement of characteristics. Without favouring anything in the nature of aggressive imperialism, I yearn to see the various branches of the Anglo-Saxon race become more innately, more intrinsically Anglo-Saxon, in spirit and in deed, in art and education and culture, than they have ever been at any period of history. We Anglo-Saxons, mainly Nordic as we are, are seldom widely divergent from Scandinavians in the main trend of our political, social, philosophic and artistic instincts. Both racial groups are, after all, *individualists* at bottom, highly responsive to the ideal of freedom (in its various interpretations), easily provoked to the adventure of experimentation, whether in the domain of colonization, of science, of mechanical inventivity, of sociology, of religion, or of art. What is our modern Anglo-Saxon enthusiasm for democracy but a recent blossoming of old-time Scandinavian representative habits of government? What is the modern 'independent' attitude of woman, the feminist movement in its various manifestations throughout the English-speaking world, but a reassertion (the numbing influence of the Southern culture of the Middle Ages having gradually become sloughed) of the old Norse self-sufficient 'hands-off' position of woman, a rebirth of the old Scandinavian woman's remarkable immunity from rough handling by her men folk?

In the main, Scandinavian and Anglo-Saxon bedrock instincts and ideals may safely, I think, be considered as identical, or very nearly so. But we must not overlook the barrier set to the realization of Anglo-Saxon ideals by the Norman Conquest of England, by the flood of parasitic non-English 'governing classes' that overran England as a result of that conquest. The confidence of the race in its ability to decide its own destinies gradually became weakened as a result of the defeat at Hastings. After the Battle of Hastings everything native was apt to spell failure, everything foreign was apt to spell success. In the face of Norman Kinghood and Knighthood, Norman dungeons and tortures, Norman oppression of every kind, Anglo-Saxon individualism, Anglo-Saxon studiousness (as exemplified in the Anglo-Saxon monasteries), Anglo-Saxon unpretentiousness, Anglo-Saxon loyalty-to-the-whole (all of which, when we examine it, not intrinsically differentiated from the individualism, studiousness, unpretentiousness and solidarity of modern Scandinavia) found, for centuries, no market for such native traits.

What the Norman rulers and their foreign hangers-on wanted from the Anglo-Saxon was, primarily, slavishness, docility and a willingness to participate blindly in the materialism (called 'adventurousness' by pro-Normans) of Norman schemes, Norman wars and Norman snobbery. And the Norman minority had the brute force behind it with which to enforce its destructive will upon the prone Anglo-Saxon majority. Norman brutality, shallowness and imperialism acted like a disintegrating poison upon the quiet, sterling characteristics of the defeated race.

Few individuals come out of a major disease with unimpaired forces of health. Few races, likewise, survive a long period of foreign domination with an undimmed vision of their own racial ideals, with an undiminished aptitude for carrying out those ideals. Thus, it is only natural, when we consider the destructiveness (from a Nordic standpoint) of the Norman domination over the Saxon, that the English-speaking stock has emerged from that sore trial less racially self-conscious, less racially self-sufficient, less racially visionary, than the various Scandinavian races have emerged from centuries of comparative immunity from extra-Scandinavian domination. The Norman Conquest and its long aftermath fully explain, as I see it, the star-gazing, tuft-hunting, snobbish proclivities of many Anglo-Saxons of today: our preference for foreign art and foreign artists; our preference for long words based on foreign roots that are utterly incomprehensible to the bulk of our populations;[1] our despising of agricultural life and work; our lack of interest in the preservation and study of our own racial habits, customs and culture (except where a record of victorious upperclass Normanism is concerned); the abnormal growth of the competitive spirit at the expense of the cooperative spirit.

It seems to me undeniable that vicious, vulgar, slovenly, slavish habits of national thought were born of the Norman Conquest and the culture-tendencies it generated. As a result of Norman rule, as a result of the Norman so naturally looking down upon the Saxon as his inferior, all systems of training and study sponsored by the Norman upper classes led steadily away from native towards foreign influences, and strove to make the Saxon forget himself, racially, altogether. Therefore, the study of Greek and Latin and the ignoring of Old English and Old Norse; there-

---

[1] Grainger's footnote: My friend Balfour Gardiner, the eminent English composer, noted down several typical cases of word-corruption on the part of a game-keeper in his father's employ, such as: 'Mr. Balfour certainly makes a fine process (meaning "progress") on them there cicycles ("bicycles")'. 'What with the late rains and the early frosts the consolation (meaning "consequence") is the fruit aint no good this season'. 'It all comes from the agricultural pressure (meaning "agricultural depression")'. These, and similar misuses and mispronunciations of words on the part of the less educated sections of British and American populations, centre chiefly in the non-Saxon and non-Scandinavian elements of the English language. It would be idle to pretend that really native words and roots are corrupted so freely and so chaotically. The truth is that the bulk of the words derived from Norman, Latin and Greek sources have *never won home* to the linguistic consciousness of the bulk of English-speaking people, over which, with certain exceptions, alone the Saxon and Scandinavian words and roots hold really vital and intimate sway.

fore, the favouring of Classic mythology at the expense of Northern mythology; therefore, the fondness for Continental art music and the indifference to native English folk music; therefore, the enthusiasm for the gracefulness of Southern European deportment and a complete lack of insight into the subtle charm and quiet dignity of truly English rural ways, culture and traditions. Yet, in spite of all these anti-native influences exerted from Norman vantage grounds through the centuries, the history of, say, the last five hundred years of the English-speaking peoples reveals a gradual return to their original type and original ideals, a gradual disengaging of themselves (most quite unconsciously) from the overlaying trammels forged by Norman domination.

I think we may safely assert that the average Anglo-Saxon of the British Empire and of America is today in a variety of ways (such as his rearoused love of sport, his insistence on democracy, his loyalty to woman's cause, his reborn kindliness to animals and his reawakened interest in folk art of all kinds) more Saxon and less Norman than he was a century, or a few centuries, ago; which means, in other words, that his present tendencies are approximating those of ancient and modern Scandinavia and veering away from Latin and Continental European tendencies and all that they imply—class war, militarism, imperialism, indoor clerical pursuits, officially controlled massed movements and enterprises; none of them natural to or compatible with Scandinavian life and culture as a whole.

If it be true (and I firmly believe it to be true) that this instinctive tendency towards Nordic characteristics is really growingly asserting itself, however unconsciously, throughout the English-speaking world, what could be more desirable than that our cultural machinery, our educational systems, should *consciously* aid this race-tendency instead of bootlessly opposing it? Take slang and dialect, for instance. Most English dialects are richer in Saxon and Scandinavian words than is standard English. Slang, again, is largely an unconscious effort towards discarding Latin and other Classic word-roots and idioms in favour of Saxon ones.[2] Consequently both slang and dialect have been looked down upon by the pundits operating our systems of education that have grown out of Norman, pro-foreign, upper-class influence. Would it not be far more consistent, in the light of this apparent tendency of the English-speaking peoples towards

---

[2] Grainger's footnote: This replacing of non-Saxon words and roots by Saxon substitutes is particularly noticeable in American slang, in hundreds of terms and phrases such as: 'six-shooter' (revolver), 'no kick coming' (no cause for complaint), 'make good' (succeed), 'rake-off', 'wire' (telegram), 'roust-about' (automobile), 'you said it' (I agree with you), 'hard luck stories', 'it's up to you', 'dead from the neck up', 'nobody home', 'I'll say it is' (it certainly is), 'he put one over me', 'let George do it', 'slip-horn' (trombone), etc.

Nordicness, to study both slang and dialects and aid and abet, in schools and colleges, whatever native linguistic virility they may be found to contain?

An English-speaking equivalent of the Norwegian Landsmaal move-ment[3] would, in my opinion, be a wonderfully invigorating thing, if it could be brought about. The English language is clogged up with non-English words and roots that have no vitality in every-day speech (which the average man-in-the-street understands as little as he does Chinese) and which merely serve to foster and emphasize class differences and mis-understandings. In this respect modern Icelandic is a model lesson to us Anglo-Saxons.

I imagine that there are fewer foreign words and roots used in Icelandic than in any living European language. Yet is it not one of the most expres-sive tongues, and one of the tersest, into the bargain? And do not the liter-ary achievements of modern Iceland, per capita of the population, now, as in the past, outdistance the per capita literary achievements of the English-speaking peoples just as the athletic achievements of the Finns and Swedes at the recent Olympic Games outdistance, on a per capita basis, the athletic achievements of the Americans and the British?[4] Icelandic sheds a wondrous beaconlight upon the path of social self-sufficiency in speech and art. Without being in any way hostile to foreign peoples and foreign influences, without being entangled in national parti-sanships of any kind, the Icelander stands before the world secure on his own legs on his own ground, achieving in a wholly native and highly subtle tongue a high-water mark of literary genius and perfection, stu-dious of his own past, a *racialist*, not a *chauvinistic nationalist*.

These are the goals that high-minded thinkers are striving for in all lands.

The literature of Iceland strikes me as standing amongst the literatures of the world much as Bach's music stands amongst the musics of the world—inscrutable in its masterly repose and balance. Goethe wrote of art: 'Man merkt die Absicht, man wird verstimmt', meaning that the spell of art is broken if the artist reveals his intention. The writer's intention is never revealed in the best Icelandic literature. The reader can only guess at the author's sympathies, at the author's favourites amongst the characters

---

[3] A movement to establish, on the basis of country dialects, a form of Norwegian distinct from Dano-Norwegian. It led to the language now known as Nynorsk (modern Norwegian). See Essay **39**.

[4] The first four nations in the points tally of the 1920 Olympic Games in Antwerp were United States (212), Finland (105), Sweden (95), England (92).

portrayed. The story unfolds itself as if with the impassive impartiality of life itself. It seems as if it were the aim of Icelandic writers to portray life rather than to judge life, and in the presence of such truthful art, the reader, on his part, learns to *study* and *understand* life rather than to *judge* it. I need hardly dilate upon the advantage it is for an artist to come in contact with an art so candid as is the ancient and modern literature of Iceland, since the ideals of art, in any country, can seldom be far separated from the pursuit of truth. Nor can the advantage of such contact to the average non-artist modern reader be easily overestimated in an age in which almost every branch of art (in the larger countries at least) swarms with propaganda and 'isms' and the pursuit of everything rather than a dispassionate presentation of life itself—a condition that is, after all, only to be expected in an age of massed enterprises and commercial slavery.

In praising these various Icelandic achievements, in wishing to see them held up as a model to my own race, in wishing to have them act upon us by the force of example, I feel that I am praising and advocating *not foreign ideals and habits* but ones so close to the temper of my own race that they may be considered really assimilable by us, may be regarded as part of *our own* racial heritage.

It is because I look upon contact with Iceland as one of the Anglo-Saxon's *natural roads to selfhood* that I advocate it so strongly, because I expect from it a heightening of that robust naturalness and fearless optimism that already characterizes the outlook of the outstanding geniuses of the Anglo-Saxon race and towards which I fondly trust the residue of the race is moving surely, however slowly.

We can never reap the full fruits of democratic systems of government unless the populations in the countries concerned possess a highly developed individualistic sense (by which I mean each man constituting a moral unit within himself, actuated by his purely personal sense of right and wrong rather than swayed by public opinion and majority domination) as well as consciousness of human unity (by which I mean a realization of the cosmic unity and harmoniousness of all human life and endeavour, that religious insight so well expressed in the following lines by Walt Whitman: 'If it is not as much to you as it is to me, it is nothing, or next to nothing'[5]).

Without the presence and development of virile individualistic qualities the race tends to drift into despotism and demagogy, and without a realization of the final unity of all human enterprises the very nature and goal

---

[5] Misquoted from 'Song of Myself' No. 17, in *Leaves of Grass* (1891–2 edn.): 'If they are not yours as much as mine they are nothing, or next to nothing'.

of democracy is misunderstood and its application becomes a mere mockery. The same applies to the various experiments of socialism, communism, cooperation, paternalism, etc., that present themselves in the different lands. None of these systems can produce ideal results unless the races to which they are applied possess in a high degree the *personal initiative* and the *philosophical perspective* unobtainable without the individualism and sense of unity above alluded to. Most modern populations are very noticeably lacking in both these fundamental requisites. This is evident in the mob violence (in the form of race riots, lynchings, imperialism and chauvinism in international relations) that raises its head with, or without, provocation as well as in the indifference paid by the public in general to all serious efforts to ameliorate the race (such as prohibition, eugenics, birth control, physical culture, elimination of poverty etc.), to preserve the spiritual achievements of the past (by the study of popular dialects, local customs, folklore, folk music, and the like), and to promote the highest possible functioning of the talents of the present and the future (by means of stipendiums for scientific and artistic experimentation on a scale worthy of the size of the nation). Nor do the literatures of modern countries, with the exception of those of Scandinavia, provide us with the example of individualism so necessary to the fulfilment of the democratic ideal. In most modern books we read of people acting and thinking in droves, the blind slaves of mob psychology and mob prejudice, just as we see them behave in everyday life. In other words, most modern literature is a reflection of the lives, thoughts and aims of servile and debilitated types. In the Icelandic sagas we encounter the very opposite to all this. We read of a race of heroes, a race of natural aristocrats, a race of *born individualists*. True, many of these individualistic heroes of the Viking Age were rare old rascals. But their unfailing individualistic force forms such a salutary contrast to the vacillating spinelessness of so much of modern life that we are apt to exclaim with Walt Whitman, in this connection: 'The man I love is bad, rather than good out of conformity or fear'.[6]

If the force of example, as displayed compellingly through the medium of a great literature, counts for anything, then the reading of Icelandic tales, ancient and modern, is precisely the dose to prescribe for the Anglo-Saxon of today, in order to resuscitate his somewhat halting individualism and, thus, to fit him to carry out the Anglo-Saxon (Scandinavian-derived)

---

[6] Misquoted from 'Song of Myself' No. 47, in *Leaves of Grass* (1891–2 edn.): 'The boy I love, the same becomes a man not through derived power but in his own right, | Wicked rather than virtuous out of conformity or fear'.

ideals of democracy to their full fruition in the face of many hostile Southern counter-influences—most of them remnants and tag-ends of the militarism and mob-rule of the ancient Roman Empire.

While unique in the spectacle of fierce individualism that it presents there is no doubt, however, that the ancient Scandinavian world as mirrored in the sagas, may justly be criticized for its lack of the sense of human unity, for the almost total absence of those harmonious qualities of cosmic religious inspiration so satisfying in Buddhist thought and in the writings of such seers as Hans Christian Andersen, Walt Whitman and Edgar Lee Masters. Therefore, a crude destructiveness stalks through the sagas and is apt to occasionally depress the modern reader in spite of the masterly portrayal of numerous lovable and noteworthy personalities.

But this imputation of destructiveness and lack of a sense of human unity can no longer be levelled at modern Iceland. Scandinavia, in general, and Iceland, in particular, show today more sense of human unity, more true constructiveness, more artistic, cultural and scientific preservative sense than any other countries known to me. Are exceptionally gifted individuals not more encouraged and better supported (by dint of national and private stipendiums and other assistance) in Northern lands than anywhere else? Have Scandinavian political experiments in the direction of race amelioration (such as votes for women, total prohibition, old-age pensions, cooperative societies, etc.) not led the civilized world for many years? Above all, does the Icelander's sense of unity manifest itself in his combination of extreme modernism with an equally extreme conservatism, in the spectacle of a nation speaking a language well-nigh unchanged for the last thousand years, yet in the forefront of modern political and economical experimentation, and reading with equal gusto the tales of the colonization of Iceland and the works of the most recent native literati.

In the unusual degree of homage he pays to learning, science and art, does the typical Icelander prove himself more spiritually visioned and racially farseeing, more truly a man of genuine culture, than the typical citizen of most modern commercial states and empires. On account of all the rare qualities of mind, spirit, character and culture that have made and kept the Icelandic race what it is today, and on account of the rich and concentrated presentation of these qualities through the medium of the Icelandic language I would, if I were an Icelander, consider the preservation of my native tongue a matter of almost sacred importance.

Let me, in closing, repeat that, as an Anglo-Saxon, I regard the study of Icelandic to be the most valuable single cultural asset of my life, an asset that I burn to see put within reach of every Anglo-Saxon the world over, because of its golden lesson in the domains of art, language, politics and philosophy.

17   *Nordic Characteristics in Music*
(1921)

I sincerely hope that many of you here[1] do not know the meaning of the term 'Nordic'. Only a little over a year ago I did not know its meaning myself and it would [be] humiliating to me to think that every one of you should know what I was so wholly ignorant of. I read of it first in that fascinating and provocative book of Madison Grant,[2] *The Passing of the Great Race*,[3] and since then I have read it used in several other books on racial study to define one [of] the three chief races of which the population of Europe is made up. These three are: (1) Mediterraneans, a small race with long narrow heads, dark hair and dark eyes, (2) Alpines, a stocky race, medium height or short, with broad round heads, dark hair and eyes, and (3) Nordics, tall, narrow long heads, fair hair ranging from flaxen to brown and fair eyes ranging from light blue to hazel, grey and green. The main characteristics as set forth in Grant's book and in other books[4] is this: That ALL the fairness in the world (all fair hair, all blue or light eyes) wherever found is due to Nordic blood; that most of the aristocracy of most European countries is more or less rich in Nordic blood; that the great thinkers, innovators, soldiers, athletes, artists, mystics, leaders of Europe have mostly had some Nordic blood; that the flowering of culture in ancient Greece, ancient Rome and several Asiatic countries was resultant upon a wave of Nordic conquering colonisation sweeping southward from near the shores of the Baltic; that as the Nordic blood got diluted by mixture with the non-Nordic conquered races in the various areas the aforesaid flowering of culture lessened and faded; that in modern life the Nordic tends to die out in competition with more Southern breeds (Mediterraneans, Alpines, Negroes, Jews, etc.), as the Southern breeds can

---

Source: Typescript dated 5 Mar. 1921. Grainger Museum, Melbourne.

[1] At Yale University, where Grainger delivered this lecture on 6 Mar. 1921. Grainger's typescript alternates between verbatim text and cues for points to be elaborated.

[2] (1865–1937), New York lawyer, with strong zoological interests.

[3] (New York: C. Scribner's Sons, 1916). Grainger's own copy was of the revised edition of 1919, which his mother had presented to him for Christmas of that year.

[4] Grainger also owned Lothrop Stoddard, *The Rising Tide of Color against White World-supremacy* (New York: Blue Ribbon Books, 1920), which contains an introduction by Grant, and later acquired Stoddard's *Racial Realities in Europe* (1924) and *The Revolt against Civilization* (1925).

stand city and factory and crowded life generally better than the Nordic, who is an out-doors man, a natural soldier and pioneer, a natural individualist and fighter for freedom, fond of adventure, fond of animals, etc.

State roughly the presence of Nordic blood in Europe and the rest of the world. *State* the defects (to my mind) in the Nordic type as portrayed by Grant. *State* the way out for the Nordic as seen by me—that he shall abandon his quest for slaves to do the rough work for him, that he shall do his rough work for himself, that he shall build up communities of *racial equalities*, consisting of Nordics and *any other races* that measure up to Nordic requirements.

I am personally not a believer in the magic of 'blood'. I believe that Jews, Negroes and plenty of other non-Nordic races could and would, if presented with Nordic surroundings and conditions, acquire all the Nordic traits. I am not going to pursue this line of thot in this lecture, however, but merely mention it here that it may be evident from what angle I approach the question of racial characteristics in music. I approach them from an utterly cosmopolitan angle, and if I lay emphasis upon the artistic advantages of racial and local traits in art it is because I am thinking of what racial traits and the fostering of local traits can do to enrich the *art of the world*, of all the world, including China and the Islands of the South Sea, Europe, and all the rest. However it may appear to my listeners, I wish to assure them in advance that I do not believe in special artistic privileges for any race; I do not believe in special artistic superiorities in any race; I do not believe in the special artistic favoring of any race. Why? Because I believe that all races are almost, if not quite, equally gifted artistically—at any rate, that the talents of all are worth having, that the talents of all should be fostered. Still further: I am inclined to believe that the artistic talents of any race can be acquired by every other race, given similar conditions and influences. I shall not argue this point, merely mention it in order to show where I stand. With regard to the power of races to acquire to perfection the artistic traits of other races, [I] will say this: One of the most truly English, one of the most truly Nordic composers is Frederick Delius. Yet he is, I believe, partly Jewish of race. One of the most typically American composers, one of the finest exponents of Nordic characteristics in American music is Rubin Goldmark, a Jew, nephew of Carl Goldmark the great Hungarian composer.[5] Why, with Jewish blood and a Continental European background and artistic tradi-

---

[5] (1830–1915), principally known for his operas.

tion in his family, is his music not European rather than American, Jewish rather than Nordic, in its characteristics? Because, it seems, local influences are more potent in determining artistic type than is blood.

Why then am I known as an exponent of racial and local characteristics in music (if I am known at all)? Why do I consistently play Anglo-Saxon and Scandinavian works on my programs whenever I can? Just for that very reason that racial and local traits, in my belief, will die out if not locally fostered; because there is nothing in *blood* that will preserve racial musical characteristics unless the conditions and surrounding favorable to their retention are preserved. But why, as a cosmopolitan artist, then, do I value local and racial traits so highly? Because I value artistic variety highly, because originality and individuality are needful to the vigorous art life of the whole world, because I wish the artists of the future to have an immense artistic palette to paint with, rather than a narrow and impoverished palette.

When I speak of Nordics in music, or speak of Nordic nations in this lecture, I am not distinguishing between pure Nordics and part-Nordics nor distinguishing between musicians whose Nordic characteristics in art are accompanied by Nordic blood and those whose Nordic artistic characteristics have been acquired, in their own generation or before. Thus, when I say Nordics I mean races preponderantly Nordic (such as the Scandinavians, the Dutch, the British, the Americans of the U.S., Canadians, Australians, New Zealanders, South Africans, etc.) and when I say Nordic music I mean music showing in preponderance those characteristics that have come to us mainly in the music of Nordics. Thus, from this standpoint a great deal of Negro music is typically Nordic, just as a large part of Negro thot and emotionality is typically Anglo-Saxon.

State Nordic characteristics in music and conditions responsible for them: pioneer life, lonely pursuits, farms etc. wide apart, athletic tastes, cold weather and chilly dwellings. Results: individualistic melody of superlative quality, lack of harmony in folk music, jigs, reels and body-warming dances generally, work-music of all sorts.

Later on in Nordic musical culture the lonely tunes (plowtunes, saeter tunes, tunes of the shepherd life) come to be used in art music for the expression of nature moods—moods inspired by contact with, contemplation of, wide expanses and *virgin nature* rather than the landscapes of villages and semiurban life.

Let us examine the titles of composers and see how these leanings come out in the matter of choice of themes for music. Here are the titles of 12

Préludes by Debussy,[6] whom we may safely class as non-Nordic, artistically and racially. As well as I can translate these titles from French, which
language I don't know, they are as follows: The dancing women of
Delphi. Veils. The wind on the plain. Sounds and perfumes in the air of
evening. The collines of Anacapri. Steps in the snow. Where the west wind
went. The girl with the hair like flax. The interrupted serenade. The
buried cathedral. The dance of Puck. Minstrels. Some of these would pass
as Nordic, but the bulk would not, and as a whole the series of subjects
could hardly be imagined without a classic background, without the
civilisation of Greece and the Roman Empire.

Let us turn to MacDowell, a typical Nordic in his choices. We find the
titles of *Woodland Sketches*[7] run as follows: To a wild rose. Will of the
wisp. At an old trysting place. In autumn. From an Indian lodge. To
waterlilly. From Uncle Remus. A deserted farm. By a meadow brook.
Told at sunset. At once in the 'deserted farm' we find the Nordic love of
expressing loneliness (one of the dominant experiences of the race from
way back). We see that MacDowell turns to the primitive Indian, to the
primitive Negro rather than to cultured man, or to the traditions of the
culture of the past, such as some of the things that inspire Debussy. *Four
Little Poems*[8] have the following titles: The eagle. The brook. Moonshine.
Winter. Not a trace of man or civilisation or culture, nothing but virgin
nature. Note that in the titles so far taken (and taken at random, at that)
MacDowell chooses 'Winter' and 'In autumn' rather than summer and
spring. Typically Nordic in all these traits. Let me take some titles of
works by Fannie Dillon,[9] born in Colorado, living in California, and a
typical Nordic in her love of nature subjects and her gift for artistically
using bird music and conjuring up lonely and vast spaces of nature in
sound: April moods. Birds at dawn. The desert. Evening. Forest mourn-
ing dove. Ocean depths. A song of the Sierras. Under the pines.[10] Heights
sublime. Birds at dusk. Harp of the pines. Brooklets, and Quiet pools.[11]

Grieg's titles are equally typically Nordic: Gnomes, shepherd boys,
mountains, dairy maids in the hills, mountaineers, sailors. The heroes and
mythology and superstitions of the ancient Scandinavian life are brought
before us in his titles all the time, and in the pieces without descriptive
titles it takes little imagination to see the moods born of vast distances,

---

[6] Book I (1910).   [7] Op. 51 (1896), for piano.   [8] Op. 32 (1887), for piano.
[9] (1881–1947), American composer and pianist, who studied in Berlin with Godowsky
during 1900–6 and also took occasional lessons with Grainger.
[10] These first eight titles are from Dillon's *Eight Descriptive Compositions*, Op. 20 (1917).
[11] These five titles are of self-standing works by Dillon.

smiling or darkling fjords, primitive living. These conjectures were borne out by all that Grieg told me of the inspiration of much of his works. One of his greatest favorites of his own works was 'Captive of the hills',[12] a lonely wanderer lost in the mountains, a work full of eerie Northern superstition and the presentation of loneliness—a kind of exaltation in the horror of loneliness, worshipping it while hating it. Whereas Debussy and Ravel paint the charms of fountains, of gardens, of temples, or semiurban scenes, of life where man's hand and mind has left its impress, in Grieg, in Delius, in MacDowell, in Scott, in Dillon, in Herman Sandby, in Ole Bull,[13] in Svendsen,[14] [in] Grainger, we see largely, if not chiefly, the influence of scenes where man's hand has played no part but of the reaction of man's emotionality to wholly non-human nature.

Speak of Carpenter's *Concertino* 2nd movement, stirred up by steamer trip near Mississippi rivers. *Speak* of Sandby's *Havstemning*;[15] *Saeterjentens Søndag*.[16] My own *Hill-songs, Sea-songs, Colonial Song.* *Quote* Delius titles: *Appalachia, Seadrift, Song of the High Hills, Dance Rhapsody, On Hearing the First Cuckoo in Spring, Summernight on the River.*

Play Grieg: 'Evening in the High Hills';[17] 'Song of the Mountaineer'.[18]

Tell story of Op. 66 No. 2 'Det er, etc.',[19] how Grieg wrote, up in the high mountains: 'I can write harmonies up here that I would not dare to do down in the plains'. *Tell story* of 'Folketone fra Valders',[20] how it is distance-music like so much of Grieg, how he met the hillman who would not play to him on his pipe but hours afterwards heard him playing the strains of 'F. fra Valders', miles and miles away.

Play slow bit of Delius Dance Rhap. as distance music.

Then there is the foot-warming, body-warming music: the jigs, reels, breakdowns, hallings, springdances, Morris dances, and the like, and all that has come out of them directly and indirectly. I do not say somewhat similar music does not exist in Spain, Italy, Germany, France and other countries to some extent. I only assert that such types do not preponderate in other races as in Nordic, are not craved by other audiences as they

---

[12] *Lost in the Hills* (*Den Bergtekne*), Op. 32, for baritone, horns and strings (1877–8).
[13] (1810–80), Norwegian violinist, composer, and founder of a Norwegian Utopian colony in Pennsylvania.
[14] Johan Svendsen (1840–1911), a 'dark' Norwegian violinist and composer.
[15] *Sea Mood*, for orchestra (pub. 1921).
[16] *The Dairymaid's Sunday*, by Ole Bull.
[17] Op. 68 No. 4 (1898), for piano.
[18] Op. 73 No. 7 (1903–5), for piano.
[19] 'Det er den störste dårlighed' ('It is the greatest folly') (1896), for piano.
[20] 'Folk Tune from Valders', Op. 73 No. 4 (1903–5), for piano.

are by Nordic audiences, who *never* seem to tire of them. Where does the Nordic foot-warming dance music differ from others, as I see it? In the *speed* of the beats. Each beat means a stamp of the foot with the weight of the body behind it, or a big kick or lunge, some *big, vigorous, heavy* movement to each beat most of the time. In French music, in Scarlatti, in Spanish music such as Albéniz and Granados, we find heaps of rapid notes, lots of vigorous passage work, but less *speed of the beats*. In other words, these less Nordic dance musics suggest that they are to accompany vigorous or vivacious or graceful gestures and actions of the lighter parts of the body rather than leaping, bounding, thumping hammerings of the entire body on the floor through the medium of the feet. I may be all wrong about much of this; my experience of the various lands isn't enough to assert all this with full confidence; I merely throw it out as a possibility, as something to think about and investigate. But I am sure that in the Nordic dance music of Scandinavia, Holland, and the English-speaking world, the beats fall much faster than in what I know of the dance music of the rest of Continental Europe.

Show the fast beats of *Turkey*,[21] Grieg Halling and Spring dance, Juba, Molly, Morris dances, Malle kits [*sic*], as compared with seguidilla, Laendler, Austrian waltz, gavotte, etc.

Mention tarantella, polka (Poland, largely Nordic);[22] old Bach gigues as possible exceptions.

What do Continental musicians think of all this jigging of ours? At home they don't hear it at all, probably because they don't like it when they do hear it. When they do hear, I think they think we have gone stark staring mad, or are very queer, rough, inartistic people. They regard it as a form of 'treat 'em rough'. That is because they lack the cultural insight, the racial insight, the historic background to sense its raison d'être. We must provide the world with this needful background, insight, all we can. We must, as Grieg put it: 'raise the folk song to the *niveau* of art music'. We must go further, and 'raise our racial art to the niveau of cosmopolitan art', so that foreign artists may recognise achievement in our art as well as talent, so that our art may show *study* and *science* as well as instinct and inspiration.

And now I wish to speak of what to me is the dark side of Nordic art—the laziness of so many Nordic musicians, the racial unconsciousness of them, the disloyalty of them to their own art, their fickleness of artistic

---

[21] *Turkey in the Straw*, by Texan composer David Guion (1895–1981).

[22] The polka is, in fact, a Bohemian dance, the word deriving from the Czech 'pŭkla', a half-step.

taste when not bolstered up by a majority of foreign influence. Who really does justice to *jazz*, realises its artistic *subtlety*, its artistic *workmanship*? Rachmaninoff (*tell story* of his love of listening to jazz after concerts). Who makes collections of American popular music? Myself and others equally *cosmopolitan* in tastes and training. Who was the first famous pianist to play a whole program of exclusively American compositions? Josef Hofmann, not an American nor an Anglo-Saxon.[23] What publishers have brought out the larger and more important works of the greatest English composers, such as Cyril Scott and Fred. Delius? German publishers, such as Schott, Mainz and Leuckart, Leipzig. Well, that is natural enough. The classic, ornate, highly cultured side of Anglo-Saxon music is only in its childhood. We cannot expect to compare in the matter of ornate publishing with lands where music is an enormous industry as well as a long-established custom. In this respect, in the matter of the publication of large works costly to produce, American publishers do nobly their full share in the bringing out of native works. I marvel when I see the size and the worth of the orchestral and choral publications of the best American firms.

But the Anglo-Saxon music lovers, in general, the Anglo-Saxon professional musicians, in general, must work a little harder, be a little more Spartan with themselves in the matter of study if they wish to *hold permanently* the heights their inborn musical gifts so easily won. No race succeeds in music more *easily* than the Anglo-Saxon; no race, as a whole, shows less manly application, on the other hand. I met one of the most gifted of young American composers the other day, a truly inspired writer of songs and piano pieces. I asked him if he was conversant with orchestration. No, and he didn't think he ever would be, as his eyes were weak and he couldn't use them as he would wish to read books on orchestration. I suggested that orchestration can also be studied by sitting close to orchestras and small instrumental bodies, by studying instrumental blends through the ear alone, by playing all sorts of instruments oneself. But he did not seem very excited about it all. There is one of the most gifted of living composers more or less complacent at the thot of being shut off from the world of orchestra and chamber music, limited to the shallow soloism of the piano and songs. Many gifted composers in England, likewise, could hardly be described as gigantic workers. They are content to let a few short pieces, hardly more than a few pages of

---

[23] (1876–1957), Polish-born pianist. In 1941 Grainger classed him—along with Rakhmaninov—as a 'blond' Jew.

manuscript, dribble from their pens each year. When we come to the *geniuses* of the Nordic world all is otherwise, of course. A composer-genius may be a drunkard, a wifebeater, a thief, a liar, *but he never can be lazy*. The great British and American geniuses, men like Delius, Cyril Scott, Carpenter, Goldmark, Vaughan Williams, are all tremendous workers, as can be readily seen in the quality as well as the quantity of their work. But the public and the lesser artists seem to me to lag far behind. In what respects, in particular? In the slovenly way they *think* of music, in their tardiness in thinking *justly* and *critically* about their own music, in their lack of response to the heroic efforts of their best musicians. This can be most clearly seen in the Anglo-Saxon attitude to the *older Anglo-Saxon masterpieces*. Why do we not rank Clay's 'I'll sing thee songs of Araby',[24] Hatton's 'To Anthea'[25] and Foster's[26] immortal songs as *song classics,* fit to rank on cosmopolitan programs beside the deathless songs of Schubert, Brahms, Grieg, Fauré, etc? I suppose because we are waiting for some *foreign non-Anglo-Saxon* artists to so treat them. Artistic *cowardice* is our great fault, and a lazy neglecting to play our *international part*, for which we are now *quite ripe*. Why is 'Bedelia'[27] not treated as popular classic alongside 'The Blue Danube'? Why is Leo Fall[28] considered a greater creative artist than Irving Berlin[29] and Harry Lauder?[30] I know of no cosmopolitan, no artistic reason.

Mention Norwegian lack of appreciation of Grieg, etc.

Permit me to state what I think ought to happen: The Nordic musicians should realise that they have two separate tasks to perform, for their own and the world of music's good. (1) To collect, study, elaborate and preserve and adequately present their own specifically Nordic characteristics in music, and add this heritage to the cosmopolitan world of music as a priceless addition. (2) To realise that, in so far as many of them are now city-dwellers and civilised folk, able to read and write, etc., they should take their share in the duties and work and expense of the cosmopolitan world of music, above all supporting consciously and continuously (not merely haphazardly and intermittently) their own musical geniuses, soci-

---

[24] Frederick Clay (1838–89), English composer of light opera and songs.

[25] John Hatton (1808–86), English composer of vocal and choral music, inc. 'To Anthea' (1850).

[26] Stephen Foster (1826–64), American composer of popular songs. Grainger's *Tribute to Foster* and associated *Lullaby* date from 1913–16.

[27] Irish 'coon song serenade' from the Broadway show *The Jersey Lily* (1903) by Jean Schwartz (1878–1956), Hungarian-born American composer.

[28] (1873–1925), Viennese composer of operetta and cabaret.

[29] (1888–1989), Russian-born, American song writer.

[30] (1870–1950), Scottish music-hall singer, particularly popular in Edwardian London.

eties and publishers, who have *already gone deep into tasks of musical culture, study and science*, who have already done their share but are still not getting the support in their home lands that men of equal talents and industry are getting in non-Nordic lands, as a general rule.

But the whole thing, as I see it, really boils itself down to work: the work of imagining and writing down, the work of appreciating and criticising, the work of listening and *remembering* and supporting. One of our major tasks is to gradually bend the public mind, at home and abroad, to the realisation of the artistic truths of our age. We must not let foreign musicians bulldose us into accepting their own verdict of our local product. These foreign musicians are like our own, neither better nor worse. Most of them are fairly ignorant of much in music (particularly of the most *recent* events in Music), fairly intolerant at the beginning but glad to learn *if we insist on teaching* what little or much we happen to know. There are, in my estimation (and I talk as a cosmopolitan musician, from first to last) no greater composers and musicians alive than the best of our Nordics (Americans, British, Scandinavians). The best of our men can not only confidently face comparison with the best contemporary creators in all other lands but also comparison with the best compositional output of all time. The goods are there. It is our business to deliver them, deliver them to the whole world. Let us see that our Nordic characteristics, that have come down to us through the icy Northern past, that have weathered all sorts of adventures in all sorts of exacting, primitive lives, that have now spread out into so many richly diversified artistic types of expression and have now entered *conscious, cultured, studious, complex* stages *are delivered in full to the world at large*, enriching cosmopolitan music in all sorts of unexpected ways, providing all sorts of new themes and forms and expressivenesses for the future of music, placing our races artistically on the map for all time—an honor and benefit to others no less than ourselves, to ourselves no less than to others.

* * *

Early in lecture should be outlined the musical characteristics of other races:

Germany: Feeling rather than sensation is the urge behind German music, a very varied range of feeling, full of the most human and romantic tendencies, on the one hand, and running up into impersonal pattern music and to half-Nordic nature music, on other hands.

Show difference of *Rhinegold* music and Grieg and Anglo-Saxon nature music.

Italy: Essentially ritual music (church music) and formal music (court music and courtly music), on the one hand, and, on the other, the music of romantic passion. No nature music to speak of, and next to no sensation music.

France: Sensation music, where the German is music of feeling. The sensations of scenes and of occasions and situations is the wellspring of most French music, as so clearly shown by the titles.

Scandinavia: Music of feeling rather than sensation, and, in so far, in line with German music—but the feelings portrayed are more intensely and more often inspired by nature scenes (virgin nature) than human promptings. But largely, it is music of action (work and sport music) and herein differing from the bulk of more Southerly musics but closely allied to Anglo-Saxon.

Anglo-Saxon (both British and American, etc.): Very similar to Scand. music in the preponderance of nature feelings and music of action. To even greater degree than Scand., music of action, though more closely drifting towards German complexity and variety and range of feeling than does Scand. music.

Negro-American: Closely allied to Anglo-Saxon in every way yet at times showing the impress of *tribal influences* and tribal life as Anglo-Saxon music does not. The gift and tendency to sing and play in groups, partly by ear and by instinct, and to sing and play for the sake of *taking part* rather than for the sake of the listener, is the truly tribal touch and is present in so much Negro-American music.[31]

[31] Grainger's typescript concluded with a summary page of 'Order of subjects, program'. Its final instruction was to 'wind up with Australian group (*Colonial Song*, '*Gumsuckers' March*)'.

Part III

1922–1930

18 Guide to Virtuosity: Foreword to Students
(1923)

Musicality before Pianism[1]

Students should always aim at keeping their general musical knowledge well in advance of their mere pianism. To develop the former they should daily devote some time to transposing (playing pieces they know in all keys—the best way of attaining an actual working knowledge of harmony), to sight-reading at the piano (not only compositions for the piano but also piano scores of the greatest musical works, such as the Bach *Passions*, Wagner music dramas, Delius nature-music, Beethoven, Brahms and Tchaikovsky symphonies, Debussy and Richard Strauss tone poems, Stravinsky ballets, etc.) and to ensemble playing with others students (duets at one or two pianos, and ensemble work with other instruments and with voices). Students should also make a point of reading writings upon music by the great composers (such as Schumann's and Wagner's writings on musical subjects, Cyril Scott's *Philosophy of Modernism*,[2] etc.) rather than too many books about mere piano technic. There is no better

---

Source: 'Foreword to Students', in H. Balfour Gardiner, *Prelude 'De Profundis'*, Percy Grainger Guide to Virtuosity No. 1 (New York: G. Schirmer, 1923), pp. iv–viii.

[1] This 'Foreword to Students' is an introduction to Grainger's highly annotated, instructive edition of H. Balfour Gardiner's *Prelude 'De Profundis'* (1905), which was intended as the first in a series of *Percy Grainger Guides to Virtuosity*.

Grainger's preliminary programme note to the 'Foreword' reads: H. Balfour Gardiner was born in London, England, November 7, 1877. The wide popular appeal of many of his compositions lies, largely perhaps, in the fact that he never puts pen to paper without a genuine inspirational impulse. His thematic invention is clear-cut and straight-forward and his music always sounds an unmistakably individual note. Of a variety of notable works for various mediums the following may be mentioned as possessing outstanding originality and charm: *Shepherd Fennel's Dance*, for orchestra; *News from Whydah*, for mixed chorus and orchestra; String Quartet in one movement; *The Stranger's Song, The Golden Vanity, Roadways, Rybbesdale, The Quiet Garden*, for voice and piano; *The Three Ravens, An Old Song Resung, The Hunt is Up, Cargoes* (Masefield) and *The Stage Coach*, for chorus *a cappella*; *English Dance*, for two pianos; *Humoresque, Prelude (De Profundis), Michaelchurch, Noël, The Joyful Homecoming, Shenadoah, A Sailors' Piece*, 'Clun' and Gavotte [from Five Pieces (1911)], for piano solo. In addition to its rich emotional and musical qualities the '*De Profundis*' Prelude draws exceptional pianistic interest from the extent to which it has utilized the resources of modern tone-strength control on the piano and the cooperation of the three pedals. It is invaluable to students as a touch-study and as a lesson in the use of the sustaining (middle) pedal.

[2] *The Philosophy of Modernism* (London: K. Paul, Trench, Trubner and Co., 1917).

method for piano students to develop both musical and pianistic knowledge, taste and sense of style than by listening repeatedly to good player-
piano and gramophone recordings by great pianists; especially is it
enlightening to compare different recordings of the same composition by
different *virtuosi*. This branch of training should be especially cultivated
by students who are not in a position continually to witness performances
'in the flesh' by the best artists, and by music schools not situated in the
great musical centers.

Phrasing

The melodic habits of instrumental music largely reflect the physical
conditions of vocal music. The human voice grows in *intensity of
quality* (quite apart from increase of volume) as its scale ascends and the
majority of instruments (for instance, stringed instruments, woodwinds,
brasses, etc.) resemble the voice in this respect. It is only natural that
most melodies designed for the voice or these comparatively voice-like
instruments should generally have their climax-notes (points of intensity)
on high notes, and that there should be a drooping of intensity as the
melodic line sinks to lower pitch altitudes. Unlike the voice, the piano
(in common with the organ, the harmonium, the harp, etc.) shows no
increase in *intensity of quality* (apart from increase in volume) as its scale
ascends. Yet most music written for the piano reflects in its melodic
instincts the basic condition of vocal music; i.e., its melodies mostly
demand an impression of growing intensity as they ascend in pitch, an
impression of climax-intensity on their highest notes. These impressions
we convey on the piano primarily by means of *crescendi* as phrases rise,
diminuendi as phrases sink. A further means of emphasizing melodic
climax notes is by very short holds (∩) on the tops of phrases—hardly
long enough to be consciously perceived by any but experienced ears,
yet just long enough to confer a certain added emphasis and importance
to the climax notes on which they occur. Sometimes the presence of
such a tiny hold on the climax note of a melodic phrase will permit the
climax note to be played with less tone-strength than would otherwise
by advisable; often an advantage in music of a delicate character, in **pp**
passages, etc.

   Then, again, a 'soft climax' may be combined with a tiny hold; in which
case the melody increases in volume towards the climax note, but the
climax note itself is played suddenly softer than the preceding and ensuing

melody notes and acquires its climax impression solely through being slightly dwelt upon. Examples of soft climaxes will be found in the footnotes to measures 24, 25, 50 and 51.[3]

A careful study of the playing of the finest pianists will reveal the fact that a large proportion of the small *rubati* employed by them in music of an expressive melodic nature is consciously or unconsciously introduced in order to invest high melody notes with climax feeling without undue increase of volume, or to make accented climax notes seem less harsh. Holds and *rubati* serving both these purposes will be found in both the gentler and most vigorous sections of this Prelude and are typical of the phrasing habits used by all sensitive concert artists. Additional, hardly perceptible *rubati*, tiny holds on the high notes of phrases (for instance, in measure 6), small swells[4] and judicious 'soft climaxes' (for instance, in measures 20 and 22) may be introduced by experienced players in numberless places not indicated.

Tone-Strength Contrasts

Much is said and written about 'tone quality', 'beauty of tone', 'individuality of touch', and the like, on the piano, but I am convinced that none of these things exist—are not possible to the mechanism of the instrument. I assert that a given note played upon a given piano at the same degree of tone-strength by a hundred different players employing a hundred different 'touches' will always necessarily have the same 'tone quality'. I feel sure that all those things that are carelessly or ignorantly described as contrasts of tone *quality* are, in reality, always contrasts of tone *quantity*; i.e., contrasts in sound-strength between successive notes in melodies, phrases and passages, or between simultaneously played notes (the latter called 'simultaneous tone-strength differentiation').

Therefore, I strongly advise students to cease wasting their time practising for 'beauty of tone', 'tone-quality', etc., and urge them to concentrate their efforts upon control of contrasts of tone *quantity*; for it is through this latter means that most musical expressiveness has its being on the piano and most impressions of musical structure are made manifest in performance. It does not matter in the least what way the student holds his fingers, hands, wrist and arm, what kind of 'touch' or 'method' he uses

---

[3] Grainger elaborated on exactly how these 'soft climaxes' might be achieved in his detailed bar-by-bar 'study hints' to the piece.

[4] Grainger indicated *crescendo* and *decrescendo* signs in parentheses.

(or thinks he uses), whether he plays 'relaxed' or 'tense', PROVIDED *he controls a variety of dynamics (louds and softs) that range from the most violent fff to the most whispered ppp*. Students should concentrate on musical results (the *actual sounds* produced in playing) rather than upon the pianistic methods employed. Wherever certain modes of holding fingers, arm and hand are prescribed in this edition they are merely recommended because experience has shown them to be practical and easy; they are never supposed to be 'the only way'. The same results can often be attained in several different ways. The important thing is to know which results to strive for, and in this connection students should remember that all truly great performers possess the *power to exaggerate* and *a range of extreme contrasts*. On the other hand, the mark of mediocrity is the tendency to underdo—to play louds too softly, softs too loudly, fast speeds too slowly, slow speeds too quickly, etc.

While most students are absolutely incapable of playing a violently loud chord that is equally *fff* in all its component notes, the capacity to do so is a sure sign of a technically well-equipped pianist. What is called 'thumping' or 'harshness of tone' is due, generally, to the unequal and *uncontrolled* distribution of tone-strengths in loud chords (the outer fingers are generally too loud for the inner fingers), NOT to the extreme loudness of the whole chord.

The simplest way to attain an extreme and controlled *fff* is to bring the hand down with as quick as possible an arm action from a height of six or more (preferably more) inches, fingers, hand and wrist being held as rigid as possible. It is easy enough to get the required strength from the arm, provided the arm is raised amply between blows; what is difficult is to get the fingers to *translate that strength to the keys*, to carry the strength of the arm-blow *intact* to the keys. Only extreme rigidity of the fingers, hand and wrist makes this possible. None would wish to drive a nail with a hammer-head or hammer-shaft made of soft rubber! Why, then, do they hope to be able to play extremely loud chords with 'relaxed' wrist, hand and fingers? Has anyone ever seen a practical pianist actually play *fff* chords with 'relaxed action'?

Extreme *fff* is more difficult to attain and control than extreme *ppp*, though both extremes are far too rare and should be ardently cultivated. In order to acquire an extreme *ppp*, try to play single notes, slowly, that are so soft as to be *hardly audible*. Do not be discouraged if some of these extremely soft notes do not sound at all; that is a good sign, showing that you are really attempting *extreme* softness. On the other hand it is a bad sign if all the notes invariably sound in *ppp* practice; it means that you are not attempting to play *soft enough*. When wooing extreme **ppp** you must 'flirt with silence'. The piano is one of the few musical instruments that can produce a barely audible, extreme **ppp** tone without impairing the purity of its pitch or without loss of the characteristic tone color of the instrument. Particularly is this true of extremely soft, low bass notes, such as those in measures 11–19, 53–62.[5] Pianists should exploit this beautiful possibility of their instrument to the full. The utmost extremes of loud and soft should be carefully studied in the Gardiner Prelude, as well as all the intervening dynamics.

Simultaneous Tone-Strength Differentiation

Skill in playing louder and softer notes at the same time, in the same hand, is one of the most valuable developments of modern piano technic, and is equally necessary to the proper rendition of the classics and of the moderns; especially imperative when performing Bach Fugues. Fortunately, it is the easiest branch of pianism to acquire quickly.

While simultaneous tone-strength differentiation can be achieved in different ways the following method of its study is recommended to students because of its simplicity. It is a fact that a fully depressed key will always give a louder note than a partially depressed key, provided both keys are struck with the same force. Therefore, when simultaneously playing louder and softer notes in one hand, fully depress the keys of louder notes but only partially depress the keys of softer notes, holding fingers, hand and wrist stiff and unyielding (thus striking all the keys involved with similarity of force) and descending from a height of at least two inches above the keys with a brisk arm action. In order to carry out this plan the fingers that play louder notes must, of course, be slightly more extended (must protrude further downwards towards the keys) than the fingers playing softer notes; these latter fingers (playing softer notes) should be comparatively withdrawn, held higher away from the keys. In other words, the position of the fingers must correspond exactly to the relative positions of the fully depressed and partially depressed keys, the fingers playing louder notes corresponding to the fully depressed keys, the fingers playing softer notes corresponding to the partially depressed keys.

---

[5] Grainger, again, gave extremely detailed 'study hints' in his bar-by-bar commentary.

When first beginning to practise simultaneous tone-strength differentiation (by means of the study shown below) hold the fingers that are going to play the softer notes so high that they only just touch the tops of their keys, without depressing them (hence, these notes will be silent), while the louder notes are sounded at full strength, their keys fully depressed. Then (while continuing to practise the study shown below) very gradually lower the fingers that are going to play the softer notes, so that the keys of these notes are first very slightly depressed (sounding **pp**), then very slightly more depressed (sounding **p**, **mp**, etc.)—meanwhile the louder notes continue at full strength, their keys fully depressed.

The following diagram gives the position of fingers to silent, softer and louder notes:

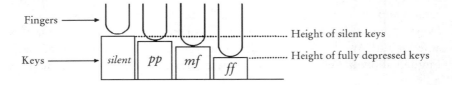

The positions for the intermediate tone-strengths may easily be imagined.

The following study should be practised by each hand separately, at slow speed, raising the hand before each chord and holding the damper pedal down during the entire study.

Simultaneous Tone-Strength Differentiation Study

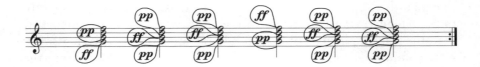

All kinds of chords and octaves, involving all kinds of positions on the white and black keys, should be practised along these lines.

When practising the above study it is essential that fingers, hand and wrist are held absolutely rigid, that a quick arm action is used and that the hand is raised from two to ten inches before each chord is struck. If the fingers are not rigid those fingers supposed only partially to depress the keys of the softer notes will 'follow through', depressing their keys more than they should, with the result that these should-be softer notes will be sounded too loudly and the whole object of the study defeated.

Damper (Right-Side) Pedal

The kind of damper pedalling mainly required throughout this Prelude is that known as 'legato pedalling', in which the damper pedal binds one chord or note to another; the pedal being changed *just as* (not before!) each chord or note (requiring change of damper pedal) is played and held down until the next indication of damper-pedal change. As this provides a complete *legato* effect to the ear if properly executed, and makes *legato* playing by the fingers unnecessary in most cases, the hands and fingers may, in such cases, be freely raised between notes and chords, thereby making simultaneous tone-strength differentiation and other tonal contrasts much easier to control. In *legato* pedalling all pedal changes must be made as quickly as possible and exactly at the prescribed moment. In order to promote speed and exactitude of damper-pedal change, scales may be practised in the following manner:

Study in Legato Pedalling

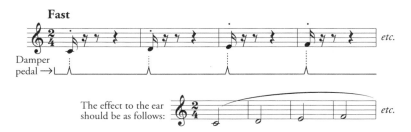

Sustaining (Middle) Pedal

The office of the sustaining pedal is to prolong the resonance of certain selected notes independently of the subsequent activities of the hands and the damper pedal. This is accomplished as follows. The keys of the notes that are to be prolonged by the sustaining pedal must be pressed down (sounded or silently) *before* the sustaining pedal is taken and held down *while* the sustaining pedal is depressed by the left foot. These keys may then be released by the hands without the resonance of their notes being impaired, as long as the sustaining pedal is held down—for the sustaining pedal, as long as it is depressed, will hold the dampers of these notes away from the strings of these notes. While the resonance of these selected notes is prolonged by the sustaining pedal in this manner the hands are free to play *staccato*, *legato*, or otherwise at will, and the damper pedal may be changed as often as desired (quite independently of the sustaining pedal). The sustaining pedal acts as a clarifying and refining influence upon piano playing, making unnecessary (and inexcusable!) many blurred pedalled passages formerly condoned and raising considerably our whole pianistic standard of harmonic cleanliness. The sustaining pedal is almost as necessary to modern pianism as is the damper pedal, and no pianist can pretend to be properly equipped who has not mastered the technic of this pedal, the joint use of all three pedals and their interplay with each other.

The following are the most important points to keep in mind when beginning to use the sustaining pedal:

1. The damper pedal must always be completely raised *before* the sustaining pedal is pressed down.
2. The keys of the notes to be sustained by the sustaining pedal (and only such keys) must always be held down *before* and *during* the pressing down of the sustaining pedal.
3. The sustaining pedal must be kept *fully depressed* until the release sign (*) is reached.

Both the sustaining pedal and the soft (left-side) pedal must be worked by the left foot. Where these two pedals are employed simultaneously the left foot must be slewed round so that the toe of the foot faces the damper pedal and the heel of the foot faces away from the player, to his left. The toe of the left foot presses down the sustaining pedal while the ball of the left foot presses down the soft pedal. The player must be freely able to take and release the soft pedal while holding the sustaining pedal, to take and release the sustaining pedal while holding the soft pedal. Players with small feet, new to this problem, are apt to think it an impossibility, but experience shows that all sizes of feet can master this double-pedal technic with sufficient practice. It is an *absolute necessity* to modern pianism. The following left-foot study should be mastered before the problems it contains are met with in actual playing.

Left-Foot Study

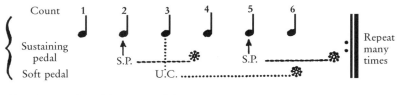

(Another notation of the same study)

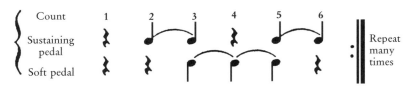

At count 1 both pedals are raised. At count 2 the sustaining pedal is depressed. At count 3 the sustaining pedal is held down fully depressed while the soft pedal is depressed. At count 4 the soft pedal is held down fully depressed while the sustaining pedal is released. At count 5 the soft pedal is held down fully depressed while the sustaining pedal is depressed. At count 6 the sustaining pedal is held down fully depressed while the soft pedal is released. During counts 1, 2 and 6 the foot is in its normal position. During counts 3, 4 and 5 the foot is in the slewed-round position, the toe pointing to the damper pedal, the heel pointing away to the player's left. During count 1 the heel should be on the floor; during counts 2, 3, 4, 5 and 6 the heel should be raised from the floor.

Soft (Left-Side) Pedal (una corda)

As the soft pedal on modern pianos no longer carries with it any characteristic tone quality (as it did on ancient pianos) and has, therefore, ceased to be a 'special effect', it may be freely used wherever soft effects are desired; the more so when playing upon large-toned pianos.

Markings

Damper pedal = ⌐_⌐_⌐	– = small accent	⌒ = extremely short hold, hardly noticeable
Sustaining *(middle)* pedal = S.P. ⸺❋	> = louder accent	⌒ = slightly longer hold, but still quite short
Soft pedal *(una corda)* = U.C. ⸺❋	*sf, sff* = very loud, harsh accents	⌒ = normal hold.

19   *What Effect is Jazz Likely to Have upon the Music of the Future?*

(1924)

From an Interview with Percy Grainger

Distinguished Pianist, Composer and Teacher in a Conference Secured Expressly for the Etude, Tells Why We May Have No Fear of the Ultimate Results of Jazz on Art Music

Editor's Note: Mr. Grainger has easily one of the most original and individual minds of the present-day music world. His intellect has not been nourished on hackneyed thought paradigms handed down from stagnant pasts. He thinks for himself. This marks his vigorous music which seems in a way like a reincarnation of melodic and harmonic existences which expired with the England of Byrd, Tallis, Bull and Purcell. He has made a graphic study of Jazz and its influence upon the music of to-day and to-morrow. In the following brief notes he characterizes this in his customarily interesting manner. Modesty, frankness, total absence of snobbery, are Mr. Grainger's natural traits; and this makes this review of a few facts relating to Jazz all the more interesting. Compare Mr. Grainger's views with those in the 'Jazz Problem' issue of last month.[1]

What is this bug-a-boo[2] of Jazz? Is it polluting the musical art of to-day? Or is it something which will vastly increase the musical interest of the future? These are interesting questions, but by no means of the vital importance that some attribute to them. It was quite natural that Jazz should first bubble up in the melting pot of America, and equally natural

Source: *Etude*, 42/9 (Sept. 1924), 593–4.

[1] The Aug. 1924, 'Jazz Problem', issue of the *Etude* led with an editorial on 'Where the *Etude* stands on Jazz' (p. 515), and included a survey of opinions on jazz from thirteen leading artists, an article 'What is Jazz doing to American Music?' by Paul Whiteman, and 'Jazz: Highbrow and Lowbrow' by Henry T. Finck.

[2] Popular slang word of the 1920s for an object of dread; title of a jazz piece of 1928 by Jelly Roll Morton.

that it should spread all over the world. The fact of the matter is that Jazz differs not essentially or sociologically from the dance music all over the world, at all periods, in that its office is to provide excitement, relaxation and sentimental appeal. In this respect it differs not from the Chinese or native American Indian music or from the *Halling*[3] of Norway, the Tarantella of Italy, Viennese Waltzes, Spanish Dances or the Hungarian Csárdás.[4] The trouble is that too much fuss is made about Jazz. Much of it is splendid music. Its melodic characteristics are chiefly Anglo-Saxon— closely akin to British and American (white) folk music.

The Finest Popular Music

In speaking of Jazz, I have in mind the extremely clever jazz manipulation of popular themes with marked rhythm that has taken place in the last few years. These orchestral arrangements are often made by musicians with unusual experience. To my mind, this form of Jazz is the finest popular music known to me in any country of to-day or even of the past. Its excellence rests on its combination of Nordic melodiousness with Negro tribal, rhythmic polyphony plus the great musical refinement and sophistication that has come through the vast army of highly trained cosmopolitan musicians who play in Jazz. There never was a popular music so *classical*.

One of the main characteristics of Jazz is that taken from the improvised habits of the Chinese and other musicians of the Far East. The seductive, exotic, desocializing elements imputed to Jazz by musical ignoramuses have no musical basis. Musically speaking, the chief characteristics of Jazz are solidity, robustness, refinement, sentiment, friendly warmth. As music it seems to me far less sensuous, passionate or abandoned than the music of many peoples. It is what one would expect from a solid, prosperous Nordic race.

What is there new about Jazz? All of the rhythms existed before. Nothing distinctly fresh and original has been contrived rhythmically. Surely the Scotch snap, such as we find in the old Scotch tune 'Comin' through the Rye', is not new. Yet this is one of the elements in the Jazz prescription. Nor is there anything new about the after beat, such as we find in the Hungarian dances of Brahms.

Though the elements out of which Jazz is made are not original when taken singly, yet, no doubt, the combination of these widely diverse and

[3] Duple-metre dance, probably originating with the Scottish reel.
[4] Stylized dance in duple time with frequent syncopations.

highly contrasted elements is new and constitutes the originality and characteristics of Jazz.

The music of all free peoples has a wide melodic sweep. By free I mean those people with strong pioneer elements—people who live alone in isolated stations. This accounts for the great melodic fecundity of the Nordic race. Folk who live in congested districts cannot be expected to write melodies with wide melodic range. Their melodies are restricted by the group. The group can sing just so high or so low. It has a narrow range. The compass is short. On the other hand, the Scandinavian, the Englishman, the Scotchman, the Irishman, whether he be in his native land, an American cowboy or an Australian boundary rider, is often wholly solitary in his music-making; and his melodies have, therefore, wider range of melodic line, as, for instance, in such a tune as 'Sally in Our Alley'[5] or the Norwegian [Swedish] 'Värmlandsvisan'.

This strong Anglo-Saxon element preserved in America was musically mixed with the equally virile rhythmic tendencies of the Negro. The Negro is not natively melodic, in the bigger sense. His melodies are largely the evolution of tunes he has absorbed from his white surroundings. His musical instinct is rhythmic first of all. (Note the Negro folksongs collected in Africa by Natalie Curtis.) To this came, doubtless, via San Francisco, about ten years ago, certain Asiatic influences, which in turn were to make some of the other elements of Jazz. Oriental music is allegedly 'in exact unison'. A great many people play the same melody at the same time, or at least they endeavour to do so. The fact is that they rarely play quite in tune with each other and a very strange effect is achieved. Somehow this got into Jazz as an occasional discordant feature, but one which gives it unlimited individuality. Beethoven, in the Scherzo to his 'Pastoral', has satirically suggested a peasant group in Europe doing the same thing. Indeed, it is a characteristic of many aboriginal groups. The Maoris, of New Zealand, when singing in alleged unison, often reveal that certain individuals are a quarter of a tone sharp or a quarter of a tone flat. The effect, especially in the distance, is far from disagreeable. There is always a kind of fuzz around the note. One hears this done deliberately in Jazz orchestras in America—of course, in a more sophisticated way.

If Jazz had done nothing more than to break down certain old orchestral jail walls, it would be justified. It is in the instrumentation of the modern Jazz orchestra that the musician is principally interested. This is momentous in every way. To me it represents an advance in instrumenta-

[5] By Henry Cary (c.1687–1743).

tion only to be compared in extent with that which occurred in another line between the instrumentation of Beethoven and the instrumentation of Wagner. It has opened up glorious instrumental possibilities.

It is amazing to me that the saxophone, the supreme achievement of the great instrument maker, Adolphe Sax (the inventor of the bass clarinet and the perfector of the brass instruments which made many of the most beautiful passages of Wagner possible),[6] should have to wait until this day and time to come into its own through the popular music of America. The same genius which Sax displayed with regard to wind instruments, America has displayed with regard to percussion instruments, such as the Deagan xylophones and marimbas, which I have prescribed for the score of my symphonic poem *The Warriors*.[7] This American genius, taking the instruments from Africa, Asia and South America, has given them reliable pitch so that they may be legitimately employed, both in vaudeville and with great orchestras, in extremely beautiful effects. Most of the ancestors of these new American instruments may be traced in great collections, such as the Ethnographical Museum of Leyden, Holland, or the Crosby Brown collection at the Metropolitan Museum of Art in New York.

The Jazz orchestra has shown us how the percussion instruments add clarity to the orchestral mass.[8] The instruments of the conventional symphony orchestra have something of a spongy character and lack the sharp, decisive qualities of the bells, xylophones and marimbas which have a clarity and sharpness, yet when well played seem to float on the mass of orchestral tone color like oil on water. The Russians have seen the possibilities of bells in their orchestral music. Bells and the percussion instruments I have mentioned cut through the tone mass but do not interfere with it. They seem to be in a different dimension of sound.

Another great achievement of Jazz is the introduction of vibrato in the wind instruments. All wind instruments should be played with vibrato; at least as much as the strings.

Jazz Makes No Impression on Classical Music

Apart from its influence upon orchestration, Jazz will not form any basis for classical music of the future, to my mind. The tendency will be to turn to something simpler. We are now musically located in an epoch which is

---

[6] (1814–1894), Belgian instrument maker.
[7] Grainger's 'Music to an imaginary Ballet' (1913–16).
[8] See Essay **21**.

not dissimilar from that which confronted the world at the time of Johann Sebastian Bach. That is, a vast horde of musical influences of great complexity seem to be coming together. Jazz is one of the manifestations of this. But Jazz is not likely to prove very fructifying to classical music. On the other hand, it has borrowed (or shall we say 'purloined'?) liberally from the classical. The public likes Jazz because of the shortness of its forms and its slender mental demands upon the hearer. No music is ever really popular which is too long or too complicated. On the other hand, length and the ability to handle complicated music are invariable characteristics of really great genius. We realize this if we compare the music of Bach, Beethoven, Wagner, Delius and Tchaikovsky with the music of such fine but smaller musical talents as Scarlatti, Jensen,[9] Roger Quilter, Reynaldo Hahn,[10] and others. Therefore, the laws which govern Jazz and other popular music can never govern music of the greatest depth or the greatest importance. I do not wish to belittle Jazz or other popular music. The world must have popular music. We should rejoice that the ragtime of ten years ago has reformed into the Jazz of to-day, but there will always exist between the best popular music and classical music that same distinction that there is between a perfect farmhouse and a perfect cathedral. The more we examine Jazz we see that its entire effect is aimed at short, sharp contrasts. There is, of course, a vast chasm between this and the Bach 'Passion Music', the Wagner 'Music Dramas' or the Delius 'Nature Poems'. In the education of the child, Jazz ought to prove an excellent ingredient. But he also needs to drink the pure water of the classical and romantic springs. He will get plenty of Jazz in America. He cannot escape it in this day in any part of the civilized world. Last summer in Germany I noted that Jazz had made a really noticeable impression upon the scores of the works of many modern composers I heard. The influence was superficial, but it was there, nevertheless, and it is steadily growing.

My chief impression of the best Jazz is that it is near-perfect and delightful popular music and dance music. It is that and nothing more—and what more should it be?

---

[9] Perhaps Adolf Jensen (1837–79), German song composer.
[10] (1875–1947), Venezuelan-born French composer, best known for his stage works.

20

To My Fellow-Composers
(1924)

Most of you know that for over twenty years it has been the dream of my artistic life to give concerts of Anglo-Saxon and Scandinavian modern music on a big scale, and that my beloved mother[1] shared that dream and fought hard to help me earn the money with which to realize it. The delightful and generous Balfour Gardiner concerts of 1912–13 in London, to which I and so many other composers owe so much of our good fortune as composers, no doubt helped to put life into this wish of mine, by showing me tangibly how much more a composer can do for other composers and for the cause of modern music than any other type of musician can.

This past season, for the first time, I found myself in a position to bear the expenses of engaging a big orchestra as a result of my successful concert tour as a pianist and my growing royalties as a composer. Following up old talks and plans between the late Dr. Mees[2] and myself I went to Mr. Warner, the president of the Bridgeport Oratorio Society, and asked him whether his fine chorus would care to join me in a Delius–Grainger–Grieg–Rachmaninoff programme in New York City and Bridgeport, I to provide the orchestra (and, in the case of the New York concert, the hall and concert expenses), and the choir to provide itself. Although I offered to provide the orchestra for Bridgeport as well as New York Mr. Warner very generously took the bulk of the Bridgeport orchestral expenses and the Bridgeport soloists' fees off my shoulders— I merely paying certain extra fees for certain good orchestral players I wanted to have in Bridgeport as well as in New York.

I shall never forget the kindliness, the helpfulness, the sympathy shown to me throughout by the Bridgeport chorus, and particularly by its moving spirits, and by its altogether splendid conductor, Mr. Frank Kasschau,[3] who has continued the work done by Dr. Arthur Mees in a

Source: *Musical Life and Arts*, 1/2 (1 Oct. 1924), 35–6, and 1/3 (15 Oct. 1924), 67.

[1] Rose (Rosa) Grainger (1861–1922).

[2] Arthur Mees (1850–1923), American conductor, associated in later years with the New York Philharmonic Orchestra.

[3] Kasschau had taken over as conductor of the Bridgeport Oratorio Society in 1923; he soon established a reputation for innovative programming of contemporary works.

truly wonderful and ideal way. Dr. Mees was, from my particular stand-point as a composer, the most ideal conductor I ever had anything to do with in any land. Experienced and manly, noble and lovable as a human being, he served music for its own sake to a quite unique degree, never felt his own importance and personality as most conductors do, but was humbly, excitedly on fire to reveal the inner message of the music on hand, and did so. I shall never hope to hear my suite, *In a Nutshell*,[4] and my *Marching Song of Democracy*[5] as perfectly, satisfyingly done as he did them in 1916 and 1917. Dr. Mees chose Frank Kasschau as his assistant in the latter years, and he chose a man of his own high line of musical thought. Kasschau, like Mees, is a composer's conductor, has a fine beat and fine judgment, and has done wonders with the Bridgeport choir.

When thinking over the dream of Anglo-Saxon Scandinavian concert-giving I often had grave doubts as to how I would shape as a conductor. I feared I would lack manliness, that I would fail to make my ideas clear to the choir or the orchestra, that I would blunder in the practical arrange-ment of the rehearsals, etc., that the whole thing would fail to 'bite' under my personality. These fears proved ungrounded. I found all the musi-cians, whether professional or amateur, warmly sympathetic from first to last; they did not seem to laugh at me unduly, and rehearsals and concerts were conducted in a solemn, devoted mood; or, at least, so it seemed to me. Many knew that the New York concert fell on my beloved mother's death day,[6] and that I planned the whole thing as a kind of consecration, and that helped, of course. My concert managers (Concert Direction Antonia Sawyer)[7] gave me noble and ideal support. They worked unusu-ally hard over the whole venture, not only putting their hearts into it as an artistic and business matter, but also as a matter of warm and loyal friend-ship to me and my dear mother's memory. My rehearsals were as follow:

April 24th—Morning, strings $2\frac{1}{2}$ hours; afternoon, wind $2\frac{1}{2}$ hours.

April 25th—Full orchestra $2\frac{1}{2}$ hours.

April 26th—Full orchestra $2\frac{1}{2}$ hours.

April 28th—(At Bridgeport before the concert there) short rehearsal with chorus (the only one together).

The rehearsals went like clockwork. I had everything mapped out beforehand—when I was to begin each section of each work, but I was always a few minutes ahead with each part of the work, and was able to

---

[4] (Completed 1916), four-movement suite for orchestra.
[5] (1901–15, scored 1915–17), for mixed chorus, orchestra, and organ.
[6] 30 Apr. (1922).
[7] Sawyer (1863–1941) was Grainger's agent for the first eleven of his American years.

close each rehearsal before the full time was used up—generally with a quarter of an hour to spare. I found my own *Marching Song of Democracy* the hardest to conduct; in fact, at the Bridgeport concert I made a sorry mess of a place near the beginning (got muddled up with the changing bars), and if the performers had paid too much attention to my beats it would have been a catastrophe. On the other hand, I think I gave a good account of both of the Delius works (having prepared myself thoroughly mentally in them), but particularly of *The Song of the High Hills*.[8] The *North Country Sketches*[9] perhaps takes more subtlety and refinement than I have in my make-up, whereas I think I realized the great sweeps and gathering climaxes of the *High Hills* in fine style. I do not ever expect to be a great, or an exquisite, or an inspiring conductor. But the concerts have made me feel that I have it in me to present fine and difficult works with good accuracy, and with the power to make the importance of the works given felt by all—to have the task respected. That is the main thing from my standpoint—to present new works in a mood of holy serious-ness, and get the performers and hearers to partake of that mood.

I have pleasure in announcing that I was thoroughly pleased with my *Marching Song of Democracy*. After hearing it under Dr. Mees at Worcester, Mass., in 1917, and after now working out its details with singers and instrumentalists, I feel I am in a position to judge. It sounds as I wanted it to, as I still want it to. It is hard to do, but not too hard, and the 'nonsense syllables' seem to me wholly successful. I do not think that the audience cares much for this work, or that other musicians prize it very highly—not even 'Graingerites'. But I like it, and naturally care more for my opinion than the whole world's.

No words can tell the elation I feel about Delius's *Song of the High Hills*. For twenty-five years I have been waiting for an Anglo-Saxon work that should not be merely gifted and original, not merely part of the musical tide-streams of the moment, but that should strike me, on mature association, as being *great, immortal, universal*—a work to be placed beside Bach, Walt Whitman, Wagner. At last, I have it. When I first heard this work (London, December 1922), it so overwhelmed me emotionally that esthetic judgment was out of the question. As I got to know it better in Frankfurt[10] (training the Ruhrscher Gesangverein in it) I was certain of its greatness, but not so certain of its practicalness, or of the perfection of

[8] (1911), for chorus and orchestra, but without text.
[9] (1913–14), for orchestra.
[10] During Grainger's extended stay there during the first half of 1923, when he frequently assisted Delius.

its details. Since then I have arranged it for two pianos, and hence know its harmonic texture intimately, and since then, again, have rehearsed it often and carefully with choir and orchestra, and listened to the final result with the tense nerves of two concert performances. And I say, without any hesitation, here is one of the few great works of all time, here is the peer to the *Matthew Passion*, the *Tristan* Overture, the *L'après-midi d'un faune*. At the same time it is typically English—in its harmonic type, in its nature-worship (think of the English poets), in its kinship with both Scandinavian music and primitive, such as Negro music.

I have long craved *size* in the best Anglo-Saxon music. Too often it is gifted and brief, or it is long and somewhat tedious—like much of Elgar, for instance. But here we have a typically Anglo-Saxon, typically Nordic work that yet measures up to the greatest Continental standards as to the bigness, breadth and sweep of the workmanship needful to realize these requirements. Of all the works I know of Delius it is the best orchestrated; his long experience is here put to the greatest ends, and beauty of momentary details and the needs of large form are balanced with true genius, with strange perfection. Yearfuls of splendidly applied varied experiences separated this *masterly* work from that inspired but uneven other nature-poem, *Appalachia*. I will not say that perfection is by any means the most golden of artistic achievements. I will not even say that the imperfections or inexperiencednesses of *Appalachia* make it less deathlessly valuable. I will say only this: It is glorious to have at last an Anglo-Saxon work that seems to combine all the qualities of greatness and satisfies every international standard as regards *size, depth of feeling, perfection, skill, inspiration, practicalness*.

The orchestration of *High Hills* is particularly interesting in view of Delius's own views on orchestration. He says he believes in 'pure colors' rather than blending. That is to say, he believes in avoiding doubling wherever practicable. But in spite of this belief we find in the *High Hills* an unusual amount of doubling—perhaps as much as in Wagner or Bach—say, the *Matthew Passion*. As I am myself a believer in doubling and a keen opponent of 'pure color' I naturally ascribe a great deal of the perfection and melt of sound in the *High Hills* to the great variety of contrasting colors Delius in this work brings to bear on almost every voice, thereby obliterating the color impression and heightening concentration upon more purely intervallic appeals, as is also the case with Bach and Wagner. Where important voices are allotted to solo instruments, or to a single quality of timbre we are left much more at the mercy of the individual player, and the conductor, to my mind, spends too much time at rehearsals and performance, trying to establish correct tonal balance and ensuring prominence to the more important voices. But where these balances, overweights, underlinings are registered into the score by the composer himself by means of blends and doublings the conductor is freer to devote himself to matters of expression rather than to matters of prominence and balance, and a more emotional interpretation results; furthermore, the composer's own conception of balance and prominences are, at that, more faithfully realized than they ever can be by any conductor dealing with a 'pure color' orchestration.

Be it as it may, the conductor's job in the *High Hills* is a particularly expressive one, and I can imagine no score that holds finer thrills for the conductor or offers him finer chances of passion, calm and wide-flung transitions. To my mind the *Song of the High Hills* is beyond all question the work of works with which to introduce Delius's muse for the first time in any country (where a choir is available) and to show the highest flights of British music, just as my *Marching Song of Democracy* is the best work to show my larger choral style and a typically Australian feeling.

I feel far less elated about the *North Country Sketches*. I fell in love with these on hearing them in Frankfurt as a piano duet (in Philip Heseltine's splendid arrangement—Augener)[11] fell in love with the exquisite harmonic texture, the delicately expressive motives, the infinite resourcefulness of the third movement (Dance). But actual orchestral experience of this work, both in Frankfurt and in America, lead me to consider it far less *telling* than the *High Hills*. To my mind it is far less perfect in orchestration. In the Dance there are passages for solo or massed woodwind, accompanied by string chords, that simply *will not* come through if the full strength of the strings is used. In Frankfurt I was prone to put this down to the lack of flexibility of the players. But the strings of the New York Philharmonic are perfect material—but even with them the same trouble remained. So I did not hesitate to play all such passages with two desks only of each string voice, with the results that seemed to me satisfactory.

At the very beginning of the Dance I found (in Frankfurt and New York) that the accompanying notes on the oboe and English horn kill the melody on the flute, so I substituted two clarionets[12] for oboe and English horn. On the third page of the score of this same movement is another

---

[11] Augener No. 15660 (pub. 1922), by fellow Delius enthusiast, the British composer-critic Peter Warlock (Philip Heseltine) (1894–1930).   [12] Clarinets.

melody on the flute (ending high with the notes E, C sharp, A) that fails to come through, so I added clarionet with the flute—a less desirable expedient, but one I felt forced to make in the interests of clarity. Problems of this kind keep recurring in *North Country Sketches*, whereas they are unknown in the *High Hills*. Therefore, I consider the *Sketches* far less advisable a choice where one is introducing Delius for the first time. At the same time I consider *North Country Sketches* truly inspired and truly beautiful, and there is nothing in music dearer to me personally than many passages in this composition.

The Grieg *Psalms*[13] and the Rachmaninoff *Songs of the Church*[14] made a great appeal under Mr. Kasschau's ripping training and leadership. Both these collections are examples of ideal *a cappella* writing, and show off to the best advantage any decent choir that tackles them.

My *Colonial Song* went splendidly in its original orchestration for two solo voices and orchestra, and made the effect it had failed to make in England (1912 or 1913)[15] with the original orchestration—partly due to several alterations in scoring I have made since then, and also largely owing to the fine vocal work of the two soloists, Anita Atwater and William Owen Gilboy. Balfour Gardiner, whose opinion on compositional matters I always greatly revere, and from whom I have learnt a lot, did not consider *Colonial Song* a satisfactory work, nor did English critics or individuals realize the importance of this piece as the first musical voicing of definite Colonial and Australian feeling. Their failure to do so, their indifference to the Australian side of an Australian composer (who had, on the other hand, devoted himself to English folk songs and English music in general), went far to make me feel 'not at home' in England. I cannot agree with Balfour as to this work. I agree with mother that it is one of the very best of my smaller pieces, and I rejoice at its really great popularity in America. It is quite typical that America should welcome an avowedly Colonial and Australian piece and feel romantically about it as an expression of British Empire feeling, while England remains indifferent to it.

I consider the public response to the Delius works all that could be expected. I hardly expected so good a response. Delius is the Bach of his era, or the musical Walt Whitman of his era; we cannot expect a Meyerbeer or R. Strauss response to such music. And what the appreciation of Delius lacks in suddenness it makes up in steadiness, I feel. As for

[13] *Four Psalms* (1906).
[14] Vesper mass, *All-night Vigil*, Op. 37 (1915).
[15] 25 Feb. 1913, with soloists Gleeson-White (sop.) and Elwes (ten.).

my purely personal feelings, I will never cease to be thankful for all the hours I spent rehearsing this lofty music. I consider it a very great privilege to have been associated with it so many hours, with its noble strains ringing in my ears at the time and for long afterwards.

What lovely and important new works have swum into my musical ken in the brief two years since my darling mother's death, and how I regret she did not live to hear some of these works. How she would have relished some of them. Very outstanding is Balfour Gardiner's *Michaelchurch*[16]—certainly by far his finest piano piece, perhaps the finest recent piano piece of the whole British school. Here is a piece fit to rank beside the best Schumann Novelette or Brahms Rhapsody, a piece full of flowing form, wide range of contrasts, comforting surging human emotions, delicious contrapuntal and choral textures. This is the sort of thing John Ireland[17] seems to me to try to do, but here done by Gardiner a thousand times better, done to perfection. If Gardiner had written nothing but this one piece I would rank him as an important and lasting composer. I long to play this piece in public, to push and push it. American works I have heard less of than usual, what with my whole year in Europe and my unusually busy concert season since my return. But a really priceless masterpiece stands out in my memory—David Guion's *Sheep and Goat Walkin' to the Pasture*[18] for piano (at least as good as his immortal *Turkey in the Straw*—to my mind even better, even stronger)— and Nathaniel Dett's setting for voice and piano of 'Zion Hallelujah'.[19] Brahms at his best in the *Deutsche Volkslieder*, and elsewhere, never wove more entrancing contrapuntal threads than Dett in this arrangement, or combined more happily warmth with suave grace. Dett told me he worked for years at this trifle—it was worth it.

As the result of my big concerts I feel more elated and hopeful artistically than I ever have in my life before. I see that I can handle a big scheme, if not inspiringly, at least safely and reliably. I see that I can combine the creative side with the conducting side, and perhaps gradually become the *active force* in modern music I have always longed to be.

In the *Song of the High Hills* I have learned that Anglo-Saxon music at its best can be as great, as inspired, as immortal as the greatest music of all the ages. All this is a real comfort to me, and I consider the whole

---

[16] For piano (1920–3), dedicated to Grainger.
[17] (1879–1962), English composer and teacher.
[18] A cowboys' and old fiddlers' breakdown, trans. for piano (pub. 1922).
[19] From his *Negro Spirituals*, arr. for solo voice (pub. 1919).

experience cheap at about $5,000 (about £1,000) which is, roughly, what the whole business cost me.

As I look forward to the future orchestral concerts (maybe two seasons from now, for next season I am planning two chamber concerts), the things I most itch to give are Grieg's entrancing *Symphonic Dances* for orchestra;[20] Cyril Scott's orchestral *Aubade*, and Herman Sandby's *Havstemning* for orchestra. Scott's Aubade seems to me the very essence of his spiritual flower—like nature, highly typical technically of his muse—and more perfect to me, more deeply beautiful, more highly personal than his splendid orchestral Passacaglias,[21] fine and effective though they be. Sandby's *Havstemning* (Sea Mood) is a work I especially long to produce, and set high hopes on. Touching melodic lines, woven over appealing shifting harmonies create an irresistibly Danish mood, while the look of the score suggests grandeur in the bigger moments and a large flow of form consistent with the title of the composition.

Next season I hope to get Roger Quilter over, and present him and his lovely songs to America. His (and in a quite different way Howard Brockway's *Lonesome Tunes* and *Kentucky Mountain Tunes*) are for me the most important and perfect songs in the English language.

We live in ages of crazes, isms, rushing after 'the latest'. I am the last to say, or feel anything against such activities. Anything is better than stagnation, deafness to the new. But while I revere Schoenberg, Hindemith, Stravinsky, etc., I am particularly desirous of presenting to the musical world works that especially abound in harmoniousness, calm, balance, melodiousness—qualities I see in abundance in the particular works I care to produce of Grieg, Delius, Cyril Scott, Sandby, Balfour Gardiner, Roger Quilter, Natalie Curtis, Guion, Dett, and others.[22]

---

[20] 1896–7.   [21] Two Passacaglias on Irish Themes (1916, pub. 1977).

[22] Grainger did arrange two chamber concerts in 1925: 26 Apr., presenting mainly his own works; and 3 May, featuring works by Dett (*Negro Folksong Derivatives*), Natalie Curtis-Burlin (*Memories of New Mexico*), Schreker (*Chamber Symphony*), Hindemith (*Chamber Music* No. 1), and Grieg (*Lost in the Hills*).

21

The Completion of the Percussion Family in the Orchestra

(1926)

The percussion family is the least complete in the orchestra. I do not refer here to more or less noisy instruments of fairly indefinite pitch, such as the snare drum, tenor drum, gong, cymbal, triangle, bass drum and so on, but to those instruments of definite pitch which are capable of melody and harmony, such as the xylophone, glockenspiel, large bells, dulcitone, celesta, piano, kettle drum, 'nabimba', tubular bells and others. The brilliant experiments of various earlier and recent composers (the celesta in Tchaikovsky's *Nutcracker Suite*, the xylophone in Saint-Saëns' *Danse Macabre*, the xylophone and piano in Stravinsky's *Petrouchka*, and the like) have already proven the usefulness of some of these instruments in orchestration and their charm in solo passages. Solo percussion is even more extensively developed in American dance music.

New instruments are generally first introduced into the orchestra for solo purposes and their combination into sections develops later. This is evident from a comparison between Bach's use of solo woodwinds and their treatment by Wagner and Strauss as an instrumental family. It also explains why percussion instruments still remain unexploited as a group, despite the fact that they have been brought to a high degree of perfection by certain instrument makers (especially J. C. Deagan in Chicago).[1] In my opinion, these will soon prove their great value as a family. It seems to me that their function is to increase the clarity and independence of sound in the orchestra. In the percussion orchestras of the Orient (the gamelan of Java, among others) this clarity and independence of sound emerges beautifully. Individual sounds stand out in relation to each other despite great rhythmical complexity. The European orchestra is the antithesis of this kind of sound; masses of strings and woodwind have a levelling effect acoustically; individual details easily disappear in a 'thick soup of sounds' from which, in rhythmically and polyphonically complex passages, no

Source: 'Die Ergänzung der Schlagwerkgruppe im Orchester', *Pult und Taktstock*, 3/1 (Jan. 1926), 5–9, trans. Bruce Clunies Ross. (An English version by Grainger has not been found.)

[1] By 1910 the Deagan catalogue featured sixty-three types of glockenspiels, eighty xylophones, and sixty chimes.

section emerges clearly. This possibility is, however, available to the percussion section, even in the *tutti* of large orchestras, now that its lower notes can be completed.

It is not, as many uninformed people think, the purpose of the percussion family to increase the noise level and confusion of the orchestra. Rather, the aim should be clarity and beauty of sound. The deeper octaves of all the percussion instruments are especially suited to enhancing this. The presence of a xylophone and glockenspiel in the orchestra without the addition of a bass xylophone (or 'wooden marimba', as it is called in America) and bass glockenspiel (steel marimba) seems ridiculous when these splendid deep instruments are known—as ridiculous as finding an oboe in an orchestra without an English horn and bassoon and a trumpet without horns, trombones and tuba. The lower registers of most percussion instruments are certainly much weaker than the higher, but they have their own tenderness and beauty and when combined with the upper octaves lend them a satisfying fullness.

Most performers on percussion instruments are, however, inclined to use hard mallets, especially in the lower registers. Through this practice the deeper frequencies naturally disappear and the higher overtones stand out strongly. In order to realize precise pitches over the full range of the percussion section it is necessary for performers to use suitable mallets for each octave and each passage.

The lower limit of the steel marimba is approximately *c* or *F* (an octave and a twelfth below middle *c*); the wooden marimba descends even lower. In the higher registers these instruments overlap the range of the xylophone and glockenspiel, respectively, so that altogether they have a full four or five octaves. In the lower register the wooden marimba has a remarkably beautiful liquid, hollow sound; the steel marimba, on the other hand, has the quality of a celesta but with a distinctly greater fullness of tone. Even richer tones than those of the steel marimba are produced by the large, heavy metal bars, similar to those of the glockenspiel, which are installed in many American organs as a harp register. The latter are especially worth recommending for use in the orchestra.

A sound similar to the glockenspiel or celesta is produced by the dulcitone; an example of this highly functional instrument made by Thomas Machel[2] and Sons in Glasgow is constructed of tuning forks and equipped with keyboard and damping pedal. It has a range of five octaves, from *A* to

---

[2] (1841–1915), who perfected the dulcitone in 1880.

a'''' and because of its fuller sound and range is preferable to the celesta in the orchestra. Ideally, however, both should be used.

The Swiss staff bells or Swiss hand-bells, cast in the shape of bells, actually have the character of church bells. The range of these effective instruments extends beyond four octaves, from about *b* to *c'''''*. By using mallets of varying degrees of hardness strong acoustical contrasts may be attempted on these Swiss staff bells. Very satisfying results can be obtained with the Swiss staff bells, steel marimbas and tubular bells (the latter should have a range of two octaves), though, in my experience, only when each of these instruments is fitted with a keyboard (operating two rows of hammers, one with lighter padding and one with harder padding) and a damper system controlled by a pedal. Only then can the desirable multiple-octave doublings be executed without using far too many performers, and only then can clarity be attained, as it is necessary to control the drawn-out resonance of these sounds through a damper system similar to that on the piano. On the other hand, because of the shortness of their sounds, a keyboard need not be fitted to the wooden marimba or the nabimba (one of these very distinctive instruments similar to the marimba, made by J. C. Deagan, has a sound quality amazingly like the clarinet and bass clarinet).

Very beautiful, characteristically gong-like sounds can be produced on the piano by playing directly on the strings with wooden marimba mallets in different degrees of hardness, covered in various thicknesses of wool or felt. The sounds produced in this way with light marimba mallets blend well with those of the steel marimba, the dulcitone and the glockenspiel, with the added advantage that they can be extended down to the deepest strings on the piano.

The percussion instruments mentioned above fall into three groups:

1. Clear sounds, similar to the glockenspiel: glockenspiel, bass-glockenspiel (steel marimba) with keyboard (from three to five octaves); celesta (four octaves), dulcitone (five octaves); piano strings played with marimba mallets (the five lower octaves of the piano). This group combines very effectively with the high overtones of the harp.

2. Less clear sounds similar to church bells: Swiss staff bells with keyboard (over four octaves); tubular bells with keyboard (two octaves).

3. Hollow, liquid sounds, typical of the xylophone: xylophone, bass xylophone (wooden marimba, three to six octaves); nabimba (three to six octaves). This group combines well with the upper octaves of the piano.

If these three groups are combined they form a percussion family which completely matches the other instrumental families, and the orchestra is enhanced by a new, bright, lively, clear and transparent cluster of sounds which is possibly suited to the resolution of various problems of modern instrumentation.[3]

In the last twenty years the piano has been used as an orchestral instrument with increasing frequency. In my experience, however, only rarely does a single piano in a large orchestra give truly satisfactory results. Three pianos sound far better. Trebling does not make a louder sound—on the contrary, it produces a greater fullness and tenderness. In 1921, at a benefit concert in New York, sixteen famous piano virtuosi played sixteen pianos in unison.[4] It was only necessary to hear this concert to be persuaded of the beautiful effect of multiple doublings of piano tone. Three pianos played in unison is enough for this enhancement to become noticeable. The hard, forced tone of a single instrument attempting to penetrate a whole orchestra disappears to be replaced by an effortless yet stronger piano tone which can be sustained even in the *tutti* of a large orchestra. The same is the case with all percussion instruments: the ideal sound is achieved through multiple doubling—doubling in unison and in the lower octaves. A single glockenspiel in the orchestra with nothing to complete its lower register is just as insufficient as a piccolo without a larger flute. It is like only playing the two upper octaves of the piano without using its other resources.

In the last generation, much has been done to fill the gaps in the percussion family by percussion instrument makers, especially Deagan in Chicago, who in this sphere has made similar advances as Sax in the sphere of brass instruments. About sixty years elapsed before musicians at large recognized the beautiful possibilities of the saxophone family. How long will it be before the manifold qualities of the completed percussion family are effectively studied and exploited?

[3] Grainger's footnote: I used expanded percussion sections like those mentioned above in three of my larger compositions: the suite *In A Nutshell*, for orchestra, piano and Deagan percussion instruments (composed 1914–1916, G. Schirmer, Inc. New York); *The Warriors*, music for an imaginary ballet for orchestra and three pianos (1913–1916, B. Schotts Söhne); *Marching Song of Democracy* for choir, orchestra and organ (1901 to 1917, Universal Edition).

[4] On 21 Dec. 1921. See, further, Essay 40.

22   *Sargent's Contributions to Music*
(1927)

John Singer Sargent[1] was one of the most outstanding musicians I have ever met; for although his musical technic was not as developed as his painting technic, he had that rarest of all esthetic gifts—individualistic, balanced, critical judgement. His musical judgements, sympathies and activities welled up instinctively out of his rich musical inner nature, and were not (as are the musical doings of many a gifted amateur musician) influenced by the opinions of professional musicians, or indeed by any ascertainable outside factors whatever. To hear Sargent play the piano was indeed a treat, for his pianism had the manliness and richness of his painting, though, naturally, it lacked that polished skillfulness that comes only with many-hourly daily practice spread over many years. He delighted especially in playing his favorite, Fauré, and in struggling with the fantastic difficulties of Albéniz's *Iberia*, which latter he had mastered to the point of making it a musical joy to listen to under his hands; a task that might stagger many a well-equipped concert pianist.

However, remarkable as his playing was, intense as his delight in active music-making was, I consider his greatest contribution to music lay in the wondrously beneficent influence he exerted on musical life in England. It is probable that he exerted this same influence in other lands, but I happened to witness it in England only.

In the benevolent paternal quality of his musical influence, Sargent was not only the ideal artist, but also the ideal American; for there is probably no people, today, that bring such a beautiful reverence and generosity to the support of music as do the Americans—possibly a modern manifestation of their original Puritan background. Sargent always seemed to me a typical Puritan, a typical New-Englander in his musical life. Music seemed to be less a recreation to him than a sacred duty, the duty of aiding especial musical talent wherever he found it. While he was nowise deaf to the appeal of the gifts of reproductive musicians it was primarily the

Source: Evan Charteris, *John Sargent* (New York: Charles Scribner's Sons, 1927), 149–51.

[1] (1856–1925), European-based American painter, who lived in London from 1885 until his death. He is best known for his portraits (including Theodore Roosevelt, John D. Rockefeller, and Grainger), water-colour scenes, and murals. Grainger came to know him soon after moving to London in 1901.

creative musicians (composers) to whom he was most powerfully drawn, and whom he aided most extensively. Out of those many musicians for whom the warmth of his musical enthusiasm was especially kindled I recall particularly the following ones: Gabriel Fauré, Charles Martin Loeffler,[2] Ethel Smyth,[3] Korbay,[4] Léon Delafosse,[5] Debussy, Cyril Scott, Albéniz, and myself.

Sargent was not content to enjoy his musical enthusiasms as merely personal pleasures; he never rested until his enthusiasms had taken practical tangible shapes beneficial to the musicians that had aroused them, and to the art of music in general. For many years (longer than I knew him) he had been the apostle of Gabriel Fauré in England, bringing over that great composer to London for public and private performances of his compositions, arranging performances of Fauré works by the Cappé Quartet, Léon Delafosse, and other exquisite artists and the like. In my opinion Sargent is chiefly responsible for the fine understanding of Fauré's music that obtains in England. He was likewise one of the first (if not the very first) to proclaim the beauty and the importance of Loeffler's muse.

Sargent used his great prestige as a unique social as well as artistic 'lion' in London, to benefit those musicians he considered worthy of help and fame. He had only to announce his approval of any musician for hostesses to spring up ready to engage these protégés, hoping that the performance of these musicians at their 'At Homes' would guarantee them Sargent's coveted presence—which it usually did, for Sargent was untiring and self-effacing in all that pertained to the support of those he considered true artists. To have Sargent's approval and support was a wonderful boon to any struggling artist; highly beneficial from a practical, mundane standpoint, and deeply comforting on purely artistic grounds—for Sargent's musical mind worked like a composer's rather than like a mere music-lover's.

The things he especially enjoyed in music, the things he emphasized in his musical comments, the details his musical memory retained, were all highly specialized points, rare sparks of genius, highlights of original workmanship that the average musician (professional or amateur) usually misses entirely, and that, as a rule, only great composers can be expected

---

[2] (1861–1935), French-born American composer and violinist. Preceding Grainger's tribute in Charteris's book was another recollection of Singer's 'musicalness', by Loeffler (pp. 147–9).

[3] (1858–1944), German-trained English composer, author, and suffragette.

[4] Ferencz Korbay (1846–1913), Hungarian composer, singer, and pianist, perhaps best known for his orchestral *Nuptiale*.   [5] (1874–c.1951), French pianist.

to appreciate consciously. But even great composers are seldom as balanced, as fair, as clear-eyed in their musical criticisms as Sargent was, and I repeat what I asserted earlier—that esthetical judgement such as his is the rarest of all musical gifts.

The fact that he bestowed upon the music of Gabriel Fauré the greatest depth and intensity of his musical admiration and devotion is a convincing example of the rightness of Sargent's artistic vision, of his ability to penetrate to musical essentials, of his unsusceptibility to shallow surface appeals, of his freedom from the 'isms' and vogues of his day. For Fauré is one of those quietly great masters (like Bach, César Franck & Frederick Delius) who, in the main, work hidden from the outer world of their own era, to emerge undyingly resplendent to future generations. But Sargent had in all musical matters the magically penetrating eye of genius. In addition he had the comforting touch of a warmly human heart, of a compassionate seer—which, by the way, explains to me, his natural sympathy with such a subject as that so illuminatingly disclosed in his painting *The Hermit*.[6]

In all the years in which I was privileged to know him, on all the many, many occasions on which I was made happy in meeting him, I never discovered in Sargent one act, one thought, one gesture, one opinion, judgment or sympathy that did not proclaim the true genius, the great man, the innate aristocrat. Few men were funnier than he, consciously and unconsciously. Probably his artistic dislikes were as strong as his likings but his disapprovals were buried in obscure grunts, in indecipherably broken sentences, while his approvals were always clearly and unmistakably conveyed; for he was, above all things, a *constructive* personality, and never oblivious to the actual effect of all he did and said. Two things stand out in my memory of him: his unfailing benevolence, where the welfare of art was concerned, and his inscrutability in all that touched his purely personal life. He was strong in all things; always giving sympathy, never evoking it; always helpful to others, and always self-contained—a strange mixture of a compassionate Christian and a stoical, Red Indian Warrior!

I cannot close this short account of my impression of Sargent without mentioning what I, in my innermost artist's heart, owe esthetically to him and his friend, William Gare Rathbone.[7]

These two, both so individualistic and uninfluencable in their musical perceptions, were yet united in many musical sympathies and enthusi-

---

[6] *Il Solitario* (1908).
[7] (1849–1919), British businessman and arts patron, to whom Grainger dedicated *Handel in the Strand*.

asms. They were alike in this—that they were the finest musical amateurs that I, personally, have ever seen; that their musicality was essentially that of the composer type; that their natural attitude towards music and musicians was constructive and benevolent. Some of my years in London were, artistically speaking, dreary and hopeless enough. But into the darkness of those times Sargent and Rathbone unfailingly shed light. To meet either of them, anywhere, was to drink a great draught of artistic and human encouragement, to feel emboldened towards further compositional experimentation, to sense our intuitive championing of all artistic genuineness and originality. For all these nobilities, which were revealed to me in moments when I was poor and desperate enough to measure their true and rare value, I shall be unforgettingly thankful as long as I have my memory.

23   *The Orchestra for Australia*
(1927)

Possibility of a New Kind of Growing Up

Editor's Note: In this very fearless article Mr. Percy Grainger wants to know why Australians should avoid the use of the simpler and more popular instruments which are in everyone's hands to-day for the purpose of formulating quite a new kind of orchestra. He does not want to replace the symphony orchestra of convention or make jazz entirely the current medium of music, but he has no hesitation in suggesting that Bach and the ukulele may be brought into sweet communion for their mutual good.

Of the utmost interest to me is the question of the Australian orchestra. It may not have been considered by others in the same light, but I feel that in Australia, as also in America, there is the possibility of a new kind of orchestra growing up.

The symphony orchestra as we know it has only grown up naturally, and without any high-horse business, out of the instruments which were played by the musical people in Europe at the time when the orchestra came into being. For instance, the clarinet was long a popular instrument that was greatly despised by the highbrows. I imagine that the clarinet was never used in Bach's time as an instrument moving in really polite society. It was then in much the same position as the saxophone is in now.[1] The trombones were never used in classical music until Mozart, I think, employed them.[2] The saxhorns[3] were never used until Wagner used them for any such serious purpose.

We stand to-day in a period in which many things, social and artistic, are changing—and, in many cases, changing for very good reasons. Why should we ask the young people of to-day to study difficult instruments when simpler and sometimes better instruments have been evolved in

Source: *Australian Musical News*, 16/8 (Mar. 1927), 11–13.

[1] The clarinet had been invented during the early 18th cent. by J. C. Denner (1655–1707).

[2] The instrument was, however, used in sacred music well before Mozart introduced it into some of his operas, most notably *Don Giovanni*.

[3] Family of valved brass instruments, developed by Adolphe Sax during 1842–5.

recent years. May it not be a sign of intelligence rather than of laziness on the part of many young people when they prefer the easy saxophone to the more difficult clarinet? Personally, I think the saxophone a much more beautiful and musical instrument than the clarinet, though I like them both. Even if the saxophone were difficult to play and the clarinet were easy to play, I should personally choose the saxophone for my own instrument.

Easy Has It

If we try to make music difficult for people in an age in which people are not particularly desirous of encountering difficulty it seems to me that we are doing an unmusical thing. The question of people preferring easiness or difficulty is not really a musical question at all, but one of character and outlook on life. Musically speaking, all we have to do is to develop people musically. If that can be done on easy instruments such as the saxophone and the xylophone, I consider the pedagogues and music teachers, critics, conductors, or whatever they are, to be very unmusical if they are going to let their conceptions of character and morals stand between possible young musicians and the easier instruments they prefer in our days.

The saxhorn was invented by Sax, the man who together with his father[4] perfected the clarinet and the bass clarinet, and who did so much to ensure perfection of tune in most orchestral wind instruments. We are told that through his efforts the brass choirs employed by Wagner and his contemporaries became possible for the first time. Sax was no popular or commercial inventor. He was an instrument maker of the most serious and thorough and untiring type. The climax of his experience was the saxophone, an instrument to which he gave his name because it embodied his ideals more than any other instrument. Sax saw that there was a tonal gap between the comparative weakness—shall we call it weakerness—of the woodwinds and the greater strength or comparative strongness, of the brass. In doing so he also created one of the most humanly expressive of all instruments.

If the public and the popular musicians have developed the saxophone, if the lowbrows have done so and the highbrows have turned unappreciatingly aside from it, that must only be accounted greatly to the credit of the former and greatly to the shame of the latter. People who do

---

[4] Charles-Joseph Sax (1791–1865).

not realise a good musical instrument when they hear it are certainly not fit to be arbiters of musical opinion.

Bach and the Ukulele

There are many other instruments that deserve the most serious use by the more profound musicians: guitars, mandolins, mandolas, ukuleles, banjos, mandolin-banjos are only some of the fine instruments evolved or developed or popularised in our time, and deserving the most serious consideration of the leaders of musical thought everywhere. To that list should be added, of course, xylophones, wooden marimbas, bells, steel marimbas, the celesta, dulcitone, reed organ and the harmonium. I think it is safe to assume that Bach and Wagner would have revelled in these instruments. What instruments were used in the days of those men that they did not lovingly and varyingly employ? Should we not be stirred by their good example rather than confine ourselves to the limited number of instruments of the time in which they worked?

Therefore, the idea occurs to one, why not an Australian or an American orchestra consisting chiefly or entirely of the instruments most played in those countries? In the formation of such a new orchestral medium let us regard ourselves as being in a period of flux, if we like. Let each country, each section of the country, each community, make its own experiments. But let us begin by using most or entirely those instruments that are most played by the most people in the community, and of which popular taste at the moment is most fond. Let us not bow blindly to popular taste in this or any other matter, but let us give it a trial to see what there is in it.

Not Pure Symphony or Blind Jazz

I am thinking now not of the high professional orchestras, such as a good jazz orchestra, but of the formation of amateur orchestras, particularly of young people, without following blindly either the example of the symphony orchestra or of the jazz orchestra. Let conductors call for young players, find out how many there are playing each instrument in each community, and use them as far as possible in the proportion in which they appear. If violins are numerous and violas are absent, use them as far as possible in the proportion in which they appear. If violins are numerous and violas absent, use them so [sic]. Use the ukuleles and the banjos and whatever else is present, and in whatever way suits the style of those instruments best. If more saxophones than violins are present, then let the orchestra consist mainly of saxophones.

We, none of us, know what the results of such a wide experimentation would be, but we may be sure that they would be very interesting. My own opinion is that an orchestra consisting very largely of saxophones, ukuleles, mandolins, pianos and harmoniums would be an extremely expressive and soulful medium.

We can easily say that it would err on the side of being too soulful and rich; on the side of not being bright and chirpy enough. The instruments of the modern young people are instruments of emotion and sentiment rather than instruments of technique and brilliance. The music would have to be in consonance with that spirit and its possibilities. We can imagine the Bach chorales and the Bach chorale-preludes sounding very magnificent on such an orchestra.

The Harmonic Background

As so many of the modern popular instruments are melody bearers we would have to be sure of throwing in a sufficient number of pianos and harmoniums to provide harmonic background. Perhaps it would be one of the characteristics of such an orchestra, as it grew up, that the keyboard instruments would provide the bulk of the harmony and that the mainly single-note instruments, such as violins, saxophones and so on, would play melodies or melodically polyphonic parts rather than harmony parts.

In handling such an orchestra, of course, we should not try to make it in any way a substitute for the symphony orchestra. For instance, we should not try to make ukuleles take the part of violins, nor should we try to make the saxophones take the part of the brass of the conventional symphony orchestra. We should try to freely evolve a new orchestra with its own system of tonal balance, its own system of contrasts, its own system of prominences.

In all modern communities there are a large number of keyboard players, organists, pianists, and harmoniumists. We should not be afraid to use all those elements to their full extent. Very likely a large number of pianists in such an orchestra—perhaps ten to fifteen pianos in many cases—would provide that element of sharpness, that dramatic rhythmic quality, that in the symphony orchestra is often provided by the brass instruments.

Music that Can be Used

In trying experiments with such an orchestra we might possibly make good use of a lot of music composed entirely or partly for the chorus; so many of the instruments that are popular or becoming popular to-day are quasi-vocal in their type. This is true of mandolins, saxophones, and ukuleles, for instance. Let us use these quasi-vocal possibilities to the full, and see whether there are not many choral compositions such as those of Brahms or Rachmaninoff (for instance, the fifteen Anthems of the Church[5]) which would be very effective on such an orchestra, and would point the way to the kind of more purely orchestral effects to be evolved later.

Other things that could be drawn on would be, of course, the melodic and soulful works, small or large, popular or otherwise, such as 'Bruyères' by Debussy, and Debussy's 'Sarabande' from the *Trois pièces Pour le piano*; 'The Song of the Volga Boatmen'; the 'Intermezzo' from *Cavalleria Rusticana*; Bach's chorale-prelude 'Wachet auf'; the E-major Fugue and the D major from the second book of *The Well-Tempered Clavier*; and 'Dirge' by Roger Quilter for mixed chorus; 'Träumerei' of Schumann; the *Liebeslied* and waltzes of Brahms; the arietta from Bizet's *L'Arlésienne Suite*; 'Aase's Death', from the *Peer Gynt* suite; the *Valse Triste* of Sibelius; the 'Good Friday Music' from *Parsifal*.

This obviously very varied list presents both popular and classical music, and is suggested simply because it seems to present the same effectiveness with regard to the instruments imagined.

Who will Provide?

Of course one may ask who is going to make the arrangements? Well, that is for the young people who show any talent in composition. They should first of all be encouraged to arrange for the orchestras and then to compose for them. They will compose much better for the orchestras if they gain the experience of arranging for them. It will not do any harm to anyone if he spends some time in this arranging work even if he does not

[5] *All-Night Vigil.*

become a creative genius. It will make him a very good musician, if nothing else.

It is a significant fact in musical history that those men who have succeeded most deeply and brilliantly as practical musicians, men such as Bach, Handel, Haydn, Mozart, Beethoven, Dvořák, Strauss, Elgar, and many others, have most of them had great experience in playing in the orchestra or in arranging for or controlling small orchestral groups. If we compare with these real practical musicians such other types of genius as César Franck, Brahms, and Delius, who did not have this practical experience in the same degree, either in the orchestra or in spending time in arranging for or conducting small orchestral groups, we see that the second type does not ever, or at least as easily, master orchestral technique as does the first.

If Australia wants to produce a race of composers able to write really practical music as well as great music, and able to take their part in the musical life of the community as well as to live the life of isolated grandeur apart from it, let those responsible for music in Australian communities encourage local composers of all kinds, ages, experience and qualities to throw their talents into practical contact with whatever orchestras exist locally, and into the work of arranging for and composing for such local bodies.

24   *The Gregarious Art of Music*
(1927)

Australia Needs the Get-Together Spirit

Editor's Note: In the course of this article Mr. Grainger lays emphasis on the fact that the more gregarious the musical disposition of musical workers—the less esteem of themselves as soloists and the more regard they possess for music in ensemble—the greater the interest of the community is likely to become in their art, in the long run. He devotes special attention to the possibilities when two or more pianists get together, and walks into the people who stiltedly declare themselves against transcriptions and arrangements. Incidental to that, it may be mentioned that the paraphrasing of music has been much practised in the best circles—by Bach, Brahms, Schumann, and Handel as well as by Liszt, Tchaikovsky, Strauss, Saint-Saëns, Gounod, and Berlioz, and a whole host of them.

A large amount of the best music we have in the world does not sound much better when twenty Kreislers[1] play it than when twenty ordinary people play it. Why, then, should so many people who do not possess extraordinary musical gifts commit themselves to a life of inevitable disappointment by trying to become Kreislers rather than devote themselves to music which is much better suited to them? There is far too much solo playing; far too little playing in association with one another.

Everywhere I go in Australia, for instance, there are very many excellent pianists from the point of view that they are not good enough to fascinate audiences but quite good enough to give delightfully artistic performances with others. Yet they go on trying to fascinate with a zealous determination which would achieve much more for their own and the community's musical culture were it diverted to the purpose of two-piano playing.

The main thing, after all, is to get a knowledge of the great works. It does not make a bit of difference if one plays them on a church organ or on a mouth organ so long as one gets the knowledge.

Source: *Australian Musical News*, 16/9 (Apr. 1927), 13–15.

[1] Fritz Kreisler (1875–1962), Austrian-born American violinist and composer.

When Brahms wanted to hear a new symphony of his own composition he did not call together a whole orchestra there and then. He
arranged it for two pianos and played it with Clara Schumann. Ravel
and others willingly spend their time arranging works for two pianos.
Balakirev was willing to arrange some of his own works for two instruments. Grieg did so, too.[2] If those men have been willing to make
arrangements of their own compositions in this manner, and not
only the compositions of others, why should the smaller flight, who
really hardly know anything about anything at all, make such an
uproar against arrangements and transcriptions? They merely doom
themselves to the night of ignorance instead of joying in comparative knowledge. When we have become familiar with the great works
of all times and countries through the medium of arrangements and
transcriptions we will find ourselves the more ready for the reception
of those works in their original scoring. What we really have to think
about is the interest of the works themselves, and not the quality of the
sound.

Bach as an Arranger

Now Bach, for instance, wrote certain chorale preludes in four or five different ways, for manuals, with pedals, and without pedals. In the case of
some of the cantatas he provided alternatives in a similar fashion. He also
arranged works for either violins or pianos—and yet, what could be more
unlike than the tone quality of the piano and the violin?

Sometimes, in fact, we find that a work sounds much better in an
arrangement than in its original form. Very often a composer is driven
into making use of a certain instrumental medium for practical reasons.
He soars out of the medium, and sometimes in his imagination conceives
a whole group of sounds of which that particular medium is really
incapable.

Busoni once very cleverly said: 'All composition is always transcription.'[3] That is fundamentally true.

So much for transcriptions. That is one side of it. The other side is that
in Australia the musical sense is languishing in all the large communities
because people will not get together and make music. What they are

---

[2] See Essay 25.
[3] Grainger may be thinking of the passage in Busoni's famous essay of 1907, *Sketch for a New
Esthetic of Music* (New York: Dover, 1962), 85.

waiting for, I don't know. If we could wake up the dormant spirit of music in Australia and elsewhere, and get a lot of the people to throw their petty jealousies and ambitions and prejudices aside in order to cooperate with one another and exchange ideas—even though some of them got down to hitting each other in the course of it—an enormous musical efflorescence would result.

Music can only progress through people making music, and the extent to which music is made in a community depends very much on the musicians and those who are inclined to be musical forgoing their miserable little frictions and their miserable little spites.

Getting Together

The thing is to get together. I do not hear half the music that I want to hear in my life. I am always eager for more music, and I know where to go for my musical experiences and pleasures; where I go is to my fellow musicians. If we want to exalt ourselves to the heights, we will not do it by withdrawing ourselves from our fellows or from those we are too apt to look upon as our inferiors. We should all be united for the purpose of considering the greatest musical thoughts of the greatest men of the past and the present.

Solo playing is all very well, but we must remember that a large part of solo music is only a reflection of forms of music that are more polyphonic. Music as we of the European races know it is the music of polyphony such as was evolved in the Middle Ages through the singing and playing together of many parts. We cannot get away from that. Nor can composers throw all that aside and write purely soloistically. They reflect what was arrived at through the playing together of people who were devoted to music for its own sake.

If we want to go to the wellsprings of music we must go back to ensemble playing and singing, whether it is by two people or by two hundred. Music is not an art of isolation. It is an art of cooperation. I do not mean to exalt music over the other arts when I say that it is more largely than they are an art of love. It even makes us love our fellow musicians, for whom we may cherish no great love at other moments; for in playing one sound yourself and hearing alongside it another sound of a different quality, thus generating a beautiful harmony or a difficult discord, is to love that person at that moment. At least, it is so with every true musician.

Cross Sounds—not Swords!

One loves oneself and one loves his fellow. I think that is the true definition of what a true musician experiences in ensemble playing. If we do not indulge in that pleasure, and cross sounds, as it were, with our neighbours, we remain ignorant of the chief delight of music and the chief origin of music.

Let us take the practical commercial side. Let us say that there is some little music teacher, pianist or violinist, living in a community. She has pupils and her friends and their friends who support her, but she has not got a wide public. But a group of such musicians working together, and each able to call on pupils, friends and supporters will collectively draw some kind of a public vastly superior to what any one of them alone will draw. What is needed is that they shall be sensible enough to play for the glory of the music, and present the works in an adequate manner. They will get their public if they do that.

Treat the Music Adequately

This problem of presenting the works adequately is not great. It is very largely a problem of choosing the best works and bringing the musicians together in such a way as to prevent their quarrelling and drifting apart. I am speaking of normal, average musicians. Let them band themselves to do the best programmes within their powers, not losing sight of the attractiveness of the music, and its value as typifying different periods and different nationalities, and further evince a full interest in the creative musical life of their own country, for this I feel is most important. They will, I am sure, find steadily growing audiences. I do not mean enormous audiences, but audiences well worth their while troubling about in the preparation of good music over and above the sheer joy of the thing. If they have the courage and the patience they will make a little financial profit in more ways than the direct one, for the more the interest in music among those who live around one, naturally the greater will be the number of those who will wish to study.

When we examine such affairs as the Bach Festival which is given at the town of Bethlehem, in Pennsylvania,[4] or the Passion Play at Oberammergau, which do we find?—an insignificant group of insignificant people in the sense of having no special talent band themselves

---

[4] Inaugurated in 1888, with the American première of the *St John Passion*.

together to do a special kind of work because of some religious belief or some artistic belief. It is because they are able to immerse themselves in some great feeling or movement like those I have mentioned that they interest not only themselves but the whole community about them, and eventually exert an influence far beyond their own borders. That is so where there is a great devotion to religion in a community. Are we musicians going to say that there is less devotion to music? If that is what we think of it, the best thing to do is to give up music altogether.

I am not saying that you can make people musical who are not musical. What I am saying is that all those elements which are musical should be sufficiently musical to come together, sink their suburbanite or hamlet-bred pettinesses and jealousies, and so on, and show practical common-sense about music. If they cannot make their ensembles in a big hall let them do so in a small hall or a house.

25

Music for Ensemble Players

(1927)

Grainger Prepares an Enticing List

Editor's Note: If the greatest instrumentalists the world has known, men such
as Liszt, Kreisler, Busoni, Rubinstein, Pablo Casals, or Paderewski, have
chosen to play in ensembles, why should the lesser lights of music disdain to
do so? This is the pointed query put by Mr. Percy Grainger in concluding his
valuable series of articles in the *Australian Musical News*, which should be
taken to heart by every musician on this continent. Many times one has heard
from pianists that there are not enough works for a combination of forces
at their instrument. Avoiding the ordinary list, adopted by our too-few
two-piano artists, Mr. Grainger presents them with another that will open
their eyes.

It is all very well to suggest that such people as two pianists should get
together for the purpose of making music. I fancy I can hear some saying,
but how are we to get the two pianos? They are costly instruments, and it
would not always be convenient to pack two of them into one room of the
usual villa or bungalow. This, however, is essential, that musical people
should unite to make music, singers with instrumentalists, instrumentalists with each other, and if it so happens that two pianos cannot be
brought together, or there are other difficulties, it may be practicable for
one of the two pianists to utilise a harmonium. A large quantity of very
beautiful music is arranged for harmonium and piano together.

When we come to music for string ensembles, the tendency is to stick
to the conventional quartet, although there is so much music for other
string combinations in existence. Take Bach's 'Brandenburg' Concertos,
finding employment for three violins, three violas, three 'cellos and
one bass. There are heaps of works by Tchaikovsky, and there are things
like the *Water Music* of Handel, which can be done in their original combination and are thus possible in every comparatively small community.
That brings me to the question why everyone wants to play the violin,
and despises the possibilities of its kindred instruments. Why, I heard

Source: *Australian Musical News*, 16/10 (May 1927), 9.

Kreisler a few years ago playing a viola part in association with Efrem Zimbalist[1] as the violinist. The harmonium is easy for the pianist to learn, but the query I am confronted with is, how many of the pianists would be willing to relegate themselves to what they seem to consider the minor role of harmonium player? Those who think in this way must be placated by being given an opportunity to play the piano on another occasion.

Great Ensemble Players

Players who spend a good deal of their time in ensemble work would soon find that they would become the better soloists. Nearly all the great soloists, such as Sarasate, Paganini, Rubinstein, Liszt, Paderewski, Kreisler, Casals, Ysaÿe, Busoni, and the conductor Koussevitsky have all been players who devoted a lot of time to ensemble art, or who have expressed themselves as conductors or composers as well as in their virtuoso capacity. In fact, when we come to compile a list of the soloists who have become great and popular, we find few who have not enjoyed and profited by the experience of ensemble playing. Therefore, I can see no reason why lesser men who possess a smaller value for mankind, and are less international, should avoid such work. In other words, the only road to music is through music, all of it and in every way possible. If a man wishes to make a business success he needs to have a lot of capital. If a man wishes to make a musical success, he also needs all the musical capital that he can lay his hands on. He must be like the business man who does not say, 'I want all gold', or 'I want all silver', but knows that all money is capital to him.

Lots of musicians fail to recognise that all music is really capital, on which they can found their musical fortunes. The man who says that he will not be willing to play in a picture orchestra[2] or a jazz orchestra because he will be in danger of undermining his musicality is a musical fool. The one great factor behind all music is that all of it is closely related, and as Rudyard Kipling says, 'What he will learn with the black and the brown will help him with the white.'[3]

Perhaps it will help to a better realisation of the great possibilities in ensemble playing if I give a list of some of the pieces which can be

---

[1] (1889–1985), Russian-born American violinist and composer.
[2] Cinema orchestra.
[3] Apparently a misquotation from 'The Ladies', in *The Seven Seas* (1896).

undertaken by various instrumental combinations. This list comprises really just a moiety of what can be done, and yet, what an inspiring one it is:

Duets at One Piano (Four Hands)

*Grieg: *Four Norwegian Dances* (Peters Ed.).
*Roger Quilter: *English Dances* (Boosey and Co.).
Gabriel Fauré: *Pavane* (Hamelle).
Stravinsky: *Petrouchka* (Edition Russe).
Stravinsky: *Le sacre du printemps* (Edition Russe).
Delius: *North Country Sketches* (Augener).
Delius: *Brigg Fair* (Universal Ed.).
*Schumann: *Studies for Pedal-piano.* (The second player plays the pedal part one octave lower than printed.)
Bach: Any organ works. (The second player plays the pedal part one octave lower than printed.)
Balakirev: *Thamar*[4] (Russian Music Agency).
Grieg: *Symphonic Dances* (Peters Ed.).
Wagner: *Siegfried Idyll*, 'Good Friday Music', 'Kaisermarsch', *Meistersinger* Overture, *Tristan* Overture, and many other arrangements (B. Schott Söhne, Peters Ed., etc.).

Six Hands at One Piano

*Grainger: *Zanzibar Boat-song*[5] (Schott and Co. Ltd., London).
*Brahms: *Handel Variations* (Lengnick).

Two Pianos (Four Hands)

César Franck: Three Chorales for organ (Durand).
*Grieg: *Romance* (Peters Ed.).
J. A. Carpenter: *Concertino* for piano and orchestra, arr. for two pianos (G. Schirmer, New York).
Cyril Scott: *Three Symphonic Dances* (B. Schott, Mayence).
Delius: *Dance Rhapsody* (Universal Ed.).
Delius: *The Song of the High Hills* (Universal Ed.).
Gabriel Fauré: Suite *'Pelléas et Mélisande'* (Haraucourt).
G. Fauré: First Quartet for piano and strings, Op. 15, arr. for two pianos (Hamelle).

---

[4] *Tamara*, symphonic poem (1867–82).   [5] 1902, pub. 1923.

Grainger: *Hill Songs I* and *II*. (G. Schirmer).
*Grainger: *Children's March* (G. Schirmer).
Grainger: *Suite 'In a Nutshell'* (G. Schirmer).
Debussy: 'Nuages', 'Fêtes', 'Sirènes'[6] (Durand).
Debussy: *L'Après-midi d'un faune* (Durand).
Richard Strauss: *Sinfonia domestica* (Universal Ed.).
R. Strauss: *Ein Heldenleben* (Universal Ed.).
Scriabin: *Le Poème de l'ecstase*.
Grainger: Bach Fugues for piano ensemble (G. Schirmer).

Six Hands at Two Pianos

*Grainger: *English Dance* (Schott and Co., London).
Grainger: *The Warriors* (Schott and Co., London).
Grainger: *Green Bushes* (Schott and Co., London).

Eight Hands at Two Pianos

Balakirev: *Thamar* (arranged by composer) (Jurgenson).
Bach: Many excellent arrangements of many organ works in several editions.

* Means originally composed for that medium.

6 *Nocturnes* (1897–9).

26

Impressions of Art in Europe

(1929)

I—Finland (February 1929)

Editor's Note: Percy Grainger at the present time is travelling in Europe, and during the course of his travels, his active and observant brain is receiving and recording impressions more or less associated with music, and some of these impressions are being set down in the form of articles which will be printed from time to time in the *Musical Courier*. The first of these follows herewith.

The first time I met Grieg (at Lady Speyer's in London, in 1906)[1] a characteristic episode occurred. At dinner, during a lull in the general conversation, a famous singing teacher, seated near Grieg, was heard remarking to his neighbor: 'After all, art is technic.' And the next moment Grieg was heard saying to the singing teacher and to the world at large: 'Art is not technic.' Grieg did not break the ensuing silence by adding what art was. But it may be guessed that he would have been more likely to have approved of the following statement: 'Art is the development and expression of selfhood.'

Certainly it may be observed every day that the artistically less successful students and artists are those who look upon art as mainly a matter of skill—something to be learned from without, something to be 'picked up' from others, like a game or a language—while the great and everlasting artists are those who, ignoring existing conventions and established skills to a large extent, dip deep into their own selfhood and bring to the surface images of their own selves, their own race, their own land, their own time, their own religions and political beliefs. The great artists are those who become universal by way of going from the particular to the general, not vice versa. And when even so avowedly artistically cosmopolitan a people as the Jews beget a great composer (such as Ernest Bloch),[2] he also is a racialist; in other words, an exponent of selfhood.

Source: *Musical Courier*, 98/22 (1 June 1929), 8; 98/25 (22 June 1929), 6; 99/1 (6 July 1929), 8; 99/13 (28 Sept. 1929), 8, 31; 99/17 (26 Oct. 1929), 10, 12.

[1] 15 May 1906. Lady Leonora Speyer and her husband, Sir Edgar Speyer (1862–1932), were leading British arts patrons.

[2] (1880–1959), Swiss-born American composer.

Viewed from this standpoint of 'selfhood', Finland is a most instructive land for any thoughtful artist to visit. Arriving at Helsingfors[3] by train he lands in a railroad station that is a glorious example of typically Finnish architecture, heroic in mood. Going into the throng-filled eating-hall of this station he is confronted by an apotheosis of Finnish scenery in the shape of an oil painting, by one of Finland's finest painters, that covers half a gigantic wall—a fiercely thriving, bristling fir tree crowning a crag in the foreground, and behind, a sunny joyance of glistening lakes and wooded islands, the whole palpitating vision aglow with balmy pinks and juicy greens. This wall decoration may be taken as a hint of what will be found to be typical of Finland and Finnish art throughout—a glorification of rude, natural strength, a noble pride in national selfhood, a fondness for all that is primitive and close-at-hand, a celebration of all that is humble and lowly, a veneration for such survivals as the 'Kalevala'[4] and kindred folk arts. Do not some of the orchestral works of Sibelius seem like great chunks of his native land transformed into tones, at times grim as the great glaciers and granite masses that molded, ages ago, the geography of his land, at other times a-shimmer like light on summer lakes, or surging and swirling like myriad streams and currents at snow-melting time? There are passages in his music that sound to me like musical translations of conversations between a rock and a tree, or the self-revelation of other equally forest-like, non-human things.

A kindred racial, national and local consciousness pervades most of the artistic achievements of this vital land. What the sculptor Eino Räsänen[5] carves so lovingly in wood is not a cosmopolitanized abstraction of the female form in general; it is a statement of the quite specifically Finnish female figure in particular. When the genius-painter Gallén-Kallela[6] depicts a 'Pock-marked youth from Savolaks' he gives us a summing-up of all that is most concentratedly Finnish in its kindly fierceness, its friendly uncouthness. Roaming through the ethnological rooms of the recently erected and excellently conceived National Museum in Helsingfors we see the folk dresses, embroideries, home utensils and farming gear not merely of the Finnish countrysides throughout several centuries, but, furthermore, similar exhibits from the various branches of the Finnish-Ugrish-speaking communities that are dotted around

---

[3] Helsinki (in Swedish).
[4] Finnish national epic (pub. 1835, 1849), compiled from oral sources by the philologist Elias Lönnrot.　　[5] 1902–70.
[6] Akseli Gallén-Kallela (1865–1931), Finnish artist.

Europe, Russia and Siberia from the arctic tundra to the sun-drenched plains of Hungary. The racial self-awareness that is so characteristically Finnish has welded together these heterogeneous relics of isolated tribes into a total showing that is as impressive to the mind as it is ravishing to the eye.

On picking up a daily Helsingfors paper one reads that Selim Palmgren's[7] opera, *Daniel Hjort* (the tale of a national hero),[8] is soon to be given, and that there are Finnish operas and Finnish theatres, as well as Swedish operas and Swedish theatres, all of them giving continuous performances, independent of each other, on repertory system lines.

Among the concert announcements, I enjoyed seeing posters of two merry-looking youths, debonair in shirtsleeves and boldly-patterned sweaters, who were scheduled to give a duet-recital on the saw and the Kantele (a national instrument of the zither type), showing that the austerity of much of Finland's artistic outlook does not preclude activity along popular and folkish lines. Nor, of course, in this field does American music need to drop a diminished head. Everywhere one goes in these Northern countries, on boats or on trains, passengers produce portable gramophones and the well-known strains of American jazz (or imitations of it) float forth. Even such tunes as Santa Lucia[9] are heard now only in their Americanized forms, it would seem. Nor is this conquest by American popular music limited to 'low-brow' circles.

A serious, well-informed young Russian composer questioned me searchingly anent jazz orchestrations, craving to know by what means Paul Whiteman[10] and others have evolved and perfected orchestral tints and blends of a delicacy and originality unknown in Europe. It seems evident to me that this world-wide victory of American jazz is thoroughly deserved esthetically. It is the result of a dove-tailing co-operation of talents, a concentrated passion of sheer hard work and experimentation, heretofore and elsewhere unknown in the domains of popular music. Furthermore, the subtle artistic results obtained by these means have been exploited and internationalized by publishers and touring jazz orchestras with typical American thoroughness and organization. I was told that Paul Whiteman's orchestra is expected in Finland soon; but there

---

[7] (1878–1951), Finnish composer, pianist, and conductor, best known for his piano pieces. Grainger had corresponded with him several times in the early 1920s.

[8] (1910, rev. 1938), three-act opera based on events in 16th-cent. Finland.

[9] Traditional Neapolitan air.

[10] (1890–1967), American bandleader, whose orchestra popularized a style of 'symphonic jazz' during the 1920s.

was no sign in the offing of any similar visit from any representative of America's loftiest musical realms, such as John Alden Carpenter, Leo Sowerby,[11] Howard Hanson,[12] Rubin Goldmark, etc. Why do such representative American composers not visit Finland and Scandinavia as Sibelius, Palmgren and Sandby have visited America? In my opinion, they, no less than Paul Whiteman, would find it worth their while. Such artistically vital countries are worth any great artist's while to visit. When composers of 'classical' American music do as much abroad for their own type of music as the jazz musicians have done for theirs in most parts of the world, we may expect to see the more involved forms of American music take a rightful place in the world's appreciation and admiration.

In connection with the problems of modern 'high-brow' music it is interesting to learn that the great creative artists of Finland (including, of course, its composers) all receive national life-long stipendiums which enable them to woo the muse of their chosen art free from the disastrous distractions of commercial considerations. This is in line with the procedure in the Scandinavian lands where such creative artists as Grieg, Ibsen, Bjørnson[13] in Norway, Herman Sandby, Evald Tang Kristensen[14] in Denmark, have long received national life-long support as a matter of course.

One cannot refrain from speculating upon the more favorable lot of creative artists in these small countries as compared with the less satisfactory conditions under which their brothers-in-art struggle in larger countries such as England, America and Germany. The favorable artistic conditions in Finland are certainly not due to the size or prosperity of the population. The total population of Finland is not as large as that of Chicago. There are few really rich people in Finland, and there is no doubt that the middle and intellectual classes have suffered much, in a material way, from the fall in value of the Finnish mark. The working classes, in town and country, though seldom really destitute, are undeniably poor to a degree that would seem alarming and terrible in Australia or America. I went into the third-class eating-hall of the railroad station one day to study faces and conditions. Almost every towering figure was gaunt; almost every face seared with hardship, privation and cruel

---

[11] (1895–1968), American conductor and composer in a wide variety of styles.

[12] (1896–1981), American conductor, teacher, and composer, strongly influenced by Grieg and Sibelius.

[13] Bjørnstjerne Bjørnson (1832–1916), the Norwegian novelist, poet, and dramatist.

[14] (1843–1929), Danish folklorist responsible for the major collection of Jutish songs, tales, and proverbs, with whom Grainger collaborated on several collecting trips during the 1920s.

weather, though seldom marked by worry or unhappiness; of the hundreds that streamed through the eating-hall each hour not more than maybe one in twenty seemed to have means or time for more than a cup of coffee. How can it be, one asks oneself, that this small, poor population can afford to spend national and personal moneys for the support of its creative artists to an extent utterly unknown and undreamed-of in larger countries? I think it is because the Finns (in common with all the Scandinavian peoples) regard the arts and the sciences as the most honorable, noble and resplendent forms of national accomplishment. Whereas in lands such as England, America and Australia art is regarded more as a polite accomplishment, more as a luxury and recreation, more as a matter of personal fancy and taste, in Finland and Scandinavia the creative side of art is conceived to be a matter of national and racial pride and concern. There is much to be said, I am sure, for both attitudes. But there can be no doubt but that the national and racial attitude towards art makes for a more vital and human solidarity between the genius and the layman and vastly increases the influence and comfort-giving powers of art as regards the whole national population.

Does the fault, if any, lie with the Anglo-Saxon creative artist, I ask myself? Is nation-wide popularity unattainable by the deeper-souled types of English-speaking geniuses because they lack, in their work, the national feeling, the national self-awareness possessed by Finnish and Scandinavian artists? These questions, I feel sure, must be answered in the negative. I am convinced that American poets such as Walt Whitman (no genius that ever lived was more national, in the noblest sense, than Whitman), Edgar Lee Masters and Vachel Lindsay;[15] American composers such as MacDowell, Carpenter, Howard Brockway, Rubin Goldmark and Nathaniel Dett typify and celebrate their land and people as loyally and genuinely as any artists ever have or could. The less satisfactory artistic conditions (less satisfactory to the public at large no less than to the creative artists) that obtain in English-speaking countries are not, I feel sure, due to any deficiency in the artists themselves, but merely to the lack of a really wide-flung national response to their achievements.

The Finnish poet Bertel Gripenberg[16] has recently translated Edgar Lee Masters' *Spoon River Anthology* into Swedish, and this translation (highly excellent, by the way, in its spiritual insight and literal faithfulness) seems already better known in Finland than is Masters' original in its

[15] (1879–1931), American poet, whose works Grainger collected and frequently quoted.
[16] (1878–1947), Finnish-Swedish writer; a frequent commentator on the difficulties experienced by Finland's Swedish community.

native land. An interesting point in this connection is that the Finnish translator is the recipient of a poet's stipendium, whereas the American creator (as far as I know) enjoys no such support.

The more one considers these national differences the more apparent it is that the Anglo-Saxon layman does not realize that the circle of art is not complete until the action put forth by the creative artists has been supplemented by some reaction to the same on the part of the general public. The average Anglo-Saxon has not yet learned that it is artistic creators (rather than interpreters) that mold the artistic future of any land and that life-long stipendiums granted to a very few quite young composers of inspired genius will accomplish infinitely more for the musical life of the land than will thousands of study-scholarships handed out to mere glib, skill-seeking, shallow-natured instrumental or vocal performers. The average Anglo-Saxon has not yet sensed that successes in the fields of sport, commerce and politics (however excellent in their own very limited way) are, in a national sense, but ephemeral alongside the comparatively everlasting monuments of national greatness raised by creative artists, thinkers and scientists. The causes of this lack of deeper knowledge of human values on the part of the English-speaking public in various lands can, I think, be explained historically without much difficulty; but not with the brevity befitting this article.

It seems to me that those things that are most lacking in English-speaking artistic life (lack of spiritual contact between the creative artists and the general public, lack of organization in the more serious and complex artistic fields, lack of racial and national self-awareness about art) would fairly soon be forthcoming if those of us who love the arts most deeply, in the countries in question, would bend our thoughts together in goal-conscious effort. A visit to so artistically thriving a land as Finland shows how fair can be the fruits of such a high-minded concentration and co-operation.

II—Sweden and Norway (March 1929)

My impressions of art in Sweden and Norway may be summed up in one word: vitality. Not merely that vitality which, father-like, throws out new ideas into the world, but also that more mother-like vitality which watches tenderly and protectingly over young intellectual stars and does not lose interest in them or patience with them until they have matured and exerted their full influence upon mankind.

These Northern peoples are spiritually thrifty (in the true and full sense of the word, linked with the idea of thriving) in that they energetically avoid cultural wastefulness and forgetfulness. We often observe countries, in which the artistic vitality suffices only to produce mere modernism or mere conservatism—that, to my mind, is a partial and ineffectual vitality. In no countries known to me are experimentation and conservatism so perfectly balanced as vital Scandinavia—those lands of normal, natural living; those lands of great uses and few abuses, where the whole population seems instinctively to follow that freedom that Tennyson described as avoiding 'the falsehood of extremes'.[17]

Great contrasts do exist—such as the immense contrast between the ultra-modern iconoclastic anti-authoritative national life of the people and their ultra-polite personal manners, which latter display an old-world courtliness, formality and gracefulness elsewhere extinct in Europe—but these contrasts are made harmonious by the perfect balance existing between them; neither the old-fashioned nor the new-fangled tendencies can become extreme, can enjoy undisputed sway, amongst a race so alert-minded, so individualistic, so quick to resent and combat abuse and injustice.

All the world knows the ability of such wholly or partly Scandinavian heroes as Nansen, Amundsen, Stefansson, Lindbergh, Rasmussen, Sven Hedin,[18] etc., to dare unchartered ways, and art-lovers have been able to measure the force for newness in Scandinavian art since the advent of such path-finding Northern geniuses as Grieg, Ibsen, Strindberg and their worthy successors. The world at large is slightly less conscious of the fact that a number of political experiments, which have since been adopted in many progressive countries, originated in Scandinavia and were first tried out there—such as Votes for Women (Finland), Old Age Pensions and Compulsory National Insurance of Workers (Denmark), Total Prohibition of Alcoholic Beverages (Iceland), and many others.

Least known of all, to those who have neither visited nor studied Scandinavia, is the unobtrusive but deeply-rooted conservatism of these Northern lands—a fierce spirit of cultural self-preservation that sets out to defy the tooth of time ('life's secret, which is vanishment and change',

[17] From the final stanza of 'Of old sat Freedom on the heights' (1842).
[18] Respectively: Fridtjof Nansen (1861–1930), Norwegian Arctic explorer; Roald Amundsen (1872–1928), Norwegian Antarctic explorer; Vilhjalmur Stefansson (1879–1962), Canadian explorer of the Northwest Territories; Charles Lindbergh (1902–74), American aviator; Knud Rasmussen (1879–1933), Danish-Eskimo explorer of Greenland; Sven Hedin (1865–1952), Swedish explorer of central Asia.

sings Edgar Lee Masters) by a support of art and artists (all art is necessarily conservative in a sense; for art is the lasting record of the fleeting moment), a passion for family and personal records (the sagas of the past; exhaustive publications of letters and memoirs in our day), a profusion of large and small museums in towns and villages, a propaganda work for old-time dialects (the Peasant-Language and Local Speech movements in Norway, Jutland, the Faeroes, etc.), a perpetuation of folk arts, folk customs and folk costumes—all of these movements unique in their extent and success.

A great work in preserving old-time loveliness is done by the Domestic Crafts Associations ('Hemslöjd' and 'Husflid') organizations that encourage and enable country-side craftsmen to carry on the local traditional arts of weaving, embroidery, wood-carving, furniture-making, metal working, etc., by displaying and selling their art products in the great cities. From the stores of these organizations, whose showrooms are as beauteous as the fairy castles of our dreams, a tradition of old-time grandeur and comeliness flows out to a thousand homes, keeping country and town, past and present, sweetly in touch along businesslike, practical lines.

While Sweden and Norway are alike in their general vitality, their ways seem to part in that the Swedish spirit runs mainly to culture of all kinds, while the Norwegian spirit runs strongly to enthusiasm. The Swede is Europe's natural aristocrat. All classes of the population are more or less aristocratic-looking, aristocratic-mannered. The national taste instinctively demands buildings, museums, concert halls, stores, art, furniture, clothes, customs that are more lordly, grand, solid, tasteful and exquisite than those elsewhere. (It was instructive to note how tawdry, gaudy and cheap some of the best modern French furniture, pottery and glassware looked after seeing the modern Swedish equivalents—the distinctive 'Swedish Tin' products, for instance.)

The main trend of Swedish thought is towards nobility, gracefulness, harmoniousness and dignity. It is, therefore, not surprising to find the Swedes noticeably lacking in a sense of humor. And I am glad to see how well they get on without it; for I have long considered 'a sense of humor' a very over-rated commodity, having my suspicions that it is, in most cases, naught else but a bad habit, on the part of the lazy, slipshod people, of slavishly 'making the best of' unseemly or disgusting situations and conditions that more properly ought to be humorlessly fought and made an end of.

If a man wants to attain to a high and wide range of culture, I would advise him to live in Stockholm. But if he wants to kindle his mind I would advise him to try Norway. Life there is one unending exhilaration. The natural enthusiasm of the Norwegians is like a foaming mountain torrent, every field of thought and action being attacked with the same burning boyish keenness. As for their delightful delight in the recent wedding of their Crown Prince to the Swedish Princess,[19] it reminded me of that memorable phrase in Gauguin's enthralling record of South Sea Island Life, *Noa Noa*: 'It was the homage of a phrenetic populace'.[20]

Full artistic vitality presupposes, it seems to me, another perfect balance—that between the native and the foreign in art. Also this balance is most satisfactorily present throughout all Scandinavia.

During my few days spent in Stockholm, foreign art was richly represented by O'Neill's play, *Strange Interlude*;[21] Aeschylus's *Agamemnon*; exhibitions of Finnish and Norwegian paintings and sculpture; of modern French furniture, pottery and glassware; displays of gorgeous Polish weavings; German, Austrian, French and Italian operas, and an excellent rendition of the English composer York Bowen's[22] melodious and effective Second Piano Concerto by Anita Harrison (a skilful English pianist living in Stockholm), and the Stockholm 'Konsertföreningen' Orchestra under the sympathetic conductorship of Adolf Wiklund[23]—surely a real and copious tribute to cosmopolitanism!

Yet the native arts were equally well represented, patronized and applauded. These included a whole program by the Konsertföreningen (Concert Association), devoted to the orchestral and choral compositions of Hugo Alfvén;[24] *Eric the Fourteenth* and other plays by Strindberg; and an exhibition by the younger Swedish painters (the so-called 'Free Group'), remarkable for the work of one man of strong genius, Bertil Norén,[25] who is able to invest large surfaces covered with sickly-colored gouache, depicting uncomfortable-looking rooms and grim views from attic windows, with that unwithstandable bewitchingness that is the mysterious hallmark of genuine art.

[19] The future Olaf V (1903–91) to Princess Martha of Sweden.
[20] Autobiographical sketch of 1900 by Paul Gauguin (1843–1903), French post-impressionist painter.
[21] Eugene O'Neill (1888–1953), American writer and dramatist, whose *Strange Interlude* was pub. in 1928.
[22] (1884–1961), English pianist and composer.
[23] (1879–1950), Swedish composer, conductor, and pianist.
[24] (1872–1960), Swedish composer and conductor.
[25] (1889–1934), Swedish painter, whose works tended towards the grotesque.

It was a real privilege to hear a whole evening of Hugo Alfvén's manly music, conducted by himself with such freshness and grip. His third symphony (E major)[26] deserves to be as popular abroad as it already is in Sweden, for it rushes along with a captivative and contagious eagerness in the quick sections which enclose one of the most delicious slow movements ever penned—rapturous in mood, rich in melody, glowing in orchestration, and abounding in ecstatic twists of polyphonic harmony that unwind themselves and drift away like silver wreaths of smoke.

Alfvén's setting, for tenor solo, male chorus and orchestra, of Geijer's[27] noble poem, *Manhem* (a paean in praise of the Nordic race and its home-lands),[28] well matched the masculine dignity and dark heroicness of the text, unfolding some marrow-stirring tone-blends of brass and choir.

It was an evening of festive music, festively rendered and festively responded to. And no wonder! For Alfvén is a type of creative musician— keen, bold, joyous, emotional, skilful, experienced—of which any country might rightly be proud.

The extent to which the public in Scandinavia exults over and enjoys its native creative geniuses, while they are still alive, is in pleasing contrast to what happens in many other lands. A stranger to the art of music arriving in some great city in Great Britain, America or Australia, observing that the bulk of serious music scheduled for performance is the product of foreigners, most of them long dead, might be justified in thinking of the art of music as having its roots in other times and places (in spite of the fact—which our stranger would, however, have no means of knowing— that the English-speaking countries produce more original, serious, masterly, influence-exerting creative geniuses than most other countries today).

Arriving in a Scandinavian capital he would get a very different impression; he would think of music as having its roots here and now (as well as elsewhere and elsewhen), for he would notice that some of the greatest drawing-cards, in the musical life of the city, are local, living, native creative artists, to whose music whole programs are devoted.

I arrived in Oslo one day too late to hear the last of several successful, hall-filling performances of David Monrad Johansen's[29] great choral work based on the Völuspa[30] (old mystical poem from the

---

[26] Op. 23 (1905).
[27] Erik Gustaf Geijer (1783–1847), Swedish historian, composer, and poet.
[28] Op. 47 (1928).   [29] (1888–1974), Norwegian composer.
[30] *Voluspaa*, Op. 15 (1923–6), for solo voices, chorus, and orchestra.

Icelandic 'Edda'[31]), but not too late to sense the artistic sensation it had created.

My three days in Oslo, however, were crowded with other offerings of native art: a whole concert of the Philharmonic Society given over to the orchestral works of Johan Halvorsen,[32] the composer conducting (looking like some great viking chieftain—hairy, burly, great-hearted, his head thrown back, his eyes flashing); a recitation-program by the poet Herman Wildenvey;[33] a farcical play in the peasant language entitled *Friarleik paa Liland* (Wooing-antics at Liland farmstead) at the Norwegian Theatre, acted with sparkling humor and trenchant characterization—always funny, never stupid; and some fragrantly sweet, rural village tunes (*Seks gamle Bygdevisur fraa Lom*)[34] set with unmistakable genius by Sparre Olsen[35] (a new name) and deliciously played by that sterling, high-minded young Norwegian pianist, Mary Barratt-Due.[36]

Not since Grieg have I heard any Norwegian composer display such rich originality as this young man [Olsen]—despite his obvious indebtedness to the harmonic innovations of Cyril Scott and Frederick Delius. But proneness to influence does not preclude originality; in fact, one is almost tempted to say that the greatest originality (such as Wagner's) consists largely in the ability to devour and use all styles, all influences, to one's own ends. In these little settings (which may be used either as songs or as piano pieces) Sparre Olsen has certainly captured the glory and the wistfulness of 'the great open spaces' and matched in his tangy harmonies the meaty concentratedness of the texts, which abound in gems such as this— as tense as any Chinese poem:

> Leirungs-valley is big and wide
> With all its bogs and marshes.
> There I have wandered many a day
> And called to my cows and bull-calves.[37]

---

[31] The Poetic or Elder Edda, compiled *c.*1270, included earlier poems such as 'Völuspa', a history of the Norse gods.

[32] (1864–1935), Norwegian violinist, composer, and conductor at the National Theatre in Oslo during 1899–1929.

[33] (1886–1959), pioneer of a lighter, more witty style of Norwegian verse.

[34] Six Old Village Songs from Lom, Op. 2 (*c.*1928).

[35] (b. 1903), Norwegian violinist and composer. In the 1930s the Graingers holidayed with Olsen, both in Norway and in England.

[36] (d. 1982), piano student of Grainger in his later London years.

[37] Cf. alternative translation in Essay 33.

Johan Halvorsen (best known outside his native country by such early works as his *Entry of the Boyars* March[38]) is that enviable type of composer that deepens and mellows as he ages. Always musical to the core, always a skilful orchestrator, his inspiration has steadily grown in majesty and subtlety, so that now, in his early sixties, he is writing his most significant works. His third symphony, completed only a few months ago, is a stately and masterly composition, based on warrior-like themes of much pith and character—much of it clanging and glistening like steel armor. Other passages, woven in clinging, vibrating sonorities, glow with a balmy, kindly warmth like Northern summer sun on purple heather. A manly and tender heart beats through the whole work. An earlier number of his, given on the same program, the *Fossegrimen* (The Goblin of the Torrent) *Suite*[39] (based on Hardanger-fiddle[40] dance tunes) is a triumph of compositional virtuosity. It is a proof of the sturdy originality possessed by both Grieg and Halvorsen that each has produced such utterly different results in dealing with the selfsame peasant-dance material. Halvorsen's *Fossegrimen Suite* (like the final march from Ippolitov-Ivanov's *Caucasian Sketches* and Rimsky-Korsakov's *Spanish Caprice*) belongs to that sparkling, bloodwarming type of athletic music that pleases audiences in all countries. It should become a household word on American orchestral programs.

I had long wanted to hear Herman Wildenvey recite his poems. It is small wonder that he is Norway's best-beloved living poet, for he—a sort of twentieth-century Robert Burns—combines a profusion of artistic and personal attributes that would ensure his popularity in any land; creative originality, directness and facility of expression, a light but warm eroticism, an out-door freshness of mood, a caressing voice, a sturdy frame, an Apollo-like beauty of face—the true poet-face, Greek-like of feature, but truly Nordic in its dreamy, deepset grey-blue eyes.

Here is a personality shaped by nature and experience to charm audiences as a lecturer no less than as a reader of his poems, for his command of English and several other languages is admirable and his general information on a host of subjects amazing in its range and exactness. This moodful, emotional poet discloses, on examination, a cosmopolitan knowledge of men and lands, an insight into things spiritual and practical,

---

[38] Op. 17 (1895).   [39] Op. 21.
[40] Norwegian national instrument; a four-stringed fiddle with between two and five resonating strings.

a memory for details and events that prime ministers and men-of-affairs ought to possess—but don't, as a rule.

The son of a farmer near Drammen, in south-eastern Norway, he brings to his art those robust, generous and warm-hearted attributes that are so often characteristic of the country-born artist. His verse bears out the accidental symbolism of his name (Wil-den-vej = I choose this path), for it is wilful, informal, natural, colloquial.

The following poem, addressed to the Universal Spirit of Life, is typical of the philosophical, cosmic side of his muse:

LIKE ONE COMING FROM A BANQUET[41]

Like one coming from a banquet,
—Not intoxicated by feasting,
But who, as he walks homewards, looks around
For a guest,
The guest of honor,
Who never came to the banquet—
 Thus I now meet many a morning.
 Life itself was the banquet,
 And the guest of honor
 That never arrived—it was *You.*

Like one bereft and defrauded,
—Not of anything he owns,
But of something he secretly yearns for;
A rare treasure
That sank to hidden depths
He cannot envision or reach—
 Thus I now meet my lonely nights.
 In darkness I dive
 For pearls and gems.
 And *You* were the treasure that sank.

Like one that has emptied his glass,
—Not craving the poison it held,
Yet toying with the death that lay in the dregs
 of the poisoned cup;
Living on out of sheer spite
In shifting sunshine and storm,
Undaunted and undiminished—

---

[41] An Eng. trans. of this poem by Joseph Auslander is included in Wildenvey's *Owls to Athens: A Book of Poems* (New York: Dodd, Mead & Co., 1935), 83–4. It is there entitled 'As One that Comes from a Feast'.

Thus I now go my way and avoid meeting you.
I mock at the torments
That come of poison and wine.
For *You* were the poison and the wine.

Like one who is afraid of dying,
—Not for fear of death itself,
But clinging to life in hopes of seeing once more
The seed of eternity
Sprout in the dawn of spring
As a shoot of the tree of resurrection—
Thus I now go my way observing life.
Yet even when fleeing from death
Towards the dawn of spring there is no escape.
For *You* are both life and death!

(Translated from the Norwegian original by
Ella Viola Ström-Grainger[42])

His career has been as romantic as his verse. On his way to America in his seventeenth year he was wrecked on Rockall Island, being one of the few survivors of the *Norge* who, from a lifeboat, saw that ill-fated steamer sink with 800 souls on board.[43] Picked up out of a stormy sea by a Grimsby (England) trawler he proceeded to America, where, after three happy years on farms in Minnesota, he enlisted in the United States Marine Corps, from which body, however, he was soon discharged, in Manila, because of heart trouble. He then worked his way as a sailor from San Francisco to Norway, by way of Central America and the Canaries. Home again in his native land, and fortified with a small sum of money saved in the United States, and with the impress of the New World still fresh upon him, he retired into a lonely valley in Gudbrandsdal in order to work out an urge towards poetry that had stirred within him since his early teens.

Wildenvey must thus be classed (with Frederick Delius, Masefield,[44] Knut Hamsun,[45] etc.), among that ever-growing number of European geniuses whose artistic energy was stimulated, whose artistic style was colored, early in life, by contact with the freshness and hopefulness of the New World. It is easy to guess that much of the unrehearsedness,

[42] (1889–1979), Grainger's Swedish-born wife, whom he had met in 1926 and married in 1928.
[43] The *Norge* sank off Scotland on 28 June 1904, with the loss of 646 lives.
[44] John Masefield (1878–1967), English novelist, dramatist, and, from 1930 until his death, Poet Laureate.
[45] (1859–1952), influential Norwegian novelist, awarded the Nobel Prize in 1920.

directness and colloquialness of his verse is traceable to such an influence. (The liberating, informalizing trend of all the young Anglo-Saxon democracies is making itself increasingly felt in the arts, no less than in economics, all over the world.)

Six months after his retirement to Gudbrandsdal, Wildenvey's first book of verse, *Nyinger* (Bonfires) appeared—young in spirit, but esthetically ripe with that mysterious perfection possible to youthful genius. Almost immediately our poet found himself famous, a national idol.

His subsequent career is an illuminating example of that aforementioned cultural maternalism with which art-loving Scandinavia knows how to watch over the material welfare of its native geniuses—being content to leave the matter of spiritual, artistic and moral welfare in the hands of the geniuses themselves, realizing that what creative artists need from the outer world is unconditional love and support, not criticism and 'competitive selection', if they are to bring their gifts to fairest blossoming.

Wildenvey, like all other originators, has, of course, had his troubles, conflicts and setbacks. Yet he can be in no doubt as to the goodwill of his native country towards him. Some six times he has won different major prizes allotted to poetry in Norway, and on the recent occasion of his fortieth birthday a fund was collected and presented to him by his artistic admirers in order that he might build himself a home to his liking. This intention is now realized in the form of a simple but charmful dwelling in lovely surroundings at Stavern on the shores of the Skagarak—'with skerries before and dwarf-treed brents behind'. His wife, herself a distinguished novelist,[46] fills his life with womanly beauty and womanly wisdom. Such is the fair lot of a great poet in a small land.

Large countries take notice!

III—Delius Reaps his Harvest (August 1929)

'As a man soweth, so shall he reap.' This seems unanswerably true of composers and their careers—especially if we include their posthumous careers. There are people who believe that ambition, influence, intrigue, money and commercial talent play a real part in introducing a serious composer to the ears of the world and in building up his fame. I, for my part, have always held that all a composer needs to do, in order to make

---

[46] Gisken Wildenvey (1895–1985), friend of Ella Grainger.

his music widely known and loved, during or after his life, is to possess a deep and loving and compassionate nature, to be helplessly fond of music, and to compose endlessly and untiringly for his own joy (as Bach did, for instance). The man who writes music merely to please himself may some day find that he has unwittingly pleased thousands of his fellow-men as well—may surprise himself in discovering that he has accidentally proved a mouthpiece for the feelings of countless unknown strangers—whereas the man who is misguided enough to compose in the hope of pleasing others generally ends by pleasing neither them nor himself. It is the old matter of 'to thine own self be true'.

Certainly no one in the world of music has ever been more unbendingly and uncompromisingly true to himself than Frederick Delius. Not on a single point (that I can recall) has he ever turned his pen aside from its inwardly-inspired goal in order to make his music more likeable, more easy to understand or to perform, more appealing to half-musical listeners by non-musical accessories.

Out of a deeply musical, loving and philosophical nature—filled to overflowing with primitive and artificial urges and stocked with a superlative richness of accumulated memories and impressions, musical and otherwise—he has poured forth a prodigious number of musical self-unfoldings that are always lovely, mellow, balanced and soul-touching, always highly and unmistakably personal and individualistic, but seldom or never startling, brilliant, 'contrasty' or 'effective'.

Beginning his creative activities much later than most composers of genius, Delius did not develop his full compositional expressiveness until somewhere around his fortieth year—in this respect over twenty years behind a Bach, a Brahms, or a Cyril Scott. Here, if ever (one might argue), was a composer destined to die before he wormed his way into the public heart—the more so as there was little or nothing in his music to attract the virtuoso conductor or virtuoso performer. In fact, there is nothing much to say in favor of his music except that it is the deepest and loftiest kind of art, voicing a noble and tender soul in accents that appeal irresistibly to other noble and tender souls. And this, it would seem, is enough. There must be many noble and tender souls strewn around the world of music in many lands; otherwise the recent and present success of Delius's music would be hard to explain.

When Delius, a few years ago, around his sixty-first year, was stricken with blindness and partial paralysis, some of his friends feared that this great genius would not live long enough to see his art acclaimed by the public-at-large. But fate has been kinder than we expected. Owing to his wonderful fund of innate bodily and spiritual vitality and owing greatly to the wise ministration of his angelic wife (herself a painter and authoress of rare gifts), Delius has regained much in bodily well-being in the last few years. Though still lacking the boon of sight, though still in the main fettered to his chair by weakness, his mind is vigorous and creative, his moods gay and masterful, his speech argumentative to the point of being delightfully teasing and mischievous.

His mail and his radio bear almost daily witness to the vast and ever-growing vogue of his music in all civilized countries. Splendid recent recordings of several of his finest orchestral and choral works, conducted by Beecham[47] and others, have replaced the less satisfactory records of some years back.

Even the compositional silence, imposed on him by his blindness, has been lifted since the advent in Grez (Delius's blossoming, tree-rich riverside home near Fontainebleau, France) of Eric Fenby,[48] a gifted composer and organist from Yorkshire, England. This young man, aged twenty-three, felt such admiration for and devotion toward the great master that he wrote offering his services as a musical and literary amanuensis for an indefinite period. Since October 1928 Fenby has been installed in the Delius home and has already accomplished wonders. Forgotten sketches have been unearthed among the Delius manuscripts (Delius was too prolific a worker to remember all the works he had drafted) and these, together with other larger or smaller unfinished works, have been completed by Fenby from Delius's dictation. Few musicians could undertake such exacting tasks, but Fenby has carried them through with sensitive intuitiveness and untiring conscientiousness. Thus several important new works have been added to the already prodigious list of Delius's compositions—for Delius is one of the most prolific artists of all time.

These works, finished or nearing completion under Fenby's amanuensis-ship during the last year, include a choral and orchestral suite based on the music to Flecker's *Hassan*,[49] a major orchestral work (the title not yet decided upon),[50] *Cynara* (words by Dowson)[51] for baritone solo and orchestra,[52] *A Late Lark*,[53] and several minor items.

---

[47] Sir Thomas Beecham (1879–1961), English conductor and entrepreneur.
[48] (1906–97). Fenby's recollections of the Graingers' visit of Aug. 1929 are found in *Delius as I Knew Him* (London: G. Bell, 1936), 75–9.
[49] Delius had completed the incidental music to J. E. Flecker's play in 1923, with some assistance from Grainger.
[50] Perhaps *A Song of Summer* (1929–30).
[51] Ernest Dowson (1867–1900), a decadent poet of the 1890s.
[52] Originally started in 1907; premièred in London on 18 Oct. 1929.
[53] For voice and orchestra (1925).

In addition to these compositional activities Delius has recently dic-
tated to his wife and to Fenby several articles, on 'Romanticism in Music',
and kindred subjects, that have appeared in magazines in various
European countries.

The growing recognition of Delius's genius in his native England found
official expression in the 1929 New Year's Honors List, when he was
made a 'Companion of Honor'.

Probably no one has so successfully championed the Delius cause
as Sir Thomas Beecham. Certainly no other conductor has so divined
the very soul of this music, has so uncannily realized every intention
of every phase of it. 'There is but one Delius, and Beecham is his
prophet.'

Therefore, the Delius Festival, to take place in London this fall,
organized and conducted by Sir Thomas Beecham, bids fair to prove the
crowning event of Delius's public career. Beginning on October 12 and
ending on November 1, it comprises four orchestral and choral concerts
at the Queen's Hall and at Central Hall, Westminster, and two chamber
concerts at the Aeolian Hall. The finest London orchestras and chamber
bodies will play and the choirs participating will be The Philharmonic
Choir, The British Broadcasting Company Choir and The London Select
Choir. Within the generous scope of this scheme will be included all the
above-mentioned recently completed works as well as such established
masterpieces as *The Mass of Life* (complete), parts of *A Village Romeo
and Juliet*, *Appalachia*, *Sea Drift*, *North Country Sketches*, *Eventyr*, the
first violin sonata, the cello sonata, *Dance Rhapsody* No. 2, *Song Before
Sunrise*.[54]

But what will make this festival historical and romantic will be the
presence of the composer himself at the rehearsals and concerts. Can
one imagine a more thrilling event than the public reappearance, after
years of seclusion, of this blind frail genius (so beautiful in his concentrated spiritual vitality) on the occasion of a great festival devoted exclusively to his works and conducted by the man who is his most inspired
interpreter, as well as his greatest artistic benefactor—at a moment, too,
when the broad public has at last wakened up to the full magnitude of
Delius's genius?

We who are his friends can only give thanks (most of which must go to
Jelka Delius, his wife) that our hero is still young and sprightly enough
in spirit and strong enough in constitution (despite his sixty-seven years

---

[54] For details of the programmes of the 1929 Delius Festival, see Thomas Beecham, *Frederick
Delius* (London: Hutchinson, 1959), 201–4.

and his misfortunes in health) to be able to enjoy this glorious esthetic festivity to the full.

IV—Music in England (March–September 1929)

It is sometimes given to a certain country to forge ahead of others in the matter of musical creation for a while. That was clearly the case with Germany in the middle of the last century, and it would seem to be equally clearly the case with England at present. What other European country today can boast of such a host of grandly and variedly gifted composers as England could (but does not; for she errs is the direction of self-belittlement as to her music)? Add together the cosmic depth of Delius, the spiritual ecstasy of Cyril Scott, the countrified nobility of Vaughan Williams, the dignity of Elgar, the telling virtuosity of Holst and Goossens,[55] the many-sidedness of Bax, the miniature perfection of Roger Quilter, the cultural insight of Frederic Austin[56] and Peter Warlock—to compile a very incomplete list. These men are all so substantial, so intrinsically inventive, such followers of true beauty, so free from 'isms' and cliquishness, so normal in spite of strong individualism, so unlike one another in spite of an all-pervading national spirit. They do not make themselves ridiculous either by exaggerated newfangledness or old-fogeyishness. Their musical behavior is natural and unstrained. They go their own gait without undue self-consciousness. They have great souls, deep moods; and these they express with manly straightforwardness.

For several years English musicians have regaled me with woeful tales of the lowered pulse of English music, of the lessened efficiency of English orchestras, since the war. But my own ears tell me that English orchestras are finer now than ever they were and that the music-making I have listened to in many parts of England during the last five months seems more genuine in feeling, more noble in character and more sensitive in technic than anything I have heard on the European continent of late years. Where else, in Europe, can such high-minded, self-effacing conductors be found—who worship music itself, not merely their own personal part in it? Just think of the almost unbelievably unselfish devotion of Sir Henry Wood[57] and Sir Thomas Beecham to the welfare of their art! They

---

[55] Eugene Goossens (1893–1962), English conductor and composer.
[56] (1872–1952), English baritone and composer.
[57] (1869–1944), English conductor, founder of the Promenade Concerts in 1895.

are not merely great conductors; they are benign fathers of music, turning cultural deserts into pastures.

Not only in London, Manchester and other large cities is this spiritualized standard of music-making upheld. There are several smaller centers that do not lag behind one whit. For nearly a lifetime Sir Dan Godfrey[58] has done a noble work in sustaining in Bournemouth a full-sized symphony orchestra of excellent quality and in furthering the cause of classical and modern British music alike. At Hastings and Harrogate Basil Cameron has developed small orchestras of singular sympathy and finish. I foresee that this superlatively gifted young stick-wielder, now in his very prime, will soon be 'snapped up' by America. He would certainly prove a god-send to some American city wanting to form or perfect a great symphony orchestra.[59] For Cameron is not only one of the most skilful and electrifying of Europe's younger conductors; he is equally a magnificent trainer and orchestra builder. His technical grasp of every section of the orchestra is exhaustive, his patience unending and his grace of manner irresistible. He is one of the few conductors who instinctively know how to keep an orchestra 'happy, though efficient'.

We are told, in economics, that it is unhealthy to 'consume without producing.' In music the composer alone is the producer, the performer being the middle-man and the public the consumer. In English musical life the vital need for composers seems more clearly understood than elsewhere. Composers—even young ones, not yet famous—are invited to conduct their works on all hands, throughout England, and the enthusiasm their performances of their own compositions arouse does not necessarily pale beside that called forth by interpretations of the most hackneyed classics by the most acclaimed virtuoso conductors. Music-lovers in England are genuinely intrigued by composers, native and foreign, and deem it a privilege to hear the first performance of a new composition under its creator's guidance—with the speeds and shadings he approves of (indeed, without them the work has not been fully heard). Concert organizers in England do not seem so prone, as elsewhere, to believe the stupid fallacy that 'composers are the worst interpreters of their own works' (the exact reverse is true, of course).

British composers and their compositions have been gaining steadily in solid popularity for many years in England. Even within the last two years a noticeable gain in this direction may be recorded. In the programs

---

[58] (1868–1939), conductor of the orchestra at Bournemouth from 1892 to 1935.
[59] Cameron (1884–1975) did soon become conductor of the San Francisco Orchestra (1930–8).

of this season's Promenade Concerts (with which no other concerts known to me anywhere can be matched as a scheme for popularizing all that is best in all music) Sir Henry Wood has scheduled no less than eighty British works for performance. At these concerts every Thursday evening is now a 'British Composers' Concert', with the program up to the interval (about six-eighths or seven-eighths of the entire program) devoted exclusively to native works. The vast audiences and the electrical enthusiasm present at these Thursday evenings leave no doubt as to the hearty response of the public to this innovation.

Why are 'American Composers' Concerts' not more general in the United States? Simply, I think, because no conductor or concert promoter has as yet known how to draw forth and organize the vast and varied appeal that lies waiting in the works of the best American composers. It is a thankful task, worth essaying.

Few in England realized the full potentialities for popularity of British music until Balfour Gardiner made them manifest at his orchestral and choral concerts of 1911–1913. Up to then most concert-givers seemed to have shown rather poor judgment in their choice of new British works. But Balfour Gardiner, being an inspired composer himself, had no difficulty in distinguishing full talent from half talent or in selecting the best examples of each gifted man's work. Therefore his concerts quickly proclaimed the full worth of such men as Bax, Holst, Vaughan Williams, Cyril Scott, Frederic Austin, Whittaker[60] and others, and his audiences were not slow to kindle in the proximity of so much sacred flame. The fires of enthusiasm for the best British music thus cunningly lit by Balfour Gardiner were subsequently kept alive by other conductors and concert-givers, and no doubt the war years also played a part in fanning them into the present pleasant conflagration.

Of music other than British that I have heard during my stay in England the following impressed me most: Ernest Bloch's jolly Concerto grosso for piano and string orchestra;[61] Respighi's lusty *Roman Festivals*;[62] Stravinsky's *Apollon Musagète* Ballet Music[63] and the same composer's entertaining Concerto for Piano and Wind Orchestra[64] (the last masterfully conducted by Goossens, the solo part scintillatingly percussed by the composer); *Apollon Musagète* was remarkable for certain

---

[60] William G. Whittaker (1876–1944), musicologist, conductor, and composer, mainly of vocal music.

[61] No. 1 (1924–5).   [62] 1928.

[63] From Stravinsky's ballet in two scenes for string orchestra (1927–8).   [64] 1923–4.

flame-like shoots of sound that keep darting upwards with strident brilliancy. A weird but not dislikable whiff of decay hovers around the musical textures of the Concerto; they haunt the memory as some sort of musical counterpart of mellow cheese.

But it is my impressions of British music that I most wish to record. Above all other examples of old English instrumental music tower the Three-, Four- and Five-part Fantasias for Strings by Purcell, recently edited and made available for modern string-quartets or string orchestras by Peter Warlock and André Mangeot[65] (Curwen Edition). They are not only the finest showing of Purcell's genius that I know; they are as good as the very best of Bach. They unfold a complex glory of polyphonic sonority for which many a modern ear is athirst and, whether lively or solemn, are shining models of the most telling kind of writing for strings. Moreover, they point an interesting lesson on the subject of abiding national characteristics in art; for the moods of some of these Fantasias, written five years before Bach was born, are, in their calm rapture, surprisingly akin to much of Delius, Scott and Vaughan Williams.

Excellent performances of Delius's works were to be heard all over the country. Especially memorable among these was the tender rendering of the Double Concerto (Violin, Cello and Orchestra) by May and Beatrice Harrison[66] and Sir Thomas Beecham at Queen's Hall, London, on June 14th—soloists, conductor and orchestra vying with each other in subtlest artistry.

The golden worth of Vaughan Williams's music becomes more evident each year. His 'Pastoral' Symphony[67] seems to me the most successful essay under this title by any composer. None other seems so genuinely pastoral in mood—not a pastoralness consisting of imitations of bird-calls and other 'natural' sounds, nor claiming to paint rural scenes in tones, but the musical outpourings of an artistic soul into which the very essence of the countryside has entered. His *Concerto Accademico*[68] for violin and strings is another happy achievement. Here is no barren 'neo-classicism' born of flagging of the creative imagination resulting in a lazy harking back to certain worn-out formulas of the 16th century—the husk of the past, not the living past itself. Here is no breaking of faith with the urge of modern music, but a truly modern work into which certain fascinating

---

[65] (1883–1970), London-resident French violinist.
[66] May Harrison (1891–1959), violinist, and Beatrice Harrison (1892–1972), cellist, to whom Delius had dedicated the work and who premièred it in 1920.
[67] No. 3 (1921).   [68] 1924–5.

archaic influences have infused a unique flavor. This is a work that should widely commend itself to violin virtuosi and to string orchestras.

A delightful experience was the *Beggar's Opera*,[69] well sung, well played, well acted at the Lyric Theatre, Hammersmith (London). With unerring judgment and sensitive musicianship Frederic Austin has adopted and expanded this old music to suit modern requirements. These same and other fine qualities mark his own independent compositions, such as his C major Symphony and Spring Rhapsody[70]—works that should become more widely known in the near future.

An amazing compositional and orchestral virtuosity pervades the score of Eugene Goossens' opera *Judith*.[71] Only a keen, vigorous mind could have conceived this music; in the main somewhat unbending in its extreme austerity and conciseness, though flowering forth occasionally into brief moments of luscious sensuousness. It seems a little aloof from the main trend of British music, both in its masterly craftsmanship and in its lack of inner emotional melt. For let it be confessed that English music (the glory of which lies in its deeper human qualities, in its tender-heartedness, its knightliness and purity of mood, its reliance upon sheer inspiration) is almost always marred, on its technical side, by some ama-teurishness, some indifference to details of craftsmanship. Possibly Elgar and Holst should be partly or wholly exempted from this generalization, both to their gain and loss. The more representative and racially revealing English music is the more may these high virtues and accompanying defects be awaited without disappointment.

Of short, telling pieces for smallish orchestras—of a type that appeals to most conductors in that it is effective with next to no rehearsing—Peter Warlock's vividly scored *Capriol Suite*[72] and Roger Quilter's lovable Three English Dances[73] struck me as outstanding.

A valuable contribution to a curiously neglected field—that of concert-hall works for voice and orchestra—is Quilter's recently composed moving setting of Shelley's poem 'I arise from dreams of thee';[74] fervent in melody, glowing in orchestration.

England has long been lucky in her song writers, quite particularly in

---

[69] Ballad opera, with dialogue and lyrics by John Gay (1685–1732) and music selected and arranged by J. C. Pepusch (1667–1752); revived by Frederic Austin in 1920.

[70] Premièred in 1907.

[71] Op. 46, with libretto by Arnold Bennett, premièred at Covent Garden in 1929.

[72] 1928.   [73] Op. 11 (1910).

[74] For tenor and orchestra (completed 1931), to a text from Shelley's *The Indian Serenade* (1819).

her women song writers. How deeply yet unsentimentally emotional, how harmonically poignant, are such gems of song as Maude Valerie White's[75] 'When the Swallows Homeward Fly', 'Let Us Forget', 'So, We'll go no More a'Roving'. What character struts in Ethel Smyth's *Anacreontic Ode*, what pathetic charm breathes in her *Chrysilla* (both for voice with chamber music accompaniment).[76] Yet most English musicians are surprised if one ranks these, and Quilter's, and others of the finest English songs, with Schubert, Schumann, Brahms, Fauré and Grieg. I ask myself, what quality do they lack that they should be debarred from highest rank? None, to my ears. English musicians should wake up and realize that they already possess a great hoard of song classics that are the equal of any other penned.

A jewel among London Concerts was the song recital given on June 17th by Plunket Greene.[77] I have heard in my life three art-singers that spelled perfection for me; in whose art the spirit of music and poetry was not smothered by the flesh of sound: Ludwig Wüllner,[78] Yvette Guilbert[79] and Plunket Greene. Of these the last named is still at his very best. He is the only singer I know who masters art-song and folksong equally well; who is equally at home in a Bach aria and an Irish patter-song. If I were a vocal student I would study with none but this knightly troubadour, whose technical and musical knowledge is so vast, whose taste is so unfailing, whose repertory of every period and nationality of song seems unlimited. Singers complain of difficulty in finding good songs in English; they would find Greene's programs a storehouse of valuable repertory suggestions.

One of England's finest composers recently said to me that of everything in modern music he would soonest hear Cyril Scott's *Festival Overture* (for chorus, orchestra and organ).[80] In that I quite concur. It is, for me, the most entrancingly lovely music I have heard for many years. It contains strains of seraphic beauty that woo the hearer's inmost soul; it is a paragon of teeming melodic invention, winsome part-weavings and flowing form.

Cyril Scott, as composer, conductor and pianist, proved the hero of the

---

[75] (1855–1937), English composer of mainly vocal and piano music, and three operas.
[76] Both dating from 1909.
[77] Harry Plunket Greene (1865–1936), baritone, with whom Grainger had performed several times during his London years.
[78] (1858–1938), German tenor.
[79] (1867–1944), French soprano.
[80] A reworking of his early *Princess Maleine Overture*.

Festival of British Music given at Harrogate on July 24th, 25th and 26th. Who, among living composers, masters so many sides of his art as gracefully as Cyril Scott? What pianist can play as frolicsomely, as individually as he? He at the piano, with Basil Cameron at the conductor's stand, gave a model rendering of the sparkling Scott piano concerto,[81] in which tenderness, sprightliness and energy relieve each other in satisfying proportions.

When I first went to London, around 1900, Cyril Scott seemed to me to be leading English compositional thought. It was largely his musical ideas and innovations that his fellow composers discussed and drew esthetic nourishment from. And now, returning to English musical life nearly thirty years later, I still find him in the van of modernistic thought. On every hand I note the influence of his original and beautiful style. Indeed, it is not too much to say that a large portion of contemporary music is but an echo of sounds he invented long ago. Scott is the very antithesis of the young composer to whom Rossini is reported to have said: 'Your music is original and beautiful; but the original parts are not beautiful and the beautiful parts are not original.' It is precisely the most beautiful elements in Scott's music that are the most original. And therein lies his power to exert, for so many years, a life-giving influence upon musical thought in England and elsewhere. For true beauty never becomes old-fashioned. He was the first Englishman, in modern times, to match in music the fantastic imaginativeness displayed in poetry and painting by such artists as Keats, Swinburne, Turner and Aubrey Beardsley. As Goossens recently so pointedly put it, in my hearing: 'Cyril Scott was the first English composer who was at once truly English and truly modern.'

We must, if we are to get our musical values straight, distinguish between a talent for musical mimicry and caricature (such as that so engagingly possessed by Stravinsky) and a genius for musical creation (such as that possessed by Cyril Scott). The bright moments in Stravinsky's music are largely imitative—the mimicry of the two simultaneously playing barrel-organs in *Petrouchka*, the caricature of a maudlin operatic duet in *The Story of a Soldier*,[82] the caricature of Bach in the Piano Concerto, of Gluck, Haydn, etc., in *Apollon Musagète*. These imitative sallies are delightful and valuable because some quality of newness and originality always goes with them in Stravinsky. All the same, any form of mimicry or caricature is far from being a main office of highly developed music. Music is primarily an ecstatic, an uplifting, an

---

[81] No. 1 (1915).   [82] *L'Histoire du soldat* (1918).

exciting, an enthusing art—a religious art, if you will. Anything that smacks of cynicism, of humor, of braininess makes music less musical. Music, at its best, should remind one of the choiring of the angels, or of the thanksgiving song of cosmic nature 'singing like the morning stars for joy that they were born' (Kipling). It may even, still at its best, sound like the mournful moaning of telegraph wires. But it must always, if it is to be at its best, voice some positive utterance of joy or sorrow. It must tell us of the soul or the heart, rather than of the mere sensations.

Viewed from this angle, Cyril Scott is the true musician, the true positivist. But it is only in his larger and more complex works (such as the *Festival Overture*, the *Nativity Hymn*,[83] the *Aubade*, the orchestra Passacaglias, the Piano Sonata, the Quintet for piano and strings[84]) that his full spiritual and artistic stature emerges. As yet the public, even in England, knows him mainly by his smaller and simpler works—those that are easiest to perform.

Scott needs a conductor-prophet who will do for his music what Sir Thomas Beecham so long and loyally has done for Delius. Just as twenty years ago I foresaw the inevitability of a world-wide recognition of Delius's claims to first-class genius, I now venture to predict a similar vogue for Scott's greatest and noblest works within the next ten or twenty years. The world needs the loveliest and loftiest kind of music just as urgently as it needs jazz and Sousa, Stravinsky and Hindemith. But what a time it takes to discover the highest flights of the art, and how tiresome it is for those who are able to recognize high genius at once to have to wait while the world toys with cocktails instead of going straight to the real meal! 'Eventually—why not now?'

[83] For chorus, soloists, and orchestra (pub. 1923).   [84] 1904, pub. 1925.

Part IV

1931–1939

27

Democracy in Music

(1931)

'A chance for all to shine in a starry whole.' Some such thought as this underlies, I suppose, our working conception of democracy. Democracy seems to our mind's eye not merely a comfortable system of ensuring personal independence & safety to each man, but also an adventure in which the oneness & harmonious togetherness of all human souls is lovingly celebrated—for it is obvious that democracies are just as patriotic & humanitarian as they are freedom-loving.

Such a banner seems fair enough for any upward-yearning soul. And, in fact, this ideal, as applied to life, art & thought, has spurred on many a genius, such as Walt Whitman, Tennyson, Martin Luther, Bach, Grieg, Edgar Lee Masters, etc.

Yet in spite of the master-minds that have championed democracy, & in spite of the fact that the measure of a country's democraticness is almost exactly the measure of its prominence in freedom, science, power & prosperity, we hardly ever meet an individual (even in those lands most nearly democratic) who whole-heartedly believes in the practical wisdom of democracy; nearly always the individual is held back from a happy embrace of democratic doctrine by the sway exerted over his nature by old-time influences that make for superstition, personal greed, leisure-worship, celebrity-hunting, slavishness & lack of selfhood. As a result, so many of those who give lip-service to democracy where the larger issues of world affairs are at stake are unwilling to practise democracy in the small & immediate affairs of their everyday life. As a result of this weakness & blindness in so many individuals we may truly say that democracy (like Christianity, like socialism, like many another noble ideal) has never yet been given 'a fair chance'. Yet its cause goes marching on.

Is it not the same with the cause of the best, the deepest, the grandest, the loveliest art music? Its cause, also, goes marching on with quiet but steady invincibility, although retarded by the blindness & smallmindedness of so many individuals—amongst whom, it always seems to me, there is too large a percentage of highly-trained professional musicians.

Source: Manuscript dated 9–10 July 1931. Grainger Museum, Melbourne. (Grainger's annotations indicate that the article was intended for Schirmer's promotional booklet *Grace Notes*, in which it evidently did not appear.)

These individuals seem to forget that art music is an essentially democratic art, an art that mingles souls while it mingles sounds, an art that in its
self-forgetful collectivism transcends individualism, an art of fusion and
cooperation, an art that feeds on soul-ecstasy but starves on mere cerebral
cleverness. In the highest forms of art music, as in democracy, 'the starry
whole' (the radiant glory of art itself, of collective humanity itself) counts
for at least as much as 'the chance for all to shine'. Technically, this means
that the various melodic lines, that make up the harmonic texture, must
enjoy, at various moments, equal opportunities to be independent, prominent & volitional; but that the splendor & beauty of the composite whole
is the goal that none may lose from mind.

I, personally, would go so far as to assert that the value of all existing art
music depends on the extent to which it is intrinsically many-voiced or
democratic—that is to say, the extent to which the harmonic texture is
created out of freely-moving voices, each of them full of character, or
vigor, or melodic loveliness. That is why I prize the best jazz as highly
as I do: because it is more many-voiced than any dance music that went
before it.

The whole world of harmony (which is the salient thing that distinguishes the art music of the European races from the musics of Asia, or
from primitive music or folk music anywhere in the world) owes its
origin to the habit of singing or playing together in freely-moving
melodic parts. That being so, it stands to reason that the music student
cannot possibly understand the inwardness of any art music (old or new,
'jazz' or 'classical') unless he himself has been through the light-shedding
experience of singing or playing freely-moving, independent melodic
parts together with others in many-voiced music. The budding musician
needs the inspiration of hearing a grand coöperation of myriad sounds
surging around him, to which he joins his own individualistic voice. This
is the *special experience* of music, without which mere lonely practising to
acquire soloistic skill must always remain esthetically barren and unsatisfying.

As already stated, not all forms of music are 'democratic'. True folksong (unaccompanied single line—for the most part non-harmonic in
its suggestions) is individualistic rather than democratic. Top-melody,
accompanied by subservient unmelodic chords & basses, cannot be called
democratic; nor can soloistic display-music (such as much of Scarlatti,
Paganini, Liszt, Verdi, etc.). Such musics are closer to musical feudalism,
aristocracy or high-priest-craft than to democracy. But all true many-
voiced (polyphonic) music (such as we find in the compositions of

Palestrina, Purcell, Bach, Wagner, Delius, Vaughan Williams, Cyril Scott, Loeffler, Arnold Schönberg & many others) may be said to be musically democratic. Such music is not only richer & more subtle in a purely musical sense than all other existing music, but also satisfies the spiritual, religious, ethical & emotional cravings of modern humanity as does no other.

There are many indications abroad that the music-loving public at large realizes this fact. The glorious growth of high-school orchestras, bands & choirs, the newly awakened fondness for 2-piano playing, the increasing interest in amateur orchestras, *a cappella* singing, group teaching & other forms of musical teamwork, all indicate that large sections of the public (better nourished, musically, by radio & other *impersonal* musical influences than ever before) are turning more & more towards *music itself* & away from the comparatively unmusical wizardry, & personality-mongering of virtuoso 'concert artists'.

But it may be questioned whether the average professional musician— the average conductor, the average teacher—really divines the goal of this upward turn of public taste. Still more may it be questioned whether the repertory of the pieces he knows includes an adequate supply of works likely to satisfy music lovers in their quest for democratic, soul-satisfying, many voiced music.

Too many a professional musician has equipped himself along skill-worshipping display-music lines, hoping to be a sort of musical high-priest, holding the public off at arm's length & making of music an enclosed mystery-trick, surrounded by irrelevant 'personality' & 'temperament' & 'tradition' side-shows. Such 'specialists' cannot, for the life of them, understand the present wholesome craving of the general musical public for nourishing musical fare or the pursuit of music for music's sake.

In spite of the success of Gershwin's *Rhapsody in Blue*,[1] of Bloch's *America*,[2] of Guion's arrangements of cowboy tunes, in spite of the vogue of jazz & Negro spirituals, these high-priests do not seem to realize that large sections of the American musical public want Americanism in music, & will not be happy until they get it.

Young Americans should be encouraged to feel the same sort of local and national pride in their native-born (not merely naturalized) composer-geniuses that they feel for their athletic heroes. As long as this natural feeling is thwarted or undeveloped we can hardly expect to find

---

[1] (1924), for jazz band and piano, commissioned by Paul Whiteman.
[2] (1926), an 'epic rhapsody' for chorus and orchestra.

real stability in musical affairs in America; public taste may be expected to swing from one exotic craze to another until the truth is widely realized that musical greatness, in any land, can never be based upon anything except the genius of native-born composers.

Full many a conductor fails to satisfy the cravings of his audiences for the deeper experiences of music—notwithstanding whatever technical virtuosity he may command in all sorts of worn-out orchestral display-pieces—because his musical mind is too closely wedded to the *banal* simplicities of the 18th & 19th centuries, and too ignorant of the deeper, grander music of the 17th & 20th centuries!

Full many a choral conductor fails to realize that he is undermining the choral enthusiasm of his choir by giving them too much 19th-century choral music—music that, despite the inspired genius of such men as Beethoven, Wagner, Schumann, Mendelssohn, Brahms, etc., is not really vocal & choral in character (mostly it gives the impression of being melody-&-accompaniment—a type of music basically unsuited to choral needs) &, therefore, falls short of revealing, to those taking part, the full musical glory & spiritual purpose of choral singing. Such a conductor does not guess the flame of choral enthusiasm he might kindle by familiarizing his singers with the best many-voiced choral music of all times—not only the gems of the pre-Bach periods, but also the best many-voiced choral compositions of modern composers such as Grieg (*Psalms* for mixed voices, *Album for Male Voices*, Opus 30), Rachmaninoff (*15 Anthems of the Church*), Cyril Scott (*Nativity Hymn*), Delius (*The Song of the High Hills*, *A Mass of Life*,[3] etc.), Roger Quilter ('Herrick' choruses[4]), Vaughan Williams, Arnold Schönberg (*Friede auf Erden*[5]), Loeffler (*Ode to One that Fell in Battle*[6]), Natalie Curtis-Burlin (*Negro Folksongs*, 4 vols.), Nathaniel Dett, Howard Brockway, etc.

Piano teachers should utilize the piano chiefly as a teamwork instrument, realizing that it is a music-study instrument second to none—even though its tone color may not always please our ears. Every phase of the student's pianistic development can be unfolded along team-work lines—*by beautiful music-making from the very start*, instead of letting him waste his time by merely *preparing* to make music.

In my opinion piano study should begin with melody playing in groups (the larger the groups, the better), since melody & not passagework (scales, etc.) is the root of music. Groups of beginners at one or more

---

[3] For four soloists, chorus, and orchestra (1904–5).   [4] Op. 7 (1905).

[5] Op. 13 (1907), for mixed a cappella chorus, with *ad lib.* instruments.

[6] (1911), for eight voices.

pianos (four or five players at each piano, playing the same melody in different octaves) should practise reading the voice part of songs (not bothering about fingering; playing everything 'with one finger', if they like) while an advanced player (the teacher or another pupil) plays the song accompaniment on another piano. In the case of American students, such American songs as Howard Brockway's *Lonesome Tunes* & *Twenty Kentucky Mountain Songs* might well form the starting point. Here we have exquisite American melodies, exquisitely harmonized. The average American music student seldom knows a single genuine American folksong & is quite ignorant of the melodic idioms, folk modes & other local characteristics that dominate American music, whether it be Negro spiritual, jazz, MacDowell or Carpenter. What would we think of German, Norwegian, or Russian music students who were totally ignorant of the folksongs of their native countries? In my eyes an American music student who knows nothing of American folksong & its influences is a ridiculous & pathetic incapable.

Beginners may learn to master the bass clef by reading (on the piano—preferably in groups) the pedal line of organ compositions such as Bach's chorale preludes & César Franck's Three Chorales.[7] There is no reason why the student should not have the advantage of filling his ears with the very loftiest music from the very start.

No one can grasp the full beauty & significance of a Bach fugue who has not played or examined each voice (of the fugue) separately. My advice to all fugue students is to make a practice of playing the Bach fugues, on pianos or harmoniums, with one player to each voice. Thus a three-part fugue will call for three players, a four-part fugue for four players, & so on. In the case of a four-part fugue, the soprano & tenor parts should be played on the 1st piano (or harmonium), the alto & bass parts on the 2nd piano (or harmonium), in order to give each player keyboard-room for his particular part (voice). The parts may sometimes be played in single notes, sometimes in octaves, single or double. (The whole procedure may be studied in Bach–Grainger: *A minor Fugue for Four or more Pianists at Two or more Pianos*.[8])

All the forty-eight fugues of the *Well-tempered Clavier* may with profit & joy be played & studied in this way (from the ordinary two-hand editions). In my opinion, no pianist should essay a solo (two-hand) performance of any fugue unless he has first familiarized himself with its many-voiced ingredients by means of such team-work study.

---

[7] (1890), for organ.   [8] Pub. 1931.

String orchestras & string quartet players should nourish their musical souls on Purcell's unsurpassable *Three-, four-, and five-part Fantasias for Strings*, recently edited by Peter Warlock & André Mangeot (Curwen Edition). This is the most sublimely beautiful many-voiced, democratic music known to me, & should become to all string players what Bach's *Well-tempered Clavier* is to pianists. String quartet players should begin their team-work experience with *such truly quartet-like* creations as these, rather than with the comparatively homophonic (& therefore less truly quartet-like) quartets of Haydn, Mozart & Beethoven.

In closing, I would not like to leave the impression that I consider 'democratic' music a suitable *final goal* for the musical aspirations of mankind. For me democratic music is only a halfway house on the road to 'free music'—music in which all intervallic, rhythmic, harmonic & formal relationships will be free, irregular, unlimited & non-conventional. Then only will the full soul of man find a universal, untrammelled musical speech. But such a goal of musical freedom is still far off; the mounting 'democratic' many-voiced music points the road in the right direction.

28

A General Study of the Manifold
Nature of Music
(1932)

The main purpose of this course[1] is set forth in Statement 1 (below). Statements 2–20 embody other salient facts, opinions, and suggestions that are presented in the lectures.

As most of the music discussed by the lecturer—and performed by him and his musical illustrators, or rendered on gramophone records—is new to the ears of those attending the course, the lecturer feels the need of presenting many of his chief conclusions (and the musical examples upon which they are based) several times during the course at somewhat widely separated intervals, so that the students may gradually digest their impressions of all this (to them) unusual music and the statements regarding it. Therefore, no attempt is made to present the subject matter of this course in chronological or geographical order. The amount of time devoted to any particular subject in a given lecture is largely governed by the response shown by the students in the form of questions, etc.,—it being impossible, when giving these lectures for the first time, to foretell the exact response that such a mass of novel material will call forth.

* * *

Statement 1. The main purpose of this course is to make the student familiar with the chief types of music of all periods and places (as far as they are known and available), to show the threads of unity running through all kinds of music (primitive music, folk music, jazz, Oriental and Western art music) and to point out the apparent goal of all musical progress (increasing discordance, ever closer intervals and the growing use of sliding tones without fixed pitch, growing informality of musical form, irregular rhythms making towards 'beatless music', until finally 'Free Music' is reached, when music will be technically advanced enough to tally the irregularity, subtlety and complexity of life and nature—

Source: Undated duplicated typescript. Grainger Museum, Melbourne.

[1] Music A–B, New York University, taken by Associate Professor Grainger between Sept. 1932 and May 1933.

including 'human nature', of course—to the degree that Greek sculpture was finally able to present all shapes, attitudes and movements true to nature). It is hoped that some general knowledge of all the world's music will promote a genuine cosmopolitan musical outlook. An effort will be made by the lecturer to discourage the intolerance and indifference that still prevails generally with regard to most music older than 1700 and younger than 1900; in particular, the prevailing prejudice against almost all American music (be it art music, folk music or jazz) will be combated.

Statement 2. The highest flights of music are a spiritualizing influence inducing contemplation and rapture and leading mankind toward a more peaceful, harmonious and angelic life (on earth). The Chinese statement anent music in the *Record of Rites* (2225 B.C.?)—'Poetry is the expression of earnest thought and singing is the prolonged utterance of that expression'[2]—is true of the finest music everywhere, at all times. Lofty music achieves sustained rapture by means of sustained notes, sustained musical moods. Therefore, melody (see Statement 3) is the main ingredient of spiritual music everywhere.

Statement 3. Melody in its purest form is musical expression by means of changing intervals (fixed intervals or vague sliding intervals), the intervallic changes happening slowly enough to be clearly heard and appreciated. Melody (whether sung by voices or played on instruments) follows the nature of man's singing voice, while 'tune', 'theme', 'motiv', 'passage', are inclined to be more instrumental in type. We do not speak of 'a melody on the bugle' or 'a melody on the drum', though we do speak of a melody on any of the more voice-like instruments, such as violin, trumpet, saxophone.[3] Melodic thought is weakened where too much rhythmic energy or preoccupation with harmony hold sway. Therefore the loftiest types of music (whether 16th or 17th or 20th-century European, or Chinese or Japanese or folksong) are melodious (single-line melody or melodious polyphony) and comparatively free from energizing rhythmic sway (see Statement 4). The following are examples of pure melody:

> Wagner's *Parsifal* Prelude, opening phrase.
> Chief theme of C. Scott's *Aubade* (orchestra).
> 'Pretty Polly', American folksong (Brockway).

    [2] Cf. Essay 31. The source of Grainger's quotation is Robert W. Marks ('Music and Musical Instruments of Ancient China', *Musical Quarterly*, 18 (1932), 593–607 (p. 594)), who draws it from Shu Ching's *The Book of History*.   [3] Cf. Essay 43.

Claude Le Jeune's (1530–1600) *La Bel' Aronde*.
Javanese Records, *Musik des Orients*,[4] Nos 9 and 10.
'Fraanar Ormen', Norwegian hero-song.

Comparatively few examples of pure melody are found in Bach, Haydn, Mozart, Beethoven, Schubert, Schumann, Mendelssohn, Brahms, Tchaikovsky, etc., because these composers are too engrossed in rhythm or harmony to express themselves often in pure melody.

Statement 4. Rhythm (especially regular rhythm) is a great energizing and slave-driving force, a great promoter of action. Therefore it has played a great part in practical life ('Sea chanties', for instance) and has been highly prized by practical-minded men. Rhythm does not promote contemplation or rapture, however, nor does it favor the 'prolonged utterance of the expression of earnest thought'. Therefore, a strong influence from dance music upon art music is inclined to lower the high traditions of the latter and to make for frivolous, displayful art music, unable to sustain a lofty mood—as in the case of 'Jazz Classics' Haydn, Mozart and Beethoven,[5] or in the case of Gershwin or Stravinsky.

Statement 5. Harmony is as potent a spiritualizing force as melody. But up to the present the technical limitations of Western music (but this is not true of the polymelodic music of Java) have harmony under rhythmic sway. It is one of the tasks of the near future to create soulful music in which melody, harmony and rhythm will not be hampered by each other (the harmonic or disharmonic changes might be arrived at by melodious part-movements that have each their own individual rhythmic life and are not controlled by beat impulses affecting all the parts simultaneously).

Statement 6. Up to the present the most soulful, spiritualizing music has belonged to the polymelodic or melodiously polyphonic types, of which the following are a few examples:

(*a*) Pre-Haydn European music: G. de Machaut, Palestrina, Byrd, William Lawes, Purcell, Bach, and many others.

(*b*) Modern European (and American) music: Wagner, C. Franck, G. Fauré, Grieg, Debussy, Scriabin, R. Strauss, Arnold Schoenberg, Rachmaninoff (15 Anthems of the Church), and others.

---

[4] *Musik des Orient: ein Schallplattenfolge orientalischer Musik von Japan bis Tunis* (SX107 DL 9505-6), issued in 1931 by Karl Lindström and Erich von Hornbostel of the Berlin Phonogram Archive. The set, of twelve 10-inch records, featured 'Native Songs and Dances of Japan, China, Java, Bali, Siam, India, Persia, Egypt and Tunis'.   [5] See Essay 34.

(*c*) Oriental music (not influenced by European harmonic thought): the Javanese polymelodic music, etc.

(*d*) 'Native' musics influenced by European harmonic thought and now creating new melodiously polyphonic types of their own: American-Negro part-singing (as recorded in Natalie Curtis's *Negro Folk Music* [*sic*], Schirmer); Russian peasant part-singing; Madagascan part-singing; Rarotongan (and other Polynesian) part-singing.

Statement 7. Tonal balance (equal tonal strength in the parts making up the polyphonic or harmonic texture) is essential in polyphonic music, old and new. The traditions of tonal balance (which were still in force in Bach's time) were lost in the mid-18th century (together with other traditions of lofty art music), and have not yet been regained. Our present symphony orchestras, choirs, military bands and chamber organizations are a riot of tonal 'top-heaviness'. It is one of the tasks of the 20th century to restore decent tonal balance in our sound bodies, so that the masterpieces of pre-Haydn times and the masterpieces of modern music can be heard without barbarous distortion. It is noteworthy that the best jazz bands have achieved refined tonal balance.

Statement 8. 'Large Form' (in which one single inspiration of form carries the music forward from start to finish) and 'Sectional Forms' (forms such as 'Sonata Form' evolved out of dance forms—forms in which a lot of separate sections are loosely knit together into a seeming whole) are contrasted. 'Large Form' may be compared to one huge, singly conceived tapestry covering a large wall, while 'Sonata Form' may be compared to many small unrelated tapestries arbitrarily sewn together so that they cover the same wall-space (but without creating an impression of greatness or unity).

Examples of 'Large Form': Most of the pre-Bach English fantasies for viols; the first chorus of Bach's *Matthew Passion*; Bach's *Chromatic Fantasia*; the Fantasia of Bach's Fantasia and Fugue in G minor for organ; Wagner's *Tristan* Prelude; Scriabin's *Poem of Ecstasy*; C. Franck's 3 Chorales for Organ; Delius's *The Song of the High Hills*; Arthur Fickénscher's *The Seventh Quintet*;[6] Herman Sandby's *Sea mood* (orchestra).[7] For the other side of the argument (for a praising of

[6] *From The Seventh Realm*, an adaptation of part of the lost *Evolutionary Quintet* by American composer, Arthur Fickénscher (1871–1954). Fickénscher was Head of the Music Department at the University of Virginia, 1920–41. See, further, Essay **31**.

[7] *Havstemning*.

the dance influence for introducing clarity & thematic pithiness into art music) the students are advised to read Sir Hubert Parry's article on 'Dance' in *Grove's Dictionary*.

Statement 9. Art and civilization. The two have little in common. The main purpose of civilization appears to be to simplify life (and make it fool-proof) by means of education, standardisation and other social and mercantile machinery, while the main object of art is to keep a record of the complexity and subtlety of life and nature. Musicians should resist all demands for 'simple' music, since good music never has been, or can be, simple, even primitive music and folk music being highly complex and subtle in their own way (a 'simple folksong' is simply an incorrectly remembered or recorded folksong).

Statement 10. The advantages of the 'crescendo pedal' (organ) type of dynamics (in which new voices, or new instruments, or new stops are artificially added in *crescendos*, artificially withdrawn in *decrescendos*) preferred (in soulful music) to the simpler type of scoring in which each voice or instrument (or group of instruments or voices) is expected to make dynamic effects by its own efforts throughout a whole phrase without the artificial addition or withdrawal of other voices or instruments. Examples of the 'crescendo pedal' method: the elaborate choral habits of the Palestrina period; Wagner's scoring.

Statement 11. The indebtedness of modern composers to Oriental music:

(a) Themes from Balakirev's *Tamara* and *Islamey* and themes from Rimsky-Korsakov's *Scheherazade* compared with a Persian record (*Musik des Orients*, No. 19).

(b) Saint-Saëns's *Algerian Suite*, based on North African music.

(c) Debussy's 'Pagodes' and 'Reflets dans l'eau' compared with Javanese records (*Musik des Orients*, Nos 9 and 10).

(d) Spanish (Moorish) influences in Debussy's 'Soirée dans Grenade' and *Ibéria*, and in Ravel's *Spanish Rhapsody* and *Boléro*.

Statement 12. 'Talents' are those who succumb to the temptation to specialize; 'geniuses' are those who proudly refuse to specialize, those who retain an all-round, balanced, manly approach to art and life. Thus D. Scarlatti and Stravinsky are talents, while Bach, Wagner and Delius are geniuses.

Statement 13. Cumulative composers (in whose art many streams of past and present music run together), experimental composers (who are building up the music of the future) and modish composers (who are content with the compositional habits of their own day, without reaching out far into the styles of the past or the future). The cumulative composers (such as Byrd, Palestrina, Bach, Wagner, Delius, Tchaikovsky, Franck, Fickénscher) are shown to produce the greatest masterworks. Thus (if we desire the loftiest music), the need of preserving an unbroken tradition of the richest possible musical culture. If the thread of the highest traditions is broken, we get a debasement of art music (as in the mid-18th century) with resultant frivolousness and technical inability to sustain a lofty mood.

Statement 14. The Nordic and Anglo-Saxon temperament in music. The lecturer ascribes Scandinavian and Anglo-Saxon colonisation partly to the wistful, peace-loving, emotional sensitive natures of these peoples, who prefer to 'run away' to the waste-places of the earth rather than to stay at home and 'fight it out'. This dreamy, yearning, wistful, tender temperament is abundantly shown in every period of Scandinavian and Anglo-Saxon music (in the fantasies of Byrd, Jenkins, William Lawes and Purcell no less than in Grieg, Ole Bull, Herman Sandby, Sparre Olsen, Cyril Scott, Roger Quilter, Delius, V. Williams, MacDowell, Howard Brockway, Rubin Goldmark, Gershwin—for Jews living in Anglo-Saxon communities take on Anglo-Saxon musical attributes) and is one of the reasons why Nordic music is so little understood by non-Nordic European musicians—for no man understands a national temperament more tender, more complex, more highly evolved than his own.

Statement 15. 'Natural' and 'de-natured' singing: the former, many-sided, vocally resourceful habits of singing we meet with in children, in Oriental art music, and in 'native' singing and folk singing almost everywhere; the latter, the monotonous, vocally unresourceful debasement of singing technic we find almost universally among art singers today (notable exceptions are Yvette Guilbert, Ludwig Wüllner, Plunket Greene).[8] 'De-natured' singing is not due to too much artificial training but simply *inadequate* training and wholesale vocal ignorance and lack of musical sense. A revival of a richer vocal technic amongst art singers is particularly desirable because of the influence of singing on melody and

---

[8] See Essay 26.

the all-important part melody plays in music of the highest type (see Statements 2 and 3).

Statement 16. Jazz is called 'the most classical of popular musics' because it embraces subtleties of harmony, polyphony and orchestration that formerly were the exclusive property of art music. This approximation of art music and popular music (jazz) is only natural in an age in which human class distinctions are more levelled than ever before; a levelling of musical 'class distinctions' naturally follows suit. The lecturer points out, however, that jazz is dance music and as such is, of course, rhythmically energetic. As long as it has this energizing quality it can never (despite surface refinements) rise to the heights of religious, contemplative, rapturous angel-music. The difference between ragtime and jazz consists mainly in the Chinese and other primitive musical influences which jazz contracted from San Francisco's China Town.

Statement 17. Syncopation: No Special Characteristic of Jazz. 'Scotch snap' in such Scottish tunes as 'The Earl of Huntley's Reel' and in English and White American folk tunes on such words as 'Father', 'Brother' (also, with less linguistic provocation, in English tunes such as 'The Rainbow', *English Folk Song Society's Journal* 12)[9] completely accounts for syncopation in ragtime and jazz tunes (without American-Negro influence— syncopation in American-Negro folk tunes is probably due to Anglo-Saxon influence rather than to African characteristics), while the rhythmic syncopations and compensations in Bach, Brahms, etc., forerun similar rhythmic traits in jazz. What is new in jazz are its sliding tones and off-pitch notes, which are valuable hints of freer (most soulful) art-music to come (see Statement 1).

Statement 18. The lecturer will attempt to trace, geographically, certain main streams of musical influence:

(*a*) Individualistically rhythmic music amongst Australian natives, Africans, American Indians.

(*b*) Gaunt, solemn, slow-toned, five-tone melodiousness reaching from China to the north of Europe (Celtic music)—often associated with harmonic instincts.

(*c*) Florid, irritable, energetic, highly virtuoso display-music reaching

[9] *Journal of The Folk-Song Society*, 3 (1908), 147–242 (pp. 180–3).

from India to Europe (by way of the Moors to Spain and Western Europe, by way of the Gypsies to many parts of Eastern and Western Europe). This music tends to be played in octaves or 'inexact unison'.

The above suggestions are made very tentatively.

Statement 19. Strange affinities between types of music widely separated in time and place.

(*a*) Rhythm in Hindu music and G. de Machaut (French, 14th-century).

(*b*) Similar phrases in G. de Machaut and Bach.

(*c*) Similar harmonic suggestions in North African and Celtic tunes.

(*d*) Similar rhythmic irregularity in Claude Le Jeune (Belgian 16th-century) and Cyril Scott (living Englishman).

(*e*) Some points of likeness between medieval European polyphonic music and similar types of music growing up in Madagascar, the South Seas, etc., where native and European musical cultures fuse.

(*f*) Scale-likeness in almost all parts of the world.

Statement 20. Books and music especially recommended for study:

(*a*) Arnold Dolmetsch: *The Interpretation of the Music of the 17th and 18th Centuries* (Novello)

(*b*) Robert Donington: *The Work and Ideas of Arnold Dolmetsch* (The Dolmetsch Foundation, West Street, Haslemere, Surrey, England).

(*c*) Cyril Scott: *The Philosophy of Modernism in [its] Connection with Music.* (London: Kegan, K. Paul, Trench, Trubner & Co.)

(*d*) Cyril Scott: *The Influence of Music on History and Morals* (Theosophical Publishing House, London).

(*e*) Knud Jeppesen: *Palestrina and the Discord.*[10]

(*f*) Joseph Yasser: *A Theory of Evolving Tonality.*

(*g*) *Journal of the (English) Folk-Song Society*, No. 12.

(*h*) Cecil J. Sharp: *English Folksongs in the Southern Appalachians.*

(*i*) Natalie Curtis: *Negro Folksongs* (4 volumes) (G. Schirmer).

[10] *The Style of Palestrina and the Dissonance*, Eng. trans. of Jeppesen's seminal study in Danish of 1923.

(*j*) Natalie Curtis: *Songs and Tales from the Dark Continent* (Schirmer)

(*k*) Natalie Curtis: *The Indians' Book* (Harper Bros.)

(*l*) Purcell: *Fantasias for Strings* (score) (Curwen Edition).

(*m*) Grieg: *Norwegische Volksweisen*, for piano, Op. 66 (Peters).

(*n*) Cyril Scott: Piano Sonata, Op. 66 (Elkin and Co.)

(*o*) (Records) *Musik des Orients* Album (Carl Lindström, Berlin)

(*p*) (Records) Album of *African Records* (The Gramophone Shop, N.Y.)[11]

---

[11] Grainger's course outline was later augmented with summaries of the main contents of his twenty-nine lectures, and, finally, with copies of the course's two examination papers, of 17 Jan. 1933 (Music A) and 16 May 1933 (Music B).

29 *Arnold Dolmetsch: Musical Confucius*
(1933)

A student of China recently pointed out that, while the great thinkers of the West usually preach more or less drastic reforms in the national life and habits of their own peoples, the philosophers of China mostly advocate a strict adherence to old Chinese traditions and customs. His explanation was simple enough: that the Western traditions and customs do not prove satisfactory to Westerners, while those handed down from past ages in China actually satisfy the Chinese—or did until recently.

With regard to music, it seems to me that we should not be afraid to admit that certain musical traditions and habits make for musical perfection as surely as others preclude it. If we concede that the harmonic consciousness of Western art music arose out of melodious part-writing, and if we further postulate that some form of melodious many-voicedness has been an important ingredient of all the greatest art music of Western peoples (that of Guillaume de Machaut, Palestrina, Byrd, Purcell, Bach, Wagner, Delius, etc.), we are logically led to the conclusion that balance of tone, between the various parts that make up any combination of voices or instruments, is essential to perfect music-making, since without it the movements and significance of the various parts cannot be clearly followed. In the light of these findings we may say, without hesitation, that the art-music habits and traditions of the sixteenth and early seventeenth centuries were favorable to musical perfection, because they insisted upon balance of tone in composing and performing, but that the art-music habits and traditions of the nineteenth century (and of the twentieth century too, so far as the latter is still dominated by the former) make inevitably for imperfection since, under their sway, balance of tone was thrown to the winds and has not yet been fully regained.

We may marvel that so all-essential a thing as tonal balance should ever have been allowed to disappear from Western art music; but perhaps we shall understand this catastrophe better if we remember the strong influence from dance music and other popular music that beat down upon art

Source: *Musical Quarterly*, 19 (1933), 187–98. (This essay was partially reproduced in 'Balance of Tone: Varying Art-Music Habits', *Australian Musical News*, 24/8 (Mar. 1934), 7–9, and 'Arnold Dolmetsch: Musical Confucius—Ancient Lore will Affect the Future', *Australian Musical News* 24/10 (May 1934), 8–9.)

music in and after Bach's time, realizing that high strident instruments, such as the violin, were practical and desirable in dance music—as making themselves better heard above the noise of the dancers than do lower and gentler instruments—thereby setting the vogue for noisy top-heavy art music in which the tune (we could not rightly call it the melody) floated, as does oil upon water, above a slavish accompaniment, mostly non-polyphonic.

Let us compare a few salient perfections of tonal balance as they obtained in the sixteenth and early seventeenth centuries—and even in Bach's and Handel's time—with the imperfections of tonal balance practised in more recent times. The 'consorts of viols' written for by the English masters of chamber music in the sixteenth and seventeenth centuries presented an evenly graded assortment of higher and lower instruments—treble, alto, tenor and bass viols—with no gap greater than half an octave between the normal register of one of these instruments and that of the next above or below it in point of tuning. Compare with this our modern string quartet (and also the massed strings of our string orchestra and symphony orchestra) in which the lack of the tenor violin (tuned a fourth below our viola and forming a part of the original violin-family quartet consisting of violin, viola, tenor and violoncello) leaves a gap of an octave between the normal registers of the viola and the violoncello. This inevitably creates a weakness in the tenor register of the harmony or the polyphony which is fatal to proper balance.[1] This top-heaviness of all modern string bodies is further aggravated by the absurd habit of employing in orchestras more violins to a part than violas and violoncellos to a part, in spite of the fact that the lower instruments (even when the proportion between higher and lower instruments is numerically even) have more difficulty in making their tones tell through the web of sound—which fact, if anyone doubts it, can readily be proved by playing through such a piece of polyphonic music as Bach's third Brandenburg Concerto (for 3 violins, 3 violas, 3 violoncellos, violone and cembalo) with a single instrument on each part. Yet reputable orchestras, all over the 'civilized' world today, do not shrink from performing this same third Brandenburg Concerto with such limping disproportions as the following: 10 first

---

[1] Grainger's footnote: Dolmetsch's light-shedding remarks on the desirability of reintroducing the tenor violin (properly tuned, of course, as above described) into chamber music and orchestra reveals his complete and sympathetic grasp of the needs of modern music. See Dolmetsch, *The Interpretation of the Music of the XVIIth and XVIIIth Centuries*, London, p. 455, and Robert Donington, *The Work and Ideas of Arnold Dolmetsch*, The Dolmetsch Foundation, Haslemere, Surrey, England, pp. 13–14.

violins, 10 second violins, 10 third violins, 4 first violas, 3 second violas, 3 third violas, 3 or 4 first 'cellos, 3 second 'cellos, 2 or 3 third 'cellos, *8 or 10 double basses*, and no cembalo or piano! We hardly need to examine accounts of the proportions of the fundamental voices (soprano, alto, tenor, bass) present in the chief Italian chapels during the fifteenth, sixteenth and seventeenth centuries[2] in order to be convinced that the melodiously polyphonic vocal music of the Renaissance (that of Josquin des Près, Palestrina, etc.) necessitated and produced perfectly balanced choirs—one glance at the music itself is enough. In Charles Sanford Terry's biography of Bach (page 201) we may read Bach's letter of August 23, 1730, to the Council of the Leipzig Thomas School, in which he defines 'the requirements of church music' and we note that he always calls for exactly the same number of voices for each of the four fundamental parts of the choir. We know that the chorus that took part in the Handel Celebration in Westminster Abbey, London, in 1784, had a decided over-weight of the lower voices (60 sopranos, 48 altos, 83 tenors, 84 basses)—taking into account, no doubt, the greater difficulty, above mentioned, that the lower voices experience in making themselves trenchantly heard in polyphonic texture. Yet in spite of these ascertainable, though still too little studied, facts regarding traditions of the polyphonic periods, famous and respected modern choirs are not ashamed to essay the choral compositions of Palestrina, Bach, Handel and other polyphonic composers with top-heavy misproportions such as 162 sopranos, 131 altos, 48 tenors, 62 basses;[3] or 107 sopranos, 63 altos, 28 tenors, 34 basses.[4] But we must turn to the modern use of wind instruments and percussion instruments in the symphony orchestra and in the military band to see nineteenth-century indifference to balance of tone run riot: flute

---

[2] Grainger's footnote: 'An equality of the numbers of the singers of the Chapel was established, realizing that any disproportion in the fundamental parts is disadvantageous to the good order of the harmony which results from equality of the parts' wrote Matteo Fornari in his history of the singers of the Pontifical Chapel of Rome (Fornari became a member of the Chapel in 1749). This statement is quoted on page 85 of *Rivista Musicale Italiana*, Torino, 1907. Of the choir of Saint Mark's, Venice, as it was constituted around the end of the seventeenth century, Giovanni Massuto remarks (page 48, Vol. I, of his *Della Musica Sacra in Italia*, Venice, 1889), 'The singers of the Chapel were limited to 36, with 9 voices to each part.' In the same work we are struck by the continually recurring multiples of four appearing in the total figures of choir membership of the leading Italian chapels during the 16th, 17th and 18th centuries. (See Vol. I, pp. 47–49; Vol. II, p. 20; Vol. III, p. 87.)

[3] Grainger's footnote: Berlin Philharmonic Choir around 1900, according to Arthur Mees, *Choirs and Choral Music*, p. 108.

[4] Grainger's footnote: A typical American choir, 1931.

and piccolo used without bass flutes;[5] 2 oboes, 1 English horn and no bass oboe or haeckelphone[6] (although both these delightful instruments are available); in the military band often as many as 8 to 10 solo B-flat clarinets, 6 to 8 first B-flat clarinets, 4 second B-flat clarinets against 1 alto clarinet and 1 bass clarinet (or no alto and bass clarinets); glockenspiel used without bass glockenspiel (metal marimba or vibraphone); xylophone used without bass xylophone (wooden marimba). Everywhere the same tonal 'top-heaviness'; which is, perhaps, not so surprising when we recall that the middle and lower parts of much 18th- and 19th-century music are as dull to play as they are boring to listen to. No wonder that players have been crowding the higher divisions of each instrumental family and that conductors have been permitting or encouraging them to do so!

It stands to reason that such crippled music-making, almost universally practised, distorts our notions of all pre-Haydn musical culture as surely as it warps the output of living composers. Wagner, it is true, was usually able, by dint of his phenomenal instinct for tone values, to rectify in his orchestration the defects of the sound bodies of his time. But his case is pretty well unique. Most composers cannot create musical perfection with imperfect musical tools, and there is no virtue in putting them to this uselessly severe test, the more so since the development of a consistently satisfying musical culture is at least as important as (in my opinion vastly more important than) the occasional creating of an isolated compositional masterpiece. In this connection we may with advantage apply to music Walt Whitman's dictum concerning literature: 'Literature is great; but language is greater than literature.'

As a result of this wholesale indifference to the first principles of serious music-making, our conductors, performers and music-lovers are, for the most part, well-nigh deaf to the appeal of the noblest and most spiritualizing type of music yet evolved—melodiously polyphonic music, whether old or new, whether 'white' or 'native'. Solemn, angelically-mooded music is seldom heard in our concert halls, with the result that our musical public is undernourished in the higher musical experiences, while surfeited with the basest of musical appeals, that of rhythm.

What cure can be prescribed for all this slipshodness, ignorance and general 'hardboiledness' that has descended upon our musical life as a

---

[5] Grainger's footnote: Contrast with this the beautifully balanced 'consorts' of 5 or more recorders (English flutes) of various sizes heard at the Dolmetsch Festivals at Haslemere.

[6] Usually spelt Hechelphone after its inventor Wilhelm Hechel and first produced in 1904.

result of nearly two hundred years of music-making under the sway of dance music and other popular music—two hundred years of divorce from the true traditions of art music as they were practised before Bach, and as they must be practised and always *are* practised (whether in Europe, America, the Orient or the South Seas) wherever melodiously many-voiced music is upheld as a serious, lofty and spiritualizing art?

To offset this long-standing musical impoverishment, I would recommend a combination of the four following experiences:

1. Copious hearing of European art music, from the earliest available examples up to and including Bach, given with the instruments, tonal proportions and traditions of the periods;

2. Repeated performances of the melodiously polyphonic masterpieces of modern music—such works as *The Song of the High Hills* by Delius, *Die junge Magd*[7] by Hindemith, *The Seventh Quintet* by Arthur Fickénscher;

3. A study of the poly-melodic music of the Orient (Javanese gamelan, etc.)[8] and of the native melodiously polyphonic music that is growing up in Madagascar,[9] the South Seas, etc., as a result of the blending of native and European musical cultures;

4. A serious study of the balance of tone and subtlety of scoring in the best jazz orchestras, such as Paul Whiteman's and Duke Ellington's.[10]

*   *   *

The first of these 'cures' is provided, ready-made, by the genius and activities of Arnold Dolmetsch, who, for more than forty years has played the rôle of a musical Confucius, holding up to our ears the perfections of a great variety of ancient European music and preaching its value with persistence, yet without exaggeration or undue partisanship. If by the term 'a genius' we mean one who has not allowed his great natural gifts to become narrowed and withered by specialization, but instead has kept a manly, full-blooded, all-round approach to art and life, then we must acclaim Arnold Dolmetsch as a genius indeed. From the very start of his

[7] Op. 23/2 (1922), for alto voice, flute, clarinet, and string quartet.

[8] Grainger's footnote: Gramophone records, *Musik des Orients* (Carl Lindström A. G., Kulturabteilung, Berlin S. O. 36), Nos 9 and 10.

[9] Grainger's footnote: Madagascar gramophone records, 'Mampahory ny Masoanoro Seranin-Javona' (Chant Malgache 50-1597) and 'Oay Lahy E' (Chant Malgache 50-1598), Disque 'Gramophone' (French 'His Master's Voice').

[10] (1899–1974), American jazz composer, bandleader, and pianist. Ellington and his jazz orchestra had taken part in one of Grainger's classes at New York University, on 25 Oct. 1932.

artistic life he has shown a breadth and universality of vision, a combination of theoretical deduction with practical handicraft, a blend of æsthetic intuition with scientific fact-hunger and unbending truthfulness that it is truly breath-taking to review.[11]

Born of musically distinguished Bohemian, German, Swiss, and French forebears at Le Mans, Western France, in 1858, Arnold Dolmetsch had his early training in drawing, mathematics, physics and chemistry. On leaving school he entered the workshop of his father, who was a pianoforte maker. There he learned wood-working and piano-making, while with his grandfather he studied and practised the building and tuning of organs. His inborn passion for music-making soon drove him to study the violin, which he did under Vieuxtemps and others in Brussels and later at the Royal College of Music in London. Always alive to the charm of such older forms of European music as were then in circulation, he discovered in 1889, in the British Museum, an immense collection of English instrumental music of the 16th and 17th centuries. At once divining its vast importance—at a time when this type of music was contemptuously ignored by the musical authorities—Dolmetsch, with inspired insight, at once determined to play them on the instruments for which they were written and set about procuring viols, lutes, virginals and clavichords, repairing the old instruments as the need arose and training himself and other music-lovers to play upon them. From these beginnings he was led, step by step, into the tremendous scope of his eventual career—a career that has profoundly altered our conceptions of many phases of ancient European art music, and which will, I am convinced, eventually radically affect the music and the musical life of the future. These many-sided activities included: the tireless examination of old manuscripts in libraries, museums, and elsewhere; the study of all discoverable treatises on the interpretation of ancient music; the collecting and repairing of old instruments; the making of clavichords, virginals, harpsichords, pianos (along his own original lines), lutes, viols, and other instruments for Chickering & Sons in Boston[12] (1905–1911) and later for the firm of Gaveau in Paris[13] (until 1914); the leading of his entire family to perform delightfully on all sorts of old instruments and to develop themselves as artist craftsmen and

---

[11] Grainger's footnote: Two excellent accounts of this astounding life of vision and fruitfulness may be consulted with advantage: *Dolmetsch and his Instruments* (written by Dolmetsch himself in 1929) and *The Work and Ideas of Arnold Dolmetsch* by Robert Donington (1932). Both procurable from 'The Dolmetsch Foundation', at the address already given.

[12] American firm, originally of piano makers, established in 1823.

[13] French firm of piano and harpsichord makers, established in 1847.

decorators in connection with the making of these instruments; the giving of many hundreds of lectures on, and programs of, ancient European art music ranging from the 13th century to Mozart (the performers sometimes attired in the dress of the period) in London, Boston, Paris and elsewhere; the publication of ancient music and books about it;[14] the training of children and grown folk to play together in groups along original, common-sense lines; and finally the crowning glory of the present activities of the entire Dolmetsch family at Haslemere, Surrey, England, where, for over a decade, harpsichords, virginals, spinets, clavichords, lutes, recorders, rebecs, viols, and other instruments (in many cases exquisitely decorated) are made with unrivalled artistry and bold experimentation at the Dolmetsch workshops, where young musicians are trained to play the old instruments with the old traditions, and where, each midsummer, a two-weeks festival of chamber music and dancing is held by the Dolmetsch family and some assistants, the like of which can be heard nowhere else in the world.[15]

* * *

At the original instigation of Robert Bridges,[16] Sir Walford Davies,[17] Sir Henry Hadow,[18] Sir Richard Terry,[19] Dr. W. G. Whittaker,[20] Mr. W. J. Whitall,[21] and others, a Dolmetsch Foundation was formed at Haslemere, in 1927, to give financial support to the Dolmetsch workshops (which, by reason of the stubborn insistence on the highest attainable perfection at any cost practised there, naturally cannot be commercial) and to give to every phase of Dolmetsch's work and aims a more established position and wider influence—for instance, by the granting of scholarships to gifted young musicians capable of learning the Dolmetsch traditions and carrying them forward into the future.[22]

[14] Grainger's footnote: Notably *The Interpretation of the Music of the XVIIth and XVIIIth Centuries*, described above.

[15] The Festival was inaugurated in 1925; Grainger first attended in 1931.

[16] (1844–1930), Poet Laureate from 1913 until his death.

[17] (1869–1941), English music academic and Master of the King's Musick from 1934.

[18] (1859–1937), English music academic and Vice-Chancellor of Sheffield University in 1919–30.

[19] (1865–1938), director of music at Westminster Cathedral during 1901–24.

[20] (1876–1944), English music scholar, choral conductor, and composer.

[21] British collector of rare violins, who had first suggested a Dolmetsch Foundation.

[22] Grainger's footnote: Members of the Foundation receive *The Consort*, a journal containing valuable examples of the old music and information about it in articles by Arnold and Mabel Dolmetsch, W. G. Whittaker, Gerald Hayes, Sir Henry Hadow, C. Sanford Terry, Robert Donington and others. Those interested should apply to the Dolmetsch Foundation, West Street, Haslemere, Surrey, England.

The Haslemere district is rightly famous for its rural charm, and this plays its part in creating that pleasant mixture of restfulness and liveliness that colours the whole festival experience. The festival concerts themselves are held in a quite small hall that is in every way ideal for the enjoyment of intimate chamber music.

The main instruments heard at the festival are:

> Lute, Archlute, Theorbo, etc.;
> Complete family of Viols: Treble, Alto, Tenor, Bass ('Viola da Gamba'), Violone (Double-bass Viol) and Lyra (a smaller, variably tuned, Bass);
> Complete family of Violins: Treble, Viola, Tenor, 'Cello, Lyra da Braccio, Rebec;
> Viola d'Amore, Viele, etc.;
> Complete family of Recorders (English flutes or Flauti d'Echo): Sopranino, Discant, Treble, Tenor, Bass;
> Choir of 24 Recorders: Oboe, Oboe d'Amore, Horn, Bassoon, Serpent, Shawm, Pipe and Tabour, etc.;
> Keyboard Instruments: Chamber Organ, Harpsichord, the Virginals (or Spinet), Clavichord.

The seven members of the Dolmetsch family have so spread their talents as musical performers over most of the instruments above mentioned, that they can at any moment render a consort of viols, or a consort of the complete violin family, or a consort of recorders without outside assistance—thereby rivalling the musical accomplishments of the family of Johann Sebastian Bach.

The wonderful playing of Arnold and Rudolph Dolmetsch[23] on the clavichord, the virginals and harpsichord is, I suppose, too well-known from gramophone records[24] to need describing here. Their eye-opening Bach-renderings delight with wayward *rubati*, sparking high speeds and vivid contrasts of *staccato* and *legato* so welcomely different from the 'bagpipe style of Bach playing' wittily ridiculed by Dolmetsch. Unforgettable are the pure-toned sonorities of the recorder consorts. These instruments produce a richer, less windy, tone than the modern flute and bear for my ears at least, a certain likeness to boys' voices. When

---

[23] (1906–42), educated at the Royal College of Music; also interested in contemporary music.

[24] Grainger's footnote: *The Columbia History of Music for Ear and Eye*. Arnold Dolmetsch is at present recording his playing of the entire *Well-Tempered Clavier*, and the *Chromatic Fantasia* on the clavichord for the Columbia Graphophone Company. Those interested in these records should apply to the 'Forty-eight' Society, 98 Clerkenwell Road, London, E.C.1. The first album, containing seven double-faced records, is now available.

they play music in several parts, the voice-movements seem to stand out with unwonted clearness and impressiveness. The singing of Cécile Dolmetsch[25] is an experience to warm the heart of every sensitive musician. Hers is a *naturally* produced voice (as different from that of the conventional concert singer as is a folk-singer's—though different again from this), fresh in all its original girlish lightness and humanity, but used, of course, with high musical skill, consciousness and conscientiousness.[26]

No less potent than the actual sounds produced by the Dolmetsch family is the mood that lies behind their musical teamwork—the serious joyousness, the informality of it all. They have entirely recaptured the spirit of seventeenth-century music-making in the home. Dolmetsch is not above stopping in the middle of a number, if all does not go to his liking, and beginning again, after having embellished the occasion with some kindly argument. He is not above chiding late-comers amongst his audience (reminding them that 'punctuality is the courtesy of Kings') although himself quite capable of starting his programs well over-time. In short, he is intimate, natural, affectionate, inconsistent, wilful and tyrannical—as we like truly great and sincere beings to be.

Of the vast, varied mass of ancient music and dances—classical and popular, religious and profane—performed at the Haslemere Chamber Music Festivals from 1925 to 1932 (inclusive) the following may be singled out as having special significance:

English Songs and Dances, from medieval times up to and including Purcell, for all kinds of solo instruments (such as the lute and the keyboard instruments), for 'consorts' of several instruments of one family and for 'broken consorts' (blends of instruments of different families);

English Intimate Music, especially the Fantasies and other compositions for four, five or six Viols by such 16th- and 17th-century composers as William Byrd, G. Coperario (John Cooper), Richard Deering,[27] John Dowland, Michael Easte, John Jenkins, William Lawes, Matthew Locke, Thomas Morley, Martin Pierson, Thomas Tomkins, Thomas Weelkes;[28]

Early Spanish Music (13th to 16th century), especially the Fantasies for Viols by Francisco de Peñalosa, Antonio de Cabezón and Diego Ortiz,

---

[25] (b. 1904); she also played the pardessus de viole.

[26] Grainger's footnote: A good gramophone record of her singing may be heard in the 1st album of *The Columbia History of Music for the Ear and Eye* [CM-231].

[27] Dering.

[28] During the 1930s Grainger made arrangements of works by most of these composers. See, further, Essay 37.

and the strangely archaic song for voice and lute by Diego Pisador (*c.* 1550) entitled 'Paséabase el Rey Moro';[29]

Early French Music, from the 13th to the 18th century, featuring chiefly such composers as Couperin, d'Anglebert, the Forquerays, J.-M. Leclair, Marin Marais, Mondonville, Rameau, and including the Court Music of Louis XIII, XIV and XV (part of this latter played by 24 violins corresponding to 'les vingt-quatre Violons du Roy' of the Louis XIII epoch);

Early Italian Music, including the remarkable 'Scherzi Musicali' for voices and instruments by Claudio Monteverdi;

Early German Music by such composers as D. Funck, Johann Kuhnau, August Kühnel, R. T. Mayer and G. P. Telemann;

Bach programs, covering the whole range of Bach's muse from the 'Comic Cantata' to the 'Passions', copiously presenting the variously scored concertos (which are a revelation when heard on the original instruments) and clearly stressing the basic difference between the clavichord compositions (*Chromatic Fantasia*, *Well-Tempered Clavier*) and the harpsichord works (French and English Suites, *Goldberg Variations*, Italian Concerto);

Haydn and Mozart programs;

Festival Dances (and other Dances) of Italy, Spain, France, and England, researched and revived by Mabel (Mrs. Arnold) Dolmetsch[30] and performed by 'The Renaissance Dancers' trained by her.

* * *

I shall pass by the impressions made by all the other kinds of music performed in order to dwell upon what, for me, is the major experience of the festivals—the soul-stirring renderings of the matchless English Fantasies[31] for Viols. Dolmetsch is not exaggerating when he describes

---

[29] Grainger arranged this piece for voice and small orchestra under the title *Peaseabase the Moorish King* in late 1934.

[30] (1874–1963), third wife of Arnold Dolmetsch, bass viol player and author of two volumes on court dances of the 16th to 18th cents.

[31] Grainger's footnote: Of all the Fantasies for Viols that I have heard, the Fantasy and Air in G minor by William Lawes (died 1645) strikes me as the most notable for its unusual combination of diverse qualities—broad flow of form, complexity of polyphonic and harmonic texture, emotional poignancy, harsh discordance, surging sonority and strong personal originality. A facsimile of the last two pages (containing a passage of surprising beauty and dissonance) of this composition, as scored by Arnold Dolmetsch (in his own handwriting) from the original manuscript, will be found on page 242.

Last two pages of the manuscript score, made by Arnold Dolmetsch, of the Fantasy and Air in G minor by William Lawes

these compositions as being 'the highest summit of pure music'. I have no hesitation in saying that they are as superior to all other compositions for any type of stringed instruments (for instance, the string quartets of Haydn, Mozart, Beethoven, Brahms) as the piano writing of Chopin is superior to all other piano writing, as the orchestral style of Wagner is superior to all other orchestral styles. There is, after all, such a thing as the perfect use of a medium, and it seems to me very important that we should not neglect to recognize perfection in art when we find it—without denying, however, that imperfect art (with, for instance, an imperfect adjustment of the outer medium to the inner inspiration) also may have its great—though lesser—value. These Fantasies are as polyphonically melodious, in their own instrumental way, as are the vocal perfections of Palestrina. They do not suffer, as does so much string writing of later periods, from being orchestrally or pianistically conceived. Above all, they unfold the angelic mood, the sustained rapture, the complexity of musical thought, the glowing sonority, the breadth of form-flow so native to the strings. Furthermore, they are blessedly devoid of all that 'humor' (a quality always incompatible with real music, I find), 'comic relief' and displayfulness that mars so much post-Bach chamber music. The English Fantasies were not written for hungry professional musicians always in need of pushing forward their tiresome skill and personality; they were created for the delight of music-loving, leisured amateurs who wanted to *play* music in groups rather than *practise* 'technic' in single wretchedness. Therefore these Fantasies are ideally fitted to the needs of high-school musicians and all the other jolly and sensible groups of younger and older amateur musicians that are springing up everywhere in American musical life and are the comfort of all well-wishers of music.

But these chamber-music masterpieces must be played on the instruments they were written for—the viols—and not on members of the violin family. The less noisy, yet more 'edgy', tone quality of the thinner-strung viols enables the intricate voice-leading of these often highly polyphonic compositions to 'tell' with an obviously superior ease.

In a few years there will be a universal stampede in the direction of these pre-Bach consorts for viols. It is as easy to foretell this to-day—on the grounds that *the finest*, in any line, always makes its mark—as it was to foresee in 1890 the coming popularity of Bach, or in 1906 to foresee the pending vogue of Delius. In the meantime Arnold Dolmetsch, who above all men knows the secrets of this and other ancient European art music, is seventy-five years of age. The obviously sensible thing to do, for all forward-looking musicians who can manage it, is to emigrate to

Haslemere[32] and learn there the Dolmetsch traditions from their foun-
tain-head while they yet may! Why go to Bayreuth or Salzburg to rehash
traditions already familiar to all normally equipped musicians? Is it not
more important to acquire knowledge of the vast body of shamefully
neglected traditions concerning almost every phase of older music
unearthed and made living by Dolmetsch that so soon will become a
necessity to every self-respecting musician?

I can think of nothing that could be more fructifying to me, personally,
as a composer, pianist and music-maker generally, than to spend some
years under the Dolmetsch tutelage; and I say this as one who is not primarily interested in ancient music as such, but as one whose hopes and
interests are concerned with the music of the future. I believe that the
music of the future will be more soul-satisfying—more melodious, more
many-voiced, more complex, more rapturous, more angelic in mood—
than any music of the past. But I feel that the best training for future
musical perfection lies in at least some working knowledge of those past
periods of musical culture that possessed some real perfection.

In the case of those unlucky enough not to be able to visit Haslemere,
I recommend a perusal of Dolmetsch's epoch-making book, *The
Interpretation of the Music of the XVII and XVIII Centuries.*[33] This
closely-packed volume, with its appendix of invaluable musical illustrations, is the outcome of a lifetime of inspired investigation and correlation
of a myriad of neglected facts and contains a mine of information for all
musicians—be they singers, instrumentalists or conductors—concerned
with any music older than Beethoven's. What conscientious musician,
reading this handbook of hitherto lost tradition for the first time, can fail
to blush as he realizes the gross errors in style, ornamentation, tempo,
rhythm and other details he has inevitably committed when performing
the works of any of the older masters?[34]

I will close with some statements by Arnold Dolmetsch—culled from
his various writings—that seem to me typical of their author's wisdom,
insight and far-sight:

[32] Grainger's footnote: The next Dolmetsch festival at Haslemere will take place from July
17th to July 30th (inclusive), 1933. Those desirous of attending the festival should write early to
the Secretary of the Haslemere Festival, 'Jesses', Haslemere, Surrey, England, for information
regarding programs, tickets, hotels, boarding houses, reduced railroad fares, etc. Haslemere is a
little over an hour's run by train from London.

[33] Grainger's footnote: Novello & Co., London (U.S. agents, The H. W. Gray Co., New
York).

[34] Grainger's footnote: Note the amusing example of the *Meistersinger* 'Preislied', misinter-
preted as we misinterpret most older music, presented on page 109 of the *op. cit.*

'No art can develop healthily unless grounded upon a real, direct comprehension of the achievement of past generations. The neglect of this truth is the principal cause of the futile striving after originality and the misguided experiments which have brought music to its present chaos.'

(In estimating pre-Bach music) 'We should take warning from the 18th century connoisseurs, who declared Gothic architecture barbarous, or the early 19th-century art critics, who could see no beauty in pre-Raphaelite art.'

'Should not modern musicians treat the works of their masters as they wish their own may be treated in future centuries? Yes, but the unreasoned conviction of their own superiority obscures their mind. . . . We can no longer allow anyone to stand between us and the composer.'

30 Can Music Become a Universal Language?

(1933)

We often hear people talk of music as a universal language. I always wonder what they mean, for I can only see that music, as it is practised throughout the White Man's world, is the *least* universal of all the arts. If you show an ordinary man a Chinese red lacquered chair he will hardly mistake it for a piece of Chippendale furniture; he will hardly mistake a Bokhara rug for a Scottish plaid; and a great many people can tell the difference between a Japanese color-print and a Rembrandt etching without any great effort. But in music the most utter ignorance and confusion prevails if we step outside the European circle. If you play a typical American or British folksong to one of our normally equipped professional musicians he will probably think he is listening to a Chinese tune. He will not be able to distinguish between North-American, African or Australian native music and he will not have even a nodding acquaintance with the great art musics of the Orient, although they are just as significant in their own way as European art music is. And what is more, they are now available in a splendid and easily procurable album of twenty-two gramophone records, entitled *Musik des Orients*, that is published in Berlin. I shall play some of these records tonight.

This widespread indifference to oriental art music is the more astonishing when we recall how much some of the greatest European composers have learnt from exotic music in the last fifty years. Rimsky-Korsakov's *Scheherazade*[1] is a good example of a popular composition that is directly indebted to oriental influences. I will play you one of the chief themes from *Scheherazade*, and then let you hear a bit from a record of Persian folk music. You will hear that the two themes are almost identical. (*Play—* 12 sec.; *play Musik des Orients*, No. 19, last $\frac{1}{4}$ inch of record— 10 sec.)

We all know that modern music got its first impetus, at the beginning of the century, from the thrust of amazing originality put forth by Claude

Source: Typescript of radio broadcast on WEVD (New York), 20 June 1933, 10.15 p.m. Grainger Museum, Melbourne.
[1] Symphonic suite, Op. 35 (1888).

Debussy. What is less known is that Debussy's originality was immensely fructified by his contact with Javanese gamelan orchestras at a Paris exposition around 1888.[2] The gentleness of the gong-sounds influenced his sonorities, the five-tone Javanese scales influenced his choice of intervals, and the sense of blissful calm that pervades the tropical music developed in Debussy his subtle power of being intense without being noisy. I will let you hear a snatch of such Javanese music, for two voices, flute and gongs. It belongs to the type we call 'polymelodic', that is, freely intertwining melodies that are not bound tightly to each other by rhythmic bonds. (Record: *Musik des Orients*, No. 10. *Start* ½ inch from beginning, then 1.00.)

Now I shall play the opening of Debussy's piano piece called 'Pagodas'. (*Play* page 1, 'Pagodas'.) The next is from Ravel's 'The Valley of Bells'.[3] (*Play* page 1, 'Valley of Bells'.) It is hard to understand how students can steep themselves in the music of Rimsky-Korsakov, Debussy and Ravel without becoming at least mildly curious regarding the oriental models that so obviously inspired these great geniuses.

In America, today, thousands of young folk in their teens play bells, marimbas and other delightful percussion instruments without being able to find any group-music really suitable to their chosen medium. If these young music-lovers will assimilate the bizarre and whimsical percussion pieces from Bali and Siam, contained in the above-mentioned gramophone album *Musik des Orients*, I think they will find just what they are looking for. Here is the tail-end of a Siamese show-piece for xylophone. (*Play* record: *Musik des Orients*, No. 16, last half of record, 1.15 min.) So far, I have presented to you oriental music that is not contaminated by contact with ours of the West. But all over the native world—in America, as well as in Africa, Asia and the South Seas—delicious forms of melodiously polyphonic music, sometimes of the most complex types, are springing up as a result of the fusing of native and European musical traditions and habits. Here is a typical sample of such hybrid music from Madagascar, played by plucked strings and sung by two women's and two men's voices. (*Play* 'Oay Lahy E', begin ⅛ inch from outer rim, first 45 seconds.)

Most Negro-American folk music belongs in this category of hybrid music. The most touching music I have heard on this continent was the singing of the so-called 'Old Hampton Quartet'[4] —four men's voices whose improvised part-singing was untrammelled by any knowledge of musical notation or conventional harmony. The full flavor

[2] 1889.   [3] From *Miroirs* (1904–5).
[4] Associated with the Hampton Institute in Virginia, where Curtis-Burlin had carried out research in the 1910s.

of their unique art has been preserved for all time by that inspired genius among collectors, Natalie Curtis, in her four wonderful volumes of *Negro Folksongs*, published by G. Schirmer. Natalie Curtis possessed an ear of exceeding sensitiveness and also a deep intuitive grasp of the soul-life of exotic races. Her collections will someday become household words over the entire musical world, I do not doubt. I will play you a tiny lullaby from her *Negro Folksongs*. (*Play* 'Lullaby', Vol. 4, two verses.)

These and a thousand other forms of exotic music deserve to be studied by our musicians and enjoyed by our music-lovers. That they are still so neglected is perhaps not so surprising when we remember how far they are removed from our own lives, both geographically and culturally. But what are we to say to our terrible ignorance of our own European and American art music? The only European music that is well known in our concert halls is that composed between 1700 and 1900 in Italy, Austria, Germany and Russia. A very little French music is also known, but hardly more than a smattering. The glorious musical achievements of all the other European countries are passed over in silence, as a rule. Music written since 1900 is almost invariably outlawed, unless it happens to be esthetically scandalous or sensational, like Ravel's *Boléro* (which I adore, by the way) or Stravinsky's *The Rite of Spring*, or unless it happens to carry a title that appeals to our touristic sense, such as *Paris* by Delius, *An American in Paris* by Gershwin, *A London Symphony* by Vaughan Williams, 'Evening in Grenada' by Debussy, or my own *Country Gardens*.

Serious, spiritual music by American, British and Scandinavian composers seems to be rigidly excluded. There is the case of the Danish composer Herman Sandby, whose exquisite chamber music is still unknown to concert-goers, in spite of the fact that he was the first, around 1898, to recapture the true chamber music spirit lost since Bach. True chamber music, as I conceive of it, should give equal delight to all the players taking part, because all the parts that make up the harmonic texture are equally melodious and vital, equally interesting and instructive to play. Such music makes its appeal through the beauty of the musical thoughts themselves, and not as a vehicle to display the skill of the performers. These characteristics of true chamber music are clearly evident in the opening passage of the Andante amoroso from Sandby's Second String Quartet, published by Carl Fischer, New York, which you will hear from a Speak-O-Phone record made by that delightful group of artists, the Willem Durieux String Quartet of New York. (*Play* Speak-O-Phone record, GNSR 17, begin $\frac{1}{8}$ inch from outer rim, then 1.00.)

Perhaps it may interest you to compare this with an excerpt from an equally perfect example of true music dating from the early 17th century—the first Fantasy for five viols[5] by the English composer John Jenkins, born 1592. This record, also was made by the splendid Willem Durieux Chamber Music Ensemble. (*Play* Speak-O-Phone record, GNSR 2, begin $\frac{7}{16}$ inch from outer rim, then 1.15.)

A vast array of glorious Spanish and English fantasies for strings are available through the Dolmetsch Foundation in England. This is exactly the sort of musical fare to give to our string groups, clarinet groups, and saxophone groups in schools and elsewhere, for such polyphonically melodious music quickly develops an interest in the lower instruments and thus creates well-balanced sound bodies. On the other hand, the top-heavy, non-polyphonic chamber music of Haydn, Mozart, Beethoven, Schubert, Schumann and Brahms, with its unmelodious lower voices, naturally kills all interest in the lower instruments. That is why we find so many orchestras with sixteen first violins and only two violas and three cellos!

The amount of unheard early European music of the first rank is positively overwhelming. That clever and well informed writer Robert Donington is not exaggerating when he says that 'The music now known, which preceded Bach, exceeds the whole of the music from his time onward.'[6] These survivals of older European music do not constitute just *one* world of music, they constitute several totally different and distinct worlds of music, each of them as perfect and satisfying as the musical world of Beethoven, Wagner or Delius. One of these early phases is revealed to us by Dom Anselm Hughes in his fascinating book on *Worcester Mediaeval Harmony*.[7] I will let you hear an example of this thirteenth-century English monkish music. (*Play* record, *Mediaeval Music*, first section, 1.15 mins.)

A much later world of early music may be heard in 'La Bel' Aronde' (Pretty Swallow) by Claude Le Jeune, a Belgian composer born 1530. This winsome spring song was composed for six voices, but is here played for us on the strings of the Willem Durieux Chamber Music Ensemble. (*Play* Speak-O-Phone record, GNSR 1, begin $\frac{7}{8}$ in from outer rim, then

---

[5] In Grainger's own edition (pub. 1944) for modern string instruments, based on Arnold Dolmetsch's transcription for viols.

[6] See Robert Donington, *The Work and Ideas of Arnold Dolmetsch* (Haslemere: The Dolmetsch Foundation, 1932), 21–2.

[7] *Worcester Mediaeval Harmony of the Thirteenth and Fourteenth Centuries* (London: Plainsong and Mediaeval Music Society, 1928). Hughes (1889–1974), an English musicologist and historian, collaborated with Grainger in the 1930s and 1940s.

33 seconds.) (For the last two numbers I am indebted to Professor Gustave Reese, lecturer on Mediaeval and Renaissance Music at New York University, College of Fine Arts.[8])

The only modern American music that can be said to be really widely known, in America or Europe, is jazz, or somewhat jazz-like compositions, such as Gershwin's *Rhapsody in Blue*. Such music is often truly inspired and thoroughly deserves its great popularity. All the same, it is only *one* side of American music, and not *the* most thrilling side at that. A superb example of the loftiest flight of the noblest American muse is *The Seventh Quintet* for piano and strings by Arthur Fickénscher, an American composer born in 1871. While I am a reverent admirer of the piano and string quintets by Bach, César Franck, Brahms, Cyril Scott and others, I must confess that this American work by Fickénscher out-soars them all, for my ears, in point of spiritual rapture and sensuous loveliness. It combines the harmonic and polyphonic traditions of Bach, Wagner, Brahms and César Franck with iconoclastic experimentation of a highly original nature, for instance in the use of intervals closer than the half-tone. The following passage from a record made of the work by the Willem Durieux Quartet and myself contains these closer intervals that I consider so prophetic of the music of the future. (*Play* Speak-O-Phone record, GNSR 14 Vse, begin $2\frac{1}{8}$ inch before end of record, then 1.20.)

I have put before you a few—a very few—of the world of music's neglected masterpieces. In my work at the Summer School of the Music Education Department of New York University I shall try to demonstrate how examples of all the world's music can be made applicable to ordinary practical everyday American music-making—for instance, how gramophone records of exotic music can be reduced for notation and fitted to our voices and instruments.

I firmly believe that music will someday become a 'universal language'. But it will not become so as long as our musical vision is limited to the output of four European countries between 1700 and 1900. The first step in the right direction is to view the music of all peoples and periods without prejudice of any kind, and to strive to put the world's known and available best music *into circulation*. Only then shall we be justified in calling music a 'universal language'.

---

[8] (1899–1977), lectured at New York University from 1927. His *Music in the Middle Ages* appeared in 1940.

Melody versus Rhythm

(1932/3)

Final Goal of Musical Art

I was interested to read in *The Musical Quarterly* the other day, in an article on Ancient Chinese Music by Robert W. Marks, the following quotation from the Chinese *Record of Rites*, said to date from 2255 B.C.: 'Poetry is the expression of earnest thought, and singing is the prolonged utterance of that expression.'[1]

That statement is just as true of the higher flights of Western music today or yesterday as it presumably was of Chinese music long ago. I take it for granted that it is the office of the higher flights of music to uplift us, to emotionalize us and to awaken and increase within us the wellsprings of dreaminess, lovingness and compassionateness—in other words, to prepare our natures for some kind of angelic life (presumably here on earth) and to turn our thoughts away from worldly and practical things of life—those things Walt Whitman called 'the terrible doubt of appearances'.[2]

It seems evident to me that it is melody and harmony rather than rhythm that is empowered to turn our natures towards the angelic state. What do we mean by melody? I think we all mean fundamentally the same thing by the term 'melody'. Even the most unmusical person will hardly speak of 'a melody on the bugle' or 'a melody on the drum'; so we may assume that even the popular conception of melody does not associate melody primarily with broken chords or with rhythm. Melody, I take it, is single-line sound that follows the nature of the human voice. The

Source: *Australian Musical News*, 24/1 (Aug. 1933), 12–14. This text largely follows Grainger's lecture of the same title, presented at Steinway Hall, New York, on 6 Dec. 1932, itself based on Grainger's notes for his New York University Music A–B lectures of 20 and 27 Sept. 1932. A modified version of Grainger's Steinway Hall lecture also appeared in 'Pointed Paragraphs', *Music News* (Chicago), 29 Sept. 1933, p. 9, and 6 Oct. 1933, p. 9. The Chicago version of Grainger's essay drew a reply from Béla Bartók: 'Béla Bartók Replies to Percy Grainger', *Béla Bartók Essays*, ed. Benjamin Suchoff (London: Faber & Faber, 1976), 224–5. See, further, James Porter, 'Bartók and Grainger: Some Correspondences and a Hypothesis', *Studia Musicologica*, 25 (1983), 221–8.

[1] See Essay **28**, n. 2.   [2] Title of poem in 'Calamus', *Leaves of Grass* (1891–2 edn.).

human voice occasionally gives out shouts and barking sounds and other detached sounds: but in the main it tends towards long, continuous, sustained legato sounds—'prolonged utterances'—and it is these sounds that we call melody.

Instruments that closely follow the sustained utterance of the human voice (such as the strings, the saxophone, the brass and wind instruments, the organ) we consider melodious instruments, while other instruments that are not modelled upon the tone-type of the human voice (such as the piano, the percussion and plucked instruments) we consider less melodic.

Broadly speaking, I think we may generalize and say that religious music, all over the world (whether in Europe, Asia, the South Seas, etc.) has been preponderatingly melodic—as we would naturally expect lofty and uplifting music to be. On the other hand, the dance songs and the working songs of the world have been comparatively rhythmic and unmelodic.

Rhythm is a great energizer, a great slave-driver; and the lower types of mankind (the tyrants; the greedy ones; the business-minded people) have not been slow to sense the practical advantages to be drawn from rhythmically-regular music as an energizing action-bearing force. When these 'hard-headed', practical people want young men to go and get themselves killed,[3] they play marches to them and they encourage sailors and road workers to sing at their jobs in order that the maximum of hard work may be forthcoming as economically as possible.

Practical Minds and the Dance

The practical-minded people welcome any type of music that will encourage themselves and others to dance rather than to dream, to act rather than to think. Don't I see the proofs of this in my own royalty returns? We composers know that (with rare exceptions) our rhythmic compositions sell by the thousands while our melodic compositions sell by the tens or the hundreds. Rhythmic-typed works such as Stravinsky's *The Rite of Spring* and Ravel's *Boléro* have been performed and discussed endlessly, while heart-transmuting, melodious works such as Arnold Schönberg's Five Orchestral Pieces and Delius' *The Song of the High Hills* have remained relatively unperformed and undiscussed.

[3] In the Chicago version of this paper the editor of 'Pointed Paragraphs', Eyvind H. Bull, added the note: 'Although it is evident that Mr. Grainger is opposed to war, he enlisted in the United States Army and served throughout the World War in various capacities in the Army Bandmasters' School.'

During the last thirty years there has been a regular orgy of rhythmic music, both in the jazz and in the classical fields. Well, the results are before us, and we of the dreamy and anti-active persuasions may ask if they really are so good—from even a 'practical' standpoint. Mankind has responded most loyally to rhythmic intoxication; millions have been killed or had their lives upset by the wars and still more millions have allowed themselves to become needlessly, and uselessly, 'hard-boiled' in all sorts of ways, responding to the calls of energy and worldliness. We may now ask ourselves whether we would have been worse off, from any standpoint, if we had listened less to the energizing suggestions of rhythm and more to the spiritualizing influences of melody.[4]

I have said that we have been through an orgy of rhythmic music. But there are clear indications that large sections of music-loving folk today are increasingly craving rapturous, sustained, spiritualizing melodious music. The case of Frederick Delius shows us the typical position of an exalted and incurable dreamer during the present economic change. Here is a composer who has written nothing that is 'effective' or spectacular, nothing that appeals to virtuoso conductors or soloists. No songs, no piano pieces, no solos of any kind that amount to anything. Most of his representative compositions are long, vague and (from a superficial viewpoint) monotonous, and they are mostly expensive and troublesome to perform. But they certainly are 'the prolonged expression of earnest thought'; they certainly are melodious, harmonious, uplifting and spiritualizing. As Delius has been blind and paralyzed for the last ten years, and as he is mainly dependent upon the proceeds from his compositions for his wherewithal, it is consoling to those of us who consider him the greatest of living composers to learn that his royalties have never been so high as in the last two years. As far as my personal experience goes, serious, dreamy, uplifting, emotional, melodic music has never prospered in my lifetime as it does today.

Melody's Thread of Unity

My programme of illustrations is selected to show the thread of unity running through the basic types of melody in many times and places. The programme may produce an impression of same-ishness, as it is not

---

[4] Grainger's original lecture script had added here: Would we have done worse if we had copied Walt Whitman when he says, 'I loafe and invite my soul?' [From 'Song of Myself' No. 1, in *Leaves of Grass* (1891–2 edn.).]

designed to present a succession of contrasts, but, on the contrary, to stress the persistence and universality of certain types of lofty, melodic habits.

As dance music is often designed to remind the dancers of repetitions in their dance steps and figures by means of repetitions of musical phrases, it is only natural that sequential and repetitious phrases (example: second theme of the first movement of Schubert's 'Unfinished' Symphony) may be expected in such music. On the other hand, such sequential and repetitious phrases (and the lack of intervallic inventiveness and inspiration that they imply) are the bane of all truly melodic music. It stands to reason that true melody steers clear of all repetitions and sequences of four-bar phrases and other cut-and-dried platitudes. Melody makes its chief appeal by means of slowly-moving, freely-curved, non-repetitious intervallic expression—by means of the contrasts between higher and lower notes and the subtle suggestions and meanings that these contrasts possess for musical ears, if they are heard at not too fast a speed. I may cite these:

1. SINGLE-LINE MELODY
    'Fraanar Ormen' (Norwegian archaic hero-song)
    Plainsong (*Columbia History of Music*, No. 1)
    Opening of *Parsifal* Prelude
    La Bel' Aronde (Claude Le Jeune)
    Javanese gamelan (*Musik des Orients*, No. 10)
    Melody in Cyril Scott's *Aubade*

2. POLY-MELODIC MUSIC (without harmonic consciousness)
    Javanese gamelan record (*Musik des Orients*, No. 9)

3. MELODIOUS POLYPHONY (the harmonies arrived at by the melodious flow of individual voices)
    Purcell: Four-part Fantasia No. 8, for strings
    Bach: D sharp minor Fugue, Second book (piano)
    Wm. Lawes: Six-part Fantasia and Air No. 1 (transcribed by Arnold Dolmetsch)[5]
    Hindemith: *Die junge Magd*, first movement.

Poly-melodic music may be visualized as somewhat similar to a life lived in a kindly country where bananas grow (without human tending) naturally on the trees and life may be lived happily and selfishly without much

[5] See Essays **29** and **32**. Grainger's own edition for modern string instruments (pub. 1944) was based on Dolmetsch's transcription for viols.

awareness of relatives, laws, duties and the needs and troubles of our fellow-men. We see that animals can witness the death and misfortunes of their fellow animals and go their way wholly, or comparatively, unaffected. Yet if we modern humans witness an automobile or other accident we are likely to feel deadly sick—an accident to a fellow man being only different in degree to an accident to ourselves, so much are we aware of the world's agony all around us and correspondingly sensitized by that awareness. A similar sensitized awareness underlies Western Melodious Polyphony. As we play our own sounds we are aware of all the other sounds around us and aware of the harmonic import of the whole. We move in a kind of blissful agony of rapturous, compassionate sound awareness that, I believe, to be highly contributory to the coming angelic-ness of mankind.

Perfect Melodious Polyphony

It seems strange that the most perfect example of Melodious Polyphony that I can find to put beside Purcell, Lawes and Bach should be the work of a modern German; for we might expect that the *Sachlichkeit*[6] of the present-day Germany would hardly make for angelic music. Yet, the fact remains that the first movement of the Hindemith *Die junge Magd* carries on in great perfection the noblest old-time polyphonic traditions and unites with them a harmonic freedom (a harmonic discordance) that is a clear, twentieth-century gain. No less than in Purcell and Bach are Hindemith's harmonics (in this piece) arrived at by the melodious flow of the parts.

In all this Melodious Polyphonic music all the voices that make up the harmonic texture are equally expressive melodically; the bass (lowest) part is as melodic as the top part and the middle parts are not less so.

This type of music seems to me the most soulfully expressive yet evolved in music, and the most stimulating towards the angelic state of mankind for which we are all striving. Of course, I believe that the Free Music (non-intervallic, non-rhythmic, melodic, harmonic or super-harmonic)[7] of the future will be still more subtle, rapturous, lovely and spiritualizing.

---

[6] Worldliness (Germ.).

[7] Grainger's lecture script has 'non-intervallic, non, rhythmic, melodic[al]ly harmonic or super-harmonic'.

4. MELODIC HARMONIC POLYPHONY (harmonic thought dominating, yet always expressing itself in melodic, or quasi-melodic, part movements)

    Bach: Air from Suite in D

    Herman Sandby: Slow movement from Second String Quartet

    Grieg: 'Evening in the High Hills'[8]

    Delius: Excerpts from Dance Rhapsody (two pianos)

5. IRREGULARLY-PULSED MELODY

    Madagascar record (Native three-part music)

    Claude Le Jeune: *La Bel' Aronde*

    Cyril Scott: Solemn Dance

The slave-driving, soul-stultifying influence of rhythm lies in regularity and repetitiousness and in all the four-bar phrases and other forms of musical platitudinousness and inventive torpor that these give rise to. On the other hand, subtle, irregular, unrepetitious rhythms hold fine influence towards freedom and rapture.

6. PROGRESSIVE (EXPERIMENTAL) MUSIC

    Cyril Scott: Excepts from Piano Sonata, Op. 66

    Arthur Fickénscher: Excerpts from *The Seventh Quintet* (piano and strings).

* * *

During and after Bach's time such strong influences from dance music and popular music beat down upon art music that most of the noblest traditions of art music were forgotten or ignored. It was a real jazz period—much as if we today were to throw overboard the accumulated musical culture found in Palestrina, Bach, Wagner, Delius, etc., and to content ourselves merely with such cultural traditions (no mean ones at that—yet inevitably more limited than the traditions derived from an unbroken contact with all available periods of music culture) as survive in Gershwin and other gifted half-jazz-like, half-classical composers.

It was only after Mendelssohn, Schumann and others in the mid-nineteenth century discovered and appraised the grander flights of Bach's genius (and that of his forerunners) that a competent insight into the nobler technical and emotional possibilities of true art music were regained and progressive experimentation of a serious and complex character resumed.

[8] Op. 68 No. 4.

Freedom and Irregularity

It seems to be the final goal of all the arts to be able to tally the freedom and irregularity of nature—to be able to produce in art something well nigh as subtle and inspired as what we see and feel around us in life and nature. Especially in our century do we see this urge manifest itself.

Arnold Schönberg has freed us from the inevitability of harmony—we can now write harmony or disharmony as we please. Cyril Scott has done much to open up realms of irregular rhythm. It is significant that it was only after the Scott Piano Sonata (composed around 1904) had been widely performed in Europe by the composer and others that highly irregular rhythms (such as we meet with in Stravinsky, Hindemith, etc.) began to appear in the works of composers on the European continent.

The rhythmic irregularity of the Scott Sonata is arrived at by using a very quick duration-unit (such as a sixteenth note[9] in a fast tempo) and grouping it irregularly.[10]

It is obvious that the melodies of the future must be able to glide freely to and from all kinds of unpredetermined intervals and to hover in an unanchored intervallic vagueness and subtlety. In other words, we cannot remain forever chained to the limitations of arbitrary scales and modes—which may be compared to stairs up and down which we may step, without being at liberty to move to distances that lie in between the regular spaces of the stairs. Arthur Fickénscher is a forward-looking genius who is freeing us from this all-too-long-endured bondage of scales and modes.

At the University of Virginia this composer has constructed an exquisite-toned harmonium (Polytone) with five pitch divisions to the half-tone (5 Cs of different pitches, 5 C sharps of different pitches, and so on) from which he draws harmonies of heartrending beauty.[11] Also in his writings for strings he uses intervals closer than the conventional ones with unmistakable inspiration and deep emotional appeal. Fickénscher's *The Seventh Quintet* for piano and strings strikes me as the most profoundly lovely and significant work for this medium known to me and as pointing the way to our melodic future with prophetic powers.[12]

---

[9] Semiquaver.

[10] Grainger's lecture script added here: (Let audience count irregular barrings in the Scherzo while P.G. plays them.)

[11] See Fickénscher's article 'The Polytone and the Potentialities of a Purer Intonation', *Musical Quarterly*, 27 (1941), 356–70.

[12] Grainger's lecture script concluded: A few short excerpts from this epoch-making work cannot do justice to the grandeur of its formal unfoldment, yet may serve to show you the subtle effect of these closer intervals that he uses and give a hint of the exalted spirituality of his muse.

32   *Characteristics of Nordic Music*
(1933)

In talking to you of the characteristics of Nordic Music I am not using the term 'Nordic' scientifically, but merely in the loose sense that we speak of Latin or Germanic or Slavonic characteristics or tendencies in art. I am not concerned with the correct definition of exactly what a Nordic is; I am not concerned with the purity or impurity of the Nordic race anywhere, or even with the percentage of Nordicness in the Nordic countries. By 'Nordic countries' I mean those countries where we see lots of people with blue eyes, fair hair, narrow heads and faces, and tall or tallish, slight body-build. The Nordic countries are, of course, Scandinavia, Holland, Great Britain, Ireland, the United States, Canada, Australia, and several other countries. Long before I had heard or read the sacred term 'Nordic' I had discovered for myself that these countries had certain striking musical characteristics in common, and to these characteristics I am now applying the term 'Nordic' as a convenient label.[1] In some of these partially-Nordic countries the Nordicness of the composers seems to be higher than that of the population at large. In England probably only about half of the total population is blond, the other half being more or less brunette. On British ships we often see that most of the stewards are dark or fairly dark while the actual sailors and the officers are almost invariably blond. Likewise in music—the spiritual leaders are blonder than the rank and file. English orchestras seem full of brunette types, and at least two of England's most famous conductors (Sir Henry Wood and Sir Thomas Beecham) are extremely dark. But I have never yet met an outstanding English composer who was not a pronounced Nordic. This is true of the following English composers: Elgar, Delius, Cyril Scott, Balfour Gardiner, Roger Quilter, Holst, Granville Bantock,[2] Bax, Vaughan Williams, Peter Warlock.

Of course a Jew, a Negro, or any other non-Nordic individual, can write typically Nordic music if he is living in a Nordic country and if his musical mind is sufficiently impregnated with the thoughts, feelings and

Source: Typescript of radio broadcast on WEVD (New York), 4 July 1933, 10.15 p.m. Grainger Museum, Melbourne.

[1] Cf. opening to Essay **17**.
[2] (1868–1946), English composer, especially of orchestral and choral works.

musical traditions of that land—just as a man of wholly German parentage, such as Frederick Delius, can write typically and unmistakably English music if born in England and deeply impressed with English influences. We may reasonably question the racial purity of the origins of any music. For instance, I think we may take it for granted that the elements that make up the folk musics of the various European countries have roamed around and interpenetrated to an almost limitless extent through the centuries. So it would probably be absurd to talk of a purely German or purely French folksong; yet it would be still more absurd to refuse to call German a typically German folksong on the ground that some of its ingredients most likely were of international origin. The nationality of the music shows in its final condition rather than in its beginnings.

So in speaking of Nordic music I am thinking less of the possible origins of such music than of the strong musical and human characteristics that unite the musical output of all the Nordic countries, now and in the past, and distinguish it clearly from the music composed in non-Nordic or less-Nordic countries such as Germany, France, Russia, and others.

If we begin to examine Nordic music we shall be struck by the fact that the melodic habits of America, Great Britain, Ireland and Scandinavia are much nearer akin to the melodic habits of China and other Mongolian countries than they are to the melodic habits of such European countries as France, Italy, Spain, Germany and Austria.

In fact, we may tentatively speak of two main streams of musical traditions in Asia and Europe: the Mongolian-Nordic musical tradition, which favors solemn or spiritual unadorned melodies with long sustained notes or at least clearly defined intervals, gapped scales and a marked tendency to some kind or other of underlying harmonic or polyphonic thought; and the Mohammedan musical tradition, which favors nervous excitable florid tunes with quickly fluctuating notes, closely filled-up scales and a tendency to seek surface complexity in technical passagework and vocal coloratura rather than in an under-current of harmonic thought. We see what I choose to call the Mongolian musical traditions holding strong sway in China, Japan, Java, Siam, and elsewhere in the Far East, and extending across Siberia and Russia to the Nordic lands of Western Europe and thence to those other parts of the world colonised by Nordics.

Before I let you hear some samples of typical Mongolian-Nordic melody I will repeat for you what I consider to be their salient characteristics: long notes, or at least clearly-defined intervals; gapped scales; solemnity or spirituality of mood; and a tendency towards underlying harmonic thought. In other words: a complex basis with a simple surface. The following Japanese song, from the *Musik des Orients* album of gramophone records, is an instance of long, sustained notes given forth in a gaunt, unadorned style. (*Play*, *Musik des Orients*, No. 1, Japan.)

The next, a Chinese popular tune, also shows quite clearly defined and unadorned intervals, despite its faster tempo. The exquisite five-tone harmonies with which the air is accompanied are provided by Joseph Yasser in his epoch-making musicological book entitled *A Theory of Evolving Tonality*.[3] (*Play*, on piano 'Fresh beautiful Flower' tune,[4] page 98).

The following record, also from *Musik des Orients*, shows us how the Mongolian tradition works in Siam, making, as usual, for calmness of mood and clearness of intervals. (*Play*, *Musik des Orients*, No. 16, Siam.)

The well-known 'Volga Boat-song', with its serene, uplifted mood and gapped, well-defined intervals, is an instance of how the Mongolian-Nordic musical tradition operates in Russia—from which country hundreds of examples could be cited.

Now I will play you the typically American folksong 'Little Sparrow' from Howard Brockway's masterly and fascinating *Lonesome Tunes*, so that you may hear how little our Anglo-Saxon melodies differ from those of the Far East in mood, intervals and method. (*Play*, on piano, 'Little Sparrow'.)

A good example from our art music, evincing the same tenderness and wistfulness, the same gapped scale and well-defined intervals is the following, the chief theme of Cyril Scott's *Aubade*, for orchestra. (*Play*, on piano.)

One of the most marked characteristics of many Nordic folksongs is their abnormally large compass—sometimes almost two octaves between the highest and lowest notes of the melody; whereas in tribal singing, where a group of voices sing songs in unison, the compass is often only half an octave, being curtailed upwards by the limitations of the lower voices of the group and curtailed downwards by the limitations of the higher voices.

A possible explanation of the exceptionally wide range of notes found

---

[3] (New York: American Library of Musicology, 1932). Yasser (b. 1893) was a Polish-born American musicologist, organist, and conductor.

[4] 'Beautiful Fresh Flower', a tune used in Puccini's *Turandot*, which Grainger arranged (after Yasser) for piano solo.

in our Nordic melodies is that they were sung by our fore-fathers while engaged in such lonely pursuits as shepherding, the full range of the individual voice being able to be used when singing without reference to other voices. The lonely pursuits of our fore-fathers, when active as shepherds, cowherds, saeter-girls, fishermen, and the like, on the waste-lands and waters of Scandinavia, Scotland, Ireland, America, Australia, etc., may account for the emotions of loneliness, homesickness, wistfulness and mournfulness that fill our melodies with touching loveliness. The tender American melodies of Stephen Foster are perfect examples of what I mean. We are not sentimentalizing unduly when we say that typical Nordic music is the voice of the wide open spaces, the soul of virgin nature made manifest in sound, and this is as true of our greatest art music (such as *The Song of the High Hills*, by Frederick Delius) as it is of our most primitive folksongs.

Here are some of our wide-range melodies of the lonely pursuits: The first is the Swedish melody 'Värmlandsvisan'. (*Play*, on piano).

The next is a typical Irish folksong, entitled 'My Lagan Love' and most poetically harmonised by Hamilton Harty.[5] This has a range of an octave and a half (*Play*, on piano). An even greater compass is found in the American folksong 'Pretty Polly', published in Howard Brockway's *Twenty Kentucky Mountain Songs*, a superb work that should be consulted by everyone interested in the noblest flights of American melody (*Play*, on piano).

The range of this tune is only two notes short of two octaves (*Play*, on piano). The same wide range of intervals is present in the popular Irish tune sometimes called 'The Londonderry Air'. (*Play*, on piano)

Now for the other side of the picture—the nervous, passionate, excitable tunes of the Mohammedan musical tradition, consisting largely of quickly changing notes that scamper about like the flitting of insects. In this restless, self-assertive music we seldom meet with long sustained notes, clearly-defined intervals and calm, spiritual, wistful moods as in the case of the Mongolian-Nordic tradition. Nor do we sense any harmonic or polyphonic thought behind this Mohammedan music. I described the Mongolian-Nordic music as having a complex basis with a simple surface. The Mohammedan music is just the other way round: it has a simple basis and a highly complicated surface. Here is an East-Indian record from *Musik des Orients*, showing the fondness for vocal fire-works and

---

[5] From *Three Traditional Ulster Airs* (1905), by Irish composer, pianist, and conductor, (Herbert) Hamilton Harty (1879–1941).

teaching us the origins of our own Southern European operatic col-oratura: (*Play, Musik des Orients*, No. 18, Vorderindien.)

The record of Spanish gypsy music that you are now to hear proves how very faithfully the traditions of music as we know them in India, Persia, Arabia, Egypt, etc., were transplanted into Spain by the Moors. (*Play*, Peteneras,[6] No. 1.)

The following record of modern Egyptian music shows the predilec-tion for arabesques and display-music in both its vocal and instrumental forms. (*Play, Musik des Orients*, No. 20, Ägypten).

Accompanying the Mohammedan traditions of music we generally find a population with big or fleshy noses, of the Semitic or Roman type. On the other hand, where the Mongolian-Nordic musical traditions hold sway we see among the populations a large proportion of people with smooth, flat faces, high cheek-bones and small turned-up noses. This is as true of Scotland, Ireland, Scandinavia and Russia as it is of the Mongolian countries.

All these unscientific thoughts about the geographical and racial origins of Asiatic and European music seem to me quite harmless, as long as we entertain them with inquiring and elastic minds and do not claim any sci-entific authority for our guess-work. Some day theories may be proved or disproved by the researches of comparative musicology, a much-needed society for the prosecution of which in America has been started by the composer Charles Seeger,[7] and others.

For the moment it is at least very convenient and illuminating to view European art music from the standpoint of these two main streams of Asiatic musical traditions. We may, according to many students and theorists, think of harmony and polyphony arising in the more northerly countries of Europe as an outcome of the Celtic or Nordic tradition, while the elaborate musical figuration of European art music (as we see it in Couperin, Bach, Chopin, and others) is obviously due to the influence exerted by the Moorish-Spanish traditions.

We read of harmony being practised in England and Northern France in the tenth century, or earlier, and the early development of polyphony as an art capable of high beauty and perfection is proved by the existence in the 14th century of such gems as the 'Alleluya psallat' you will now hear, which was deciphered by that inspired musicologist Dom Anselm

---

[6] Traditional Spanish song, named after a 19th-cent. singer.

[7] (1886–1979), broad-ranging American musical figure. He founded and chaired the New York Musicological Society in 1930–4, from which emerged the American Musicological Society in 1934. He was also president of the American Society for Comparative Musicology in 1935.

Hughes and published in his book on *Worcester Mediaeval Harmony*, issued by the Plainsong and Mediaeval Music Society in England.[8] This record was sung by the monks of Nashdom Abbey under the direction of Dom Anselm Hughes. (*Play*, record *Fourteenth-century Music*, first section.)

Knud Jeppesen[9] (the great Danish authority on Palestrina) has some light-shedding words to say about the origin of the madrigal. He says: 'Through contact between Netherland and Italian composers the madrigal was born. It arose out of a blending of the northern erudition and northern love of the charm of complexity with the southern taste for euphony and southern craving for tonal clarity'. This sentence of Knud Jeppesen's goes to the very root of the matter and explains why it is so difficult to get non-Nordic musicians to appreciate our Nordic music—of any type or period; it is too genuinely complicated for them. It is not a Nordic view—one that we hear propounded in and out of season—that artistic greatness shows itself in the choice of simple mediums. We Nordic composers prefer complexity at all costs—even if it results in monotony and lack of tonal clarity. That is why it is so painful for us to listen for long to the simplicities of Southern European music—it does not seem to nourish us musically and our minds wander away from its platitudes and redundancies. This mutual lack of understanding between Nordic and Southern musicians is not necessarily due to intolerance or chauvinism on either side, but is the natural result of two different types of musical minds. Whether this divergence is the result of inherent racial differences or mere exterior influences, I am unable to say.

It seems as if we Nordics naturally view life and nature as onlookers rather than as participants and that this impersonal and stoical habit of mind in us makes for metaphysical, cosmic musical expression. Certainly, our music seems to have been intrinsically complex at all known periods. We saw this in the 14th-century English partsong noted by Dom Anselm Hughes. We hear the same delicious complexity in the string fantasies written by English chamber-music composers in the 16th and 17th centuries. Here is the ending of the First Fantasy and Air for six viols by William Lawes, one of the greatest musical geniuses of all time, an English composer who died in 1645. This masterpiece was transcribed for me by Arnold Dolmetsch, that giant among musicologists, and it is here played

[8] See Essay 30. Grainger's edition of this three-part motet 'for practical music-making' was published in 1943.

[9] (1892–1974), Danish composer and musicologist.

from a Speak-O-Phone record made by the superb Willem Durieux
String Quartet of New York. (*Play*, Speak-O-Phone record, GNSR 4, last
half.)

The harsh yet exquisite discordance of this music by William Lawes is
as startling, as daring, as radical—in its own calm way—as the dissonances
of the most ultra-modern atonal composer living today. The same intrinsic complexity of Nordic musical thinking is present in that amazing
work, entitled *The Seventh Quintet*, by Arthur Fickénscher, an American
composer born in 1871. On July 23, at 8 o'clock, from this same station,
Mr Ludvik Schwab, the Willem Durieux String Quartet and I are going
to give the first broadcast of this glorious work in its entirety. For the
moment, I shall content myself with a tiny excerpt from it. (*Play*, Speak-
O-Phone record, GNSR 13, Fickénscher Quintet.)

The continual complexity of the Nordic musical mind makes for monotony, of course, and the constant interweaving of polyphonic voices
induces vagueness and a lack of clarity. It is easy to understand that
the everlasting musical expression of the emotions of purity, loftiness,
loneliness and wistfulness can become extremely boring to those in
whose natures these emotions do not preponderate and who look, in
music, for simple appeals such as effectiveness, brilliance, passion and
dramatic contrasts. But I plead that we Nordics must be pardoned for
liking our music to correspond to our own natures. Our music is like
our Nordic civilisations—more scientific, more highly complicated and
organised, more restrained, more tender and tolerant than any other
known music and civilisation. If we admire these high qualities in our civilisation it seems to me that we should enjoy their manifestation in music,
particularly as music is an art peculiarly well-fitted to voice these subtle
qualities.

Is it the scientific bias of our age and civilisation that makes Nordic
composers turn to nature rather than to human impulses for musical
inspiration, or is it the atavistically-acquired memory of our lonely
pursuits of the past, such as shepherding, before alluded to tonight?
One thing is certain: that no other racial group has been so consistently
inspired to write music about the elements and about rivers, mountains
and plains as we have. A glance at the titles of works by Nordic
composers will soon convince us of this. Think of MacDowell's *Sea
Pictures*[10] and *Woodland Sketches*, Grieg's 'Evening in the Mountains' and

---

[10] *Sea Pieces*, Op. 55 (1898).

Lost in the Hills, Sandby's *Sea Mood*, Schjelderup's[11] *Sunrise on the Himalayas*, Delius's *Summer Night on the River*, *On Hearing the First Cuckoo in Spring*, *The Song of the High Hills* and *Appalachia* (the last-named a tone-poem about the Mississippi River), Vaughan Williams's 'Pastoral' Symphony, and the like. Contrast with these the typical titles of modern French music, from which we gather that the artifice of man or allusions to classical antiquity have to be associated with nature or the elements before they become creatively inspiring to Gallic composers. Consider in this light Debussy's *Afternoon of a Faun*, 'Fireworks', 'The Sunken Cathedral', 'Evening in Grenada' and Ravel's *The Fountains*, 'The Valley of Bells', 'Ondine', etc.[12]

German, Austrian and Bohemian composers seem fairly evenly divided between nature music and the human emotions. On the other hand, Russian composers seldom seem to want to voice nature impressions in their music.

Not alone as inspiring themes, but also in a more direct way do nature impressions hold sway in Nordic music, for instance in the manner in which sounds actually heard in nature enter into our music—particularly the moaning sounds of the wind and similar whining noises that glide up and down in pitch and do not settle on a definite note. Such sounds are heard in the singing of birds, the lowing of cattle, the howling of dogs, as well as in an accelerating automobile engine and in other mechanical noises. As soon as chromatic harmony became well developed in the last century, Nordic composers began to take up these nature sounds into their music. As these sounds are best made by strings or voices I will begin with a short example from the slow movement of Herman Sandby's Second String Quartet, published by Carl Fischer. Here you will hear consistently sliding sounds in three of the parts. (*Play*, Speak-O-Phone record, GNSR 17.)

This same type of sliding chromatic chords appears often in the music of Frederick Delius, notably in the first movement of his orchestral *North Country Sketches*, which is entitled: 'Autumn—the Wind soughs in the Trees'.[13] (*Play*, on piano, pages 3–5, duet.)

In Grieg these sliding voices that imitate nature sounds often occur in the bass, as in the opening of his Ballad, Op. [24]. (*Play*, on piano.) Or they appear in the middle voices of the harmony. I shall play you a few

---

[11] Gerhard Schjelderup (1859-1933), Norwegian composer.
[12] Cf. Essay **17**.   [13] 1913–14.

such harmonies of Grieg's, humming the gliding voice, so that you may more readily sense its kinship with the nature sounds. (Examples from 'Veslemöy' (*Haugtussa*)[14] and 'De norske Fjelde'.[15])

These gliding tones of more or less indefinite pitch are delightfully present in American jazz, though here it is sometimes difficult to know whether to assign to them a Nordic or Negro origin. You will hear these gliding tones in the following excerpt from Duke Ellington's fascinating 'Creole Love Call'. (*Play*, Brunswick, 'Creole Love Call'.[16])

No doubt Nordic composers will push these nature-inspired sounds so far that we will soon be able to compose entirely in soaring, floating sonorities, if we wish, and dispense with the slavish limitation of set intervals, which are perhaps merely a remnant of music's infancy. To float freely through musical space seems a more alluring prospect than to be sentenced to the treadmill of uniformly distanced tone-steps, as we are at present. Nordic composers such as Cyril Scott have made great strides in the irregularisation of rhythm and in other forms of tonal freedom. Very soon Nordic music will no longer be chained to the present arbitrary limitations of scale, rhythm and harmony but will be able to freely tally in music the freedom and irregularity of nature as we sense it in us and around us. By that I do not merely mean that music will be able (if we so wish) to imitate all nature sounds and take them up into its tonal palette; that is the least important potentiality of free music. More important will be the power to give free musical expression to all the dictates of the human heart and to our human impressions of any and every phase of nature. When free music is capable of all this it will have become as completely nature-imbued as Greek sculpture was at the time of its fullest development, when all shapes and movements seen in nature could be tallied without limitations imposed by technical shortcomings or by tyrannic habits of stylisation. When music shall have reached a comparable freedom and development we may presume that it will completely satisfy our Nordic esthetic cravings and that it will then call for no further technical progress.

[14] No. 2 from *Haugtussa*, Op. 67 (1895–8).
[15] No. 2 from *Children's Songs*, Op. 61 (1894).
[16] First recorded for Victor in 1927; extensively revised and extended for the 1932 Brunswick recording.

Can Music be Debunked?
(1933/4)

Let it Function in a Natural Way[1]

Editor's Note: In this, the first of several articles the eminent Australian composer and pianist has promised to contribute to the *Australian Musical News*,
he says a number of things which are provocative and stimulating. Some will
contend, of course, that in order to 'debunk' singing, for instance, or to
'debunk' piano playing and other forms of musical expression as we understand it, the art of composition would have to be abolished altogether, and all
set compositions beyond the simplest would have to be forgotten. That may
be left to the musicians themselves to fight out, if they so desire.

When I ask the question 'can music be debunked?' I suppose I must first
state what 'bunk' in music consists of. In my opinion anything is bunk
that wraps music round with mysterious formulas that prevent its function in a natural way. You may ask: How does music function in a natural
way? Well, music, when it is natural, functions very much like natural
speech—with this difference, of course, that the feelings and thoughts that
tend to express themselves in music are different to those that tend to
express themselves in speech. As regards natural speech, when we have
anything on our minds, we just say it, without any sense that speech is
grammatical or literary or mysterious in any way. It is the same with
music in those parts of the world where music is still in what we may call
the natural state.

The South Seas is such a place. If a Samoan visits a friend he sings a
greeting as he approaches the house. His friend likewise welcomes him in
song. They sing together a song of food-anticipation before they eat, and
when the meal is over they sing a song of food-satisfaction. When they
part they again sing at each other, just as naturally, and I fear just as
conventionally, as we say 'au revoir' and 'bon voyage' or any of those

Source: *Australian Musical News*, 24/7 (Feb. 1934), 14a–d, reproducing with some minor modifications the typescript of broadcast on WEVD (New York), 27 June 1933, 10.15 p.m. Grainger
Museum, Melbourne.

[1] This subtitle was only given in the published, not the broadcast, version.

other absurd mispronunciations of French that we, as Anglo-Saxons, feel called upon to emit on such occasions. In our case, mispronounced French seems a heightening of speech that fits the ceremonious occasion; in the case of a Samoan, song seems a heightening of speech that fits the ceremonious occasion. I will let you hear a phonograph record of such natural music-making from the South Seas. When the Maoris migrated southward to New Zealand some 500 years ago they passed through the Cook Islands, some of them remaining there. Around 1906 a group of Rarotongans from the Cook Islands were taken to New Zealand to take part in an exposition. While there they recited the names of their fore-fathers, just as Americans talk of 'The May-flower' or Englishmen talk of 'coming over with William the Conqueror'. Some Maoris who stood by listening heard the names of their own forefathers recited, as the record dipped behind the 500-year period. Excited at meeting such long-separated kinsmen the Maoris took the clothes off their own backs and gave them to the Rarotongans who, coming from a much warmer climate, were lucky enough to possess hardly any. The Rarotongans, not guessing what a torment clothes really are, rose as a man to give ceremonious thanks in song for this wonderful gift. A New Zealand friend of mine, Mr A. J. Knocks of Otaki,[2] a handsome seer-like man full of scientific and artistic intuitions, at once sensed the aesthetic value of this spontaneous outburst of improvised music and got the Rarotongans to sing their songs of thanks into his phonograph.

It provides only the thrice-removed copy of a faint and poor original, yet enables us to sense the ant-like liveliness of this wholly unpremeditated polyphonic improvisation.

We Can All Sing

I once took a recording phonograph into a native hostelry in New Zealand and asked a roomful of Maoris, that were squatting on the floor all round the room with their backs leaning against the walls, if anyone would like to sing into my phonograph. The entire population arose. They all thought they could sing, and why not? Can't we *all* sing? Of course we can, and it is simply nonsensical submission to 19th century professional propaganda that has induced otherwise reasonable human beings to believe that they cannot sing until they have had their voices

[2] See Essay 6.

trained, or 'placed', or whatever else the voice-destroying process is called. The fact that hardly anyone can sing after they have been trained vocally naturally increases public admiration for those few vocal imperturbables whose natural vocalism is so robust that it can even survive lessons from the most famous and expensive teachers.

It is obvious that no trained singer ever sings really pleasantly, as children and natives and folksingers do. But then our musical public doesn't seem to listen consciously to children when they sing and it never gets an opportunity to hear the exquisitely resourceful vocalism of folksingers and natives; so it has no means of realising by contrast how hideous and monotonous and skill-less is the singing of most of our art-singers, famous or otherwise.

I will play you a tiny piano piece by Grieg, a lullaby based on a song sung by a Norwegian hill-woman to her baby. The words run as follows: 'The little one lies low in his cradle; sometimes he cries, sometimes he smiles'. This lullaby is Grieg's Opus 66, No. 19, 'Gjendines Baadnlaat'.

Here is another natural Norwegian song—a herdsman singing to himself as he roams around the hills. It is about a valley called 'Leirungsdal'. This little ditty was harmonised by Sparre Olsen, a young Norwegian composer with a rare genius for poignant expression.

This 'Leirungsdal', or 'Leirung's Valley', runs:

> Leirung's valley is long and broad
> With all its moors and marshes;
> There have I wandered many a day
> In search of strayed cows and bull-calves.[3]

Of course, this kind of natural singing and music-making, closer to natural speech than to conscious art, went on for many thousands of years all over the world. This is the way folksingers in America, Great Britain, Scandinavia and Russia still sing, and the way Negro Americans still sing their Spirituals. This is the way native musicians play and sing everywhere. All these natural musicians improvise to some extent every time they sing or play, each performance differing from every other performance in its details, each performance thus being a musical effort that is at once creative and executive. Such conditions survived to some extent in European art music as late as Bach's time—that is to say, about two hundred years ago. To be a great musician in Bach's time was to be capable of brilliant spontaneous improvisation, and when two famous musicians

[3] Cf. alternative translation in Essay **26**.

met in competition it was largely in the art of improvising that they vied
with each other, and not chiefly in the art of memorising and interpreting
the music of past generations in a set and unvarying form, which latter is
the manner in which present-day singers, instrumentalists and conductors
practise their art.

Even as late as Beethoven's time, or a little more than a hundred years
ago, every violinist or harpsichordist playing a concerto was expected to
improvise his own cadenza.

Music before Bach's Time

For several hundreds of years before Bach's time music, even when it was
composed in a final, set form, was written mainly with the intention of
giving delight to the performers taking part rather than to make an
impression on an audience; or it was intended to serve God and mankind
in an impersonal way—as church music, marching music, dancing music,
and the like. I don't suppose that composers or performers, during that
long period, ever dreamed that they were expressing their own personalities by way of music—as, for instance, Berlioz and Schumann did in the
19th century.

But when the industrial revolution came along, introducing catch-
as-catch-can methods of living and suddenly forcing hundreds of thousands of hitherto honest folk to earn their livelihood by their wits, a great
change came over the face of music so that the whole presentation of the
art became more or less falsified.

All of us who are real musicians know that music is an art of feeling and
thinking, and only to a very limited extent an art hinging upon mere
skill. If skill at all, it is the skill of musical thinking that counts and not the
skill of scampering over a musical instrument or the skill of imitating on
the voice the scamperings that had developed on instruments. All this is
because art, however experimental it may appear on the surface, is, at
bottom, essentially conservative or even atavistic and because the roots of
music grow out of the sound type natural to the human voice, which
sound type we call melody.

Musical expression, up to and including Bach's time, realised the
melodic basis of music; the musician was regarded as some sort of spiritual servant, and it was only when the economic uncertainties of the
industrial revolution forced musicians to advertise or starve that we
find them beginning to appear as mountebanks, temperamentalists and

wizards. Strong personalities, such as Beethoven, came to be worshipped for their romantic human qualities, without too critical a regard for the musical quality of their output. Skill-mongers like Paganini took on an importance out of all proportion to the intrinsically musical attributes they possessed. A race of unmusical but socially exacting and capricious prima donnas and virtuosi arose, and are with us still. So are tyrannic-natured conductors, even those who are physically violent to the members of their orchestras; who are not only tolerated, but are venerated above all others! Why? On the very dubitable assumption that such brutish natures are more emotional than others and that extreme emotionality fits an interpreter to disclose the hidden meanings and moods of musical masterpieces. At last we have arrived at the magic word 'interpretation'. This was the great musical discovery of the 19th century—the extraordinary idea that good music needs to be 'interpreted'. The mother of a young pianist recently attended with her son a piano master class in Chicago, and, no doubt, heard the 'master teacher' repeatedly harp on the word 'interpretation' when haranguing his class. So when the class was over she went up to the teacher and said to him, in rapt awe: 'Ain't interpretation wonderful?' It certainly is. But all genuine musicians are still wondering what bearing it has upon music.

The Sacrilege of 'Interpretation'

Music is an art that speaks directly and completely to the soul of every genuine musician, be he layman or expert. We pick up a manuscript of the 13th century that contains no indications as to speed or expression; but if we are natural musicians we know by instinct what the nature of the music is and more or less how it should sound. Or we hear a piece of a type hitherto unknown to us—perhaps a piece of Chinese or other strange music: The moment we hear it, if we are true musicians, we catch the musical message it conveys, its spiritual or emotional import. This message lies in the music itself—in the musical thoughts that gave the music birth—and interpretation plays little or no part in helping us to divine this inner nature of the music.

Imagine that someone you love has died and that he or she has given a message for you to a third person. Do you want that message interpreted, dramatised, elocuted when it is told to you? Of course not. Any elocution, any interpretation on the part of the message-bearer would seem to you a sacrilege, an affront. You want the message just as it is, unedited, bare and true. And so it is with music. The great composers of the past are for us who love their works beloved personalities who have died and left intimate messages for us. The more solemn and lofty the messages contained in their compositions the less they permit of interpretation, the more interpretation is felt to be a brutal and tasteless intrusion. A composition like the D sharp minor Fugue from the 2nd book of Bach's *Well-tempered Clavichord* seems to me to belong to the noblest musical type, melodious in its phrases, rich and varied in its harmonies, and carrying a soul-message of great tenderness and subtlety. Such a musical gem needs no interpretation at all. The less we put into it, the more seems to come out. The less we deck it out with contrasting lights and shades of tone the more its intrinsic tonal contours seem to emerge. A natural musician, playing such delicate and wistful music, realises that he must suppress his own personality as far as possible and become merely the passive agent of Bach's thoughts. It is *Bach's* musical mind that must be permitted to talk to us, not the irrelevant notions of some performing interpolator.

The Parasitic Repertory

While it is true that the loftiest types of music are independent of interpretation and discourage it, so is it equally true that the lower types of music depend far more upon being interpreted, and thus put a premium on those musically-speaking simple and undeveloped types of humanity that are naturally cut out to be successful public performers. These thick-skinned empty-headed parasites have been ruling our world of music for a long time now, and in that time they have assembled together an amazing repertory of what they call 'classical' music or 'good' music—weeding out the flowers of music and preserving the weeds with an infallible flair for all that is second-rate and vulgar; not, of course, because they wanted to specialize in the lower walks of music, but merely because their intrinsically unmusical and unspiritual natures genuinely prefer all that is simple, coarse and silly in our art.

It stands to reason that only rather inartistic natures are fitted to be successful public performers—at least as long as we expect our soloists to play in public by heart, without notes; for Otto Weininger[4] was right when he declared that almost every artistic person he had known had complained to him of poor memorizing powers. Furthermore, all truly

---

[4] (1880–1903), author of *Sex and Character* (1903). Grainger misrepresents Weininger's point, however.

musical natures are shy and sensitive, and these traits make it impossible for them to do their best before an audience. That is why Chopin, whom we may guess to have been the most delicious pianist of all time, was not successful as a public pianist and preferred to perform to a small chosen circle. It is the same today. The most graceful, luscious, tender-toned pianist I have ever heard is Cyril Scott, the great English composer. Yet such a man is not worshipped by pianistically-interested concert-goers, partly because he is not ambitious enough to waste his time concertising, and partly also because concert-goers have been trained to admire only quite conventional pianistic skill along old-fashioned lines and are deaf to beauty of sound and the rapturous flight of rare musical imagination. Cyril Scott is a superb improviser, as Bach was before him, and I think an impression of this gift of spontaneous extemporization pervades his marvellous Piano Sonata, Op. 66.

Inspired Piano-Playing

Henry Cowell, David Guion and Howard Brockway are three American composers whose piano playing is unique, brilliant and inspired; yet America does not go crazy about their pianism. Grieg was a first-class conductor; yet the world did not go crazy about his conducting—because the commercialised music-making of the 19th century has led concert-goers to ignore music itself and worship only tricks of interpretation in which no composer can possibly be interested, and to which, therefore, he cannot lend himself.

For the last fifty or more years the career of a professional musician has been a marvellous means of turning a poor boy into a successful capitalist or a premier of Poland,[5] and this has naturally drawn a lot of ambitious and inartistic natures into the ranks of the musicians. Such basically unmusical natures have, of course, leant towards those sides of music, such as opera, that are largely concerned with the musical portrayal of the passions and affairs of every-day life; just as the deeply musical natures, on the other hand, have veered towards the more purely musical forms of music—realising that the greatest boon that music holds out to us is its power to create within us a separate world, rapturous and Nirvana-like, in which dramatic and worldly conflicts have no part. Music is harmony, not conflict, and all attempts to associate music with the humdrum,

---

[5] Grainger refers to the pianist Ignacy Paderewski (1860–1941), who was briefly prime minister of Poland in 1919.

competitive sides of life only succeed in lowering the art. But opera, and the other commercialised branches of music, have raised for us a crop of worldly-minded performing musicians who, partly out of their own natural conceit, no doubt, have spread the legend that music is a special mystery to which they alone have the special key. These self-satisfied, highly advertised professional musicians act as high-priests of music, raising a wall of mystery, 'bunk' and taboo between the lovely art of music itself and its natural devotees. These high-priests, by enlarging upon the shortcomings of amateurs, have succeeded in discouraging many music-lovers from enjoying amateur music-making in a natural and wholesome way.

But the spell of this self-elected musical high-priesthood seems to be broken, or breaking, today—thanks to the wholesome influence of jazz and radio. Young Anglo-Saxons,[6] listening to music over the air, cannot fail to be struck by the obvious fact that the jazz sounds made by Anglo-Saxon musicians are sweeter, more subtle and more complex than the dull, vulgar, brutal sounds made by so many famous, highly-priced foreign musicians. These young Anglo-Saxons are led by their own gentle, kindly Nordic natures to naturally prefer the affectionate and gentle sounds of jazz and crooning to the noisy, militaristic blaring of the European-style symphony orchestra and the bull-like bawling of opera singers.

Debunking Began in Schools

The real 'de-bunking' of music in America began in earnest with the wildfire spread of high school orchestras and choirs a few years ago. Even the most musically humble ears could hear for themselves that the music made by these fresh and jolly youngsters was every bit as musical, just as full of heart-throbs and emotional messages, as the performances of any expensive, blasé, professional crack orchestra. At any rate, the younger generation discovered that it could get real delight and mental nourishment out of its own amateur music-making.

The further 'de-bunking' of music demands, however, that a wider knowledge of all sorts of music really suited to amateur music-making shall reach young music-lovers in schools, high schools, colleges, universities, and elsewhere; at present too many young players and singers are wasting their time on mere display-music, written to fill the commercial

---

[6] Grainger used 'Americans' in the broadcast version of the rest of this paragraph.

needs of professional performers in the 18th and 19th centuries—stuff that lacks real musical food-value. It should become ever more widely realised that music itself is the better part of music and that details of performance are only secondary considerations. We should begin to doubt the innate musicality of any musician who is serious about setting a high price upon his musical activities, since experience proves that true musicians are always willing to make music for nothing—just as a real golfer is willing to play golf for the fun of it. Above all, the musical public at large should be informed of the fact that the period of music most performed by our conventional professional foreign musicians—the period that lies between Bach and the beginning of the 20th century—mainly distinguishes itself in having produced more dull, shallow, pretentious, platitudinous, vulgar, redundant and slovenly music than any other known period of musical history. Copious hearings of music of many periods and places will reveal the fact that many varied kinds of music of high spiritual significance throng the thousand years preceding Haydn and that the 20th century has recaptured the spirituality, complexity and deep emotionality of those earlier types.

34   *Sublime and Frivolous Elements in Music*
(1934)
The Jazz Classics (Haydn, Mozart, Beethoven)

What could be more delightful, from a certain point of view, than an English or Danish straw-thatched, white-washed farmhouse, protected by trees, and embellished with a duck-pond? No reasonable architect would resent our relishing the farmhouse—he might not even object to our preferring it to a cathedral. But he would certainly be justified in exploding the notion that a farmhouse can vie with a cathedral in the loftier architectural attributes—in size, majesty, sublimity, complexity. The purpose of this article is to urge the habit of distinguishing between musical farmhouses and musical cathedrals.

In most of the arts, the contrasts between the sublime and the frivolous—even the relative values of the gradation between them—seem well, or fairly well, realised. Tragedies and comedies carry on their faces different suggestions of seriousness and levity. A humorist like Mark Twain is rated on another plane than a seer like Walt Whitman. And the flippancy, cynicism and jingliness of such a poem as Byron's 'Don Juan'[1] automatically precludes its being classed on a par with 'Beowulf' or 'The Song of Solomon'. This does not, of course, prevent many readers preferring Mark Twain to Walt Whitman, Edgar Wallace[2] to Homer. But critical opinion does not permit such readers to make a virtue of their low-brow tastes—as it does in music, in which art-frivolous geniuses are not only more popular than sublime geniuses, but are more admired, written about, and romanced over.

Not that the contrasts between the sublime and frivolous in music are not clearly enough defined in every quarter of the globe, in all periods and amongst all races; for I do not believe that the most untrained ear would fail to guess correctly whether the music set before it were music of spir-

Source: *Australian Musical News*, 24/9 (April 1934), 4–8.

[1] Unfinished epic satire (pub. 1819–24).

[2] (1875–1932), prolific novelist, playwright, and journalist, who specialized in thrillers and was co-author of the script of the film *King Kong*.

itual rapture or active music (dance music, march music, occupational musics of all kinds).

The Film of Soul-Blindness

The influence of these two main types of music is obvious enough: the active music spurs us on to carry on the struggle of life—the so-called 'practical' side—while the contemplative or rapturous music induces love, harmony, unity, peacefulness, bliss, nirvana.

We would be thankless if we denied the practical value of the energizing sway that active music holds over us. Yet the most cursory glance at the world around us is enough to convince us that we stand in far greater need of the spiritualizing gifts that sublime music has to bestow. It must be evident to every observant eye that the practicalists of life—the inventors, the scientists, the nature-subduers—have succeeded in surrounding us to-day with a hitherto undreamt-of potential prosperity, the full fruits of which we are prevented from enjoying only by mankind's lack of harmony, unity, selflessness, and universality.

Spiritual music (religious, philosophical, rapturously emotional music) is clearly one of the influences that will enable us to shed that film of soul-blindness that still separates us from the immediate attainment of flawless human bliss. Angelic music prepares us to enjoy lives of heavenly happiness here on earth—just as definitely as frivolous, jiggy, restless music drives us to lead hum-drum, dull, bootless lives without revolt or protest.

Singing and Seriousness

Spiritual leaders have, of course, understood these simple truths in all times and places—hence the great similarity, before-mentioned, between all types of sublime music, old or new, and from whatever quarter of the globe.

That Chinese description of the nature of lofty music that I quoted in a former article ('poetry is the expression of earnest thought, and singing is the prolonged utterance of that expression'[3]) is as true to-day of Western music as it was of Chinese music when stated some four thousand years ago.

---

[3] See Essays 28 and 31.

It seems to me that we can draw up the following generalisations regarding sublime music of all periods, wherever practised:

(1) That long, sustained notes and phrases induce concentration (while short, jerky, jiggy, quickly-moving notes and phrases irritate the soul-self, and destroy concentration).

(2) That ceaselessly inventive, non-repetitive melody leads the mind of the listener on to inquisitive, spiritual or scientific wonder (while often-repeated and otherwise inventively lazy phrases destroy imagination and encourage platitudinous non-thinking).

(3) That irregularity of intervals, rhythms, bar-groupings, phrases and harmonies attunes our minds to the unforeknowableness of nature, enabling us to take a sympathetic joy in the mysteries of the universe, instead of being repelled or frightened by them (the regular elements in music, on the other hand, tend to limit our appreciation to the artificial, man-made aspects of life).

If we examine the opening phrase of Wagner's *Parsifal* Prelude, we will find that it conforms to all the habits of spiritual music as above (admittedly incompletely) defined: its notes and phrases are long, sustained and non-rhythmic, and its melodic invention is vigorous, never stooping to repetition. The whole thing seems to float freely in space, tethered to key, pattern, and beat as little as may be.

No Canaries in Churches

These are the universally followed characteristics of *the typical slow movement*, the purpose of which is to immerse the hearer in a soul-bath of calm and rapture. The first essential in such music is, naturally, a continuity of mood that eschews all 'comic relief', dramatic contrasts, bravura display passage-work, and other irrelevant distractions. Laughter-producing humour must not play too large a part in a religious sermon; canaries (however charmingly they sing) are not welcomed in churches; the injunction 'silence' confronts us in every public reading room. This is because experience has convinced humanity that solemnity, rapture, and concentration cannot prosper without some special immunity from distracting or vulgarizing appeals. It is the same with sublime music—it can make its lofty effect only if showy, noisy, flighty musical elements are banned from its make-up. Furthermore, the slow, calm and sublime nature of the music must persist, unbrokenly, long enough to produce a well-established emotional impression upon the hearer (after which, of course, it can be varied if desired—as in the case of Purcell's 8th Fantasy for string quartet, which, after being a perfect slow movement of the loftiest and loveliest type throughout its greater length, is closed by a short, lively tailpiece in fast *tempo*).

The following pieces of music—of the most diverse origin, periods and styles—are all true 'slow movements' in the sense above set forth:

'Sekar gadung' and 'Kinanti madumurti' (records of Javanese gamelan music, *Musik des Orients* Album, Nos 9 and 10).

Beata viscera, late 13th-century English *conductus* for three voices[4] (gramophone record by Dom Anselm Hughes, The Plainsong and Mediaeval Music Society, Nashdom Abbey, Burnham, Bucks, England).

'Zulu Love Song' (two-part canon), recorded phonographically by Natalie Curtis-Burlin (*Songs and Tales from the Dark Continent*, G. Schirmer).

Guillaume de Machaut (French, 1300-1377): Ballade No. 17 (three-part canon) for three voices.[5]

Most of the Fantasies for Strings by Byrd, R. Deering, Thomas Tomkins, John Jenkins, William Lawes, Purcell, de Cabezón, Diego Ortiz, and other 16th and 17th-century English and Spanish composers.

Bach: Air, for strings, D major Suite (chamber orchestra).

Wagner: Preludes to 3rd act of *Meistersinger* and 3rd act of *Tristan*.

Chopin: Nocturnes, Largo from B minor Sonata, etc.

Brahms: Slow movements of the symphonies, sonatas, chamber works.

C. Franck: Three Chorales, for organ.

Scriabin: *Poem of Ecstasy*, for orchestra. (Here the almost insect-like surface floridity never obscures the singing, yearning basis of the entire piece.)

Debussy: *Afternoon of a Faun*, for orchestra.

Gabriel Fauré: Adagio of Second Quartet, piano and strings.

Herman Sandby: *Sea Mood*, for orchestra.

C. Scott: *Aubade*, for orchestra

Rachmaninoff: Fifteen Songs of the Church (mixed voices).

Paul Hindemith: *Die junge Magd*, for mezzo soprano, flute, clarinet and string quartet.

Such music is not only the most spiritual type of music known to us; it is also the most 'musical', in the sense that its sonorities are closest to

---

[4] Grainger's edition 'for practical music-making' was published in 1943.
[5] Scored by Grainger for strings (1934).

those of the human voice, and in that it makes its effect solely, or mainly, as 'absolute music'—that is, by way of the *musical thoughts and feelings* it contains and not at all, or comparatively little, by way of extra-musical appeals, such as text, 'human' sentiment, stage action, and dance movements.

The Active Music

In extreme contrast to this soulful music is the active music of the world—dance music, march music, occupational music, music accompanying action or pantomime on the stage, music designed to show off the mechanical skill of the performer (display-music)—that makes its appeal to the bodily, athletic side of man's nature.

In between these two extremes lie, of course, the intermediate types: songs with strong text-appeal, programme-music (depicting non-musical events and feelings by means of music), pattern-music and skill-compositions (in which themes and motives are treated with contrapuntal or 'constructive' ingenuity) and styles consisting of a blend of athleticism and ingenuity (for instance, the typical first movement of a conventional symphony). These intermediate types speak to the intellect and the imagi-nation rather than to the soul or the physical impulses.

Great composers in culturally well-balanced periods divide their crea-tive activities between all these three kinds of musical expression. But in certain periods the instinct for balance becomes upset, and we then find undue pre-occupation with just one side of music. Thus, Domenico Scarlatti seemed well-nigh indifferent to all except florid display-music, while Frederick Delius, on the other hand, stoops to nothing below soulful music of the very loftiest kind.

Beethoven a 'Jazz Classic'

One of the peculiarities of jazz, as we have experienced it during the last fifteen or more years, has been the attempt to force all types of musical thought to conform to the narrow confines of current dance forms—the most undancelike types of 'classical', or other, music being adapted (jazzed) to that end. Somewhat before, and during the Haydn–Mozart–Beethoven period a somewhat similar dancification overtook almost all forms of art music, and that is why I take the liberty of calling these three great composers 'the jazz classics'. The habits and traditions that had governed religious and other emotional music for a thousand years or more in Europe were set aside overnight in favour of the vulgar traditions of dance music, and other popular 'active' music.

The many-voiced melodiousness and soul-gripping harmonic expressibility of Bach, William Lawes, and Purcell, the exquisite vocal subtlety of Palestrina and Claude Le Jeune—these and a host of other golden compositional traditions were recklessly abandoned in order to accommodate just one despotic ideal: that of *popular simplicity*. And on the debilitated musical fare resulting from this disastrous choice, our audiences have mainly subsisted for one hundred years! It is a wonder that concert-going did not die of musical undernourishment.

Not that the great composers of the pre-Haydn periods were unconversant with dance-music traditions. When Bach, or Byrd, or 13th-century English composers (see 'Puellare' in Dom Anselm Hughes's *Worcester Mediaeval Harmony*) were composing dance music they conformed to its styles and traditions as faithfully as any Haydn, Stravinsky or Gershwin. But—having a sense of style—they did not allow these lower traditions to overflow into music of a higher nature.

But Haydn, Mozart, and Beethoven knew (or conformed to) no traditions other than those of active music, and therefore they were seldom able to sustain a solemn, dreamy or spiritual mood for more than a few brief moments. They were, therefore, seldom able to write a *typical slow movement*, judged by the standards of earlier and later geniuses. In the thirty-two Beethoven piano sonatas I can discover only one genuine slow movement (displaying the sustained emotion, singing sonority and reposeful continuity of type as we find them in the slow movements of Java, India, de Machaut, Byrd, Bach, Brahms, Delius, etc.)—the first movement of the so-called 'Moonlight' Sonata.[6] (We must not make the mistake of regarding the continuous triplets of this movement as restless display-passages. On the contrary: they provide just that steady tonal murmur that lends an almost mesmeric reposefulness to the finest Javanese music, and to the first Prelude in Bach's *Well-tempered Clavier*.)

One Perfect Slow Movement

It is fortunate that Beethoven himself has supplied us with at least one example of a perfect slow movement (judged by universal standards) with which we may compare his other efforts in a like direction.

---

[6] Sonata No. 14, Op. 27 No. 2 (1801).

Viewed in the light of the first movement of the 'Moonlight', I find that the 'slow movements' of the thirty-one other piano sonatas fall into three classes:

(1) No slow movement at all: Sonatas Nos 6, 9, 10, 12, 18, 19, 20, 22, 24, 25, 27.

(2) Those whose slow and touching opening phrases fade out into frivolous-mooded, unemotional display-passages that are utterly irrelevant to the original tenor of the movement: Sonatas Nos 1, 3 (where restless 'fireworks' are introduced as early as the 11th bar, immediately after the first statement of the opening theme), 11, 13, 15, 16, 17, 23, 26, 28, 29, 30, 31. The Andante of the 'Appassionata' (No. 23)[7] is typical of this class: After sixteen bars of exquisite, soulful solemnity the texture gradually weakens out into displayfulness, until by the 53rd bar (the third variation) we are prattling along with a flippant brilliance that utterly dispels the magic of the opening theme.

(3) Those whose slow and emotional initial mood is interrupted by violent, noisy, dramatic outbursts—similar to those we hear in opera, or in the talkies, when disaster, crime and upset are at hand. (In this connection it is interesting to recall Goethe's statement: that he saw 'in Beethoven's works only violence, brutality and anger'.[8]) Often associated with these are highly syncopated rhythms of a dance-like character, and display passages similar to those in class 2: Sonatas Nos 2, 4, 5, 7, 8, 21, 32.

Unstable and Spasmodic Art

Perhaps the mood behind most of the Beethoven slow movements might be compared to the behaviour of a spoilt opera prima donna, capable of movements of true kindness, affection, and gentleness, but invariably given over to outbursts of violence, capriciousness, coyness and skittishness. In judging such unstable and spasmodic art, we should, of course, remember that the early 19th century was the age of rampant individualism—individualism at all costs. A world in the turmoil of political revolution, a world suffering from the horrible upsets induced by the industrial revolution, was, perhaps, not seeking pure beauty or the solace of calm contemplation. Goethe said of Beethoven's music 'that it represented the sentimentality and aesthetic disintegration of his age'. Perhaps it was a

---

[7] Op. 57 (1804–5).
[8] Grainger's footnote: Paul Landormy on 'Bettina Brentano', in *The Sackbut*, London, July, 1932.

proof of Beethoven's transcending giftedness that he was able to accomplish just that. His unquenchable courage, indestructible high spirits and irrepressible horseplay (all of which we clearly hear in his music) must have been a veritable godsend to the tortured, topsy-turvy age in which he lived.

But we, who live in the luckier, happier, more orderly, more harmonious-minded 20th century, must be excused for no longer needing Beethoven's frenzied invitations to superheroic liveliness. We are living in an age of leisure (of 'enforced leisure', if you will—in the age of the 'dole', world-wide unemployment and reduced working hours), and it is only natural that we should wish to spend a reasonable proportion of our leisure with serious, sublime art that ennobles and elevates the soul.

There is no doubt that repetitions of musical phrases and motives have a real practical value as slave-driving influences in work-songs and other occupational music; for repetitions of phrases stimulate repetitions of physical action. And there can be little doubt that repetitions of well-established phrases in dance music remind the dancers of recurring figures in the dance. But there is no need whatever for all these slave-driving propensities in 'absolute music' of a spiritual type, and here such habits of redundancy merely lead to inventive stagnation and melodic impoverishment.

Unashamed Redundancy

I suppose the last movement of the Beethoven Violin Concerto[9] holds the world's record for unashamed redundancy. The opening bar (starting from the up-beat) is repeated forty times, without any variation in its harmonic support, throughout the movement, during which there are additional sixty-seven bars in which this same theme, and tags of it, are sounded with only trifling intervallic variations—again without the presence of interesting harmonies. Thus, in a movement of 360 bars, the listener has to endure 107 bars given over to repetitions of a tiresome hunting-horn-like motive with next to no harmonic or rhythmic resourcefulness to break the appalling monotony. Let it be admitted that treatments or imitations of repetitious folk-dance tunes have been undertaken by art-music composers of many (if not all) periods. But in fine periods, the art-music traditions assert themselves in the richness or

---

[9] Op. 61 (1806).

complexity of the harmonic or textural treatment. This will be evident if we examine the first William Lawes Fantasy for six strings; the last movement of Bach's Sixth Brandenburg Concerto, and Nos 1, 8, 10, 12, 16 of Grieg's *Norwegian Folksongs*, Op. 66.

The emotional power and technical resourcefulness that Lawes (who died in 1645) brought to his task are positively overwhelming—especially with regard to harmonic variety and complexity. Yet the musical world goes on in almost total ignorance of the masterworks of this transcending English genius (whose muse is grander and deeper than Bach's, just as Bach's is grander and deeper than Haydn's), while forced to listen again and again to the piffling emptiness of the last movement of the Beethoven violin concerto!

The Ninth and 'Yankee Doodle'

It is hard for us more serious-minded 20th-century composers to understand the childishness with which vulgar tune-types were introduced into the most serious art music a little over one hundred years ago. Admirers of Beethoven, who consider the Ninth Symphony[10] one of his loftiest achievements, will hardly deny that the tune associated with the words beginning 'Freude, schöner Götterfunken? Tochter aus Elysium' (Joy, lovely divine spark, daughter from Elysium) plays a highly important role in the climax of the whole symphony. Yet this tune is so close to that of 'Yankee Doodle' in line, rhythm, type, and form, that the one forms a perfect continuation to the other. I would like to ask my readers to hum the first half of 'Yankee Doodle', follow it with the first eight bars of the Beethoven tune, then conclude with the refrain of 'Yankee Doodle'. I cannot conceive of any unprejudiced ear detecting any great discrepancy in style, mood and form between the American tune and the Beethoven theme. Yet all attempts to make 'Yankee Doodle' an official American national anthem have been vetoed on the ground that it is too frivolous, vulgar and undignified for such use, while the conventional opinion regarding the Beethoven theme is that it is suitable thematic material for incorporation in one of music's sublimest creations. Such divergent opinions about such similar tunes reveal the harsh and unsympathetic criticism meted out to almost all forms of Anglo-Saxon music on the one hand, and, on the other, the 'King can do no wrong' sort of attitude that is applied to all German or Austrian music, however unworthy.

[10] Op. 125 (1822–4).

We must say this for the jazz of our own age: that it has unfolded subtleties of chamber orchestration never before known, either in art music or popular music. Jazz orchestrators, such as Grofe,[11] have been scrupulous, painstaking craftsmen in the matter of tone-colour blending. We need only compare the dull, thick, stodgy orchestration of a 19th-century Viennese waltz (the *Blue Danube*, for instance) with the tonal delicacies of a representative Whiteman or Duke Ellington record to see what amazing strides in refinement have been made by the best jazz orchestrators. We can hardly praise the 18th-century jazz classics for similar virtues. The love of noise and coarse, violent effects, the craving for brilliance at all costs, disfigure all, or almost all, Haydn, Mozart, and Beethoven scores. Think of the terrible tub-thumping of the kettledrums (which destroys all chord clarity) and the blatant hammering of the open notes of horns and trumpets in all their tuttis—barbarisms never practised before or since in art music!

Frivolous Haydn

The frivolousness of Haydn's approach to the symphony is well-instanced in the unexpected whack on the drum in the 'Surprise' Symphony[12] (imagine the soul-benefit derived by the innocent listener from such a nerve-shock!) and in that last movement,[13] in which one orchestral player after another blows out his candle and leaves the orchestra, until the end is silence.[14] Beethoven's *The Wrath over the Lost Farthing*[15] is an example of a similar 'low-brow' attitude—as if it were the office of music (the most angelic of the arts) to remind mankind of its miserable money!

It is possible that all this circus-mongering, horseplay, vulgarity and frivolousness filled some human need at the time when such works were written. But that subsequent generations soon felt the need for something more emotional and heartfelt seems proved by the romantic and sentimental titles invented (without the composer's sanction) around Beethoven's innocent works—the 'Moonlight', 'Appassionata', 'Pastoral

[11] Ferde Grofe (1892–1972), American arranger, composer, pianist, and violinist, who made arrangements for Paul Whiteman in the 1919–33 period.

[12] No. 94 (1791).

[13] Of the 'Farewell' Symphony, No. 45 (1772).

[14] Grainger's footnote: Nevertheless, my admiration for Haydn as a composer of active music is proved by the extent to which I have based many of my own folk-music settings (*Molly on the Shore*, *Shepherd's Hey*, and the like) on his style.

[15] *Rondo a capriccio*, Op. 129 (1795; pub. 1828).

Sonata' [*sic*], and the like. We must remember that these post-Beethovenians had little music other than the more or less frivolous compositions of the jazz-classic age to engage their attention. They knew little or nothing of the grander flights of Bach's genius, and still less of the great musical giants who preceded Bach far down the centuries (Byrd, Tallis, Vittoria, Willaert, Josquin des Près, Ockeghem, Dufay, Dunstable, etc.). So they felt constrained to weave imaginative thoughts around the comparatively unemotional music they *did* know, in order to satisfy their growing romanticness.

Tolstoy's 'Kreutzer' Idea

That this impulse to endow quite jolly and commonplace music with mystical and almost superhuman emotional attributes was carried to quite absurd lengths is seen in Tolstoy's novel, *The Kreutzer Sonata*.[16] I cannot do better than quote George Moore (*Avowals*, chapter 7):[17]

'The teller of Tolstoy's new story is a man who murdered his wife because he committed the fatal mistake of falling in love with her at an evening party, her pretty figure, which a jersey showed off to advantage, being the active cause of the wedding. He tells a casual acquaintance, a passenger in the train, that he loved and hated his wife by turns, and that, at last, she could bear with him no longer, and took to herself a lover, a violinist, and that at one of her parties a piece of music is played by the lovers, one more or less known to all cultivated people, and looked upon by them as a natural and witty piece of music, in the humour of a Shakespearean comedy. In no other way do we look upon the *Kreutzer Sonata*, yourself and myself, reader; but the murderer, speaking through Tolstoy, heard a violent aphrodisiac in the music, and was at last driven to killing his wife with a stiletto, driving it through and through the jersey which had provoked his love of her.'

Haydn's boundless praise of Handel ('he is the master of us all') and Beethoven's tribute to Bach ('he is no brook, but an ocean'—something that could not reasonably have been said of Haydn's or Mozart's dainty and playful music) suggests that the great jazz-classical composers themselves guessed that finer musical traditions than their own lay hidden behind them in the past. That Beethoven, in his last works, was continually reaching out for more soulful forms of expression than the musical

---

[16] (1889), by Leo Tolstoy (1828–1910).
[17] 1919.

idioms of his day provided is evident enough. It stands to reason that his deeply inspired individual yearnings for more sublime musical utterance were constantly frustrated by his unfamiliarity with musical traditions dealing with long, sustained, singing notes and phrases. Thus Beethoven, in his latest quartets, is only able to indicate, in a groping, sketchy incompleteness, those moods of angelic rapture that Purcell was able to voice with full maturity and perfection in those priceless four-part string fantasies (surely the world's most sublime, beautiful and satisfying string quartets!) that he penned in 1680—about five years before Bach was born. The shortcomings of Beethoven's late works are too often laid at the door of his growing deafness. Surely it would be more sensible to attribute them to his lack of musical culture, to his ignorance of the great musical resources of the past.

What Composers Think To-day

The attitude I am taking towards the 'jazz classics' is not in any sense original or personal with me. I am merely voicing the usual opinion of composers of my generation. I do not know a single distinguished modern composer who places Beethoven high among the great composer-geniuses; though no thoughtful musician would deny his superlative gifts. Debussy's aesthetic repudiation of Beethoven is too well known to need quoting.[18] Frederick Delius recently said to me: 'When a man tells me that he admires Mozart, I know in advance that he is a bad musician.' Yet Delius loves Grieg above all composers, and Grieg's favourite composer was Mozart! So we see that even the opinions of the greatest composers must not be taken blindly. But that does not mean that such opinions should be withheld from the public; for what the composers think to-day the public will think twenty or thirty years later. Doubtless there are unchangeable values in art, but perhaps aesthetic opinions are not part of these; perhaps it is right that opinions should vary, in different generations, so that new aspects of music may result from these changing opinions. Perhaps it does not matter that Beethoven was placed on an absurd pedestal for a time—provided this folly does not persist too long. And perhaps it does not matter that the leading musical minds of to-day are over-hostile to Beethoven. It will all right itself in time. My own view of Beethoven is that he is one of art's strongest *personalities*, though not in

---

[18] Grainger is, perhaps, thinking of Debussy's categorization of Beethoven as a genius 'without taste'.

all senses a *musician* of the front rank. Certainly he is one of the most original of known composers. I cannot conceive of anyone creating themes of a more arresting quality, of more pith. But I do not believe that music gains from being thus overthemed; I think it far more important that the *whole texture* (not merely the themes) should be expressive and vital.

I have the deepest reverence for some of Beethoven's works—the *Missa Solemnis*,[19] for instance. My favourite of all piano concertos is the G major Beethoven, and my sole reason for not playing it publicly is my fear that I might not do justice to its beauty and brilliance.[20] But, in spite of his amazing giftedness, his output as a whole seems to me to suffer from the fact that it lacks a rich traditional backing. A mountain that starts to rise out of a low plain is not likely to equal the heights reached by a mountain that starts to rise in the midst of an elevated mountain chain. The worship of individualism in the 19th century favoured the idea of a single individual, unaided by great cultural backing, rising singlehandedly to the greatest heights. An age of 'self-made men' in the economic field liked the idea of self-made men in music also. But I believe that any ample study of musical history will reveal the fact that music at its best is always a cumulative, rather than an individualistic, affair. Knud Jeppesen wrote of Palestrina: 'In him all the streams run together', and this is true of all those other greatest composers who satisfy most and longest. An art like music cannot prosper fully when its roots are cut away from under it.

When the composers that followed after Bach wilfully cut themselves loose from all the rich traditions of sublime music that had accumulated in an unbroken continuity for at least nine hundred years (possibly much longer), in order to concentrate solely, or mainly, on the pretty-prettiness and lively appeal of active music (when—to put it slightly otherwise—they abandoned a singing, sustained type of sonority in favour of short, jerky, hammering sounds), they were committing some kind of artistic suicide. And it was only when the grandeurs of Bach's sublimest muse were revealed by Mendelssohn's performance of the *Matthew Passion*, in the early middle of the past century,[21] that composers such as Chopin, Schumann, Wagner, César Franck, and Brahms began to repossess the full heritage of all the musical ages, and thus were able to express mankind's loftiest emotions in a musical language adequate to such a task.

[19] Op. 123 (1819–23).
[20] Grainger had, however, played this Fourth Piano Concerto (1805–6) during his London years.
[21] His resuscitation of the *St Matthew Passion* in 1829, one hundred years after its première.

But is it not every musician's duty to carry on the task of musical light shedding so nobly begun by Mendelssohn? Should it not be our pleasure, as well as our duty, to perform and popularize all specially significant examples of sublime music as they swim into our ken—whether from the pens of living composers, or as result of the prolific researches of music-historians?

The great creative musical minds of yesterday and to-day have nourished themselves on a vast mass of myriad musics: Oriental, folk, and primitive, mediaeval and renaissance, jazz and classical, modern and futuristic. Of this vast mass of inspired music the musical public know only a tiny corner well: European art music from 1700 to 1900, not even the folk music of that period. The favourite masterpieces of this short period are played so often that there is not room on programmes to accommodate a hundredth part of those masterpieces of the older past and of the present that the public does not yet know. Why shall the musical public *forever* be denied contact with musical experiences that have long proved inspiring to our greatest musical minds? To take just one example: Debussy altered his style and enriched his compositional resources as a result of the Javanese gamelan orchestras he heard at a Paris Exposition in 1888.[22] Yet our musical public is still ignorant of this lovely (and easily performable) music that instructed Debussy forty-six years ago, and, through him, altered the face of modern music. How much longer shall the musical public have to wait?

In particular, it seems incongruous that the Australians, who are such appreciative admirers of British greatness in other fields, shall continue to remain in ignorance of the most outstanding pinnacles of British greatness in music—an art in which the British have specially distinguished themselves, on and off, for the past twelve hundred years; an art to the progress of which they have contributed more fundamentally (if we can believe the statements of eminent students of early European music) than any other European people.

There is something distressing in the thought that, while the comparatively frivolous and spiritually empty compositions of the 'Viennese classics' are performed and re-performed with more than yearly regularity, the far sublimer masterworks of infinitely greater British geniuses (ranging from the Worcester church music of the 13th century to *The Song of the High Hills* of Delius) are still awaiting their first performance in Australia.

---

[22] 1889.

35 Roger Quilter: The Greatest Songwriter of our Age

(1936)

Few well informed students of the world's music would deny, I suppose, that Roger Quilter is the greatest songwriter living today in any known part of the world, and that his place is secure amongst the greatest songwriters of all time.

His outstanding achievements in the domain of song have several obvious roots: his exquisite taste in choosing texts; his unique sensitiveness in translating the moods of these texts into music; the singableness of his vocal line; the many-voiced melodiousness of his accompaniments.

Melodious polyphony he has inherited from the habits of English artsong from its earliest traceable beginnings. The bewitching 13th-century *Beata viscera* (as published in Don Anselm Hughes's *Worcester Mediæval Harmony*); Lyonel Power's unsurpassable *Anima mea liquefacta est* (about 1420) for voice & three strings;[1] John Dowland's winsome ditties for voice & lute (around 1597);[2] these are but three out of innumerable quotable examples of the sway held by many-voiced melodiousness upon English artsong at various periods.

In this respect English artsong (in which the moaning voices of an accompaniment form a continuous emotional commentary upon the musical statements of the singer) is in complete contrast to English folksong, in which the whole appeal is concentrated upon the melodiousness of the single (unaccompanied) tonal line. As compared with a typical English folksong, no English (or other) artsong can show true melody—if by melody we mean beauty of curving, soaring tonal line that does not depend at all upon either harmonic or rhythmic accompaniment to make its mark. Many composers do not realise this natural gulf between folksong & artsong, & they impoverish their artsong by emulating, in it, the superior melodiousness of folksong at the expense of the complexity of their accompaniments. Not so Roger Quilter, who is unfailing in his

Source: Manuscript dated 27 July 1936 (at Haslemere). Grainger Museum, Melbourne.

[1] Transcribed by Grainger in 1934.
[2] Including *Now, O Now, I Needs Must Part*, freely set by Grainger for piano, in both easy and concert versions (pub. 1937).

æsthetic instincts. He—in common with the best English songwriters of the past—has a flawless grasp of the compromise between single-line melodiousness & accompanying polyphony, without which artsong cannot rise to its loftiest heights.

If single-line melody may be compared to an emptying of the heart in solitude, polyphonically accompanied song, such as Quilter's, may be likened to an outpouring of feeling in the presence of sympathetic listeners, who add their tender commentaries to the original, emotional statement. Quilter's music is such fellowship, such communion, such compassionateness turned into sound.

When Quilter's accompaniments are limited to the piano, their polyphonic nature is more implied than realised—just as is the hidden polyphony in Chopin's subtle piano style. But when string voices are blended with the keyboard accompaniments, the full vitality of Quilter's polyphonic mind is realised in a flash.

It is, of course, this same strangely rich subterranean many-voiced thought that makes Quilter's partsongs so delicious—for they are just as truly the equal of the finest Tudor partsongs as his solo songs are a rebirth of the sweetest traditions of Dunstable and Dowland.

The same depth & subtlety of many-voiced thinking informs his instrumental creations—think of the more sustained sections in his entrancing Three English Dances,[3] the yearning harmonisations in the *Children's Overture*,[4] & the 'space-straining expansiveness' in certain episodes in *Where the Rainbow Ends*.[5]

William James[6] wrote that religion & art are not direct expression of what is felt in life, but voice reactions from such feelings. In this sense Quilter's music is 'artistic' to the highest degree; in this respect, also, it is truly Western European music (spiritually akin to the wistful & romantic utterances of such characteristically Western composers as Guillaume de Machaut, Dufay, C. Franck, G. Fauré & Grieg, & having comparatively little in common with the simpler cruder & more bombastic musical speech of the more militaristic & aggressive European nations). If, as Cyril Scott asserts, 'music influences, in a secret way, future thought & morals',[7] then Roger Quilter's music holds a spiritual & social import far

---

[3] Op. 11 (1910), for small orchestra.
[4] Op. 17 (1919).
[5] Music to a children's fairy play (1911); also orchestral suite.
[6] (1842–1910), American pragmatist philosopher and psychologist. Grainger refers to his *Varieties of Religious Experience* (1902).
[7] In his *The Influence of Music in History and Morals: A Vindication of Plato* (1928).

beyond its mere physical proportions—for it foreshadows just such a world of affectionateness, compassionateness, tenderness, kindliness, heartiness & warmth as all true civilisation aims at. It is the music of 'heaven on earth'.

36

Free Music
(1938)

Music is an art not yet grown up; its condition is comparable to that stage of Egyptian bas-reliefs when the head and legs were shown in profile while the torso appeared 'front face'—the stage of development in which the myriad irregular suggestions of nature can only be taken up in regularized or conventionalized forms. With Free Music we enter the phase of technical maturity, such as that enjoyed by the Greek sculptures when all aspects and attitudes of the human body could be shown in arrested movement.

Existing conventional music (whether 'classical' or popular) is tied down by set scales, a tyrannical (whether metrical or irregular) rhythmic pulse that holds the whole tonal fabric in a vice-like grasp and a set of harmonic procedures (whether key-bound or atonal) that are merely habits, and certainly do not deserve to be called laws. Many composers have loosened, here and there, the cords that tie music down. Cyril Scott and Duke Ellington indulge in sliding tones: Arthur Fickénscher and others use intervals closer than the half tone; Cyril Scott (following my lead) writes very irregular rhythms that have been echoed, on the European continent, by Stravinsky, Hindemith, and others. Schönberg has liberated us from the tyranny of conventional harmony. But no non-Australian composer has been willing to combine *all* these innovations into a consistent whole that can be called *Free Music*.

It seems to me absurd to live in an age of flying and yet not be able to execute tonal glides and curves—just as absurd as it would be to have to paint a portrait in little squares (as in the case of mosaic) and not be able to use every type of curved lines. If, in the theatre, several actors (on stage together) had to continually move in a set metrical relation to one another (to be incapable of individualistic independent movement) we would think it ridiculous; yet this absurd goose-stepping still persists in music. Out in nature we hear all kinds of lovely and touching 'free' (non-harmonic) combinations of tones; yet we are unable to take up these beauties and expressiveness into the art of music because of our archaic notions of harmony.

Source: Typescript Museum legend dated 6 Dec. 1938 (reproduced in *Recorded Sound*, 45–6 (1972), p. 16). Grainger Museum, Melbourne.

Personally I have heard free music in my head since I was a boy of eleven or twelve in Auburn, Melbourne. It is my only important contribution to music. My impression is that this world of tonal freedom was suggested to me by wave movements in the sea that I first observed as a young child at Brighton, Victoria, and Albert Park, Melbourne.

Yet the matter of Free Music is hardly a personal one. If I do not write it someone else certainly will, for it is the goal that all music is clearly heading for now and has been heading for through the centuries. It seems to me the only music logically suitable to a scientific age.

The first time an example of my Free Music was performed on man-played instruments was when Percy Code[1] conducted it (most skilfully and sympathetically) at one of my Melbourne broadcasting lectures for the Australian Broadcasting Commission in January 1935.[2] But Free Music demands a non-human performance. Like most true music, it is an emotional, not a cerebral, product and should pass direct from the imagination of the composer to the ear of the listener by way of delicately controlled musical machines. Too long has music been subject to the limitations of the human hand, and subject to the interfering interpretations of a middle-man: the performer. A composer wants to speak to his public direct. Machines (if properly constructed and properly written for) are capable of niceties of emotional expression impossible to a human performer. That is why I write my Free Music for theremins[3]—the most perfect tonal instruments I know. In the original scores each voice (both on the pitch staves and on the sound-strength staves) is written in its own specially coloured ink, so that the voices are easily distinguishable, one from the other.

---

[1] (1887–1953), Australian Broadcasting Commission orchestral conductor, 1929–50.

[2] Grainger's *Free Music* No. 1 was performed by a string quartet as the last example of Grainger's last lecture of this broadcast series. Grainger's lecture synopsis explained that '"Free music" (towards which all musical progress clearly points) will be the full musical expression of the scientific nature-worship begun by the Greeks and carried forward by the Nordic races. It will be the musical counterpart of Nordic pioneering, athleticism, nudism.'

[3] Early form of electronic musical instrument, invented by Léon Thérémin (1896–1993), which Grainger was particular interested in because of its possibilities of glissando. Both his *Free Music* No. 1 and *Free Music* No. 2 were scored for theremins in 1936–7.

Part V

1940 AND AFTER

37

The Culturizing Possibilities of the
Instrumentally Supplemented
A Cappella *Choir*
(1942)

Forgetting William Byrd's unchangingly true words, 'There is not any Musicke of Instruments whatsoever, comparable to that which is made of the voyces of Men, where the voyces are good, and the same well sorted and ordered',[1] symphony orchestras in America are apt to describe themselves as being—and no doubt sincerely conceive of themselves as being—music's major culture-bearers. One of our most famous orchestras, in one of its recent programs,[2] quoted the following typically pretentious statement from an editorial in one of its local newspapers: 'The orchestral symphony (it is a fact which bears repeating) is the one art-form in which our age surpasses every previous epoch.'[3] One wonders what this curious statement may be supposed to mean. It cannot take 'our age' to mean the 20th century—for no one, I suppose, would claim that the symphonies written in the 20th century (Strauss's *Sinfonia Domestica*, Stravinsky's *Symphony of Psalms*, and the symphonies of Miaskovsky,[4] Roy Harris,[5] Vaughan Williams, Elgar, Milhaud, etc.) are superior to those of the 19th century (Beethoven, Schubert, Brahms, César Franck, Tchaikovsky, etc.). If 'our age' is taken to mean the 19th century, could it be claimed that the symphonies of that century surpass the best examples of the great art-forms of previous epochs—such as Bach's *St Matthew Passion*, Claude Le Jeune's *Printemps*, Handel's *Messiah*, Mozart's operas? (Not every classicist would admit that any 19th-century symphony eclipses Mozart's G minor Symphony.)

If, on the other hand, 'our age' is taken to mean what is loosely spoken of as 'the age of great music'—meaning from Bach to Rachmaninoff—

Source: *Musical Quarterly*, 28 (1942), 160–73.

[1] The seventh of Byrd's eight 'Reasons briefely set downe by th' auctor to perswade euery one to learne to singe', in his preface to *Songs of Sadness and Piety* (pub. 1588).

[2] In his manuscript draft, dated 12 April 1941, Grainger identifies this orchestra as the Boston Symphony Orchestra.

[3] *Boston Globe*, 26 Mar. 1941.

[4] Nicolay Miaskovsky (1881–1950), Russian composer of twenty-seven symphonies.

[5] (1898–1979), American composer, whose output included fourteen symphonies.

then it would certainly be untenable to assert that the 'symphonies' in Bach's and Handel's oratorios and cantatas surpass the masses of Josquin des Près, Byrd, and Palestrina. Taken any way you like, the sentence quoted is as difficult to subscribe to as it is to understand. Yet just such vague and misleading statements, appearing all over the world in dignified settings, give the general public the feeling that the symphony orchestra is performing a higher function than is performed by choral and chamber societies. The main impression (left by statements pleading the all-importance of the symphony orchestra) is that this type of organization gives us the widest possible musical fare, the fullest representation of all that is great in 'classical' music. But nothing could be further from the truth. Not only do our symphony orchestras fail to combine (as they should) with large choral bodies for the presentation of the greatest modern masterpieces composed for chorus and orchestra (works such as Delius's *Mass of Life* and *The Song of the High Hills*, Arthur Fickénscher's *Aucassin and Nicolette*,[6] David Monrad Johansen's *Voluspaa*,[7] Debussy's *Printemps* in its original form, Sparre Olsen's *Draumkvaedet* ('The Dream-Lay'),[8] Cyril Scott's *A Nativity Hymn*) but they equally fail to give us a true picture of the genius of Bach—whose claim to be faithfully presented to the musical public surely no one will deny. If the symphony orchestra is to be regarded as *the* supreme musical culture-bearer, it should bestir itself to present undisputed instrumental masterpieces such as Bach's Brandenburg Concertos without undue distortion of tonal balance. When Bach's Third Brandenburg Concerto (for 3 violins, 3 violas, 3 'cellos, and continuo) is played by a symphony orchestra in Europe, America, or Australia, the total number of violins (about 32) is spread over the three violin parts (giving a little better than 10 violins to a part), the total number of violas (about twelve) is spread over the three viola parts (about 4 violas to a part), the total number of 'cellos (about twelve) is spread over the three 'cello parts (about 4 'cellos to a part), and the total number of double-basses (about ten or twelve) combines on the double-bass part. This means that the double-bass part and each of the violin parts are performed with tonal resources more than double those of each of the viola and 'cello parts. It is obvious that such a distortion of tonal balance is fatal to music of a polyphonic character. Yet this is the type of conscienceless procedure regarded as normal for a symphony orchestra. (Let us turn the tables. What would we think if

---

[6] Orchestral-choral symphony poem, to a text by Andrew Lang.
[7] See Essay 26.
[8] Setting of 14th-cent. folk poem for speaker, chorus, and orchestra, Op. 22 (1937).

Beethoven's, Wagner's, and Brahms's scores were given with 4 first violins, 4 second violins, 10 violas, 10 'cellos, 4 double-basses?)[9]

We know what forces Bach regarded as suitable to the presentation of his church music, from a letter that he wrote to his church council. (It may be consulted in Terry's *Bach: A Biography*.[10]) We know what forces were used in the 'Handel Commemoration' that took place in London twenty-five years after Handel's death: 26 oboes, 26 bassoons, 12 trumpets, 48 first violins, etc. In neither of these cases was the oboe part swamped by violins (in one, there were equal tonal resources; in the other, a ratio of less than 2 violins to 1 oboe). But our symphony orchestras think nothing of accompanying an oboe solo with 16 first violins in Bach. If we were to apply the ratio of the 'Handel Commemoration' (say 10 oboes to 16 first violins) to Schubert's 'Unfinished' Symphony, the cry of 'sacrilege' would be raised. So it would be if saxophones were substituted for oboes and bassoons in Beethoven, Schubert, Brahms, and Tchaikovsky symphonies. Yet it is not considered sacrilegious (or in any way indefensible) to substitute clarinets for double-reeds (oboe da caccia, oboe d'amore, etc.) in Bach's works—in spite of the fact that the clarinet, in Bach's day, was as despised an instrument as is the saxophone with us today. In what are these inconsistencies rooted? In the assumption that Bach was a groper, not rightly knowing what he was doing, and that Mozart and Robert Franz[11] (when they re-orchestrated Handel and Bach for the conditions of their own period) knew better? (See 'Additional Accompaniments' in the 1928 edition of *Grove's Dictionary of Music*.[12])

One of America's favorite symphony orchestras, on a recent national tour, presented the Air from Bach's Third Overture (popularly known as 'Air for the G String') in an arrangement for full orchestra by a member of the orchestra. Yet Bach's own scoring, for four-part strings, is one of the wonders of music and could most tellingly have been performed by the orchestra in question. I am not querying anyone's right to re-orchestrate or re-arrange any piece of music—by whichever genius. (Bach himself was too inveterate an arranger of other men's music for us to protest any arranging of Bach's—even the wildest.) I am merely amazed that nobody thinks it a liberty to present arrangements and re-scorings of Bach's masterworks, while nobody (in the symphony orchestra field) would adopt a

---

[9] For this, and the following paragraph, see, further, Essay **29**.
[10] London, 1928.
[11] (1815–92), German composer and arranger of much Baroque music.
[12] Where Franz's additional accompaniments to numerous rescored works are claimed to be 'definitely rejected'.

like attitude to orchestral scores by Beethoven, Schubert, Wagner, and Brahms. General usage does not frown on performances with three pianos of works by Bach intended for three harpsichords—in spite of the fact that the piano (lacking octave couplers) is as bad a substitute for a harpsichord as can possibly be imagined, as regards both tone color and tonal range. While I do not protest against the occasional, or even frequent, performance of Bach in re-arranged orchestrations, I *do* consider it a calamity that he is as good as never heard in his original scoring, in his original tonal proportions. The original manuscript parts of Bach's *St Matthew Passion* were unearthed some years ago, and from these the number of performers (vocal soloists, double chorus, double orchestra) taking part in the original performances under Bach's direction may be roughly computed—some placing the number as low as 32, others as high as 50. We know that Handel conducted some fifteen performances of his *Messiah* and that on none of these occasions did the chorus exceed 30 in number. But I seldom hear of any of our societies giving either of these undisputed masterworks with the proportions used by the composers themselves.[13] On what grounds? Do our conductors feel that Bach and Handel did not know what they were doing? I repeat: I do not protest against the *St Matthew Passion* and the *Messiah* being performed with different proportions used by the composers; I merely consider it unfortu-

[13] Grainger's footnote: There are a few—a very few—professional musicians who *do* sense and fulfil their responsibilities to the musical public as well as to the music of the past, the present, and the future. In New York, The Cantata Singers, pledged, under the well-informed, painstaking, and inspiring conductorship of Arthur Mendel, to 'perform the choral music of the 17th and 18th centuries under conditions as close as possible to those of the original presentation', have given illuminating renderings of church cantatas (no less than twelve), oratorios, and the *St John Passion* of Bach, and of works by Heinrich Schütz, Giacomo Carissimi, Purcell, Mozart, and other composers. Still more light-shedding—because of the wider range of period and style covered—are the path-breaking activities of the A Cappella Choir of Gustavus Adolphus College, Saint Peter, Minn. (G. Adolph Nelson, conductor). Supporting its singularly sweet-toned band of singers with a chamber orchestra (consisting of 2 flutes, 2 oboes, 2 clarinets, bass clarinet, 2 bassoons, 2 horns, 3 trumpets, 2 trombones, 4 violins, 2 violas, 2 'cellos, double-bass, 2 pianos, and reed organ) this organization has recently presented in eight cities (Saint Peter, Minn.; Mitchell, S.D.; Omaha, Neb.; Des Moines, Iowa; Rockford, Ill.; Chicago, Ill.; Madison, Wis.; Minneapolis, Minn.) a program that opened with Bach's Church Cantata No. 147 (complete) and then gave the music of the various centuries in the following generous allotments: 13th century, 2 compositions; 14th century, 1; 15th century, 1; 16th century, 1; 17th century, 1; 19th century, 1; 20th century, 14; origin (in time) indeterminable (Russian and Negro American folk harmonizations), 4. A music-lover who has heard such a program has, afterward, some inkling of musical history, some awareness of the path of compositional unfoldment. In addition to the catholicity of his programs, Professor Nelson displays other unique powers that imbue his musical undertakings with rare value. He shows an unfailing sense of tonal beauty and a greater practical skill and more subtle esthetic intuition than any conductor I have ever observed dealing with the sometimes baffling problems inseparable from the association of small vocal and instrumental bodies along novel lines.

nate that these works are so seldom heard in the proportions used by the composers themselves. In particular, I protest against the notion that the great geniuses in the 17th and 18th centuries (William Lawes, John Jenkins, Purcell, Bach, Handel, etc.) had not reached perfection or expressiveness in orchestration and that, therefore, it is needful to adapt their scores to the superior practices of the 19th century.

Still more indefensible than the liberties taken with pre-Haydn orchestration is the alteration of *the music itself*, when presenting music by Bach and by pre-Bach composers. I cannot think of a better instance than Bach's 'Jesu, Joy of Man's Desiring', which has become very popular of late years in arrangements for piano solo, military band, orchestra, etc. In nothing does a great genius show his greatness more than in the way he presents contrasts between simplicity and complexity, and in combinations of the two. (May we not generalize and say that, while the public mostly seems to prefer simplicity and small creative talents lean towards it, the great geniuses always give much attention to complexity? Might it not be said that modern life tries to simplify everything, to make all things fool-proof? And that genius, acting as a corrective to this lop-sided tendency, tries to hold up the mirror of truth to life's many-sidedness—presenting both simplicity and complexity? Is this not the case in all periods of music—in Guillaume de Machaut's and Bach's times, no less than in Delius's and Fickénscher's times?) If this premise be true, how subversive is the tendency to eliminate the element of complexity from the compositions of the greatest geniuses! In Bach's original 'Jesu, Joy of Man's Desiring' the elements of simplicity may (I suppose) be said to predominate until we reach the coda, where a racy example of Bach's inborn complexity ('divine obscurity', if you will) delights the Bach-lover. I allude to the trellising voices of the first and second violins, 12 and 11 measures from the end of the number:

This crossing of the violin parts provides a charming confusion to the ear and balances well with the clarity of the rest of the composition. In most of the published arrangements of this composition (Myra Hess's, Harold Bauer's, Isador Freed's, Leonard Borwick's, and Albert-Lévêque's for piano solo; Elizabeth Gest's for 2 pianos; Charles J. Roberts' for orchestra; Erik Leidzen's for band) this crossing of the voices is eliminated, either by leaving out the second violin voice altogether or by placing it an octave lower than in Bach's original[14]—whereby the listener gets a wrong impression of the proportions of the simple and the complex in Bach's make-up. In other words, in these arrangements the listener gets a different philosophic message from the one he receives from Bach's original. From Bach's original he learns that life, however simple it may appear, always contains something baffling, something elusive. From the arrangements, above referred to, he gets the (as I think, more dangerous) impression that life at its best may be 'plain sailing'.

Again I ask: What is wrong with Bach that arrangers and conductors should feel it necessary to present his music in 'bowdlerized' versions, while not taking the same liberties with Haydn, Mozart, Beethoven, and other later composers? Why, in spite of the vast popularity of the single number 'Jesu, Joy of Man's Desiring', do societies not consider it attractive to present *the whole Church Cantata* (No. 147) in which it occurs? What would we think of organizations that repeatedly performed the slow movement of Dvořák's 'New World' Symphony, but never, or seldom, the whole symphony? Is the whole layout (the togetherness) of a composite work of Bach's less worth knowing than the layout of a Dvořák symphony?

Let my questions enter another field, another period. Grieg's Piano Concerto (although hardly one of its composer's most exquisite works) is repeatedly given by symphony orchestras; for the reason, no doubt, that it falls into the conventional symphonic framework. Likewise the *Peer Gynt Suite* is frequently given; for the reason (I would guess) that everything connected with the theatre and the stage was 'well seen' in the late 19th century and, therefore (if the music is at all presentable), falls to the taste of conventional symphony-followers. On the other hand, four compositions that Grieg himself considered to be the pinnacles of his creative work are consistently ignored by symphony orchestras (why do we almost invariably find serious modern compositions rejected by symphony orchestras, while frivolous works by the same composers are welcomed by these 'culture-bearers'?[15]):

(1) *Den Bergtekne* (*Lost in the Hills*) for baritone, 2 horns, and strings;
(2) Album for Male Chorus, Op. 30 (folk-songs);
(3) Symphonic Dances, for orchestra;[16]
(4) *Evening in the High Hills*, for oboe, horn, and strings.[17]

---

[14] Grainger's footnote: In Myra Hess's, Elsie Horne's, and Richard G. Appel's arrangements for 2 pianos; however, Bach's original texture, at this point, is preserved.

[15] See, further, Essay 39.   [16] Op. 64 (1896–7).

[17] Orchestration of Op. 68 No. 4, as No. 1 of *Two Lyric Pieces* (1898).

Of these, numbers 1, 3, and 4 seem, on the surface, quite eligible for presentation by symphony orchestras. They show Grieg in his deepest moods and they show his greatest mastery of the harmonic culture that unites him with such classics as Bach, Wagner, Chopin, and César Franck. On general reasoning (on the grounds that the symphony orchestra favors all that is earnest, large, noble, learned, and complex in music for its medium) these works of Grieg should appeal to symphony-orchestra taste more than the *Peer Gynt Suite*. But the fact is that symphony orchestras will not touch these grander, deeper, more subtle creations of Grieg.

And this brings me to the crux of my whole question: if the symphony organizations and the conventional choral and chamber societies cannot, or will not, present the huge bulk of unknown masterpieces (partly older music unearthed by energetic musicologists of late; partly modern music from the pens of the greatest 20th-century composers), who will, who should, do so? My answer is: They should be presented by *a cappella* choirs, organized to accommodate enough instrumentalists:

(1)   to provide instrumental backgrounds to choral and other vocal works (such as G. de Machaut's Ballade No. 17; such as the Bach Church Cantatas; such as Fauré's *Pavan*) by pre-Haydn and 20th-century composers;

(2)   to provide instrumental chamber music as a tonal contrast to choral numbers.

This expanding of the *a cappella* choir, so as to include choral works with chamber-music accompaniment and also instrumental chamber works without voices, is recommended for two main reasons:

(1)   to combat the monotony of conventional *a cappella* programs. These merely follow, blindly, the general monotony worship (horse-hair furniture-like, in type) of the 19th century. The unbearable monotony of a straight recital (whether by a pianist, a lieder singer, a string quartet, or an *a cappella* choir) is apparent to everyone but professional musicians. To discover what kind of tonal fare is reasonably appealing to normal humanity, we need only consult Bach's Church Cantatas and Passions, and remember the old mixed touring companies (presenting a pianist, a violinist, a soprano, a contralto, a tenor, a bass) accompanying vocal stars (Patti,[18] Clara Butt,[19] etc.) a generation or so ago and recall music-hall and vaudeville programs in England

---

[18]   Adelina Patti (1843–1919), Italian soprano, with whose party Grainger had toured provincial Britain in 1902.

[19]   (1872–1936), English contralto.

and America. In all these, the need for tonal contrast was recognized. One of the main reasons for the monotonous straight recital was probably a commercial one: the ability of the single soloist to earn more (per capita) than a group of soloists; the capacity of a string quartet to earn more (per capita) than a sextet or octet. But this consideration is not present in the case of an *a cappella* choir—at least, not when it is part of a college, university, high school, or other educational institution. On the contrary, the more the *a cappella* choir (in an educational institution) gives chances to *many soloists*, to varied musical gifts, the better it is fulfilling its educational functions;

(2) to provide a suitable frame in which to present the vast mass of unknown musical masterworks (old music from about 1200 to 1700 as well as 20th-century music) that deserve a hearing. A whole evening of pre-Bach instrumental chamber music (the trios, quartets, quintets, sextets of G. de Machaut, A. de Cabezón, Josquin des Près, Heinrich Finck, Byrd, Ferrabosco, Lawes, Jenkins, Purcell, etc.) would be as monotonous as a whole evening of Haydn-to-Hindemith quartets.

The proper frame in which to enjoy this exquisite early chamber music is in programs in which the new and the old, the vocal and the instrumental, the melodious and the technical, are blended and contrasted with artistry. In many cases *likeness of mood* (rather than sameness of scoring) should draw a group of pieces together. For instance, a group of 'Hill Pieces' might be presented, such as:

(a) 'The Hillman's Song' (*Lyric Pieces*), piano solo		Grieg
(b) *Evening in the High Hills*, oboe, horn, 8 strings		Grieg
(c) *Lost in the Hills*, baritone, 2 horns, 9 strings		Grieg
(d) 'A Hill Tune',[20] piano solo		Bax

Before facing the problem of presenting the vast mass of unknown masterpieces, old and new, we might first consider the three main classes of performers by whom music is rendered:

(1) by normal amateurs who cannot read well, and who lack high technical skill, but who perfect themselves in individual numbers by rehearsing them so often that they commit their parts more or less to memory and who master, as best they may, technical problems, not in advance, but as they arise in each new number essayed;

[20] (1920), for piano.

(2) by professionals, or expert amateurs, who are so technically developed, and who read so well, that they can give a creditable performance with scant rehearsing—in some cases, with a 'once through' rehearsal; in some cases, with no rehearsal at all;

(3) by expert professional soloists who, while able to read creditably by sight, still rehearse together so much that they perform their numbers more or less 'by heart'. (String-quartet organizations belong to this group.)

It is pretty obvious that while known masterpieces can be tolerably well rendered by class 2, unknown masterpieces, old and new, cannot. Many performances of known oratorios, cantatas, etc. are, indeed, wrecked by a class 2 orchestra being associated (at the last moment) with a class 1 chorus. Many concerto and other soloistic performances are spoiled by a class 3 soloist (often having memorized his part a bit inaccurately) being associated with a class 1 or class 2 orchestra. Performances of instrumental sextets, septets, and octets are usually somewhat marred when two or more class 2 string players are added to a class 3 string quartet.

Works such as the church cantatas of Bach, or Hindemith's *Die junge Magd*, cannot be tellingly given when a class 1 choir or when class 1 or 3 vocal soloists are suddenly (at the last moment) accompanied by a class 2 orchestra or instrumental group. *All unknown masterpieces demand a class 1 or class 3 presentation.* Only repeated trying of certain passages, in unknown masterworks, will reveal what type of performance and tonal adjustment is needful. That is why an *a cappella* choir, expanded so as to include from 3 to 8 strings, a few woodwinds, a reed organ, 2 pianists, and a harpsichord, would be an ideal medium for the presentation of a bird's-eye view of all unknown chamber-music masterworks from the 13th century to the present day. The older chamber music in which voices and instruments may be blended together or alternated one with the other (Pérotin[21]—at least, as some interpret his music—, G. de Machaut, Worcester Medieval Harmony, Dufay, Dunstable, Isaac, A. de Cabezón, Pisador, Heinrich Finck, Byrd, Ferrabosco, Claude Le Jeune, Adrian Willaert, Josquin des Près, William Lawes, John Jenkins, etc.) can come to full fruition only at the hands of organizations in which singers and instrumentalists rehearse together all the time—as the Dolmetsch family do at Haslemere. In the matter of choice of numbers and style of performance, many helpful hints may be drawn from Arnold Schering's *History*

---

[21] Perotinus Magnus, French composer, *fl. c.*1200.

of Music in Examples (Breitkopf & Härtel)[22] and from the *Anthologie sonore*, a series of gramophone records prepared by Curt Sachs.[23] The *Anthologie sonore* records are particularly instructive in showing what beauty can be achieved with the 'broken consort' type of scoring—the association of very dissimilar-toned instruments (with each other, or with a voice or voices). In the older music the choice of the instruments to be employed is not stated—this choice being left to the performers. The score of Dufay's 'Le jour s'endort' (as seen in Schering, for instance) might lead one to accompany the voice with 3 strings, or with 3 winds. Here Curt Sachs, in the *Anthologie Sonore* record of this gem, shows us how very effective an extremely broken consort can be: flute, tenor voice, and trombone![24]

However, our main duty with regard to unknown masterworks, new or old, is not to squabble about methods of performance (as to how far the 'broken consort' method should be followed, or its reverse), but to get down to performances *of the music itself*, using a variety of approaches and forming our taste upon tireless experimentation. It does not matter so much whether we accompany the baritone voice with single strings, or massed strings, in Grieg's *Den Bergtekne*. What matters is that we *break silence* with this superb masterwork! What matters is that we learn how to unfold the whole range of available great music to the ears of music-lovers. What matters is that we, at last, make of music a universal language, a cosmopolitan experience, and (as far as possible) a timeless art.

The following is a sample program, using several different types of music suitable to an instrumentally supplemented *a cappella* choir:

(1) Church Cantata, No. 147, 'Herz und Mund und Tat und Leben',[25] for 4 solo voices, mixed chorus, oboe, English horn, bassoon, trumpet, 5 strings, and harpsichord or reed organ   Bach

(2) Early European Chamber Music

    (*a*) 'Fowles in the Frith',[26] for baritone and viola (or oboe)

                                          English, 13th century

---

[22] (Leipzig: 1931, Eng. trans. 1950), by Arnold Shering (1877–1941), German musicologist.

[23] (1881–1959), German musicologist, from 1937 resident in the United States. *L'Anthologie sonore*, recorded in Paris from 1933 onwards, consisted of thirteen volumes of ten 12-inch records each.

[24] Series record A5-3, in Vol. I. The Dufay piece was performed by Max Meile (tenor), Jan Merry (flute), F. Seidersbeck (viol), and A. Lafosse (trombone).

[25] Grainger's footnote: Breitkopf & Härtel.

[26] Grainger's footnote: *English Gothic Music* by Dom Anselm Hughes and Percy Aldridge Grainger (G. Schirmer, Inc., in preparation [1943]).

(*b*) 'Alleluia psallat',[27] for 6-part chorus and strings

English, 13th century

(*c*) 'Beata viscera',[28] for 3-part mixed chorus and harp

English, 13th century

(*d*) Rondeau, 'Ma fin est mon commencement',[29] for tenor voice, 3 plucked strings, 3 bowed strings

Guillaume de Machaut (French, 1300–1377)

(*e*) 'La Bernardina',[30] for oboe, clarinet, and bassoon

Josquin des Près (Flemish, *c.*1450–1521)

(*f*) 'O schönes Weib',[31] for tenor voice and 3 strings (or 3 winds)

Heinrich Finck (German, 1445–1527)

(*g*) 'Paséabase el Rey Moro' ('The Moorish King goes walking'),[32] for baritone voice and lute (or plucked strings)

Diego Pisador (Spanish, *c.*1550)

(*h*) 'O salutaris hostia',[33] for 2-part chorus (altos, tenors), 2 trumpets, 2 trombones   Adrian Willaert (Netherlands, *c.*1480–1562)

(*i*) 'O glorious golden Era',[34] for tenor solo, 2 violas, 2 cellos

Francesco Corteccia (Italian, d. 1571)

(*j*) Fantasy in 5 parts, No. 1,[35] for 5 strings

John Jenkins (English, 1592–1678)

(3) 'Mirabelle' ('A Quaint Cantata')[36] for mixed chorus (5 or more strings *ad lib.*)   Cyril Scott (English, b. 1879)

(4) *Die junge Magd* (The Young Servant Girl)[37] for mezzo-soprano voice, flute, clarinet, 4 strings, and glockenspiel

Paul Hindemith (German, b. 1895)

---

[27] As n. 26.   [28] As n. 26.

[29] Grainger's footnote: *Guillaume de Machaut: Musikalische Werke*, edited by Friedrich Ludwig, 1. Band, p. 63, Breitkopf & Härtel, or *Music in the Middle Ages* (p. 351) by Gustave Reese (W. W. Norton & Co., New York).

[30] Grainger's footnote: *Geschichte der Musik in Beispielen*, by Arnold Schering (Breitkopf & Härtel).

[31] As n. 30.

[32] Grainger's foonote: *Les Luthistes espagnols du XVIe siècle*, edited by G. Morphy, Vol. II, p. 179.

[33] As n. 30.

[34] As n. 30.

[35] Grainger's footnote: *The Dolmetsch Collection of English Consorts* (G. Schirmer, Inc., in preparation [1944]).

[36] Grainger's footnote: Novello & Co., London.

[37] Grainger's footnote: B. Schott's Söhne, Mayence.

(5) Folk-harmonization (improved part-singing 'frozen' into the phono-
     graph) and its influence, for unaccompanied chorus

  (a) Lullaby,[38] Negro-American folk-harmonization, noted by
       Natalie Curtis-Burlin, for mixed chorus, 8-part

  (b) 'De Lawd's agwine to move all de troubles away',[39] Negro-
       American folk-harmonization, noted by Natalie Curtis-Burlin,
       for men's voices, 4-part

  (c) 'Kindling Wood', Great-Russian folk-harmonization, noted by
       Madam Lineva, for women's voices, 3-part

  (d) 'The Flowers of the Field', Great-Russian folk-harmonization,
       noted by Madam Lineva, for mixed chorus, 4-part

  (e) 'Laud Ye the Name of the Lord',[40] from *Songs of the Church*,
       off-shoot from Russian folk-harmonization, for mixed chorus
                                      Rachmaninoff (Russian, b. 1873)

(6) 'The Chamber Blue',[41] for mezzo-soprano voice, viola, and piano
                                Arthur Fickénscher (American, b. 1871)

(7) *Pavan*,[42] for small chorus and chamber orchestra
                                Gabriel Fauré (French, 1845–1924)

   In making up programs for an instrumentally supplemented *a cappella*
choir, it would be a fatal mistake to choose *only* instrumentally accompanied partsongs. Such samishness would be as wearying as that of a
whole program of unaccompanied part-songs. In building programs, conductors should emulate the variety and contrasts of tone color and tone
size shown by Bach, Handel, and their contemporaries in planning their
cantatas, Passion music, etc. (numbers for solo voices and instruments
contrasted with numbers for massed voices or instruments; vocal
numbers contrasted with instrumental numbers) and by modern composers in their orchestral suites (Bizet's first *L'Arlésienne*, with one movement for string orchestra, enclosed by three for full orchestra; Grieg's first
Peer Gynt, with two numbers for string orchestra sandwiched between

---

[38] Grainger's footnote: G. Schirmer, Inc.
[39] As n. 38.
[40] Grainger's footnote: The H. W. Gray Co., New York.
[41] Grainger's footnote: Procurable from Professor Arthur Fickénscher, Fairfax, Marin
County, California.
[42] Grainger's footnote: J. Hamelle, Paris.

two for full orchestra; Tchaikovsky's *Nutcracker*, in which 'cellos and basses are omitted in the first movement, but present in all others).[43]

Compositions of every type and mood, dating from 1200 to the present day, suitable for inclusion in programs by an instrumentally backgrounded *a cappella* choir must run into thousands—indeed, be legion. Out of these I herewith present a small list of choice but neglected masterpieces (intentionally avoiding better known examples, such as Schoenberg's *Pierrot lunaire*):

'Puellare gremium',[44] for 6-part mixed voices, trumpet, trombone
English, 13th century

Ballade[45] (No. 17 in Friedrich Ludwig's edition), for 3 men's voices, or 6 mixed voices (3, or 6, or 9 strings *ad lib.*)
Guillaume de Machaut (French, 1300–1377)

'Veni sancte spiritus',[46] for mixed voices and 4 to 12 strings
John Dunstable (English, d. 1453)

'Aus fahr' ich hin',[47] for baritone voice and viola   German song (1460)

'Le Printemps',[48] a whole cycle of *a cappella* numbers
Claude Le Jeune (Belgian, 1528-c.1600)

Rhapsodies for voice, oboe, viola and piano[49]
Charles Martin Loeffler (American, 1861–1935)

'East of the Sun, West of the Moon',[50] for solo voices, mixed chorus, and chamber orchestra   Arthur Fickénscher (American, b. 1871)

[43] Grainger's footnote: A past master in the type of program-orchestration above advocated is Dr. Harry Seitz, the musical director of the Detroit (Mich.) Central High School. In the concerts given by his forces under his direction, small choirs are contrasted with large choirs, female voices with male voices, band with orchestra and chamber music. Certain groups undertake drastic re-arrangement (including improvisation) of the music they sing and play. One of the most thrilling features of his programs is 'choral speech'—often by choirs 300 to 600 strong. The tonal variety of such programs may be imagined. What cannot be imagined (until experienced) is the exquisite euphony that Dr. Seitz coaxes from all the groups he controls.

[44] Grainger's footnote: *English Gothic Music* by Dom Anselm Hughes and Percy Aldridge Grainger (G. Schirmer, Inc., in preparation [1950/1]).

[45] Grainger's footnote: *Guillaume de Machaut: Musikalische Werke*, edited by Friedrich Ludwig, 1. Band, p. 16 (Breitkopf & Härtel).

[46] As n. 44.

[47] Grainger's footnote: *Geschichte der Musik in Beispielen* by Arnold Schering (Breitkopf & Härtel).

[48] Grainger's footnote: *Les maîtres musiciens de la renaissance française*, edited by M. H. Expert (Editions Maurice Sénart, Paris).

[49] Grainger's footnote: G. Schirmer, Inc.

[50] Grainger's footnote: Procurable from Professor Arthur Fickénscher, Fairfax, Marin County, California.

'Fair Helen of Kirkconnel',[51] for baritone voice and chamber orchestra
                                      Cyril Scott (English, b. 1879)

'The Rat Catcher',[52] for baritone voice and flute   Cyril Scott

Fantasy for mixed voices and strings[53]
                                T. Stanley Skinner (American, b. 1882)

'Mountain-Norway',[54] for mixed voices and chamber orchestra
                                      Sparre Olsen (Norwegian, b. 1903)

Two Fantasies, for 6 strings[55]   William Byrd (English, 1543–1623)

'The Four Note Pavan',[56] for 5 strings
                                Alfonso Ferrabosco (English, d. 1628)

Fantasy and Air,[57] 6-part, No. 1, for 6 strings
                                      William Lawes (English, d. 1645)

Fantasias for strings[58] (2-part, 3-part, 4-part, 5-part)
                                Henry Purcell (English, 1658–1695)

'Longing' and 'The Elf-Hill',[59] for 9 strings
                                      Herman Sandby (Danish, b. 1881)

'Le Bal de Béatrice d'Este',[60] Suite for 10 wind instruments, percussion, 2
   harps, and piano   Reynaldo Hahn (Argentinian,[61] b. 1875)

Javanese, Balinese, Siamese Percussion Pieces (from gramophone
album, 'Music of the Orient'[62]) transc. for American percussion
instruments.

If the instrumentally supplemented *a cappella* choir could take upon
itself to give programs of the type above suggested—catholic in taste and
presenting the best music of all nations and periods—it could claim to be
the main musical culture-bearer in any community. It could popularize
the unknown masterworks of music to an extent never possible to the

[51] Grainger's footnote: Elkin & Co., London.
[52] As n. 51.
[53] Grainger's footnote: Procurable from Dean T. Stanley Skinner, Music Department, Drury
College, Springfield, Mo.
[54] Grainger's footnote: B. Schott's Söhne, Mayence.
[55] Grainger's footnote: Stainer & Bell, London.
[56] Grainger's footnote: *The Dolmetsch Collection of English Consorts* (G. Schirmer, Inc., in
preparation [1944]).
[57] As n. 56.
[58] Grainger's footnote: Curwen Edition, London.
[59] Grainger's footnote: Skandinavisk og Borups Musikforlag, Copenhagen, Denmark.
[60] Grainger's footnote: J. Hamelle, Paris.
[61] Venezuelan-born French.
[62] Grainger's footnote: Decca.

symphony orchestra or the conventional choral and chamber-music societies, for the simple reason that the bulk of the finest compositions
written within the last one thousand years are conceived for single-voice
groups or small exquisitely balanced choirs (rather than for giant choirs)
and for instrumental groups larger than (or different from) the conventional chamber groups of the 19th century (string quartet, piano and
string trios, quartets and quintets, wind quintets) yet infinitely smaller
than our ill-balanced symphony orchestras.

38   *The Specialist and the All-Round Man*
(1943)

In the lower level of the Grand Central Terminal station in New York City, near the information booth, stands a square marble pillar on which some directions are printed in black paint: 'New Haven Railroad Ticket Offices, Telegraph', etc., followed by a leftward-pointing arrow; 'Parcel Room, Telephones', etc., followed by a rightward-pointing arrow. But the leftward-pointing arrow is so far removed from the list of destinations to which it refers and so close to the list of destinations to which it does not refer as to be quite misleading. This must be the work of a 'specialist' and 'expert'.

On the map of the Chesapeake & Ohio Railroad timetable the station Richmond, Indiana, is next to the station Williamsburg, Indiana, and the station Richmond, Virginia, is next to the station Williamsburg, Virginia. In the timetables themselves both Richmonds and both Williamsburgs are printed without mention of their states, with the result that the inexperienced reader is apt to confuse the Indiana pair of cities with the Virginia pair, or *vice versa*. Men (professionals) are *paid* to commit such blunders—the reason for which is termed 'brevity' or 'conservation of space' by the experts.

Judging from the way travellers in trains behave with their shoes (that is, they take them off), one must infer that specialist-made footwear is not easy to wear on the feet. Nor is expert book-binding any more satisfactory. One takes a manuscript orchestral score to a reputable bookbinder. When it comes home it looks all right, but it will not stay open on the conductor's desk. After a few sessions with our masterful 'expert' conductors it will stay open, but by this time the score is sundered into two or three sections that hang loosely together by some strips of broken material. Yet any amateur—with a little gummed tape, adhesive tape, cardboard, and a little sewing—can bind a score that will lie open immediately and yet survive the virility of conductors.

As a composer one has similar experiences with amateur and professional musical performers. A few years ago I was asked to prepare a band

Source: *A Birthday Offering to C[arl] E[ngel]*, ed. Gustave Reese (New York: G. Schirmer, 1943), 115–19.

composition for a bandmasters' convention in Milwaukee.[1] I never like to 'sell a pig in a poke'; so I tried out the work on several student bands (among others, on the superb student band of the Ernest Williams School of Music in Brooklyn[2]) and on high-school bands in Texas, New York state, and elsewhere. Two of the movements, in my work, presented unusual rhythmic problems, but none of the non-professional bands had any real trouble with them. But the professional bandsmen in Milwaukee could not solve these problems at all, and two movements had to be left out.

When, in 1934 and 1935, I presented European chamber music of the 13th, 14th, 15th, 16th, and 17th centuries to audiences in Australia, I was as amazed at the ability of amateur groups to negotiate this unusual music successfully as I was at the inability of the finest professional chamber groups to do so. In Adelaide the most famous and admired of Australian professional quartets dragged their way through a program of pre-Bach chamber music,[3] in which no piece escaped without at least one member of the organization 'getting out'. In Sydney another famous professional quartet reached an even dizzier height of inefficiency: in every single item of a pre-Bach program the group went to pieces, stopped and made verbal apologies.[4] Yet these same medieval and renaissance chamber works were played without tonal shipwreck by comparatively inexperienced amateurs or students in Perth, Tasmania, Brisbane, and even in Mount Gambier[5]—the latter a town of some five thousand inhabitants.

So it is not merely that one deplores the fact that, in the professional, the specialist, the expert, 'human feeling is sacrificed on the altar of skill'; one deplores that specialization makes the specialist so feeble that even skill forsakes him.

So much twaddle has been written and believed, in the last hundred years, about 'the achievements of specialization' that it takes a stubborn individual to resist it all and remain an 'all-round man'. Yet cultural history—with its accounts of the romantic yet almost unbelievably

---

[1] 7 Mar. 1937, at the annual convention of the American Bandmasters' Association. Grainger refers to his *Lincolnshire Posy*, which was premièred at this concert, along with his '*Lads of Wamphray' March*.

[2] Grainger conducted three movements from *Lincolnshire Posy* as guest conductor in an Ernest Williams School of Music concert on 19 Mar. 1937.

[3] 3 and 5 June 1935. The programme does not identify by name the six string players who took part in these broad-ranging concerts.

[4] 13 and 16 Mar. 1935.

[5] 27 Feb. 1935. Mount Gambier is in the south-east corner of South Australia.

victorious lives of the King Alfreds, Snorri Sturlusons,[6] Leonardo da Vincis, Johann Sebastian Bachs, Richard Wagners, Walt Whitmans, of this world—makes it clear enough that life and nature favor the all-round man. It is in the nature of things that we should all of us be the slaves-of-life. But by no set of circumstances, other than by his own inborn wit-lessness, is a man forced to so demean himself as to become the slave-of-a-job.

One might expect this obvious truth to be patent to everyone. Yet it seems far from being the case. My personal experience with thousands of piano students leads me to believe that hardly any of them have an inkling of what it is (*i.e.*, all-round manhood) that raises giants like Paderewski and Rachmaninoff high above the rabble of pianistic skill-mongers whose mere keyboard wizardry fails (incidentally) even to create audiences.

It was no surprise that Paderewski became Polish premier; long before that he had shown by his compositions (the Variations, the Polish Phantasy),[7] by his patriotism and his philanthropy that he was a great man, an all-round man.

Was it Lawrence Gilman[8] who described Rachmaninoff as 'a first-rate pianist, but a sixth-rate composer'?—a feat of mis-criticism worth remembering. Before 1895, Rachmaninoff had penned the greatest piano piece of modern times—is that not what the C-sharp minor Prelude[9] is? Long before the 1918[10] revolution drove him from Russia, he had com-posed one of the greatest of Russian symphonies and perhaps the most satisfying volume of Russian Church music—the Fifteen Songs of the Church. When the economic blow fell, this great composer was so much of an all-round man that he was able to pose as a specialist in what, for him, was merely a side-line—pianism.

While blind and unreasoning belief in the advantages of specialization has doomed countless men and women to utterly needlessly boring, monotonous, and frustrated lives, our era, like all other eras, has heaped spectacular rewards (of happiness, prosperity, richness of experience) upon those brave enough, clear-sighted enough, selfish enough, joy-worshipping enough to risk leading all-round lives. I will cite but three examples, all from our contemporary or recent world of art.

[6] (1179–1241), the most important figure in Old Icelandic literature, author of the *Prose Edda* and *Heimskringla*, who survived numerous attempts on his life until finally assassinated on the orders of King Hákon of Norway.

[7] Probably, Variations and Fugue on an original theme, Op. 11 (c.1883) and *Fantaisie polonaise*, Op. 19 (1893).

[8] (1878–1939), New York music critic.

[9] Op. 3 No. 2 (1892).   [10] 1917.

Cyril Scott, the English composer (born 1879), was a 'wonder child', as a pianist and composer. Since then, in the last forty-five years or so, he has probably written (in addition to a host of songs and piano pieces) more large works—symphonies, operas, cantatas, concertos, chamber works—than any of his time-mates. In these works he introduced innovations in the form of irregular rhythm, sliding intervals, and discordant harmony that foreshadowed the atonalism and musical futurism of his imitators. He is one of the most exquisite pianists of all time. His writings (largely anonymous) on theosophical subjects are widely read and remembered. Of late years he has written 'best-selling' books on the subjects of doctors and cancer.[11] He has published several volumes of highly individual poetry. He is active as painter and etcher.

French-born Arnold Dolmetsch (1858–1940) roamed the whole domain of European 'ancient music' (from Welsh Bardic harp music, that he believed to be a survival from the 6th century, up to Beethoven) as the Red Indians roamed the prairies. Trained as an organ-builder and piano-maker, and as a violinist as well, he made, mended, and revived almost every ancient type of European musical instrument (wind, string, plucked, keyboard) known to musical history. As a musicologist he deciphered musical manuscripts and tablatures and choreographic notations of many centuries. But—unlike many musicologists—he never failed to put his notations and transcriptions of ancient music to the acid test of public performance. Himself a fascinating performer on the lute, the viols, the violin family, the shawms, the recorders, the early keyboard instruments, the early harps, the chamber organ, he taught his entire large family to play expressively and euphoniously on these and other instruments, and with his family organized the Festivals of Ancient Music at Haslemere, England. To many musicians these festivals were the richest and most light-shedding concerts of our era. Dolmetsch's book *The Interpretation of the Music of the 17th and 18th Centuries*[12] bears witness to the amazing scope of his investigations, research, and intuition.

Norman Lindsay (born 1879),[13] the most fearless and arrogant artist Australia has produced, has spread himself victoriously over many fields. A transcendental virtuoso with pen, brush, etching needle, and wood-carver's knife, he won fame as a cartoonist on the Sydney *Bulletin*.[14] Then

---

[11] Scott's books about health include *Doctors, Disease and Health*, *Victory over Cancer*, *Cancer Prevention*, *Sleeplessness*, *Constipation and Common Sense*, and *Cider Vinegar*.

[12] (London: Novello, 1915). See, further, Essay **29**.

[13] d. 1969.

[14] Lindsay was associated with the *Bulletin* between 1901 and 1967.

followed a flood of drawings, paintings, etchings, so full of exuberant and reckless vitality as to raise a host of opponents as well as admirers. An electrifying author as well, his books (sublimating Australian larrikinism[15] into the realms of loftiest art) are devoured in Denmark, Britain, and America, while banned (most of them) in his native land. Lindsay is a tireless wood-carver, and his huge, ornately-carved models (ten feet long, or longer) of ancient Greek and Roman galleys and Spanish galleons, and the like, are centers of interest in several Australian art galleries and museums. As a self-financing book publisher, he has brought out some of Australia's most noteworthy books,—among them Hugh Patton's stark and arresting *Land-Takers*.[16]

Society offers such careers of joy, variety, and expansiveness to courageous individuals of non-specialist proclivities. Yet it may seem that there is but little official recognition of the fact that it is non-specializing all-roundness that lies at the root of human greatness.

But in the field of American music education we are lucky. It can hardly be denied that in the schools and high-schools of America young music-lovers are encouraged to enjoy, understand, and practise music as cultured amateurs rather than to develop themselves into hard-driven specialized professionals. Perhaps it is not too much to say that the present attitude of the music educators of America towards music is one of the strongest endorsements of all-roundness, as opposed to specialization, to be found anywhere in the world.

That being the case, it is a matter for rejoicing—since publication and education are so closely linked—that America's foremost music-publishing house has as its President an all-round genius of prodigious scope and experience, a graceful philosopher, a profound scholar and amazing linguist, a fascinating author, a never-baffled organizer, and (last but not least) an exquisite and many-sided composer. Think of the range of styles compassed by the virile *Academic Processional March*,[17] the mysterious nature sounds of 'Sea-shell',[18] the expressive polyphony of 'At the Seashore',[19] the harmonic subtlety of 'Lecture du soir',[20] the sensitively emotional yet aristocratically restrained *Triptych* for violin and piano![21]

Incidentally, think of the joy of a composer, coming in to Schirmers to

[15] Australian colloquial word indicating anti-authoritarian cheek.
[16] *Landtakers* (1934) by Brian Penton (1904–51).
[17] Written by Engel for Oberlin College (pub. 1936).
[18] Song for medium voice.
[19] No. 1 of *The Never-lonely Child* (pub. 1919).
[20] No. 1 of *Trois Sonnets*, for voice and piano (pub. 1914).
[21] Pub. 1920.

discuss some matter of publication, secure in the certainty that in Carl Engel, its President,[22] he will meet a fellow-artist whose advice on all subjects (be it a compositional problem, or the choice of ink for a cover design, or a detail of cataloguing, or an adjustment of interests between publishing houses) is invariably wise, inspired, sympathetic, practical, helpful and kindly! Above all, *kindly*; for is not kindness the invariable concomitant of genius? I have never known it to fail.

[22] (1883–1944), chief of the music division at the Library of Congress (1922–34), and president of the publisher G. Schirmer (1929–44).

39 Grieg: Nationalist and Cosmopolitan
(1943)

Personal Recollections of Edvard Grieg in Celebration of the Centennial of the Great Norwegian Master

Editor's Note: Few living musicians of prominence knew Edvard Grieg, and there certainly is no one for whom he expressed greater artistic appreciation or personal fondness than he did for his young friend, Australian-born Percy Grainger. The *Etude* feels that it is a distinct honor to present this article, written in Mr. Grainger's inimitable style. These recollections will be continued in equally notable instalments. The picture of Grieg and Grainger on the cover of this issue is said to be the last portrait of the Norwegian master.

I often am asked the question, 'What kind of man was Grieg?'[1] And I think the simplest, yet fullest answer is to say, 'He was a United Nations type of man.' For he was constantly striving in his life, his art, his thoughts for the same things as the United Nations are fighting for to-day. Grieg consistently championed the Jews against their persecutors and supported the young, the unknown, the untried, in whatever struggle they had with the old, the famous, and the experienced. This was not because he was a rebel but because he was a true progressive, and because he realized that progress depends upon a reasonable degree of opportunity being granted to the forces of change, as against the forces of established authority.

Grieg was very impatient with needless authority. The little railroad that operated between Bergen (Norway) and Hop (where his summer home, 'Troldhaugen', was situated) issued serial railroad tickets in a book, which tickets only the train conductor was supposed to tear out. But when the conductor drew nigh to collect the tickets, Grieg himself would ostentatiously tear the tickets out of the book and hand them to the conductor.

Source: *Etude*, 61/6 (June 1943), 386, 416–18; 61/7 (July 1943), 428, 472; 61/8 (Aug. 1943), 492, 535, 543; 61/9 (Sept. 1943), 569, 616.

[1] Grainger's published writings about Grieg spanned fifty years, from his 'Personal Recollections of Grieg', *Musical Times*, 48 (1907), 720, to 'Edvard Grieg: A Tribute', *Musical Times*, 98 (1957), 482–3.

In his resistance to the prerogatives of 'high society', Grieg was positively impish. When he and his wife[2] (she a charming singer) first visited England—two young artists precariously uncertain of their economic future—they fell into the clutches of a socially prominent lady, who invited them to a party at her home and kept them both playing and singing to her guests until long after midnight. The Griegs, with typical Scandinavian politeness and obligingness, did not like to refuse, though weary and inwardly rebellious. The master related that years later, in Paris, they met their London hostess, now high in diplomatic circles. She rushed up to Grieg, saying 'I am so delighted to see you again! Do you remember that divine evening, years ago, in London, when you and Madame Grieg entertained us so wonderfully?' Grieg looked at her stonily and said, 'No, I don't remember you.' But (he added) at that moment he caught sight of her husband, a tall man (Grieg was almost a dwarf), and the composer made his escape down a back staircase.

A Man of Opinions

As a protagonist for the Jewish cause in the Dreyfus case,[3] Grieg's actions are probably known to most musicians; but I mention them briefly here for the benefit of those who may not have heard of this so typical episode. In 1899, when Dreyfus was still a prisoner, the French conductor, Édouard Colonne,[4] invited Grieg to conduct a program of Grieg music at the Châtelet Theater in Paris; to which invitation the composer replied: 'Like all other non-Frenchmen I am shocked at the injustice in your country and do not feel myself able to enter into any relations whatsoever with the French public.' In 1903 he again was approached by Colonne, and this time he accepted. But his pro-Dreyfus letter was remembered, and hissing and shouting, as well as applause, broke forth as Grieg appeared on the platform to conduct his music. Grieg (never a rabble-fearer) simply waited until the hostile demonstration had subsided somewhat, whereupon he embarked upon the loud opening of his *In Autumn Overture*, thereby drowning out what remained of the shouting and hissing. At the end of the concert, of course, he was acclaimed with that frenetic applause which crowds reserve for those who are indifferent to

[2] Nina, née Hagerup (1845–1935).
[3] Concerning a French army officer of Jewish origin, Alfred Dreyfus (1859–1935), convicted erroneously of treason in 1894, but only rehabilitated in 1906.
[4] (1838–1910), French violinist and conductor, who established the Concerts Colonne and the Association Artistique, which pioneered performances of much contemporary music.

them. The full story of his connection with the 'Dreyfus Affair' may be enjoyed in David Monrad-Johansen's book, *Edvard Grieg* (an English translation of which was issued in 1938 by the Princeton University Press).[5] All interested in Grieg and his music should read this stimulating and highly informative book, which is a model of musical history.

There was in Copenhagen a Danish operatic composer who was well known for his plagiarisms.[6] Shortly after the performance of one of his unoriginal operas, this composer dined with Grieg at the latter's hotel. During the dinner Grieg, who was always a charming host, said nothing derogatory. But when the Dane had bid his host good-bye and was looking for his umbrella, which he could not find, Grieg heard him accuse one of the hotel bellhops[7] of having stolen it. This was too much for Grieg, who always was on the side of the 'under dog'. He burst forth from behind a curtain and thus admonished the surprised plagiarist, 'You dare to call anyone a thief! You, who steal from us all!'

A few years before the master's death one of the world's greatest piano manufacturing houses offered to present him with a lovely grand piano, an offer which Grieg accepted. But the piano house, or their local agent, neglected to pay the import duty on the piano. This aroused in Grieg his typical Norwegian 'independence', and also that blend of frugality with generosity that is so deliciously Scandinavian. 'I wouldn't dream of paying import duty on a presentation piano', he declared. Forthwith he proceeded to write to a few of his friends, saying he would be glad to pass on the piano to the one who would care to pay the import duty. So his closest friend (in the double sense of being the dearest friend as well as the nearest neighbour to 'Troldhaugen'), Frants Beyer,[8] acquired this magnificent instrument on which I often had the pleasure of playing to the Grieg and Beyer families.

His Love for Individuality

After one of these pianistic sessions (in which my programs ranged from Bach, Scarlatti, and folksong to the then Modernists, Debussy, Ravel, Cyril Scott, Roger Quilter, and Albéniz) Grieg praised to the skies my rendering of his own *Norwegian Folksongs*, Op. 66, and *Norwegian*

---

[5] pp. 352–4.
[6] Perhaps Peter Lange-Müller (1850–1926), composer of some sixteen stage works between 1878 and 1901.
[7] Hotel pages.
[8] (1851–1918), an amateur pianist and former pupil of Grieg.

Peasant Dances, Op. 72. The interpretation of this folk music presented no riddle to me, as it did to most conventional concert pianists, because as a folksong collector I was familiar with the traditions of English folk music in the field; and the traditions of English and Norwegian folk music are very similar. Later we were descending in the dark the steep path leading from the Beyer home to the rowboat in which Grieg was to row us (despite his asthma) across the water to 'Troldhaugen', when he suddenly stopped in his tracks and said to me in his most impulsive (but never sententious) manner, 'Mind you! You don't play my folksongs according to my intentions! But don't alter anything. I love individuality.'

Grieg was invited to supervise a Festival of Norwegian Music to be held in one of the larger Norwegian cities. He accepted the invitation on the condition that the Amsterdam Concertgebouw would be the orchestra employed, with Willem Mengelberg[9] (just then rising into fame) as the conductor. This raised a storm of protest from some Norwegian musicians who wanted to know why a foreign conductor must be engaged to carry out a festival of Norwegian music. Grieg's reply was typical: 'Because there is in Norway no conductor or orchestra worthy of the task, and because I consider the best service we can do for Norwegian music is to let a Norwegian audience hear it, for once, as it ought to sound.'

The final anecdote brings me to the important matter of Grieg's dual nature, as an ardent patriot and as a confirmed cosmopolitan. No one could ever be in doubt of his flaming 'Norwegianness'. I cannot remember his talking about his own music without invariably associating it with some Norwegian purpose, such as 'to carry the musical message of the Norwegian peasant into the *niveau* of art music'; or 'to write music that would tally the characteristics of Norwegian scenery'; or 'to translate the austerity of Jotunheim (the Norwegian Alps) into tones'; or 'to provide a Norwegian musical utterance for future generations'. In the realm of politics Grieg was a fervent nationalist, all his satisfaction seeming to hinge on the independence Norway had gained in 1905[10] (the year before I first met him).

Yet all Grieg's family traditions and early musical background and training were cosmopolitan. Both of the families from which he sprang—the Griegs and the Hagerups—belonged to that circle of originally foreign administrative and merchant families (the English *Bulls*, the

---

[9] (1871–1951), Dutch conductor of Amsterdam's Concertgebouw Orchestra for half a century from 1895.

[10] When the union with Sweden was dissolved.

Scottish *Christies*, the Dutch *Halses*, the German *Kroepelins*, the Danish
Hagerups) whose presence in the coastal towns, especially in Bergen,
Grieg's birthplace, gives the population a character so different from that
of the dwellers in the fjords, the uplands, and the mountains. His Scottish
ancestor, who came to Norway in the second half of the eighteenth
century, was Alexander Grieg. Grieg's father, as well as his grandfather
and great-grandfather, were British Consuls in Bergen. His father repeatedly paid visits to England, Grieg himself told me. 'What for?' I asked.
'Partly to attend concerts and to buy music', he said.

It was then that I asked Grieg if he were aware of what seemed to be
Scottish influence in his music. I cited the downward phrase (to the
words, 'Bonnie Saint Johnston stands on Tay') in the Scottish folksong,
'The Twa Sisters o' Binnorie':

Close of Scottish folksong
'The twa Sisters o'Binnorie'

which Grieg repeatedly appeared to echo in some of his works. In the Trio
of the slow movement of the Sonata in C minor for Violin and Piano:[11]

and the close of the first section of the *tranquillo* movement in the fourth
of the Symphonic Dances for orchestra,

this similarity is evident. Also may be noted the close kinship between the
pianissimo passage, just before the *crescendo* leading into the recapitula-
tion of the main theme of the *Norwegian Bridal Procession*,[12]

[11] Op. 45 (1886–7).
[12] Op. 19 No. 2 (1872). See, further, Grainger's essay 'Grieg's *Norwegian Bridal Procession*: A
Master Lesson', *Etude*, 38/11 (Nov. 1920), 741–5.

and the Scottish Reel, 'Tullochgorum',

not merely in the almost identical rhythm, but also in the suggestion of a drastic harmonic 'shift' common to both. But Grieg knew (or remembered) nothing of such Scottish music. This does not prove, however, that his father did not bring back such Scottish types of music from his sojourns in Britain and that Grieg was not influenced by them in his impressionable years. Whence, otherwise, did he draw such influences?[13] I know nothing in Norwegian folk music that could have provided them. As a matter of fact, Grieg's indebtedness to Norwegian folk music has been greatly exaggerated. The probability is that he, with his vast resources of harmonic expressiveness and formal skill—drawn from his early familiarity with the 'classic' masters of art music—enriched Norwegian folk music in his arrangements of it far more than it enriched him.

An interesting commentary on the origins of 'local color' in the folk arts and cultures was provided by a Norwegian professor, when he announced that he had been able to trace every known Norwegian peasant costume, from every dale in Norway, back to some French court dress of the seventeenth and eighteenth centuries. The peasants had seen their local gentry (administrators, doctors, large farm-owners) wear these imported French court dresses, and had copied them as best they could; from which were gradually evolved what are now called 'peasant costumes'. We are prone to regard bagpipes and kilts as things racially characteristic of Highland Scotland. Yet both, we have been given to understand, are comparatively recent importations from France.

---

[13] In his article of 1907 Grainger raised this issue of possible Scottish influence, but reported that Grieg 'much liked the idea of its being, maybe, a throwing-back in him to his originally Scottish blood, of which he was proud and fond of dwelling upon'.

Those contending streams of esthetic stimulation, localism, and cosmopolitanism are of course implied in the origins and history of all the arts, which inherit their broad expressiveness from cumulative cosmopolitan skill and traditions, and their individuality and originality from local influences. But it is easy to forget this and to over-emphasize, in one's mind, one of these two factors. Take folksong, for instance. Many regard folksong as something that has grown, as it were, by 'active natural causes', out of the native soil alone, and they see it reaching back, in its present habitat, into prehistoric ages. Then there is the other viewpoint (and one sponsored by some of folksong's leading students) that all European folksong originated in Provence, at the time of the troubadours, as an offshoot of Moorish dance music in Spain, and thence spread North and East. Possibly only a combination of these two views will ever explain the compositeness of folksong.

*   *   *

Editor's Note: This is the second section of a most interesting article by Mr. Grainger, who was, in a sense, an artistic foster son of the great Norwegian composer.

Grieg was much chagrined by his inability to identify himself with the Norwegian peasants and to feel at home with them in their daily life. Grieg was by birth and association a middle-class man. (By 'middle-class' I mean that large human element in all modern nations in which personal, individualistic, material ambitions outweigh a sense for larger group responsibilities—such responsibilities as are apt to sway the artist, the aristocrat, the soldier, the sailor, and even the poorest and most ignorant peasant or yeoman). The genius in Grieg (that heightened moral sense that drives a single man to feel responsible for the feeling and thinking of his whole nation or race) urged him to rise out of his middle-class beginnings into becoming an all-round Norwegian. So, as part of this all-roundness, he tried to mix with the peasants—to take part in their festivities. On such occasions the communal beer-bowl is passed around the table and every feaster is expected to drink from it. But here Grieg's middle-class squeamishness (his sense of 'personal cleanliness') found him out. 'When I saw the great bowl approach me, its rim dark with tobacco juice, my heart sank within me', he told me. This urge 'to feel at one with the peasants' is a more vital necessity for a Norwegian artist than a non-Norwegian might be able to guess. In Norway the peasants always have been the backbone of the country—artistically and otherwise. The population of Norway is very sharply divided between peasant and townsman. The two elements look amazingly different. The peasants, living on frugal fare, have broad, calm faces and magnificent frames; the town-dwellers—overfed, as usual—look comparatively peaked and undernourished.

True Norwegians

The peasants regard themselves as the true Norwegians and look upon the townsfolk of the coasts as interlopers, as survivals of the foreign settlements foisted upon Norway during the Hansa League period and the Danish occupation. The language dispute—whether Dano-Norwegian ('Realm-Speech') or the Rural Speech (or 'New Norse') should be chosen as the official tongue of the country—has rocked Norway for over a hundred years. The difference between the two languages is about as great as that between standard English (corresponding to Dano-Norwegian) and the 'Broad Scots' (corresponding to Rural Speech) in which Bobby Burns wrote his poems. Grieg—because of his coastal town and middle-class origins and partly, perhaps, due to Bjørnstjerne Bjørnson's[14] influence—was always on the Dano-Norwegian side in the language dispute. Yet many of his very finest songs were composed to poems in the Rural Speech—notably the eight songs of the *Haugtussa* ('Maid of the Mountains') cycle[15] (poems by the Jaederen peasant-poet, Arne Garborg[16]); and the twelve unsurpassable songs to words by the rural Telemarken poet, A. O. Vinje.[17] These latter include such gems as 'Spring' ('Last Spring'), 'Wounds' ('Heart-wounds'), 'The Old Mother', and 'On the Way Home'.[18] So here again, Grieg's dual personality—divided between 'local color' and cosmopolitanism—was in evidence, and caused him worry and frustration, though it possibly contributed also to the richness and many-sidedness of his artistic output.

> Much I owe to the Lands that grew—
> More to the Lives that fed—

---

[14] See Essay **26**. Bjørnson provided many of the texts of Grieg's stage and vocal works.
[15] Op. 67 (1895).
[16] (1851–1924), and early pioneer of the literary use of the rural 'Landsmaal'. See Essay **26**.
[17] (1818–1870). Like Grainger, Vinje was an ardent walker, and covered much of the country collecting material for the first grammar of *Nynorsk* (New Norse).
[18] Part of Grieg's Op. 33 (1873–80).

But most to Allah, who gave me two
Separate sides to my head.
—Kipling[19]

Grieg's musical affinities and preferences show how innately cosmopolitan was the very fibre of his tonal life. He worshipped Mozart with
especial zeal, which is not so surprising when we remember the clear and
'pure' sonorities (the absence of 'muddy' timbres) common to them both.
Bach, Chopin, and Schumann were other prime favorites. Among his
time-mates he felt the closest affinity with César Franck and cited the
pianissimo variation in Franck's *Variations Symphoniques*, in which the
violoncellos play the melody, starting with the notes C-sharp, B-sharp,
A and G-sharp, against downward-flowing arpeggios in the piano, as a
passage which he (Grieg) himself might have written, both in the matter
of its harmonic and melodic characteristics and the mood it utters.

Much might be said about the 'North Sea mood' that informs composers hailing from the North-Sea girding lands—composers such as
Brahms, César Franck, Grieg, Frederick Delius, and Herman Sandby.
There seems to be some climatic influence at work here—some
Rembrandtian fog of the sea, the soil, and the soul—that continually and
uniquely, in such composers, produces a soaring ecstasy of yearning wistfulness that is quite distinct from, let us say, the occasional melancholy of

---

[19] 'The Two-Sided Man' (1901).

Russian music and the sombreness of Spanish music. We discern this North-Sea mood strongly at the root of such creations as Brahms's Rhapsody for alto, male chorus, and orchestra,[20] the César Franck Symphony, Grieg's *Den Bergtekne* ('Taken in the Hills'), Delius's *The Song of the High Hills*, Vaughan Williams's first 'Norfolk' Rhapsody,[21] and Herman Sandby's *Sea Mood*.

When I asked Grieg which orchestral suite he admired most he answered: 'Beyond all question, Saint-Saëns's "Algerian Suite".' (Is it not a strange proof of the isolationism of our musical life that the present situation in North Africa[22] does not inspire our orchestral conductors to present such timely masterpieces as Saint-Saëns's *Algerian Suite* and Gustav Holst's *Beni Mora Suite*?[23])

Of all the great composers that he had met 'in the flesh' he found Tchaikovsky the most sympathetic and stimulating. Grieg said that their meeting in Leipzig was an unbroken stream of enthusiasm and mutual response.

But we do not need the above testimony of Grieg's expressed special preferences among composers (one Austrian, two German, one Polish, one Belgian, one French, one Russian) to divine the cosmopolitan scope of his compositional life. This is evident enough in his own music, in which the winsome melodiousness of genuine folksong (as distinct from the elements of truly popular melody as we find them in Haydn, Beethoven, Schubert, and so on) is paired with the seven-hundred-year-old polyphonic-harmony traditions of the Northern French, British, Burgundian, and Netherlands schools of compositions, as they came filtered to him through Bach, Wagner, and other more recent composers, and is mixed with the elaborate formal thinking of the sonata-symphony inheritances.

Vincent d'Indy, perhaps uneasily stirred by some awareness of the strange Franck–Grieg affinity that Grieg himself so keenly sensed, in his otherwise excellent and beautifully devoted book on César Franck,[24] repeatedly asserts that 'Grieg is no symphonist'. If that be true—if Grieg be not thoroughly at home in the thematic argumentations, modulatory excursions, and balancing of form lengths evolved by the 'classicists'— why was it that so many of his earliest and most enduring successes were achieved in sonata-form works—in the three violin and piano sonatas, the

---

[20] Op. 53 (1869).　　[21] 1905–6.

[22] The North African desert campaign, 1940–3.

[23] An 'oriental suite', Op. 29 No. 1 (1909–10).

[24] Paris, 1906; Eng. trans., with an introduction by Rosa Newmarch, London, 1910.

piano concerto, and the piano sonata? There is little doubt in my mind (especially when I recall the subtle development section of the last movement) that the piano sonata, had it been scored for orchestra, would have proved a favorite among later nineteenth-century symphonies. It was a work in sonata form (the Sonata in F major for Violin and Piano, Op. 8) that stirred Liszt to write Grieg the letter which, read in the Norwegian Parliament, secured for Grieg, at about the age of twenty-six, a life-long stipend from the Norwegian Government.

Significant Contributions

Despite all this, it is not in the bold externalism of musical form (which we may compare to the get-rich-quick, catch-as-catch-can adventurous opportunism of the earlier nineteenth century—the era of millionaire manufacturers, colonial imperialism, and railroad expansion), nor in his exploitation of folk melody that Grieg achieved his most significant contributions to the art of music, but rather in his transcending developments of the resources of modern harmony—resources that he received, undoubtedly, from Bach, Schubert, Chopin, and Wagner, but to which he added mighty additions of his own. Apropos of the exploitation of folksong, one is reminded of the aptness of the saying attributed to Sir Thomas Beecham: 'These little tunes have done more to ruin music in my lifetime, than any other single factor.'

If, in seeking musical counterparts of the elements we know in human life, the ecclesiastical polyphony of the thirteenth to seventeenth centuries be linked with the medieval ideal of Christian brotherhood, and the theme-dominated form-music of the Protestant era be linked with the personality-led mercantilism founded on the Industrial Revolution, then modern harmony may be considered analogous to that surge of modern compassion (vastly expanded from the Christian brotherhood ideal of the Middle Ages) that has given us the League of Nations, the rights of small nations, votes for women, child labor laws, the Societies for the Prevention of Cruelty to Children and Animals, conscientious objection to war, socialism, coöperative organizations, and meat-abhorring vegetarianism.

Some may feel that this compassion (they may prefer to call it 'squeamishness') has gone too far in some respects. Certainly 'the cult of the chord' (which I would describe as the musical equivalent of Tolstoyism and Woodrow Wilsonism) went so far, in the hands of Scriabin, Cyril

Scott, Debussy, and others, as to justify the swing-away-from-the-chord, inaugurated or developed by Schoenberg, Stravinsky, Arthur Fickénscher, and Roy Harris. But the cult of the chord, vitally furthered by Grieg, was a marvellous device for engendering musical sensitivity and compassion.

In this humanizing development, Grieg's most personal contribution was the creation of what we call 'unnatural harmony'. Natural harmony is that in which the harmonic suggestions of the melody (its key and node anchorages, its modulative sallies) are obediently carried out in the harmony. This system perhaps is seen at its best in such composers as Beethoven, Schubert, Brahms. Unnatural harmony is that in which the harmonic behavior runs partly or wholly counter to the harmonic suggestion of the melody. A 'natural' harmonization of the melody notes E, G, C would be the triads of III, V, VI, in C major.

An 'unnatural' harmonization of the same melody notes would be the triads of C major, E flat major, and A flat major.

The human purpose behind unnatural harmonization (if one may be so bold as to guess at such elusive stirs of the life-force!) seems to be similar to that behind paradox in literature: to shed new light upon old subjects, to open new doors for an escape from suffocating platitudes. When Bernard Shaw pens the following typically Shavian paradox, 'the reasonable man tries to adapt himself to the world. The unreasonable man tries to adapt the world to himself. Therefore all progress depends on the unreasonable man,'[25] he throws desirable light upon the limitations of

---

[25] Slightly misquoted, from Shaw's 'Maxims for Revolutionists', a postscript to *Man and Superman* (1903).

reasonableness. In the tone world unnatural harmonization accomplishes a somewhat similar end—it enables us to sense quite new suggestions in the most well-worn, million-times-used, diatonic and pentatonic intervals. This light-shedding effect may be gauged if we take the folk-melody employed in Grieg's Ballade for Piano, Op. 24,[26] first giving it natural harmonies, one to each quarter note (such as I, IV, V, I, and so on).

and then comparing these with the moaning 'nature voices' (imitation of the wailing sounds heard in nature) that Grieg, through the device of unnatural harmonization, was able to clothe the melody with in its first presentation.

An Interesting Remark

In connection with this Ballade, Op. 24, I pass on an interesting remark that Grieg let fall in conversation with me. He had told me that the folk-song used in the Ballade was, originally, a rowdy drinking song, with words to match. I asked him why he had not stated these facts in a footnote to his composition. 'Because the original mood of the song and its text was so totally at variance with the mood I had evolved in the Ballade', Grieg replied. 'But that clash is of great musico-historical interest', I continued. Whereupon Grieg came to the pithy part of our conversation: 'That is the difference between you and me, in our approach to folksong. You approach it as a scientist, while I still approach it wholly as a romanticist.'

The two opening chords of Grieg's previously mentioned *Den Bergtekne* are another epoch-making example of unnatural harmonization.

* * *

The mention of 'nature voices' brings me to another of Grieg's major contributions to musical progress—his approximations to 'Free Music', that

---

[26] In the Form of Variations on a Norwegian Melody (1875–6).

is, music in which all intervals are freed from the limitations of scale, in which all part-writing is freed from the conventions we call 'harmony'; and in which all rhythms are freed from the inevitableness of regular pulse-beats, particularly in the direction of sliding intervals (an inspired modern use of which we may study in the exquisite slow movement of Cyril Scott's Quintet for Strings and Piano); and intervals closer than the half tone, so transcendingly employed in the American Arthur Fickénscher's *From the Seventh Realm*, for string and piano quintet.[27] Many passages in Grieg are nudging their way towards sliding and closer intervals. Perhaps no better example could be found in his music than the chords in measures 12 to 20 of his arrestingly original song, 'The Maid of the Mountains' ('Veslemöy'), Op. 67, No. 2. The Free Music-presaging potentialities of this chromatic part-writing are not fully apparent on the piano, of course. But if we play the accompaniment on five theremins[28] (or other instruments capable of sliding tones) and play it slidingly, we find ourselves fairly within the domain of the music of the future.

The connection between such approximations to Free Music and the goals of human progress is obvious enough: such musical procedures help to attune men's thoughts and feelings to a keener understanding of the processes of nature. Freudianism, Einstein's relativity, children's interest in everything connected with flying, and the modern passion for speed are all manifestations—each in its respective field—of the same urge: the urge to know nature better, to live on closer terms with her, and if need be, to master her. Musical history clearly shows us the path from superstition and the propitiation of hostile forces (primitive music and much of folk music) through the conception, in religion, of a beneficent Deity (worship-music, from Perotinus to Palestrina) on to the fearless all-embracingness of science (Free Music). The path of this progress is always in the same direction: from fear to confidence, from distress to bliss.

In Tune with Nature

To enjoy nature (whether by that we mean the maintenance of our physical good health, or our ability to fly to the moon and control the lightning—I am looking well ahead!) we must understand nature—put ourselves in tune with her. But to do this latter we must first divest ourselves of such arbitrary conceptions of 'right' and 'wrong' as blind us to

---

[27] The correct title of the so-called *Seventh Quintet*.
[28] See Essay **36**.

the factual stirs of nature. Instead of the old-fashioned world of endless strife between good and evil, science envisages a state of heavenly bliss in which all things will be deemed good because rendered understandable through scientific thinking. In the realm of music the current limitations of scale, harmony, and rhythm bar the way to that understanding and exploitations of the full tonal world that would constitute tonal 'heavenly bliss'. A deeply inspired genius like Grieg yearned and strove intuitively towards the attainment of such musical progress and musical bliss as that outlined above. And other inspired composers in other lands (Scriabin and Stravinsky in Russia, Ravel and Debussy in France, Delius and Cyril Scott in England, Puccini in Italy, Albéniz in Spain, Béla Bartók in Hungary, MacDowell, John Alden Carpenter, and Gershwin in America) were not slow to take the hints that Grieg had thrown out. That, perhaps, is the main reason why some degree of Griegness seems founded in well-nigh all those known progressive composers.

Relative to the above, an amusing conversation between some French composers, including Maurice Ravel and Frederick Delius, was repeated to me by the last named. Talk turned on the subject dear to modernist French musicians: What are the antecedents of modern French music? The composers present gave the usual shopworn reply of the period (the early years of our century): 'Debussy and Ravel are a rebirth of the spirit and traditions of Couperin and Rameau.' Then Delius strode into the conversation with 'Fiddlesticks! Modern French music is simply Grieg, plus the *Prelude* to the third act of *Tristan*,' to which Maurice Ravel (always a discerning genius) replied: 'C'est vrai. Nous sommes toujours très injuste envers Grieg.' (It is true. We are always very unjust concerning Grieg.) At least, that is how Delius, in his Anglo-French, retold the sentence.

If the progress-bearing influence of Grieg upon Russian music be doubted, let the doubter compare the first twenty-three bars (surely the loveliest of the whole work) of Stravinsky's *Le Sacre du Printemps* with Grieg's *Evening in the High Hills*, Op. 68, No. 4 (the melody of which is Grieg's own, not a folk tune), 'Lualaat' ('The Hillman's Song'), Op. 65, No. 2,[29] the introduction to 'The Journey of the Bride of Darkness to Vossevangen', Op. 72, No. 14, and the opening of the G major Violin and Piano Sonata, Op. 13.

Grieg's influence upon Frederick Delius is freely admitted—perhaps the largest-souled genius of the era in which he lived; certainly the only heir within his period to the grand-scale form-flow of Bach and Wagner.

---

[29] Grainger probably meant Op. 73 No. 7.

Grieg and Gershwin

Grieg's influence upon one of the most sensitive and many-sided of recent composer-geniuses, the late George Gershwin, seems not to be so clearly comprehended. The opening (which is also the closing) theme of the *Rhapsody in Blue* is clearly derived from the theme with which the Grieg Piano Concerto closes. Both themes cruise through the intervals 5, 8, flat 7, 6, 5. Both have two groups of triplets following (in Gershwin) upon one long note, or (in Grieg) upon two long notes. In both, the triplets float over a clash of a seventh below (in Grieg, G, F-sharp; in Gershwin, A-natural, A-flat). A closer similarity of thematic procedure—and in two works for the same medium—can hardly be imagined. The first section of the refrain from Gershwin's immortal song, 'The Man I Love',[30] is similarly indebted to measures 26 and 29 of the slow movement of Grieg's Sonata in C minor for Violin and Piano. In both these inspired phrases (Grieg's and Gershwin's) the basic procedure is the same: the melody rises from the interval of the fifth to that of the seventh, and while it pauses on the seventh, the alto voice of the four-part harmony drops from the major third of the tonic triad to the minor third, while the two lower voices sustain the drone 1, 5. Such similarity almost amounts to identicalness!

I am not calling attention to these similarities in order to disparage Gershwin, whose music I worship. Quite the contrary. I consider it a sign of a genius in a composer to base his procedures upon an older, *original* composer, rather than upon platitudes.

These, and many other instances of Gershwin's indebtedness to Grieg that I could mention, go to show how well Gershwin knew his Grieg. That does not mean that he actually thumbed the pages of all the works of Grieg that he, unconsciously, took up into his system. If Gershwin had a bright and retentive ear it would have been enough for him to have heard a lot of Grieg over the air. This is not unlikely, for a musician connected with broadcast-program matters in New York told me, some eighteen or twenty years ago, that the most frequently performed composers over the air in America were Grieg and Tchaikovsky—those two tender hearts that felt so sympathetic to each other when they met!

* * *

Perhaps the reader will opine that this condition of being so frequently performed, that came to Grieg, may have led him to feel that he had succeeded in his life's main work—to give Norway a world-voice in music.

[30] 1924.

But quite the contrary! Grieg was one of the most disappointed and frustrated of men. In a tragic tone of voice he said to me: 'Do not make the mistake I made. Do not neglect the great for the small!' This shortcoming on his part, he freely admitted, arose mainly out of his poor health, resulting from severe damage to one lung during pneumonia suffered when he was a boy of about sixteen, studying in Leipzig. 'If I work longer than four hours at a stretch I suffer for it for days', he said, giving that as the main reason why he abandoned the large-form works of his early manhood for compositions of smaller dimensions in later life. 'One cannot write symphonies and operas if one is limited to four hours of work daily', he remarked sadly.

But the smaller dimensions of his later works were not the only cause of his sharp consciousness of defeat. He felt bitterly insulted at the consistent non-performance of those of his creations that he set greatest store by and considered to be the truest expression of Norwegianness. These were:

1. *Den Bergtekne* (*Taken in the Hills*, or *Lost in the Hills*), for baritone, two horns, and strings; the setting of an archaic folk-poem describing a man led astray in the hills by 'giants' daughters' (symbolizing the hostile elements of nature), and unable to find his way back to the haunts of men.

> Fishes in the fair blue waters
>   And herrings seaward win;
> Many a one greets kith and kin,
>   Yet knows not they are kin.

> Fishes in the fair blue waters
>   And squirrels up on high—
> Everyone has a mate so dear;
>   Never a one have I!

This doom-fraught ballad may, if we wish, be viewed as a lament for the tragic fate of Nordic men who—all over the world—are drowned in the seas as sailors, killed in the wars as soldiers, turned mad by loneliness as 'boundary riders' on Australian sheep stations (ranches), or otherwise destroyed or wasted through their unaccountable preference for dangerous and loveless pursuits. Whether this appetite for self-torture in the Nordic be meaningless, or replete with meaning, it certainly is within the province of art to record a mood inspired by contemplation of the forlorn fate of this most persecuted of all races—surely the most 'despised and rejected of men'. This is what Grieg has done in this immense trifle.

2. Album for Male Voices, Op. 30[31] (settings of Norwegian folksongs)

---

[31] 1877–8.

for baritone solo and men's chorus. Here the extreme tenderness of Grieg's muse finds in the honey-sweet sonority of voices a smoother and more rounded expression than could have been attained with instruments. In this collection the song, 'It is the Greatest Folly',[32] is one of the rarest of Grieg's harmonic gems.

3. Symphonic Dances for orchestra (they are also arranged beautifully for piano duet by the composer). These four numbers Grieg felt (and many of his admirers feel) constitute his highest achievement in the orchestral field. The orchestral texture is luscious and brilliant. The contrapuntal and harmonic subtleties in the gentler sections of the third Dance, and in the Trio of the fourth, are shining examples of inspired erudition. The winsomeness of the second Dance is like sunlight upon a fjord.

Grieg resented bitterly that the three masterworks enumerated above were next-to-never performed. (For my own part, I must state that I have moved in the musical centers of the world for fifty years without ever hearing a conductor give any of these works in its entirety. I have heard the second Symphonic Dance played separately, and 'The Great White Host'[33] divorced from its fellows in Opus 30.)

A Strange Neglect

'I wrote', said Grieg, 'many piano pieces and songs for democratic reasons; so that my music might be able to be played and sung in every fisherman's and peasant's hut in Norway where there was a piano. But in so doing I did not intend that my richer and more complicated works should be ignored. Every male choir in Norway has sung my comparatively simple *Land-Sighting*[34] until I am sick of hearing it. But they do not seem to be aware of the existence of my much finer Album for Male Voices. Every orchestral conductor feels called upon to repeat and repeat my *Peer Gynt* suites with tiresome monotony, yet never deigning to look into my best orchestral opus, the Four Symphonic Dances.'

Grieg was not priggish about his own music, or about any music. He did not despise the simple to exalt the complex. He wrote comparatively suburban and drawing-room-like pieces such as 'Erotikon', 'Butterfly', 'She Dances', with the same care and sincerity he lavished upon *Lost in the Hills*, or the larger works in sonata form. What he could not foresee was

[32] No. 5.   [33] No. 10.
[34] Op. 31 (1872, rev. 1881), to a text by Bjørnson.

that, even in Norway (that most enlightened and artistic of lands), the highest flights of his emotionality would be passed over consistently in favor of his trifles and his salon pieces. He felt that his talents (the gifts he longed to place on the lap of his beloved native land) were being rejected. And he was right. In the years during which I toured Norway as a concert pianist (1910–1914) there was always the tendency to belittle the romantic and many-sided Grieg and to exalt the one-sided and pedantic Sinding.[35] Why? Because he fitted more obediently into the German mold, I suppose.

Anent the reception of his own music in Germany, Grieg said to me: 'They tried to fit my music into first one of their drawers (*Schubladen*), then into another; but always in vain. So they said: "He does not fit into any of our drawers. Therefore he is no good." '

In the realm of music, Norwegian servility to German opinion (in this respect identical with British, Danish, American, Australian, and other Nordic servility) knew no bounds. One evening, when I had just finished a piano recital in a town on the Norwegian south-west coast, a peasant came up to me and asked if he could put a question. This turned out to be: 'Does Grieg's reputation as a composer amount to anything out in the big world?' I answered: 'His case is similar to that of all other Nordic geniuses; the nitwits belittle him, while his fellow geniuses copy him. But why do you ask, especially?' 'Well, the German gunboat Ersatz-Sachsen was here last summer and the assistant band leader of the band aboard her told me that Grieg didn't cut much ice', was the reply. Against this Nordic passion for self-belittlement, this passion for fawning upon the most insignificant non-Nordic, Grieg was helpless, as all we other Nordic composers in our various countries are helpless.

As a result of English-speaking withdrawal from classical music for about two hundred years, roughly from 1680, when Purcell composed his seraphic string fantasies, the swansong of the older English music, to 1879, when Cyril Scott, 'the father of modern music', was born, the bulk of English-speaking music-lovers (equally in Britain, Ireland, the United States, Canada, Australia, New Zealand, and elsewhere throughout the world) are still in the stage when they fear they may not be able to recognize Beethoven (and his ilk) when they hear him. They have not in the least got around to the stage in which they could be concerned with doing esthetic justice to Grieg, Cyril Scott, Delius, Fickénscher, Roy Harris, or any other composer-genius of their own racial (Nordic) group. As a result

[35] Christian Sinding (1856–1941).

of our so recent reëntry into the domains of the highest art music, our people, broadly speaking, do not yet regard 'high brow' music as a vehicle for emotional revelation, but more as a social accomplishment—as a part of 'white-collar' refinement. But for us to pursue indefinitely this superficial appraisement of music is hardly fair to that small but ever-increasing body of Anglo-Saxons who *do* draw soul nourishment from music, nor reasonable, in view of the immense amount of time (in high schools) and money (spent on symphony orchestras, radio performances, and the like) now lavished upon the art of music in our midst.

At this moment America and her Allies are engaged in a war-to-the-death with backwardness—for it is just backwardness (lack of the gift to see the world as it is—in its gradual but loving progress from harsh to tender) that dooms important nations, in this day and age, to pin their hopes, as our opponents do, upon militaristic aggression. We have in America a variety of tone works by native-born American composers that express the American way of life as clearly and convincingly as Hans Sachs's oration towards the end of *The Mastersingers* expressed the German way of life in Wagner's era. Of these I will single out just four:

Rubin Goldmark—*A Gettysburg Requiem*, for orchestra.

Roy Harris—*American Creed*, for orchestra.[36]

John Alden Carpenter—*A Song of Faith*, for chorus and orchestra.[37]

Arthur Fickénscher—*From the Seventh Realm*, quintet for strings and piano.

These works are not merely impassioned utterances of American liberalism, altruism, humanitarianism. They are equally great and deathless masterpieces of cosmopolitan music, in the same sense that Grieg's expressions of the Norwegian spirit and Wagner's expression of the German spirit are great and deathless masterpieces of cosmopolitan music.

But when shall we be allowed to widely hear and enjoy these American masterpieces? If they were performed now, during the present emergency, they not only would help to speed the ball of progress (for musical progress depends to some extent upon hearing music while it is still 'fresh'), but would help to confirm music-loving Americans in their belief in the loftiest aspects of Americanism. If this were being done it could then not be denied that music was doing something really constructive in the war effort.

[36] 1940.   [37] 1932.

40 · English Pianism and Harold Bauer
(1945)

It is not likely that the English-speaking peoples, who have not lost a war since 1066 (except to themselves; for when Britain lost to America in the Revolutionary War they were losing to themselves), & who, of late centuries, have invented or developed all the notions & devices the whole modern world thinks about (flirting, wholesale divorce, machinery, trams, trains, steamships, submarines, flying, teetotalism, antivivisectionism, co-operative societies, League of Nations, vegetarianism, afternoon tea, sport, golf, football, tennis, baseball, cricket, votes for women, Home Rule for Ireland, India, Egypt, Iceland, Faeroe Islands—to which must be added social systems such as socialism & communism worked out by foreigners such as Karl Marx, Lenin & Trotsky while living in exile in Britain or USA), would be found failing to lead in such an important art as the art of music. In other articles I have striven to show how English-speaking composers (such as John Dunstable, the 13th-century Worcester & Winchester church music composers, William Lawes, John Field, myself, Cyril Scott, Arthur Fickénscher, George Gershwin & other American popular composers) have been responsible for all known epoch-making innovations in music since the advent of decipherable musical notation (1260?). In this sketch I will deal merely with the part played by English-speakers in modern pianism.

During my lifetime (i.e. since 1882) the greatest pianists of the world have come mainly from 3 areas:

(1) Men and women pianists from USA, Britain & Australia (Fanny Davies, Gertrude Peppercorn, Myra Hess, etc.; Eugen D'Albert, Frederic Lamond, Leonard Borwick, Cyril Scott, Harold Bauer, etc.; Ernest Hutcheson, Kitty Eisdell,[1] etc.; H. Cowell, Gershwin)

(2) Mainly men pianists from Poland & Russia (Paderewski, de Pachman, Josef Hofmann, Gabrilovich, Scriabin, Rachmaninoff, Godowsky, & many others)

(3) Women pianists from South America (Carreño, Novaës, etc.)

In view of the vast musical civilisation developed in the Western,

Source: Typescript dated 19 Feb. 1945. Grainger Museum, Melbourne.

[1] Kitty Parker (1889–1971), Australian-born pianist, who studied with Grainger in London for several years from 1909.

Southern & Central parts of the European continent in the 18th & 19th centuries, it is amazing how few first-class pianists these areas produced in the late 19th century. Only from Britain, America, Russia & Poland have *thoughtful, creative, progressive, innovation-bringing* pianists come, to any extent (Stravinsky with the original role played by the piano in his orchestrations, the creations of Rachmaninoff, Scriabin, Godowsky, Moszkovsky, Scharwenka; the new & exquisite sonorities invented by Cyril Scott & Henry Cowell, the learned conclusions reached and the life-giving influence exerted by Harold Bauer in his thoughtful editings, the natural pianism of Gershwin & other American composers); all the other areas have, in the main, been content to produce merely *conventional-minded* pianists who followed in the ruts already worn by their more creative & progressive fellows.

My own experience of the more talentedness of English pianists (as compared with German, French, Italian pianists) came—& unexpectedly, for I grew up hearing the English & Australians dubbed 'unmusical' & hearing all musical foreigners lauded to the skies—when I was about seven or eight years old, in Melbourne, a newly arrived English surgeon (Dr Hamilton Russell[2]) charmed us with his amateur playing—especially of Schumann. At that time Sir Charles Hallé (the Anglicised German stick-in-the-mud)[3] was announced to tour Australia. I said to Dr Russell: 'I don't believe he plays any better than you', & Dr Russell answered (with that usual English useless modesty, where music is concerned): 'You won't listen to me when you've heard Sir Charles'. But Hallé's somewhat soulless pedanticness didn't stir me, & after hearing him I said to Dr Russell: 'I guessed right; he is not nearly as good as you are.' (And in 1926, when I heard Dr Russell, then aged about 70, for the last time, his sweet, calm, balanced English artistry still confirmed my boyish judgement of about 1888.)

Here I must contradict myself to say that around 1892 (when I was ten), I met a German pianist—*Louis Pabst*[4] (the brother of the transcriber of Tchaikovsky's *Eugen Onegin* waltz)—who seemed to me a *truly great* musician. Working with him for about a year, & hearing his magnificent renderings of Bach during that period, gave me whatever is good in my Bach playing. A year or so later the Australian pianist Ernest

[2] (1860–1933), English-born Australian physician and medical academic, friend of the Graingers from the late 1880s onwards.

[3] (1819–95), German-born English pianist and conductor of the Hallé orchestra in Manchester. Hallé visited Australia in 1890.

[4] (1846–1903), resident during 1884–94 in Melbourne, where he taught Grainger piano and theory (1892–4).

Hutcheson[5] arrived in Melbourne after study in Germany, & my friend Dr Hamilton Russell took me to meet Hutcheson. My memory of the beauty, perfection, smoothness of his Bach playing has never dimmed.

In 1895 my mother took me to Germany, to continue my piano studies. Before that, for some years, my mother had earned the living for herself & me by giving piano lessons in Melbourne. In our six years in Germany (1895–1902)[6] she earned for herself & me by giving English lessons. We were poor & never knew where next week's money was to come from. But my mother (unlike me) was happy in Frankfurt-am-Main. 'I feel free for the first time in my life', she said. As a girl in Adelaide, she had taken naturally to Beethoven, Schubert, Mozart, etc., although surrounded by a family satisfied with 'Donne e mobile'. Although coming from South English parents on both sides, although married to my North English father (also English wholly), although speaking no foreign language & familiar with no foreign group in Australia, my mother was always a *natural cosmopolitan* whose leanings in music were naturally towards the deep, the slow, the sustained, the welt-schmerz-ful, the romantic. As a girl she had always specially loved Heine's & Goethe's poetry. (On second thoughts it is not impossible that she may have had some early contacts with Germans in South Australia that fostered these tastes in literature & music. Yet the Heine & Goethe books seem to have been mainly gifts from my father to my mother's family.)

So my mother was just naturally 'all set' to enjoy Germany, the German theatre & German music. Even so, her first impression of the Hochschen Conservatorium at Frankfurt was of amazement at Frankfurt's musical backwardness, slovenliness & ungiftedness. My piano teacher—the Hollander James Kwast[7]—advised my mother & me to go to the Übungsabende & Vortragsabende[8] of the Conservatorium, at which concerts the students performed. After the first one, Kwast asked my mother what she thought of it. 'The standard is much lower than in Melbourne', she answered. 'The only pianist I really liked was Balfour Gardiner' (this was our first contact with that heaven-gifted composer, destined to be the good angel of the British composer of his generation). This was an unpopular remark, as Gardiner was studying with Engesser,[9] a rival (& not loved) teacher.

[5] (1871–1951), Melbourne-born American pianist and teacher, who studied in Leipzig. He became Dean of the Juilliard School from 1927 and its President during 1937–45.

[6] 1895–1901.

[7] (1852–1927), a teacher at the Hoch Conservatory from 1883 to 1903.

[8] Trial and introductory recitals (Germ.).

[9] Ernst Engesser, with whom Quilter also studied piano.

As for myself, I went to Frankfurt ready to worship everything German. The two great impressions of my life, at that time, were the Icelandic sagas (in Dasent's English translations)[10] & the Battle of Hastings (1066) & its results as told in *The Anglo-Saxon Chronicle*[11] & Freeman's *History of the Norman Conquest*.[12] My one goal was to learn all the Teutonic languages (which I have since done, more or less), to be able to read the sagas in Icelandic, to eradicate from the English language words of French, Latin & Greek origin & generally to 'wipe out' the effects of the Norman conquest. I was all agog to see the 'Kriegspiele' that I had read took place between German boys in the streets of German towns (instead, I was amazed to find the German boys the greatest 'sillies' I had ever seen!). I went to Frankfurt expecting to find the German music students gifted & innately musical. But I soon found that the English students in Frankfurt were the only ones with any talent at all. When Cyril Scott returned to Frankfurt (about 1897) we were all enchanted with his euphonious & dexterous playing of Bach & Mozart, & with his own sparkling improvisations. (I suppose his own playing of such things as his Piano Sonata Op. 66, & of such trifles as his 'Rainbow Trout', 'English Waltz', 'Water-wagtail' constituted the highest pinnacle of sheer giftedness & natural adroitness in pianism I have ever witnessed, anywhere.) When Ethel Liggins (later Ethel Liginska) turned up from Hull, around 1898 or 1899,[13] she eclipsed us all with her girlishly winsome Mozart playing (she was about 12 or 13 years old). But I must mention one exception to the ungiftedness of the German pupils: Frieda Hodapp[14]—then about 18–19, & studying with Kwast. She was the most prodigious talent amongst women pianists I have ever encountered. She learned Chopin's B minor Sonata in a week. Yet her renderings were never shallow, but always deeply expressive & human. But with the exception of Hodapp, the English held the whole field at Frankfurt. Cyril Scott out-soared all others in composition; but all the other gifted composer-students were

[10] Elsewhere, Grainger clarifies that he means George Webb Dasent's *Popular Romances of the Middle Ages* (1880). In fact, this book was by G. W. Cox and E. H. Jones, and contained only a paraphrase of the saga. Dasent had, however, published *Popular Tales from the Norse* (1859) and a translation of *The Story of Burnt Njal* (1861). See Bruce Clunies Ross, 'Percy Grainger's "Nordic Revolution against Civilization"', *Musicology Australia*, 9 (1986), 53–65.

[11] Grainger owned two copies of the two-volume *Anglo-Saxon Chronicle*, ed. and trans. Benjamin Thorpe (London, 1861).

[12] E. A. Freeman's (1823–92) five-volume study of the Norman conquest appeared between 1867 and 1879. His prose style, which eschewed words of Latin derivation, probably influenced Grainger's 'Blue-eyed' English.

[13] (1890–1970), English pianist, conductor, teacher, and composer, student of Kwast at the Hoch Conservatory during 1900–4.

[14] (1880–1949), later one of Germany's leading concert pianists and Kwast's second wife.

English, too—Norman O'Neill,[15] Roger Quilter, Balfour Gardiner. One would hear the teachers talk of the English as 'unmusical'; but the next moment they would mention Leonard Borwick[16] as the only student of the Conservatorium who had played at the Museums Gesellschaft (orchestral concerts) while still a student. D'Albert[17] gave a piano recital soon after I got to Frankfurt & I was enthralled by his slap-dash English style ('I like your style, so wicked & free') in his own Piano Sonata, with his feet & hands flying all over the place, and wrong notes one or two to the dozen. (Of course, D'Albert was full of un-English blood & un-English backgrounds. Yet his overweeningness—his 'Unverschämtheit'—his Cockney patter, his flirtuousness, his overpowering energy were all as truly English as his early influences & his early pianistic training.) When I saw D'Albert swash around over the piano, with the wrong notes flying to right & left, & the whole thing a welter of recklessness, I said to myself: 'That's the way I must play'. I am afraid I learnt his propensity for wrong notes all too thoroughly! When I heard Frederic Lamond[18] (about 1898) I was less impressed with his playing, though very struck with his typically British sweetness, kindliness & tenderness of manner to me personally when I (a miserably raw pianist) was stupid enough to play to him.

My impressions of the English musicians I met in my Frankfurt days is the same impression I get of English & Americans in all other fields. The British end World War I with tanks. So the Germans start World War II with tanks. But the British start World War II with Radar! Studying in Frankfurt, I had no inkling of what modern music (Tchaikovsky, Grieg, Fauré) was like (with the exception of Richard Strauss) until the English boys arrived. They found me composing in a sort of Handel–Mozart style (I was only 14). So Cyril Scott asked me, 'Don't you like modern music?' 'What do you mean by modern music?', I said. And he sat down & played me the beginning of Grieg's Ballade[19] & Tchaikovsky's Air & Variations.[20] It was not that the English were ism-y & 'modernistic'. They were just *normal* about music (as they are about all else), enjoying a range from the

---

[15] (1875–1934), who studied in Frankfurt during 1893–7, and was the more distant, fifth member of the 'Frankfurt Group'.

[16] (1868–1925), English student at the Hoch Conservatory in Frankfurt, under Clara Schumann.

[17] (1864–1932), Scottish-born pianist.

[18] (1868–1948), Scottish pianist and composer, educated at the Raff Conservatory in Frankfurt. He lived in Germany from 1904 until the 1930s.

[19] Op. 24 (1875–6).

[20] Perhaps his Theme and Variations, Op. 18 No. 6 (1873).

earliest enjoyable music to the latest enjoyable music. Thus when we went to England & Scotland for a short trip in 1900 & when we (my mother & I) settled in London in 1902,[21] that *liberal* musical education which the Germans had never given me (because they—embroiled in anti-Wagner or anti-Brahms strife—never knew it existed), but which my English fellow-students in Frankfurt had started me on, was continued in all my contacts with orchestras, choirs, musicians, etc. I quickly got to know all that world of Tchaikovsky, Gabriel Fauré, Debussy, Ravel, Scriabin, Balakirev, Albéniz, Puccini, that had been a closed book to me in Frankfurt.

I have mentioned all these early impressions of English-speaking musicians as a prelude to my remarks about the pianism & artistry of Harold Bauer,[22] because all his characteristics struck me as a continuation of those impressions of normalness & liberalism that I had received from English musicians & English musicianship in general. It is true that Harold Bauer is not merely an 'English musician'. He is, as his name implies, a combination of foreign origins with English influences. But to me he was, from the start, part of the experimentalism, the daringness, the tolerance, the normalness, the liberalism of English music. I am (of course) speaking entirely as an Australian in all these matters. My early impressions (in Australia, up to 1895) were all of German music. Then came my six years in Germany. I never saw England until I was eighteen years old, by which time I was a mature composer. So I naturally view Englishness & English music from the outside—as something having different characteristics to my own. Just as I also view everything European as outside myself & foreign to me. I suppose I feel closest to Chinese & Japanese music—for it seems to me I heard Oriental music (in 'China Town' in Melbourne, or in a 'Japanese Village' that came to Melbourne in my very early childhood), or got a strong impression of it, before European music reached me or made an impression. Just as I feel closer to Polynesian feeling & culture (Maori, Tongan, Rarotongan, Samoan, Tahitian, Hawaiian, etc.) than I do to European or American culture & feeling. As a white man surrounded by native cultures, the Australian is more race-conscious than other English-speakers. Therefore it is natural in me, as an Australian, to view Harold Bauer (or any other artist) less as an individual & more as a product of racial, national, cultural & geographical influences. So my first,

---

[21] 1901.

[22] (1873–1951), Anglo-American pianist, with a particular interest in contemporary music. Like Grainger, he settled in the United States as the First World War broke out. His name is most associated with performances of the music of Schumann, Brahms, and Franck.

& my lasting, impressions of Harold Bauer, are of a cosmopolitan musician whose great gifts have been shaped by the many-sidedness, the universality, the normalness, the tolerance, the progressiveness of English
musical thought. He has always shone, for me, as a beacon of musical
common-sense—as when he said (or is reported to have said): 'Why
should scales be played perfectly evenly? Scales are sometimes likened to
a string of pearls. Are pearls perfectly even?' In my eyes, Harold Bauer
has always stood for what is *wise* in music—as contrasted with what is
merely brilliant or smart-alecky. All his transcriptions & editions of Bach
& other early music show this wisdom—this penetration into the living
conditions of music in that period, this discrimination between harpsichord & clavichord compositions, this realisation of the necessity for an
octaved rendition of such Bach textures as those in the Prelude of the first
Partita. It is good news that Harold Bauer is engaged in editing a complete
edition of Schumann's piano works; for it has always seemed to me that
Harold Bauer plays as Schumann would have played, had Schumann not
injured his hand & had Schumann unfolded an impeccable modern
pianistic technic. When sixteen of us pianists gave our services to a Benefit
Concert for Moszkovsky in Carnegie Hall in 1919 (?),[23] & when several of
the greatest each played one section of Schumann's *Carnaval*, it was
evident to my ears that Bauer's interpretation was more soul-satisfyingly
Schumannesque than that of any of the others; it was like Schumann
himself arising from Bauer's keyboard.

What is the main characteristic of Schumann's piano writing, as contrasted with earlier & later composers for the instrument? Does it not lie
partly in being rich-toned without becoming percussive? It is not
winsome, tinkly & dainty like Haydn's, Mozart's, Scarlatti's piano style.
It is not agitated & furious like Beethoven's. It is not as florid, or as harp-
like as Chopin's. It is not traffic-like as Bach's is (with several lines moving
about, each line representing, as it were, a separate identity, a separate
purpose), but seems to represent (Schumann's does) a single big body
bounding about, a single body having its own wanton & large & rich reactions. (We might say that if Bach tallies a kind of group or communal
feeling, that Schumann tallies the utterly individual, de-grouped, person.)
Schumann's piano writing is not percussive in its impression, as is so
much of Tchaikovsky's, Balakirev's, Stravinsky's. It does not reflect the
Hungarian cembalo,[24] or guitar sonorities, or the aeolian harp, as we find

---

[23] 21 Dec. 1921, a 'testimonial concert' for Moritz Moszkovsky (1854–1925), involving such
pianists as Backhaus, Casella, Friedman, Gabrilovich, Hutcheson, and Lhévinne, as well as Bauer
and Grainger.
[24] Grainger perhaps meant cimbalom.

them echoed in some of Liszt, Albéniz, Brahms, etc. Also, it seems to me, Schumann has freed himself from the plucked string suggestions that hung over from lute, harpsichord & clavichord music for a long time. And he is freer than Chopin from tone-color suggestions from other mediums, such as guitar accompaniment, cello-like passages, snatches of monks chanting, & the like.

Taking it all in all, it would appear to me that in Schumann, for the first time, the modern (German, or American) piano tone is used *in its own right*, with the minimum of imitations of other instrumental timbres, with the minimum of percussiveness, and with the maximum of expressiveness. In what I call 'the modern piano tone' (as found in Bluethners, Bechsteins, Steinways, Mason & Hamlins, etc.) the brittle harpsichord effects & the lighter mobility of the French piano tone (that Chopin, no doubt, composed for) have been sloughed in favor of a somewhat woodwind-like, somewhat horn-like melodiousness that is a truly expressive medium when composers like Schumann (& often Brahms) use it & when a pianist like Harold Bauer knows how to conjure it up. When I speak of 'the soul of Schumann arising from Bauer's keyboard' I mean just that: that he is able to draw from Schumann's music the expressive, non-percussive qualities that Schumann, above all composers, sensed & unearthed in the piano. Moreover, a certain moderate mean of tone is called for in Schumann: It is the soul of a big, sturdy man speaking in tones. Big, but not forced—for big things do not have to over-exert themselves. Tender, but not tinkly. And this sense of a normal, man-natural, tone-strength, so called for in Schumann, is an ever-present delight in Bauer's playing. You never feel that he is exerting himself. You never feel that he is curbing himself. Yet the size of the tone-waves he produces are forever waxing & waning. Nothing is ever static in his playing. All is in flux, continually. Harold Bauer's playing is unbelievably accurate; yet you never sense that he is playing accurately. He has the most impeccable technic; yet you never think of technic when you hear him. You merely know that, without worry or trouble, without effort or restraint, *he is calling grand music to life*—a sea of tonal life in which the listener floats with perfect security, perfect bliss, swung on the tides of *music's greatness, music's balm, music's heavenliness*.

Two memories of the perfection & soul-satisfying manliness of Harold Bauer's pianism remain etched in my memory, both—curiously enough— of compositions in the key of D minor: The first Piano Concerto of Brahms & Bach's D minor Piano Concerto. Nothing grander than the works themselves, or their interpretation at Bauer's hands, can ever be imagined.

I have spoken so far of Harold Bauer in his relation to the pianistic 'classics'; yet it was as a revealer of the new & the unknown that I first heard of him, & heard him. It must have been around 1902, in London, at which time I had heard no César Franck (destined to become my favorite of late 19th century composers—at least those 3 last works of his, the Chorales for organ). Harold Bauer's name was mentioned to me as the great authority on Franck & as a great enthusiast for Franck's music. I went & heard him play his part in Franck's Piano & String Quintet[25]—in the old St James' Hall, I think. And I was won over to Franck & Bauer for life.

A further sign of Bauer's closeness to all that was loveliest & loftiest in French music at the turn of the century is Ravel's dedication to him of 'Ondine', which certainly is the finest of all the exquisite 'water pieces' created by Debussy & Ravel (*Jeux d'eau*, 'Reflets dans l'eau', etc.).

Back & forth, across the whole range of keyboard music from oldest to newest, the interpretive creative genius of Harold Bauer shuttles with perfect at-home-ness in every style & period. What is it that unites all this music & its revealment at Bauer's hands? Is it not a certain sweetness, humanness & smoothness, despite all grandeur & loftiness? A complete absence of all that is brittle, harsh, overdone, unfriendly & strained. And this sweetness, kindliness, smoothness—this eschewal of all that is harsh & exaggerated—is equally patent in Harold Bauer the man. He is witty & trenchant, realistic & unconventional. But has anyone ever heard his wit put to a harsh use? A kind of Cockney kindliness (if I may be forgiven the expression) presides over it. Harold Bauer is part of the great harmony of life—as music itself is. He is no mere player of music; he is music itself. He is a *composer's musician*.

[25] 1878–9.

The following are my opinions and experiences on this subject.

To have a secure concert memory I find it needful (to myself, as well as to students) to approach memorizing from several different angles, so that if one form of memory fails, there are other forms to fall back on.

1. *Physical (Non-Mental) Memory.* This is the subconscious memory that the hands and fingers acquire from playing a passage through countless times. I do not consider this form of memory established unless I can read a book at the same time, or be read aloud to by somebody else. When playing subconsciously, I often go from one movement (of a concerto or sonata) to another, without being aware of it. When stopped in the middle of such playing, I often do not know what piece I have been playing. *Slow, loud practicing, and playing each hand separately* are excellent adjuncts to this branch of memorizing. This memory 'tides one over' when one's mind 'becomes a blank'.

2. *Form-Conscious Memory.* Awareness of the structure, form-shapes, and key changes of the music one is playing. (Sample: One says to oneself, 'The first time the second theme appears it is in C major; the second time in A major.')

3. *Note-Spelling Memory away from the Keyboard.* The ability to spell out each note. Thus, the beginning of Chopin's A-flat Polonaise would run something like this: 'Three-four time. Beat one, octave E-flats in both hands. Beat two, eighth note rest in both hands, then six sixteenth notes running up in both hands, starting C-sharp, E-natural, A-natural, ending G, B-flat, E-flat on first beat of second measure', and so on.

4. *Sectional Memorizing.* Special memorizing of the beginning of each section of the music, so that one is always able to begin *securely* with the beginning of the next section, if anything goes wrong with the memory in the section one is in. One must be able to say to oneself, 'The next section begins in A major, E in the right hand, C-sharp in the left hand', and so on.

5. *Awareness of Bar Groupings.* Knowing the bar group is a three group, a six group, or a four group. In practicing this kind of memorizing one says to oneself: 'Four group, bar 1, bar 2, bar 3, bar 4', etc. This comes

Source: James Francis Cooke, *How to Memorize Music: A Symposium upon Memorizing* (Philadelphia: Theodore Presser, 1948), 84–7.

in very helpful when playing a concerto with orchestra. If one's memory fails, inside a bar group one knows how many bars to wait (silently, or orienting oneself by soft playing) until the next bar group, or section, begins.

6. *Transposing Memory*. To be able to play all one's passages and pieces in any key. This gives one a special grasp of the tides of modulation within a piece.

When all these six forms of memorizing are used, a fairly reliable memory ought to result. Even so, disastrous slips of memory may occur to the best memorizer. In my opinion music has been greatly worsened by public performances without notes. When music is played without notes, all concerned suffer:

1. The performer suffers agonies of apprehension and therefore cannot devote his whole mind to the emotional and esthetic messages of the music.

2. The public suffers, because memorized performances are inferior to those where notes are used.

3. The music suffers the most—from wrong notes, left-out passages or phrases, and from inadequate interpretation because the performers are concentrating on the *feat* of memory instead of upon the *revelation of art*.

I have never known a great creative genius (Grieg, Richard Strauss, Cyril Scott, Ravel, Gabriel Fauré, Herman Sandby, Arthur Fickénscher, Griffes) who did not prefer to play his piano pieces, or piano parts (in chamber music) from notes.

Conductor-memorizing is different. The orchestra *plays the notes*, and all the conductor has to do is to listen to the orchestra, follow along with it, and look inspired. (I can get up and conduct a piece of mine I haven't thought about for twenty years, without the least preparation. But I couldn't play the same piece on the piano, without preparation, to save my life.) That is why so many famous pianists have become conductors— to escape from the endless misery and unreliability of keyboard memorizing into the comparative easiness and laziness of conductor-memorizing!

Music Heard in England

(1949)

These are impressions received in England between the middle of August and the end of November 1948 from listening to music in concerts, moving pictures, BBC broadcasts and radio relays from nearby countries.

The lively interest shown by a large body of music-lovers in England in new works by currently productive composers, such as Vaughan Williams, William Walton and Benjamin Britten, might lead to the conclusion that the British musical public is preponderantly novelty-minded. In support of this view one might point to numerous incidents in English musical history: to that wave of Italianism that led Purcell so suddenly to change his style around 1680; to the instant capitulation to Handel's *Messiah*, to the commissioning of Beethoven to write his Ninth Symphony; to the frenetic vogue of Mendelssohn; to the prodigious distribution of Debussy's music in Britain some forty years ago; to the excitement in London over Schönberg's *Fünf Orchesterstücke* in 1912, and the like. But a survey of the numbers of concert and broadcast performances noted during the last months of 1948 shows that against forty-two performances of Vaughan Williams and twenty of Benjamin Britten there were thirty-three of Charles Villiers Stanford (never at any time a modernist) and forty-three of Gabriel Fauré[1]—that suavely original classicist whose music is so strangely under-performed in certain countries, for instance, in the United States, in Australia and in Scandinavia.

Taking into consideration, also, the unswerving devotion in England to the established 'classics' and the ever increasing hearings there of pre-Bach music (by the Dolmetsches and other older music groups) perhaps it might be nearest to the truth to describe as *cumulative* the main tendency in English musical life. Eschewing what Tennyson called 'the falsehood of extremes', it would seem that the British ear loves to pile experience upon experience, without too selective a winnowing-out process. English music-lovers do not seem to feel called upon, as much as do their fellows in some other countries, to shed some old enthusiasm every time they

Source: *Australian Musical News and Digest*, 39/12 (June 1949), 32–4.

[1] In a letter to Herman Sandby of 24 Dec. 1948 Grainger elaborated the results of his survey of broadcast and concert performances, including Bax 11, Ireland 6, Quilter 21, Grainger 13, Delius 23, Elgar 34, Holst 19, Parry 14, Moeran 16, and Rubbra 7.

embrace a new one. There seems to be a constant enrichment through the novel and the experimental, without loss of fealty to what is old and already beloved.

We are continually told in England that the musical trend of today is anti-romantic. Nevertheless, frankly romantic composers such as John Ireland (*The Forgotten Rite, These Things shall Be*, Piano Concerto in E flat, Sonata for 'Cello and Piano), Arnold Bax (Seventh Symphony, *The Island of Fand,*[2] Overture to a Picaresque Comedy, film music to *Oliver Twist*), E. J. Moeran (Serenade in G for Orchestra, String Quartet) and Frederic Austin (*The Beggar's Opera, Sea Venturers* Overture) are steadily performed and enthusiastically received.

John Ireland's *These Things shall Be*, for chorus and orchestra,[3] is a masterwork of unsurpassed grandeur. Cast in a choral style not wholly unakin to Handel's and Elgar's in trenchant masculinity, the dark and atavistic mood expressed in the chord-life is utterly the composer's own, revealing a prophetic insight into heroic and tragic events to come (it was written before the last war).

Arnold Bax's film music to *Oliver Twist*[4] stands apart from all other film music I have ever heard—unique in its introspective quality (for it sounds more like a tonal adumbration of philosophical musings upon the more subtle inner implications of the story than a musical accompaniment to the more obvious and physical happenings portrayed upon the screen); unique in the exquisite sonorities arrived at by hitherto untried combinations of small woodwind ensembles with piano—the piano part fastidiously rendered by Harriet Cohen.[5]

There is a morning freshness and outdoor intoxication about E. J. Moeran's Serenade in G that is irresistible. The musical thoughts are typical of this composer's rare originality and the scoring is daring but invariably effective. Here is a re-birth of the 'Merrie England' mood, enriched by a deeper emotional awareness.

Amongst successful 'romantic' works must be included a new Overture, *Sea Venturers*,[6] by Frederic Austin, whose original revival of *The Beggar's Opera* is still unsurpassed by all later versions in effectiveness and popular appeal. Austin's output as a composer is not large, but contains a setting of *The Twelve Days of Christmas* that is a model of nar-

---

[2] *The Garden of Fand*, tone poem (1913–16).
[3] To a text by Symonds (1936–7).
[4] Both the film and Bax's orchestral suite date from 1948. Grainger saw the film twice.
[5] (1895–1967), a close friend of Bax.
[6] First performed at the Bournemouth Festival in 1936.

rative song and a singularly austere symphony. His new work, most brilliantly presented by Sir Thomas Beecham in several music centres, is as sharp a contrast to the symphony as can be imagined, being a glamorous and effervescent treatment of a theme (the maritime exploits of the Frobisher–Drake period) that might have been expected to have tempted British composers long ere this. But it has remained for Frederic Austin, in his mid-seventies, to be the first to sound this gaily boastful and exuberant note, and to do so with a boyish dash and lyric wistfulness enhanced by a long background of orchestral craftsmanship. The sounds produced from the orchestra are at times violent and explosive, at other times yearning and polyphonically melodious. Here a master of form and scoring has indulged in musical speech that is intimate, untrammelled, debonair and infectious; for the response to this music is immediate.

In a category so personal and individual as to defy all ordinary classification stands Cyril Scott's Oboe Concerto,[7] transcendentally played by Leon Goossens[8] at its first performance (London Promenade Concert, September 13). It is so rich in Celtic-druidical suggestions as to positively reek of woad. Spiritually it may be said to be akin to Aubrey Beardsley's *Morte d'Arthur* illustrations[9] and to the poems of Stefan George.[10] Overflowing with inspired melodic rapture from its first to its last bar, its spontaneity of form and harmonic originality are as surprising as they are captivating. The utter newness of Scott's music—as contrasted with mere neo-classicism and neo-romanticism—is as striking today as it was some thirty years ago when Eugene Goossens said of it: 'Modern music in England began with Cyril Scott.'

Utterly different as are Cyril Scott and Benjamin Britten in emotional background and musical texture, they have one rare attribute in common: a realistic visualisation of tone qualities. With both of them there is next to no discrepancy between the sounds envisaged in the 'inner ear' and the notes set down on paper. This infallibility of tonal imagination makes for music that is easy in rehearsal, exhilarating in performance. All Britten's works, small or large, that I have heard (from his early *Our Hunting Fathers*,[11] to *Peter Grimes*[12] and his re-hash of *The Beggar's Opera*[13]) present this condition of facile and rewarding performability. The scoring

---

[7] 1946.

[8] (1897–1988), the leading English oboist of his generation.

[9] To a new edition of Thomas Malory's work (1893–4).

[10] (1868–1933), German lyric poet; friend of Scott, who translated over two hundred of George's poems into English.

[11] Op. 8, to a text by Auden (1936).

[12] Op. 33 (1944–5).   [13] Op. 43 (1948).

of *Peter Grimes* has a freshness and vividness that might be compared to a
picture painted in pure (unmixed) colors.

Many years ago Sir Thomas Beecham is reported to have said, anent
English folksongs: 'These little tunes have done more to spoil British
music than any other single factor' (or words to that effect). And Martin
Cooper discerningly mentions archaism (as which must be classed the
cult of folksong) as one of the pitfalls of much recent British music.[14]
Nevertheless, it is possible to point to the last three symphonies of
Vaughan Williams (the Fourth, in F minor; the Fifth, in D major; the
Sixth, in E minor[15]) as examples of a basic artistic amelioration springing
from a long association with folksong and archaic polyphony.

In primitive music, in folksong and in Gregorian chant, true melody is
still unimpaired—if by 'true melody' we mean expression by means of a
tonal line that is complete in itself, full of its own volition and unenslaved
by outside domination (for instance, domination by harmony or rhythm).
In Africa and Java can be heard poly-melodic music in which the melodic
initiative is uncurtailed. But with the injection of harmonic consciousness
into European music (at the time of the beginnings of harmony) it was
inevitable that the melodic intervallic choices would be limited to intervals lending themselves to those few combinations then considered concordant, and that the rhythmic life would be tied down to stereotyped and
foreknowable beat-groupings in order that the voices making up the
musical texture might know, without too much uncertainty, when to
carry out chord changes. By the end of the nineteenth century—in spite of
wonderful gifts of harmonic expressiveness and rhythmic variety having
been added to the tonal palette—the impoverishment of melody had
become so complete that composers as diverse in temperament and aesthetic goals as Grieg, Rimsky-Korsakov, Delius, Ravel and Martin
Loeffler all felt that they had to turn to a study of primitive music, folksong or Gregorian chant in order to establish within themselves a familiarity with the nature and workings of pristine melody. Ravel's *Boléro* is a
shining result of a familiarity thus acquired. Other composers had to turn
to a study of pre-Bach polyphony to counteract the nineteenth-century
tune-on-top obsession—an obsession clearly mirrored in the modern
Icelandic word for music accompaniment: 'undirspil' (under-play). To see
what an immersion in folkish and early polyphonic traditions has accom-

[14] 'Current Chronicle—England', *Musical Quarterly*, 34 (1948), 423–9. Cooper calls archaism
and amateurishness 'the twin blights of so much music produced in England since the beginnings
of our musical renaissance' (p. 429).
[15] Respectively: 1931–4, 1938–43, rev. 1951, 1944–7, rev. 1950.

plished for Vaughan Williams we need only examine the first movement of his Fifth Symphony (D major), where extended melodiousness, full of curve-beauty (analogous to Hogarth's 'curve of beauty' in the pictorial arts[16]) has replaced the short-breathed themes of the classic symphony and where the nineteenth-century tune-on-top procedure is replaced by a polyphonic texture in which all the voices enjoy an exact equality of melodic pregnance and importance. Similar conditions of true melodiousness and all-permeating many-voicedness are consistently present throughout the last three Vaughan Williams symphonies. If this great genius has been able to restore true melody and genuine polyphony to the symphonic idiom he may be said to have accomplished a major amelioration—not merely a betterment of his own music, but a basic betterment of the whole art of music itself.

I consider it not unlikely that in time Vaughan Williams's Sixth Symphony will come to be regarded as his greatest; for it seems to leave this planet—a locality to which this composer's muse has never been firmly tethered—and to float off into the realms of space, providing his listeners with a veritable music-of-the-spheres. If Cyril Scott's contention that music is prophetic (that it foretells world trends and world events) is true, then such music as Vaughan Williams's Sixth may well presage a period of journeys to the moon and similar explorations by mankind of worlds hitherto unvisited ('further than ever comet flared or vagrant stardust swirled').

If Vaughan Williams may be said to have restored a more potent practice of melody to symphonic writing, William Walton, in works such as his recent Violin Concerto and his String Quartet in A minor,[17] may be said to have invested these same forms with a new beauty originating in a supreme extension of the possibilities of rhythmic development. His Quartet tallies what Bach conceivably might have accomplished if his polyphony had been mainly rhythmic instead of mainly intervallic. The drastic use of orchestral unisons in the *tutti* of Walton's exciting Violin Concerto[18] reminded me of the overwhelming effect of chant-unisons in Maori war dances. In these newer Walton works—despite their extreme sophistication and finely chiselled details—the composer reveals anew that primitive forcefulness that made his *Belshazzar's Feast*[19] so breathtaking.

---

[16] Outlined in *The Analysis of Beauty* (1753) by English painter and engraver William Hogarth. See also Essay **46**.

[17] 1938–9 and 1945–7, respectively.

[18] 1938–9.   [19] 1930–1.

During my stay in England the brilliance, raciness and touching humanism of contemporary American music were well represented by numerous performances of works by Aaron Copland, Walter Piston, Menotti,[20] Morton Gould, Gershwin, and others. But the most advanced of all American experimental composers known to me—Arthur Fickénscher—seemed totally unrepresented.

One of the pleasantest surprises offered by music heard in England was the acclaim given to three composers from three countries hitherto inconspicuous for the production of outstanding musical genius: Sweden, Denmark, Switzerland. In two months Swedish composer Dag Wirén's[21] Serenade for String Orchestra[22] netted no less than five broadcast performances. And well this work merits the attention it is receiving, for in sunny-clear musical speech it conveys a deeply moving emotional message. I know of no previous Swedish composition that rises to such heights of universal appeal.

The unmistakable Danishness of Herman Sandby's musical idiom is in electrifying contrast to the pale cosmopolitanism of earlier Danish composers, such as Niels Wilhelm Gade and J. P. Hartmann[23] and to the more recent Germanisms of Carl Nielsen and others. Here, at last, is Danish music that, in its glowing warmth and robust sweetness, tallies the bland vigour of the Danish scene. Most men's music sounds man-made; but Sandby's carries with it the illusion of nature herself singing. Out of his orchestra came sounds as of the sea, as of the winds. And this illusion is very germane to the intentions of this composer, for since his late teens he has consistently devoted his great gifts to celebrating in tones the seascapes and shore-scapes of his native Zealand.[24] The originality of this nature music is documented by the fact that several of his most remarkable works in this field (such as *Youth* and *Sea-mood*) were penned several years before the great nature tone poems of Delius (*Brigg Fair*, *The Song of the High Hills*, *North Country Sketches*, etc.). In Sandby's later works (the three symphonies,[25] *Pastorale d'automne*,[26] *By the Sea Shore*, *Sunrise by the Sea*) his mastery of orchestration and the integrity and freshness of his musical ideas combine to evoke a positively overwhelming impression of cosmic force, purity and passion.

The Swiss composer Frank Martin's *Petite Symphonie Concertante*,[27]

[20] Gian Carlo Menotti (b. 1911).

[21] b. 1905.   [22] 1937.

[23] (1805–1900). In his typescript Grainger gave the example of Peter Lange-Müller instead of Hartmann.

[24] Sjælland.   [25] 1930, 1938, and 1942/3.

[26] For orchestra (1937).   [27] 1945.

for harp, harpsichord, piano and double string quintet, is one of the most exquisite chamber music works of all time. The pithiness of its themes, the deft unfoldment of its form, the originality of its harmonic texture exert a compelling fascination upon the listener throughout the twenty-two minutes' duration of the composition. It has been exhaustively examined and revealingly described by Jacques de Menasce in the April 1948 issue of the New York *Musical Quarterly*.[28]

---

[28] 'Current Chronicle—Switzerland', *Musical Quarterly*, 34 (1948), 271–8. Grainger's type-script for this essay continued thus: I will touch here on only one aspect of its many-sided appeals: the allurement of its harp-harpsichord-piano combinations. There is a baffling likeness and unlikeness between the sonorities of these three instruments that constitutes a delectable teasement to the listening ear and provides that slight element of confusion that is so pleasing in the more complicated flights of our art. In the plucked-and-hammered-string group the harpsi-chord fills out a tone-color gap between the harp and the piano—much as, in the military band, the saxophones fill out a tone-size gap between the weaker woodwinds and the stronger brasses, and much as marimba and vibraharp, in the 'tuneful percussion' family, fill out a tone-height gap between glockenspiel and xylophone on the one hand and tubular chimes and Swiss hand-bells on the other.

Ferruccio Busoni's caustic witticism at the expense of Swiss music, made on the occasion of a festival of Swiss music in Switzerland in the early nineteen-twenties ('After all, the best Swiss music is the Overture to *William Tell*') seems much less funny since the appearance of Frank Martin's masterwork.

43 *The Saxophone's Business in the Band*
(1949)

Editor's Note: The world-renowned composer knows all about bands and writes for them. The sax family, he says, is indispensable, but must be balanced and complete.

We are told that Adolphe Sax created the saxophones with the definite intention of providing a group of instruments midway in tonal strength between the weaker sonorities of the reeds and the stronger sonorities of the brass. This office the saxophone family most satisfactorily performs—that is to say, as long as the family is complete and tonally well-balanced within itself. It is obvious that if the soprano saxophone is missing, the tone-strength gap between the oboe and the cornet will be unfilled, and that Adolphe Sax's laudable intention (of providing a delicately gauged transition from weaker to stronger instruments within each register) will be frustrated in the soprano tonal area. Likewise, if the baritone saxophone be missing, the midway tone-strength between the bassoon and the trombone will be lacking and Sax's subtle scheme brought to nought in the bass tonal area.

Balance of Tone

As regards the balance of tone within the saxophone family itself, as intended by Sax: It is obvious that planless aggregations of saxophones, such as are all too often encountered in carelessly organized bands—say 6 altos, 3 tenors, and 1 baritone—can never produce a good balance of tone. And one cannot but wonder what it is that makes budding saxophonists so unreasonably inclined to mass on one or two voices of an instrumental family, every member of which is amenable and highly rewarding to play—a family, moreover, in which the changing from one voice to another is singularly easy and convenient.

I think this tendency to mass upon the alto and tenor saxophones and to neglect the other members of the family is the result of an old-fashioned 'soloistic' view of music and an inability to grasp the chief

Source: *Instrumentalist*, 4/1 (Sept.–Oct. 1949), 6–7.

advantage to be gained from band playing, which latter is rich harmonic experience.

Harmonic Experience in Band

Band conductors fail in their esthetic duty if they do not impress upon band members an understanding of the major role played by harmony in all types of art music from the 13th century onward—whether the five hundred years of exquisite church music that preceded Bach; whether the great giants of the 'classical' and 'romantic' periods, such as Beethoven, Schubert, Wagner, Brahms, or César Franck; whether the tonal harmonies of Arnold Schoenberg or the rich expressiveness of American jazz and swing harmonies.

Need of Complete Family

Band conductors also should be able to convince saxophone players of the utter necessity of maintaining a complete saxophone family in each band. As a soloist, a player may justifiably prefer one saxophone voice to another, but band leaders must prevent this soloistic viewpoint from playing havoc with the effectiveness of the saxophone group as a whole and of the band as a whole.

The neglect of the soprano saxophone is an extraordinary example of musical shortsightedness; for what is any family of instruments without its soprano? What would the brass section be without cornets or trumpets? What would a choir of voices be without its sopranos? What would a string quartet be without its first violin? There are differences of opinion concerning the tonal quality of the soprano saxophone. Personally, I consider it the most beautiful and characteristic voice of the entire saxophone family. It has a rich bucolic timbre that enables it to take, in the band, a place similar to that occupied by the oboe in the orchestra.

(In passing, it may be remarked that the oboe plays a very different role in the band from that which it does in the orchestra. In the orchestra it gives the impression of great intensity and considerable prominence—owing to the gentle tonal background of the strings. In the band the oboe sounds much thinner—and produces an impression of distance and frailty—owing to the larger number of brass instruments and the massing of clarinets. This is where the soprano saxophone, with its stronger-than-oboe sonority, is able to prove its unique value in the band—as a kind of band oboe.)

Ensembles and Pre-Bach Music

Adolphe Sax was deeply wise in arranging the tonal ranges of his saxophone voices in conformity with the vocal ranges—the soprano saxophone covering the range of the soprano voice, the tenor saxophone covering the range of the tenor voice and so on. Because of Sax's foresight in this particular, it is possible for saxophone ensembles to play, without rearrangement, the entire vocal polyphonic literature of the Christian Church from the 13th century up to and including Bach. This embraces the finest works of such giants as Guillaume de Machaut, Guillaume Dufay, Bedingham,[1] John Dunstable, Josquin des Près, Antonio de Cabezón, Adrian Willaert, Alfonzo Ferrabosco, and many others. These masterworks sound as satisfying on saxophone groups as they do on the voices for which they were originally written.

Roots of Saxophone Popularity

The world-wide and ever-growing popularity of the saxophone must, I think, be considered part of that great revival of interest in melody that characterizes our century. For just as the zenith of interest in technical display—on the voice, the piano, the violin, etc.—must be placed in the 19th century, so the 20th century may be described as a period of vital concern with every type of melodiousness: in Gregorian chant, in primitive music, in folksong, and in polyphonic melodiousness (as in Vaughan Williams, for instance). There is some connection between what we call 'melody' (as distinct from 'tune', 'theme', 'motive') and the human voice; in fact, true melody may be described as 'that kind of music which naturally suits the human voice'. Since the saxophones are perhaps the most voice-like of all musical instruments, it naturally follows that they have a great role to play in the present-day revival of interest in melodiousness.

---

[1] Johannes Bedyngham (d. 1459/60), English composer.

Music Trends and World Peace

In every age there appears to be some main urge behind the combined activities of humanity. There is little doubt in my mind that in our age the main urge behind all humanity is a longing and striving for world peace. Musically speaking, this urge seems to me to manifest itself not only in the yearning soulfulness and affectionate emotionalism of the greatest composers of our era (men such as Frederick Delius, Sibelius, Cyril Scott, Herman Sandby, Sparre Olsen, Arthur Fickénscher, George Gershwin and Duke Ellington), but also in the current fondness shown for sustained, singing, emotionally expressive instruments such as the saxophones. The war-loving periods of Frederick the Great and Napoleon were heralded by the war-like music of Bach (Brandenburg Concertos), Haydn, Mozart, Beethoven and Rossini—music in which militaristic fanfares, march-like drum-beating and mass-dragooned rhythms prevail. This war-attuned musical trend swayed the 'military' band in its early days, to which band programs of the last century clearly attest. But what a change has come over band music and band programs in our lifetime! The band has become the vehicle *par excellence* for music of a peaceable, loving, yearning, intimate nature. Think of the *English Folksong Suite* of Vaughan Williams,[2] the *Suite Française* of Darius Milhaud,[3] the *Shoonthree* of Henry Cowell,[4] the band Fantasy on *Porgy and Bess*![5]

To this deepening and beautifying of the Band's message, the saxophone family (with its yearning voices, its exquisitely balanced harmonies, its heart-throb sonorities) has most valuably contributed. This, in my opinion, is the main office of the saxophone family in the military band: To refine our emotional susceptibilities, thereby making music-lovers (and perhaps mankind, in general) more receptive to all those delicate stirs that make for world-peace and for a gentler and happier life on this globe.

It may sound fantastic, to many readers, to wish to trace some connection between music and world trends. On the other hand, there must be some deep-rooted instinct abroad in humanity today that makes it willing and anxious to spend so much time and money upon the art of music.

I have noticed that those who attempt to ascribe world trends to economic factors are usually unable to foretell human history at all accurately, while philosophers like Cyril Scott—who take a soulful or esoteric

---

[2] For military band (1923).   [3] For band (pub. 1947).
[4] For band/orchestra (1939, pub. 1943).   [5] 1936.

view of life—seem much cleverer at being able to forecast world movements and events before they happen. Is this, perhaps, because we live in a
subtle rather than in a simple world—a world in which the underlying
forces are emotional rather than materialistic?

About Delius

(1950–52)

Although Delius[1] did not have a drop of English blood in him, he epito-
mized for me the English gentleman-of-leisure, his birth and up-growing
in Yorkshire having so completely anglicized him. I do not know a note of
his music, I do not recall an incident in his life (as it was known to me personally), that is not somehow rooted in a preoccupation with pleasure.
His life knew no obligations, no irresistible urges, no onerous devotions.
He floated on the top of life, a rich man's son, able to indulge his every
whim and with no religious or moral scruples to limit his pursuit of pleasure. In place of the more enslaving feelings and instincts (that bind most
men to the wheel of life) Delius responded to a myriad of interests that
kept him amused but left him free. A vast range of subjects constantly
engaged his mind, each subject tolerantly viewed from his vantage point
of utter leisure. His approach to life—to the different continents, races,
and cultures—was not only leisured but positively touristic. His absorbing interest in the Negro (as instanced in *Florida*,[2] *Koanga*,[3] and
Appalachia) was purely that of an onlooker—a highly sympathetic
onlooker, but merely an onlooker none the less. The same detachment
(that of a rich man able to relish to the full what the world subserviently
had to offer him in the way of entertainment) characterized his fondness
for Scandinavia, as revealed in his songs to Jens Peter Jacobsen's (Danish)
poems[4] and in *Eventyr*,[5] *Fennimore and Gerda*,[6] *The Song of the High
Hills*, etc. I once asked Delius whether his *Song of the High Hills* pur-
ported to be the high hills 'singing about themselves' or whether the

Source: Peter Warlock, *Delius*, rev. and supplemented by Hubert Foss (London: Bodley Head,
1952), 170–80.

[1] In revising Peter Warlock's (Philip Heseltine's) book about Delius, originally published in
1923, Hubert Foss asked Grainger to contribute this memoir. Grainger's essay, dated 23–25 June
1950, sometimes draws heavily on ideas found in his longer article, 'The Personality of Frederick
Delius' (*Australian Musical News*, 24/12 (July 1934), 10–15), written shortly after Delius's
death.

[2] (1887, rev. 1889), orchestral suite.

[3] (1895–7), lyric drama.

[4] As in most of the *Seven Danish Songs* (1897) and *An Arabesk* (1911). Jacobsen (1847–85),
poet and novelist, was initiator of the Naturalist movement in Denmark.

[5] (1917), for orchestra.

[6] (1909–10), opera on Delius's text after Jacobsen's *Niels Lyhne*.

music tallied the impressions of a man under the spell of Alpine scenery. His reply was expectable: 'The impressions of a man walking through the hills.' The touristic quality of his *Paris*[7] is obvious.

This Marcus Aurelius of music was indeed the musical aristocrat of his era. He did not so much create new ideas and idioms as respond exquisitely to those brought to him by others. He was a man of taste culling the honey gathered for him by worker-bees, himself no worker-bee. Delius was not the kind of man ever to collect folksongs 'in the field'. He would not even appreciate a folksong unless it came to him already harmonized. Thus he fell in love with my setting of *Brigg Fair*[8] and at once asked my permission to use the tune in a more spun-out form. This was typical. We are told that Jelka[9] would select a text for him that she thought would inspire his muse (such as the text of *Songs of Sunset*[10]) and leave it on his desk. Delius would find it lying there, would respond exquisitely to it, and without a word passing between him and Jelka would start to compose it.

My own experience with Delius follows a similar course. Around 1910 he had complained to me that his orchestral works were neglected in England. I wrote him saying that England was studded with fine amateur orchestras that would rejoice to do Delius works, but lacked the 3rd clarinet, 3rd bassoon, and 5th and 6th horns that his scores so often called for. 'Write some short pieces for small orchestra', I urged, 'and English orchestras will devour them.' His next letter told that he had taken my advice, had already finished a short piece for small orchestra (based on a Norwegian melody) entitled *On Hearing the First Cuckoo in Spring*, and was at work on a second one, *Summer Night on the River*.[11] His receptive, rather than originative, attitude was manifest again in his choice of the Norwegian folksong around which *On Hearing the First Cuckoo* was woven. He did not take a folksong that he himself had collected in Jotunheim (Norwegian Alps), but one already bewitchingly harmonized by Grieg in his *Norwegian Folk Songs*, Opus 66—which volume I had played to Delius when I first met him in 1907. In similar receptive (rather than originative) vein did Delius conceive his transcendental *Song of the High Hills*; for all his seventeen mountaineering trips to Norway it did not occur to him to write a work about the hills until he had heard my two

---

[7] 'The Song of a Great City' (1899), for orchestra.
[8] (1906, pub. 1911), the seventh of Grainger's British Folk-Music Settings.
[9] Delius, née Rosen.
[10] (1906–7), to text by Dowson.
[11] These two works comprise Delius's *Two Pieces for Small Orchestra* (1911–12).

Hill-Songs, the first written in 1901–1902, the second 1901–1907. *The Song of the High Hills* was written around 1912.

There is no criticism implied in my calling Delius a receptive and derivative, rather than an originative and creative, composer. Some geniuses (Guillaume de Machaut, William Lawes, Schumann, Grieg, César Franck, Debussy) are born to be innovators, while other, equally great geniuses (Guillaume Dufay, Bach, Wagner, Gabriel Fauré, Ravel) are cut out to be perfecters, culminaters. (As when Wagner played to Liszt a passage in his *Ring* that was strongly reminiscent of a theme of Liszt's, and Liszt remarked, 'I am thankful to see it immortalized.')

It is light-shedding to compare with each other these two transcendental feats of emotional harmonization of the same tune ('In Ola Valley'): Grieg's in his Opus 66[12] and Delius's in the *First Cuckoo*. Both are ineclipsably lovely, resourceful, touching, sensitive. But while Grieg's is concentrated, pristine, miniature, and drastic, Delius's has the opulent richness of an almost over-ripe fruit and the luxurious long decline of a sunset.

Indeed, much of Delius's music has the quality of sunsets and sunrises. When asked why so many of his compositions 'faded out', rather than closing with some more definite ending, Delius would answer, 'Most things in nature happen gradually, not abruptly.' He wanted his musical forms to tally the processes of organic change so prevalent in nature as we see it.

And the larger part of Delius's music has the wistfulness of a sunset. This, again, was part of his aristocratic detachment, his touristically coloured emotionalism, his nostalgia of a rich man's leisured son. For Delius, like all hedonists, was lonely in his pursuit of pleasure. Meaning was not lent to his life by kin or children, or by allegiance to 'isms', beliefs, movements, or causes. He saw the infinite sadness of life without the slightest participation in those intoxicating enthusiasms that lead to life's catastrophes. When in his *Pagan Requiem*[13] he mourned all the young men killed in the wars, he did so without sensing, behind the wars, any pardonable necessity. At the same time his freedom from religious belief, moral convictions, and nationalistic frenzies left him singularly untragic, even in his laments. His sadness—even at the deaths of the young men lost in the wars—was always mild. 'Sad, but not crushed by sadness.'

With such aristocratic detachment as was his, it is not surprising that Delius was somewhat mischievous in his non-creative, non-nostalgic

---

[12] No. 14.   [13] 1914–16.

moments. Of Sir Hubert Parry[14] he is reported to have said to Elgar: 'It is a good thing Parry died when he did; otherwise he might have set the whole Bible to music.' To me Delius told of seeing, at Havre, during the first German war, an under-sized Cockney soldier chatting with a gigantic Sikh. Turning to Delius, the Cockney said: 'I tell you, them chaps is proud to talk to the likes of us.' Hearing that a certain musician who was visiting him at Grez was an ardent Christian Scientist (a fact that the musician had not mentioned to him, however), Delius regaled his guest with 'Of all the stupid things in the world, Christian Science is the stupidest.' And he went on by the hour teasing the man. But had the man admitted his belief and stuck up for it, Delius would have listened to him quite tolerantly, and a jolly and graceful discussion might have ensued. For Delius was never afraid of argument, nor impatient in it. Nor was he thin-skinned. In my own case, knowing I was a vegetarian and a teetotaller, he would ask me at meal-times what I was eating and drinking. When I replied, 'Bread and milk and a glass of water' (or the like), he would lay into me with 'Why be such a kill-joy? Why don't you enjoy a nice big steak and a mug of beer?' If I retorted, 'Yes, and be blind and paralyzed like you at the age of seventy', he would merely chuckle.

On the occasion of his sixtieth birthday, a dinner in his honour was given in Frankfurt-on-Maine, where he and Jelka were then (1923) living for a while, and among the speeches made was one by a German poet that cruised around the thought 'Into our midst has come one of the rich ones of this world—rich in feelings, rich in genius, rich in experience, and a member of a rich nation.' In replying, Delius did not waste much time in politeness and euphemisms, but passed quickly into a dissertation of the witlessness of the various European countries. First, he enlarged on the mistakes of the Allies, bringing smiles of satisfaction to the faces of his German listeners, who were beginning to comfort themselves with the thought 'At last, a foreigner who sympathizes with us.' But these smiles vanished when Delius added, 'But the Germans have been the stupidest of them all.'

A side of Delius that seems to me to be too seldom mentioned was his touching devotion to his childhood memories of Yorkshire. He was never tired of praising the kindliness of the mill-hands in his father's mills in Bradford, and his unwaning love for the scenery of the Yorkshire moors is nobly witnessed in his *North-Country Sketches*—a masterwork still too rarely heard.

---

[14] (1848–1918), English composer and academic.

Delius's innate tolerance and passiveness were shown in countless little ways. During the earlier years of his paralysis and blindness he was nursed by a succession of German male nurses who came to tend him as part of their duties as members of a religious brotherhood. A ministration by one of these 'Brothers' that Delius especially appreciated was the reading aloud of stories by Edgar Wallace. In these reading-aloud sessions the author's name was invariably pronounced 'Vall-lah-kay', and the names of the characters in the stories were equally translated into the unrecognizable. But it never occurred to Delius to correct the Brother's pronunciation.

Delius's unruffled courage was evidenced not only in the stoical (one might almost say 'unfeeling') way he accepted the collapse of his own health—so robust in earlier years—but also in many small and unforeseeable incidents of his daily life. One day, during his complete blindness and helplessness, a group of us had him seated in a chair in the middle of his boat while we rowed him about on the river Loing. The oar of a passing sculler grazed his chest. In the mildest, most unmoved voice Delius asked 'What was that?'

Delius's typically English irresponsibility was shown in a thousand ways, but never more amusingly than when interrogated about details of his scores by his unfailing benefactor and friend, H. Balfour Gardiner,[15] when the latter was correcting proofs of reprints of Delius's orchestral works. Gardiner kept asking about a kettle-drum passage in *The Song of the High Hills* in which the kettle-drummer, with only four drums, was required to play five different notes and with no time to tune between them. Gardiner insisted that the passage, as printed, could not be played. But all he could get out of Delius was: 'I don't know how he plays them; I only know he *does* play them.' Gardiner was disconsolate: 'The trouble is that the drummer does *not* play the 5th note, but Fred never notices it.'

I have dwelt at some length upon the more negative side of Delius's nature—upon his indifference, detachment, irresponsibility, and mischievousness. But I must not fail to mention his positive and humane qualities. In some ways he was the kindest and most protective man I have ever met. When in 1923, after a great tragedy in my life,[16] I confided to Delius that I was not sure that I would have the courage to return to my life in America, Delius said, quick as a shot: 'My dear lad, you can always

[15] Gardiner had even bought Delius's house at Grez so that the Deliuses would not have to move in their final years.

[16] The suicide of Grainger's mother in April 1922.

find employment here with me. You can be my amanuensis, or my gar-
dener, or my chauffeur, or anything you like.'

No colleague ever did so much for my music as Delius did. When he
and I first met in 1907, I had never heard a work of mine performed,
except some small choruses at the most rural of Competition Festivals—
in spite of the fact that my chief works had long been composed (my main
compositional activity lying between the ages of sixteen and twenty). This
condition of being unperformed was of my own choosing. Both my
parents were invalids and my first interest in life was to be able to provide
for them and their comfort. This I was doing by means of my pianistic
career, which I feared would be upset if my compositions (with their
irregular rhythms, endless chains of unresolved discords, and monotonous form-lengths—things then unheard of) were performed and
aroused great opposition. This argument left Delius unmoved. After
seeing my *Hill-songs* I and II, *English Dance*, *Marching Song of
Democracy*, *Green Bushes*, *Father and Daughter*,[17] etc., he insisted that
my first duty was to put my innovations to the acid test of performance.
'You are the only one who can judge whether they sound as you want
them to or not. And you can only tell after you have them performed.' So
when Elgar, in 1908 or 1909, asked Delius to join him in forming a
'League of British Music' Delius's only stipulation was that representative
works of mine should be given at the first Festival of the League. That is
how my *Irish Tune from County Derry* and *Brigg Fair* came to be sung at
the Liverpool Festival of 1909.

In 1923—although his health was then fast failing—Delius arranged to
have two of my most important and least saleable works published in
Vienna.[18] And in the same year he attended all the six orchestral rehearsals
of *Hill-song* I, *Marching Song of Democracy*, and *The Warriors* that I held
in Frankfurt-on-Maine, although he had to be taken from his house to the
rehearsal hall in a wheeled chair and carried up and down stairs at the
latter place. Composer never had truer colleague than I had in Frederick
Delius, and when he died I felt that my music had lost its best friend.

Our artistic comradeship was based not merely upon the great similarity of certain elements in our music (when I first saw *Appalachia* in 1907, I
thought Delius's and my harmonic idiom well-nigh identical), but equally
upon like-mindedness in other fields. Our outlook on life was very

---

[17] (1908–9), the first of Grainger's Settings of Dance Folksongs from the Faeroe Islands.

[18] *Marching Song of Democracy* (pub. 1925), and *Hill-Song* No. 1 (pub. 1924), both issued by
Universal Edition. Universal Edition also published Grainger's arrangement for two pianos of
Delius's *A Dance Rhapsody* in 1923.

similar, our artistic tastes met at many points. Both of us considered the Icelandic sagas the pinnacle of narrative prose. Both of us knew the Scandinavian languages and admired the culture of Scandinavia as the flower of Europeanism. Both of us worshipped Walt Whitman, Wagner, Grieg, and Jens Peter Jacobsen. Both of us detested the music of the Haydn-Mozart-Beethoven period.[19] 'If a man tells me he likes Mozart, I know in advance that he is a bad musician', Delius was fond of saying.

During the years 1923–1927—when Delius's health was failing so rapidly and before he enjoyed the boon of Eric Fenby's saintly presence at Grez-sur-Loing—Balfour Gardiner and I used to travel yearly to Grez in order to play to Delius on two pianos. Our offerings consisted mainly of arrangements of Delius's works: the first *Dance Rhapsody*, *The Song of the High Hills*, *On Hearing the First Cuckoo in Spring*, *Summer Night on the River*, *Brigg Fair*, the 'Cello Sonata, the 'Cello Concerto, etc.

Outside his own music Delius was not easy to cater to musically, for he indulged himself in a good deal of enfant-terrible-ism in his artist attitudes and excelled in altering his taste from one year to another. One year he would ask for Bach; the next year he would say, 'You know, Bach always bores me.' But Chopin and Grieg he never turned against. He preferred Ravel to Debussy. He had no patience with Richard Strauss, Mahler, or Hindemith. He scoffed at 'the wrong-note craze'. He cared everything for the final artistic product and nothing for those efforts that aim at building new tonal media for the future. Thus, he took no interest in my 'large chamber music', in which I endeavoured to achieve with larger groups of single instruments a tonal balance more delicate than that natural to the symphony orchestra, with its top-heavy and ill-balanced sonorities. 'Why do you bother with experimental forms of orchestration?' he would say to me, 'I find the conventional orchestra does everything I want it to.' And so it did, in his case.

To my ears it seems that in Delius's music the most tender and subtle feelings of modern life are voiced in the most poignant and soul-reaching tonal speech. As Bach and Wagner did in their time, so Delius in his time seems to have succeeded in gathering together all that is of celestial beauty in the tonal idiom of his generation, and to have succeeded equally in divesting his muse of all that is pedantic, ugly, dry, and mechanical. And I feel that the loftiness and spirituality of his music rise directly out of the beauty of his inner being—out of his freedom from ambition, ignoble eagerness, and other forms of worldliness; out of his passiveness,

---

[19] See Essay **34**.

tolerance, compassionateness, and tenderness; out of the inborn gaiety and gracefulness of his aristocratic nature.

As a result of Delius's being widely seen in public and memorably photographed in the last years of his life, when he was such a frail invalid, and as a result of Delius-worshippers in their writings having emphasized the last and painful phases of his illness, it seems that a needlessly mournful and gloomy Delius-legend has been allowed to grow up, a legend not necessarily false to his condition at the close of his life perhaps, but certainly very misleading as an interpretation of his complete personality during the main part of his life, including the period in which he produced his greatest masterpieces—from 1890 to 1922.

I did not see Delius during the last year-and-a-half of his life, being in Australia at that time. But from 1907 to 1932 I was continually in touch with him, both by means of personal contact and by letters. And in all that time I noticed nothing of the grimness and sternness that some saw in him. Delius, as I knew him, was remarkable for his gracious and graceful companionship, for the gaiety and lightness of his moods, for his good-humoured delight in fair and open-minded argument, for his unfailingly humane outlook on world affairs and his flair for foreseeing future events and conditions, for his complete cosmopolitanism ('I am a good European', was his frequent quotation), for his light-shedding anecdotes, for his perfect at-one-ness with Jelka (to see them sitting together, listening to his music, was to be present at a sort of sacrament), for his wish to see all people free and happy ('do what you want' was his constant advice to one and all), for his helpfulness to those he admired, and (as already dwelt upon) for his frank pursuit of pleasure. To be with Delius was to feel oneself participating in a constant ritual celebrating enjoyment. In spite of this, one had a feeling that the depths of his nature—the nostalgic and compassionate sides—were being hidden away, in ordinary daily intercourse. For the central core of his soul—his perception of the infinite sadness of life—one had to turn to his music.

45 Henry Balfour Gardiner: Champion of British Music

(1951)

(or, Henry Balfour Gardiner: True Socialist of Music)

In the passing of Henry Balfour Gardiner[1] we have lost one of the most vital, original & emotionally compelling composers of our era and a heroic figure in musical history. His was a life-changing personality. No one could hear this man's music and not sense the immense well-spring of goodness that filled his soul; no one could meet him and not realise his transcending benevolence, and also his almost alarming sincerity. He was a great force in the British recovery of musical leadership in Europe, both in his own captivating creations and in what he was able to help his fellow British composers to accomplish.

I always feel that the irresistible appeal of Balfour Gardiner's music—behind all its flowing melody, heart-searching harmonies and surging orchestration—lay largely in what I would call the 'social justice' underlying his choice of subjects and texts. He felt so sharply the injustice meted out to countryfied, heroic and athletic types in our Nordic civilisation—the country lad to be hung for stealing a sheep (*The Stranger's Song*[2]), the parlous lives of sea-faring adventurers (*News from Whydah*,[3] *An Old Song Resung*[4]), and the like. This deep compassionate sympathy with the misfortunes of heroic types informs even his most lively and vigorous pieces with a singular poignancy. I doubt whether any other composer, in any country, has mourned these tragedies of courageous lives so drastically and consistently in music. Such music, consciously or unconsciously, provides a subtle but powerful persuasion in the direction of those social changes that have altered all our lives so fundamentally in the last half century. If it did not do this, and did not help us to better understand the stirs for betterment within us and around us, it would indeed be a sorry waste of time in an age as crucial and as over-busy as our own.

Source: Typescript dated 9–11 Apr. 1951. Grainger Museum, Melbourne.

[1] On 28 June 1950.
[2] To a text by Thomas Hardy (1902–3).
[3] Ballad for chorus and orchestra (1911), to a text by Masefield.
[4] (Pub. 1920), for unaccompanied chorus, to a text by Masefield.

A similar, passionate urge to counteract injustice coloured all his attitudes towards his fellow composers. He saw that British music, by 1911, had risen to great heights, but that its achievements were not fully recognised. So he set out to make these achievements manifest, and he succeeded as none before him had done. British compositions had had outstanding successes before the Balfour Gardiner concerts of 1912–13, of course. But never before had the whole body of contemporary British music had a chance to display the entire gamut of its vast and many-sided appeal.[5]

An important factor in Gardiner's ability to force recognition for his fellow composers lay in the fact that he (unlike so many modern musicians) had never allowed himself to sink into the degradation of specialisation. He was an all-round musician in the way that Wagner, Bach and Adrian Willaert were. He was always a magnificent pianist, a resourceful conductor, a keen critic, an incorrigible musical hedonist and a thoroughly practical music-maker—in addition to being one of the most inspired and heart-throb-some composers of his generation.

Unlike the conductors, singers and instrumentalists who can perform music but do not understand its soul-life, and unlike the composers (like Frederick Delius) who perfectly understand the soul-life of music yet have no knack of forth-sounding it, Balfour Gardiner struck a perfect balance between the inner and outer life of music, between the creative and the executive impulses.

The ordinary professional, specialised conductors had been far too far removed from the creative side of the musical age they lived in, far too unfamiliar with the personalities of the greatest composers of their era, to be able to present convincingly the works of these great men in their true guise. The specialised conductors could conduct glibly enough; but they nearly always took wrong *tempi* and aimed at effects foreign to the nature of the music. So the inner message of the new works was only half sounded, half heard, in many cases.

But there was none of that groping uncertainty in Balfour Gardiner's renderings. He knew the emotional backgrounds of his colleagues' works intimately and knew which of their compositions were most representative and telling. He knew their 'intentions' from repeated sessions with them at the piano and from endless discussions with them. And what he did not already know he found out through inquiry. The sight of Gardiner conducting rehearsals for his 1912–13 concerts, with half an eye

---

[5] The eight Balfour Gardiner Choral and Orchestral Concerts, the programmes of which are reproduced in Stephen Lloyd, *H. Balfour Gardiner* (Cambridge: Cambridge University Press, 1984), 242–5.

on the orchestra and the other half on the composer of the work in hand—
with every nerve strained to realise the most minute intentions of the
latter—was an object lesson in the art of winning artistic (as distinct from
mere professional) victories. The overwhelming success of his concerts
came largely from Gardiner's ability to completely sink his immense personality into the national task, the super-personal issue.

No doubt this super-personal viewpoint arose partly from Balfour
Gardiner's unique ability to form noble and enduring friendships with
composers of outstanding genius—Cyril Scott, Norman O'Neill, Roger
Quilter, Frederick Austin, Frederick Delius, Arnold Bax, Gustav Holst,
William Henry Bell,[6] Benjamin Dale,[7] Denis Blood.[8] Goethe said that no
man understands a greatness not his own, and it may be that it was
Balfour Gardiner's own greatness as a composer that enabled him to
gauge the true significance in the works of his colleagues.

It was difficult to get Gardiner to explain the exact purpose of his concerts; but there was never any doubt in my mind that the impulse behind
them was deeply patriotic. And when I said to him 'Aren't your concerts
like a kind of flag?', he answered 'Yes, I suppose that is as near as we will
get to it'. And how meticulous he was in carrying out his brave scheme—
how protective of the manuscripts entrusted to his care, how passive to
the will of each composer, how aristocratically stern in his subordination
of the performers to the behests of the score, how careful and tasteful in
his selection of works and building up of programmes!

And what programmes! Fancy a series of only 8 concerts that could
boast of giving for the first time anywhere, or for the first time in London,
such works as *Life's Dance* by Delius, *Fantasia on a Theme of Thomas
Tallis* and the first and second *Norfolk Rhapsodies* by Vaughan Williams,
the first Symphonic Dance and *Fair Helen of Kirconnel* by Cyril Scott,
News from Whydah by Balfour Gardiner, *Enchanted Summer* and
Christmas Eve on the Mountains by Arnold Bax, *Beni-Mora* and *The
Cloud Messenger* by Gustav Holst, *The Baron of Brackley* by William
Henry Bell, and *Father and Daughter* and *Mock Morris* by myself! The
public acclaim of several of these works was almost frenetic and all the
works presented may be said to have made their mark.

Gardiner's own reaction to the reception of certain numbers at his concerts was typical of his impersonal, all-fatherly heart. He came to me, after
the end of his first (1912) series with a very perplexed face, saying: 'Your
and my short pieces have had far too much popular success, and it isn't

---

[6] (1873–1946), English teacher and composer, resident in South Africa from 1912.

[7] (1885–1943), English teacher and, in his earlier years, composer.

[8] (b. 1917), English composer-friend of Gardiner during his final decade.

fair to the larger works of other composers. So next season I propose to put your and my things at the beginnings and ends of programmes, where they can't make as much effect.'

The effect of the Balfour Gardiner concerts on English musical life was electrical. Conductors & other concert-givers—who, with rare exceptions, up to then had regarded the giving of contemporary British music as a rather painful duty—suddenly realised the vital appeal of this music to the British public. The 'British Composers' Night' at Sir Henry Wood's 'Promenades'[9] that followed soon after the Balfour Gardiner concerts, was typical of the change in attitude.

Gardiner's concerts, and his staunch support of noble musical organisations such as the Royal Philharmonic Society[10] and Kennedy Scott's[11] exquisite 'Oriana Choir',[12] were not his only benevolent contributions to the welfare of British musical life. If any gifted composer fell ill, or needed a rest, Gardiner would whisk him (and, if desirable, his family with him) off to Spain, or Algiers, or whatever part of the world seemed most favourable to recuperation.

Balfour Gardiner did not derive the pleasure from composing that the wholesome strains of his music might lead us to expect he would. He always insisted that composing made him feel wretched. No doubt he was too severe a critic of his own creations to be happy for long about his art works. And in the mid nineteen-twenties he suffered a sore compositional set-back that he himself described in the following characteristic words: 'My muse left me.' From then on he did little actual composing, though he threw his unique orchestrating skill with much enthusiasm into the task of scoring the music of others.

As a result of his sharply critical attitude towards his own compositional output several of his finest masterpieces in large form (such as *English Dance, Philomela, A Berkshire Idyll, Dream-Tryst*) still remain unpublished, and in some cases unperformed. We, Balfour Gardiner's friends, who are aware of the full import of his genius, should see to it that these significant works are brought before the musical public that he served so long, so unstintingly and in such a variety of ways.[13]

---

[9] See Essay **26**.

[10] Gardiner had provided financial support for the Society during the First World War.

[11] Charles Kennedy Scott (1876–1965).

[12] Choir initiated in 1904 by Scott, Beecham, and others with the initial intention of singing solely English madrigals and advocating music of the Elizabethan school.

[13] Grainger appended a list of Gardiner's approximately fifty published and unpublished compositions.

Questionnaire

(1955)

A. Persons (artists and others) whom you like very much and who have contributed to form your personality:[1]

1. My mother, whose brave, tragic, anti-Christian, anti-legal, loving, benevolent, freedom-loving, heroic, volatile, ruthless, art-worshipping attitude to life & art influenced every aspect of my life and art.

2. A. E. Aldis[2] (an English painter in Melbourne, Australia) who boarded at our house for a time (when I was eight or nine), who often spoke in the Maori (New Zealand) language & started a 'native' (non-white) view of life & art in me.

3. Our Irish-Australian friends in Melbourne, who gave me a Roman-Catholic, heroic, reckless view of life.

4. Thomas A. Sisley[3] (English elocution teacher, trainer for the stage) who possibly aroused my interest in the Icelandic sagas & in Anglo-Saxon literature.

The composers you like and who have been of special importance to your musical development:

Among the dead: J.S. Bach, Handel, Wagner, Brahms, folksong, mediaeval music, native music (Javanese, African, South Sea), César Franck, Gabriel Fauré, Debussy, Ravel, Édouard Moullé, American jazz, Scottish bagpipes, oriental pipe music, Richard Strauss, Natalie Curtis's notations of four-voice Negro spirituals, John Jenkins, William Lawes, Antonio Ferrabosco, Purcell, Antonio de Cabezón, Schumann, Puccini, Mascagni. Contemporaries: Cyril Scott, Arnold Schönberg.[4]

Source: Undated typescript. Grainger Museum, Melbourne.

[1] Grainger prepared these answers for the volume *Musikkens Verden: Musik fra A–Z*, ed. S. Hagerup (Oslo, 1955). His answers suggest that he filled out the questionnaire in the early 1950s. His review of influences upon his life is very similar to that given in a letter to Cyril Scott of 10–11 Dec. 1951 (*The All-Round Man: Selected Letters of Percy Grainger, 1914–1961*, ed. Malcolm Gillies and David Pear (Oxford: Clarendon Press, 1994), 252–8).

[2] (*fl. c.*1890–1920), botanical and landscape painter, who moved to Australia in the late 1880s. In his Museum legend to Aldis, dated 24 Apr. 1956, Grainger claims that it was Aldis's 'reciting of of Maori chants that constituted his greatest influence upon me—& a life-long one'.

[3] (d. 1925), singer, dramatist and painter; he taught Grainger in Melbourne in the early 1890s.

[4] Schoenberg's presence among implicitly 'living' contemporaries suggests a date of 1951, or before, for Grainger's draft.

Perhaps literary & pictorial influences have an almost greater sway over my music than purely musical influences. Chief among these are: Greek vase-drawings & statues, the Icelandic sagas, the Anglo-Saxon Chronicle, Ibsen's *En Folkefjende*,[5] Evald Tang Kristensen's collections of Danish folksongs & folklore, Walt Whitman's *Leaves of Grass*, Edgar Lee Masters' poetry, Kipling, Swinburne, Thorsten Johnson's studies of criminal types,[6] George Moore, Laxness,[7] Johannes V. Jensen,[8] J.P. Jacobsen, the Scottish Border Ballads.

B. Which of your works do you consider the most important and characteristic?

	When composed	First performance
(*a*) *Marching Song of Democracy* (Chorus, organ & orchestra)	(1901–1917)	Worcester, Mass. 1917
(*b*) *Hill-song No. 1* (24 single instruments)	(1901–1902)	New York City, 1924
(*c*) *Hill-song No. 2* (24 single instruments)	(1901–1907)	London (Balfour Gardiner Concerts) 1913.
(*d*) *English Dance* (orchestra)	(1901–1909)	London (Palladium, Thomas Beecham) 1911.
(*e*) *Sketch for 'Sea-song'* (strings)	(1907)	(never performed)
(*f*) *Kipling 'Jungle-Book' Cycle* (14 numbers for small chorus & chamber music)	(1898–1945)	(Gustavus Adolphus College Choir, G.A. Nelson, cond.) St. Peter, Minn. [1942]
(*g*) *British Folkmusic settings* (about 50 numbers for various combinations)	(1898–1950)	Scandinavia, England, U.S.A. 1904–1950
(*h*) Example of 'Free Music' (string quartet)	(1935)	Australian Broadcasting Commission, Melbourne, 1935.
(*i*) *The Bride's Tragedy* (chorus & orch.)	(1908–1913)	1st Perf. London B.B.C, 1936[9]

[5] *An Enemy of the People* (1882).
[6] Thorsten Jonsson (1910–50), Swedish poet and journalist; New York correspondent for *Dagens Nyheter*.
[7] Halldór Kiljàn Laxness (b. 1902), Icelandic novelist.
[8] (1873–1950), Danish poet and novelist; Nobel Prize winner in 1944.
[9] Elsewhere Grainger claims the première of this work at the Evanston Music Festival in 1922.

*C. In order to enable the public to understand better the spirit of
these works, what explanations would you give if there was
a possibility of explaining your works before a performance,
for instance, in the programme?*

(*a*) Most of my music (*Kipling 'Jungle Book' Cycle, Hill-songs* 1 & 2,
English Dance, etc.) should be conceived as a Nordic revolt against
civilisation.

(*b*) The 'gliding intervals' in my 'Free Music' (begun about 1892) are an
attempt to introduce Hogarth's 'curve of beauty' into music.

(*c*) In my 'Free Music' the lack of rhythmic conformity (the lack of
beats in common between the parts that make up the musical texture) &
the lack of harmony (as practised heretofore) are in agreement with my
anti-moral & anti-social views of life.

(*d*) The emotional moods in my music represents (in my opinion) a
soft & yielding 'Pacific Ocean' attitude towards life, as contrasted with
the harsh & strife-some 'Atlantic Ocean' view of life common to
Europeans & Americans.

(*e*) My music should be fiercely & wildly performed, rather than in a
staid & modest manner.

*D. If you have a musical creed, a special artistic point of view, or some
remarks in connection with the manner of playing your music, we shall
appreciate it very much if you would explain yourself in a few words in
order to help your public to understand your music better.*

My musical creed (to which I do not consistently live up) is 'musical
democracy', my definition of 'democracy' being 'a chance for all to
shine in a starry whole'. I would like each voice, at all times throughout
my music, to enjoy equal importance & prominence. If this cannot
be realized, I would like each voice, at given moments, to have its
moments of prominence & importance, no less than all other voices.
In other words, the ideal of 'equality' is the keystone of my musical
endeavours.

In my 'Free Music' (the only music of mine to which I attach importance) I strive to tally the irregularity, the formlessness & the unforeknowableness of nature, as it is revealed to us. The driving force behind
my work as a composer is racialism & nationalism: I would not write any
music at all if it were not to express the unity of the Nordic (blue-eyed)
race, wherever found, to express the tragic position of the Nordic race

(out-numbered in a hostile world), & in the hopes of bringing honor and fame to my native land: Australia.[10]

Sketch for *Sea-song*, 1907

---

[10] Grainger elaborated his Australian view of 'Free Music' at the conclusion of an unpublished address to the American Guild of Organists on 29 Dec. 1952: 'From an Australian democratic standpoint it seems to me that the music of the future might justifiably aim at the following freedoms: 1. Melody freed from the tyranny of harmony; 2. Harmony freed from the narrow conceptions of concordance; 3. Intervallic freedom unrestrained by the hampering confines of scale & key; 4. Rhythm freed from the constant in-step-ness-with-Jim (coincidence between the rhythms of the various voices); 5. Musical form freed from unsuitable 'architectural' conceptions. In other words: FREE MUSIC.'

Appendix

List of Grainger's Writings

DAVID PEAR

This chronological list surveys the broader range of Grainger's published and unpublished writings, from which the selection on musical themes of this volume has been drawn. Grainger's letters, programme notes, and introductions to scores of his own or others' music have been excluded. As well as his lectures, talks, broadcasts, and formal essays, the list includes Grainger's forewords to books and the legends which he wrote for the collections of his Melbourne Museum. While every attempt has been made to compile a comprehensive list, the disparate nature of Grainger's written output, his propensity to dispatch articles or parts of articles to more than one journal, and the continuing rate of reclamation of his literary legacy ensure that the list will be found to be incomplete. All listed manuscripts or typescripts are held in the Grainger Museum, University of Melbourne.[1]

Essays reproduced or translated in this volume are identified with an asterisk (*) and following essay number. Essays reproduced, in part or in full, in *A Musical Genius from Australia: Selected Writings by and about Percy Grainger*, ed. Teresa Balough (Perth: University of Western Australia, 1982) are identified with a dagger (†).

'Brahms' F minor Sonata Op. 5', manuscript notebook entry dated 23 Sept. 1898.
*1 'A Recognition', undated manuscript notebook entry, c.1898–1900.
'Idea for a Sea Song (for when I can Handle It)', manuscript notebook entry dated 22 Dec. 1899.
'Methods of Teaching and Other Things' (including 'Inventions & Technical Sundries'), manuscript and typescript collection, 1901–4 ('Piano-teaching', 'Pitch-less, Beat-less Music', 'Results of Lessons with Th. Gerold', 'On Form & Themes in Form', *2 'A Few Formal Conceptions (sketches for an article, 'Theme as Related to Form in Music')' (1901), *3 'My Musical Outlook' (dated 10 Sept. 1902 to Feb. 1904), 'Instances of the Different Outlooks of Composers', and *4 'Beatless-Notation Machine' (1902/3).
'Intentions', manuscript collection, 1902–4.

---

[1] I am grateful to Helen Reeves Lawrence for the valuable bibliographic information provided in 'The "Past-Hoard-House": A Study of the Grainger Museum' (diss., James Cook University, 1984), 155–65, to Simon Perry for his bibliographic work as part of the Grainger Studies project, and to Malcolm Gillies and Bruce Clunies Ross for their many suggestions.

'Beatless-Music Typer', manuscript dated 25 Apr. 1904.

'Doings & Sayings at the Griegs, Troldhaugen, 25.7.07–4.8.07', contemporaneous manuscript.

'Personal Recollections of Grieg', *Musical Times*, 48 (1907), 720.

'Collecting with the Phonograph', *Journal of the Folk-Song Society*, 3 (1908), 147–242, comprising † 'Collecting with the Phonograph', 147–62, 'The Impress of Personality in Traditional Singing', 163–6, 'Signs and Accents used in this Journal', 167–9, † (in part) notations of songs, 170–242.

'My Most Treasured Possession', *Royal Magazine*, May 1908, 89–90.

*5 'The Music of Cyril Scott', *Music Student*, 5/2 (Oct. 1912), 31–3.

'Cyril Scott und seine Musik', *Rheinische Musik-und-Theater Zeitung*, 14/3 (18 Jan. 1913), 38–41.

*6 † 'The Impress of Personality in Unwritten Music', *Musical Quarterly*, 1 (1915), 416–35.

*7 'Modernism in Pianoforte Study', *Etude*, 33/9 (Sept. 1915), 631–2.

*8 'A Blossom Time in Pianoforte Literature', *Etude*, 33/10 (Oct. 1915), 709–10.

'The Genius of Frederick Delius', undated manuscript, *c.* late 1915.

*9 'Modern and Universal Impulses in Music', *Etude*, 34/5 (May 1916), 343–4, repr. as 'Universal Impulses in Music', *Musical Herald*, 1 Mar. 1917, p. 73.

Paragraph in 'Will the Music of Ultra-Modernists Survive? A Symposium by Eminent Musicians', *Etude*, 34/5 (May 1916), 331.

*10 'The World Music of To-morrow', *Etude*, 34/6 (June 1916), 412.

† 'Modernism in Pianoforte Study', in *Great Pianists on Piano Playing*, ed. James Francis Cooke (Philadelphia: Theodore Presser, [1917]), 364–81 (includes both Sept. 1915 and Oct. 1915 *Etude* articles plus additional material).

*11 'Richard Strauss: Seer and Idealist', in Henry T. Finck, *Richard Strauss: The Man and his Works* (Boston: Little, Brown & Co., 1917), pp. xvii–xxv.

'Freedom of Thought in Piano Study', in Harriette Brower, *Piano Mastery: Second Series* (New York: Frederick A. Stokes, 1917), 1–17.

'Percy Grainger and his Mother', undated typescript probably by Grainger, *c.* late 1917.

'Re *Irish Tune from Co. Derry* and *Shepherd's Hey*', undated manuscript, *c.* early 1918.

'The Two-Fold Vitality of Anglo-Saxon Music', *Etude*, 36/2 (Feb. 1918), 81–2, repr. in *Australian Musical News*, 7/11 (May 1918), 285, 291–2.

*12 'The Unique Value of Natalie Curtis' Notations of American Negro Folksongs', *New York Times Book Review*. 14 Apr. 1918.

*13 'Possibilities of the Concert Wind Band from the Standpoint of a Modern Composer', *Metronome Orchestra Monthly*, 34/11 (Nov. 1918), 22–3.

'Has the Art of the Piano Reached its Zenith or is it Capable of Further Development?', *Etude*, 36/12 (Dec. 1918), 755–6.

'Grettir the Strong', manuscript dated 9 Dec. 1919.

*14 'Let Us Sit in Wait No Longer for the Advent of Great American Composers—They are with Us Already', *Quarter-notes of the Brooklyn Music School Settlement*, 10 Dec. 1919, pp. 1–3.

'The Potential Influence of Anglo-Saxon Folk Music upon Art Music', typescript and manuscript dated 4 Oct. 1920, revised as 'The Influence of Anglo-Saxon Folk Music' (see below).

'Possibilities of Variety & Balance of Tone-Color in Modern Scoring', manuscript dated 21 Oct. 1920.

*15 'The Influence of Anglo-Saxon Folk Music', Music Number, *Evening Post* (New York), 30 Oct. 1920, pp. 1–2.

'Grieg's *Norwegian Bridal Procession*: A Master Lesson', *Etude*, 38/11 (Nov. 1920), 741–5.

*16 'þýðing íslenzkrar tungu fyrir Engil-Saxa' [The Value of Icelandic to an Anglo-Saxon], *Timarit* (Winnipeg) 2 (1920), 60–8, repr. in Grainger's original English on *From a Southern Shore* (Melbourne), 1 (1985), 30–8.

Paragraph on 'Mechanical Damper for the Harp', *Eolian Review*, 29 (1921), 29.

*17 'Nordic Characteristics in Music', typescript dated 5 Mar. 1921 for lecture delivered at Yale University on 6 Mar. 1921.

'A General Education for Music Students', *Musical Courier*, 83/5 (31 July 1921).

'Rough Ideas for Capt. [Jerome] Hart's Article in *The Globe*, Sept. 17, 1921', typescript dated 31 Aug. 1921, partially repr. in Jerome Hart, 'Beatless Music as Heard by Grainger', *The Globe and Commercial Advertiser*, 17 Sept. 1921.

'Glimpses of Genius', *Etude*, 39/10 (Oct. 1921), 631–2, and 39/11 (Nov. 1921), 707–8.

'Method rather than Proficiency', manuscript probably dated 18 Nov. 1921.

*18 'Foreword to Students', in H. Balfour Gardiner, *Prelude 'De Profundis'*, Percy Grainger Guide to Virtuosity No. 1 (New York: G. Schirmer, 1923), pp. iv–viii.

'Dates of Important Events and Movements in the Life of Rose Grainger' and 'Summary of Rose Grainger's Cultural Tastes', in *Photos of Rose Grainger and of 3 Short Accounts of her Life by Herself, in her own Handwriting*, ed. Percy Grainger (private publication, 1923), 3–6.

Manuscript notebook entries of reminiscences dated Dec. 1922 to 19 May 1923.

'Facts about Percy Grainger's Year in Europe for Interviews', manuscript dated 24 Aug. 1923.

'You Can't Win without High Ideals', *Musician*, 28/11 (Nov. 1923), 11–12.

Contribution to 'A World Court of Eminent Musicians discuss "The Ten Great Masterpieces"', *Etude*, 42/3 (Mar. 1924), 150–1.

'Grainger tells of Beauties of Tahiti and Surroundings: Noted Pianist now in Australia writes of his Experience in Quaint and Distant Islands', *Daily Reporter* (White Plains), 5 Aug. 1924, p. 2.

*19 'What Effect is Jazz Likely to Have upon the Music of the Future?', *Etude*, 42/9 (Sept. 1924), 593–4.

*20 'To My Fellow-Composers', *Musical Life and Arts*, 1/2 (1 Oct. 1924), 35–6, and 1/3 (15 Oct. 1924), 67.

'Percy Grainger's Fighting Creed: His Guiding Principles as a Composer', *Autralian Musical News*, 14/3 (Oct. 1924), 17–18.

'Jazz and the Music of the Future', in *Great Men and Famous Musicians*, ed. James Francis Cooke (Philadelphia: Theodore Presser, 1925), 308–14.

'Foreword' to unidentified book by Charles L. Buchanan, typescript dated 2 Mar. 1925.

'Jazz', *Musikblätter des Anbruch*, 7/4 (Apr. 1925), 210–12.

*21 'Die Ergänzung der Schlagwerkgruppe im Orchester' [The Completion of the Percussion Family in the Orchestra], *Pult und Taktstock*, 3/1 (Jan. 1926), 5–9.

'More Important than Personality', *Australian Musical News*, 15/6 (Jan. 1926), 33.

'Sketches for The Life of My Mother & Her Son', manuscript dated 9 Feb. to 16 Mar. 1926.

'Percy Grainger on Ideals: You Can't Live without High Ones', *Australian Musical News*, 15/11 (June 1926), 45, 47.

'Never has Popular Music been as Classical as Jazz', *Metronome Orchestra Monthly*, 42/13 (July 1926), 10.

'Paderewski: King of Living Pianists', *American Legion Monthly*, 1/2 (Aug. 1926), 24–5.

'My Musical Discoveries', *Sun* (Brisbane), 26 Sept. 1926.

*22 'Sargent's Contributions to Music', in Evan Charteris, *John Sargent* (New York: Charles Scribner's Sons, 1927), 149–51.

'Vachel Lindsay: Troubadour', undated typescript, *c.*1927.

'Orchestral Problems in Smaller Centres: Use All the Means Available for a Good End', *Australian Musical News*, 16/6 (Jan. 1927), 11, 13.

'Orchestral Problems in Smaller Centres: On a Better Way of Securing True Rhythms', *Australian Musical News*, 16/7 (Feb. 1927), 11–13.

*23 'The Orchestra for Australia: Possibilities of a New Kind of Growing Up', *Australian Musical News*, 16/8 (Mar. 1927), 11–13.

*24 'The Gregarious Art of Music: Australia Needs the Get-Together Spirit', *Australian Musical News*, 16/9 (Apr. 1927), 13–15.

*25 'Music for Ensemble Players: Grainger Prepares an Enticing List', *Australian Musical News*, 16/10 (May 1927), 9.

'Percy Grainger's Pending Marriage', typescript dated 13 Mar. 1928.

'The Love-Life of Helen and Paris', manuscript dated 8 Nov. 1927 to 25 May 1928.

*26 'Impressions of Art in Europe', *Musical Courier*, 98/22 (1 June 1929), 8; 98/25 (22 June 1929), 6; 99/1 (6 July 1929), 8; 99/13 (28 Sept. 1929), 8, 31; 99/17 (26 Oct. 1929), 10, 12, also serialized, in part, in the *Argus* (Melbourne), Oct.–Nov. 1929.

'Anent Elastic Scoring', typescript and manuscript dating from Autumn 1929.

'Folk Music & Art Music', manuscript for lecture delivered at Yale University on 16 Dec. 1929.

'The Growth of our Westchester Groups', *Westchester County Recreation Community Year Book* (1930), 30, 57.

'Rough Sketch for Possible Speech by Percy Grainger at Poultney Bigelow's, Malden-on-Hudson, N.Y., Oct. 4, 1930', typescript dated 4 Oct. 1930.

'The Piano as Musical Joy-Bringer to Beginners', manuscript for American radio broadcast dated 27 Jan. 1931.

*27 'Democracy in Music', manuscript dated 9–10 July 1931.

'Read this if Ella Grainger or Percy Grainger are found Dead Covered with Whip Marks', manuscript dated 21 Aug. 1932.

*28 (in part) 'A General Study of the Manifold Nature of Music', typescript of course aims, summary of lectures, and examination papers, New York University, 20 Sept. 1932 to 9 May 1933.

*29 'Arnold Dolmetsch: Musical Confucius', *Musical Quarterly*, 19 (1933), 187–98, partially repr. in 'Balance of Tone: Varying Art-Music Habits', *Australian Musical News*, 24/8 (Mar. 1934), 7–9, and 'Arnold Dolmetsch: Musical Confucius—Ancient Lore will Affect the Future', *Australian Musical News*, 24/10 (May 1934), 8–9.

*30 † 'Can Music Become a Universal Language?', typescript of New York radio broadcast of 20 June 1933.

*31 'Melody versus Rhythm', typescript of New York lecture of 6 Dec. 1932, repr. with modifications in 'Melody versus Rhythm: Final Goal of Musical Art', *Australian Musical News*, 24/1 (Aug. 1933), 12–14, and with other modifications in 'Pointed Paragraphs', *Music News* (Chicago), 29 Sept. 1933, p. 9, and 6 Oct. 1933, p. 9.

*32 'Characteristics of Nordic Music', typescript of New York radio broadcast of 4 July 1933.

*33 'Can Music be Debunked?', typescript of New York radio broadcast of 27 June 1933, repr. with modifications as 'Can Music be Debunked? Let it Function in a Natural Way', *Australian Musical News*, 24/7 (Feb. 1934), 14*a*–*d*.

'The Goal of Musical Progress', manuscript of New York radio broadcast of 11 July 1933.

'Aldridge–Grainger–Ström Saga', manuscript dated 28 Sept. 1933 to 5 Jan. 1934.

*34 'Sublime and Frivolous Elements in Music: The Jazz Classics (Haydn, Mozart, Beethoven)', *Australian Musical News*, 24/9 (Apr. 1934), 4–8.

'The Personality of Frederick Delius', *Australian Musical News*, 24/12 (July 1934), 10–15.

'Music of the Past and the Ultra-Modern', *Wireless Weekly*, 7 Sept. 1934, 11–12.

'Grainger's Broadcast', *Listener In*, 8 Sept. 1934, p. 9.

Music: A Commonsense View of all Types (Melbourne: Australian Broadcasting Commission, 1934), consisting of synopses of twelve illustrated radio lectures: 'The Universalist Attitude toward Music', 4–12, 'Scales in the Past, the Present and the Future', 13–14, 'The Mongolian and Mohammedan Influences upon European Music', 15–16, 'Melody versus Rhythm', 17–20, 'Sublime and Frivolous Elements in Music', 20–4, 'The Superiority of Nordic Music', 24–5, 'The Development of European String Music', 25–7, 'Echo-Music', 27, 'Various Systems of Harmony', 28, 'Songs with Instrumental Accompaniment', 29, ' "Tuneful Percussion" ', 30–1, 'The Goal of Musical Progress', 31–2.

'Message to Pupils of the Correspondence Classes from Mr Percy Grainger, the World-Famous Composer-Pianist', *Our Rural Magazine* (Perth), 10/7 (Aug. 1935), 1.

*35 'Roger Quilter: The Greatest Songwriter of our Age', manuscript dated 27 July 1936.

'The Superiority of Nordic Music', *Quest*, 7/2 (Nov. 1937), 7–8.

'Foreword', in Richard F. Goldman, *The Band's Music* (New York: Pitman, 1938), pp. ix–xv.

Testimonial for Graham T. Overgard, typescript dated 25 Feb. 1938.

'Nordic English: Thots on Tone-Art', manuscript and collected press items dated 10 July 1935 to 11 April 1938.

'Sketches for my Book, *The Life of My Mother & Her Son*', manuscript dated 11 July 1922 to May 1938.

'Copy of Paul Gauguin's *Nevermore* Picture by Jelka Delius', typescript Museum legend dated Nov. 1938.

'Percy Aldridge Grainger's Published Compositions, 1st Editions', typescript Museum legend dated 2 Nov. 1938.

'Louis Pabst', typescript Museum legend, 3 Dec. 1938.

'William Gair Rathbone', typescript Museum legend dated 3 Dec. 1938.

'Programs of the Balfour Gardiner Concerts', typescript Museum legend dated 5 Dec. 1938.

*36 † 'Free Music', typescript Museum legend dated 6 Dec. 1938, repr. in *Recorded Sound*, 45–6 (1972), p. 16.

'Edvard Grieg's Desk', typescript Museum legend dated 8 Dec. 1938.

'Native Art and Stage Fright', typescript Museum legend dated 9 Dec. 1938.

'Alto Viol given by Arnold Dolmetsch', typescript Museum legend dated 25 Dec. 1938.

'When Yule-Tide Comes, by Sparre Olsen', *Australian Musical News*, 29/8 (Mar. 1939), 7.

'Why it Pays to Know North-Pinky (Scandinavian) Tongues', manuscript dated 20 May 1939.

'Thots & Call-to-Mindments: Sketches & Helps for "Aldridge–Grainger–Ström Saga" ', manuscript and collected press items dated 20 Nov. 1936 to 25 Dec. 1939.

'Nordic English', manuscript dated 5 Aug. 1940.

'Reaching your Goal at the Keyboard', *Etude*, 59/2 (Feb. 1941), 79–80, 134.

'The Purpose of Piano Ensemble Playing', typescript dated 5 Sept. 1941.

'Deemths', Book 1, manuscript and collected press items dated 18 Dec. 1940 to 28 Sept. 1942.

*37 † 'The Culturizing Possibilities of the Instrumentally Supplemented *A Cappella* Choir', *Musical Quarterly*, 28 (1942), 160–73.

'Three Stages of Music: Superstition, Religion, Science', manuscript notes for lecture delivered to the Women's City Club, Detroit, 18 Jan. 1942.

*38 'The Specialist and the All-Round Man', in *A Birthday Offering to C[arl] E[ngel]*, ed. Gustave Reese (New York: G. Schirmer, 1943), 115–19.

'Thunks', manuscript and collected press items dated 15 June 1937 to 29 Mar. 1943.

*39 'Grieg: Nationalist and Cosmopolitan', *Etude*, 61/6 (June 1943), 386, 416–18; 61/7 (July 1943), 428, 472; 61/8 (Aug. 1943), 492, 535, 543; 61/9 (Sept. 1943), 569, 616.

'English-Speaking Music & the War Effort', typescript for Australian broadcast dated 21 Oct. 1943.

'Deemths', Book 2, manuscript and collected press items dated 8 Oct. 1942 to 5 Apr. 1944.

'English-Speaking Leadership in Tone-Art', manuscript dated 20–1 Sept. 1944, repr. in Thomas C. Slattery, *Percy Grainger: The Inveterate Innovator* (Evanston, Ill.: Instrumentalist Co., 1974), 265–86.

'Compositional Life of Percy Aldridge Grainger', undated typescript, *c.* 1945.

'Ere-I-Forget', manuscript and typescript, 1944–7.

*40 'English Pianism and Harold Bauer', typescript dated 19 Feb. 1945.

'Sketch for Tail-Piece [of *Thanksgiving Song*]', manuscript dated 24–25 Feb. 1945.

'How I Became a Meat-Shunner', *American Vegetarian*, 5/4 (Dec. 1946), 4.

'Bird's-Eye View of the Together-Life of Rose Grainger and Percy Grainger', typescript dated 5–9 Jan. 1947.

*41 'How to Memorize Music', in James Francis Cooke, *How to Memorize Music: A Symposium upon Memorizing* (Philadelphia: Theodore Presser, 1948), 84–7.

'Notes on Whip-Lust', manuscript dated 24 Dec. 1948.

*42 'Music Heard in England', *Australian Musical News and Digest*, 39/12 (June 1949), 32–4.

† 'Remarks on Hill-Song No. 1', typescript and manuscript dated Sept. 1949, repr. in Thomas C. Slattery, *Percy Grainger: The Inveterate Innovator* (Evanston, Ill.: Instrumentalist Co., 1974), 260–4.

*43 'The Saxophone's Business in the Band', *Instrumentalist*, 4/1 (Sept.–Oct. 1949), 6–7.

*44 'About Delius', manuscript dated 23–24 June 1950, in Peter Warlock, *Delius*, rev. and supplemented by Hubert Foss (London: Bodley Head, 1952), 170–80.

*45 'Henry Balfour Gardiner: Champion of British Music', typescript dated 9–11 Apr. 1951.

'My Wretched Tone-Life', manuscript dated 16–22 July 1951, repr. in Thomas C. Slattery, *Percy Grainger: The Inveterate Innovator* (Evanston, Ill.: Instrumentalist Co., 1974), 258–60.

'The Organ as a Background Instrument', typescript and manuscript dated 29 Dec. 1952.

'Tone-Cribs (an attempt to show how composers "lift" musical ideas from each other, & from themselves)', typescript and musical examples, 12 Aug. 1954.

'Anecdotes', typescript and manuscript with entries dating between 8 Oct. 1949 and 6 Nov. 1954.

'National Characteristics in Modern Flagellantic Literature', manuscript dated 11 May 1955.

† 'The Aims of the Grainger Museum', typescript dated Oct. 1955, repr. in *Australian Journal of Music Education*, no. 18 (Apr. 1976), pp. 5, 7.

*46 'Questionnaire', undated typescript prepared for *Musikkens Verden: Musik fra A–Z*, ed. S. Hagerup (Oslo, 1955).

'H. Balfour Gardiner: The "Folk-Hero" of British Music', typescript Museum legend dated 23 Nov. 1955.

'Cyril Scott: Musical Originator', typescript Museum legend dated 10 Jan. 1956.

'R. Vaughan Williams: Greatness in Simplicity', typescript Museum legend dated Feb. 1956.

'Roger Quilter: Melodist', typescript Museum legend dated 10 Feb. 1956.

'Rose Grainger', typescript Museum legend dated 11 Feb. 1956.

'Evald Tang Kristensen: Danish Folksong Collector', typescript Museum legend dated 11 Mar. 1956.

'John H. Grainger', typescript Museum legend dated 15 Mar. 1956.

'From London Music-Room' and 'Contents of London Music-Room', manuscript and typescript Museum legends, 23 Mar. 1956.

'Arnold Dolmetsch: Musical Confucius', typescript Museum legend dated 18 Apr. 1956.

'English Folk-Singers', typescript Museum legend dated 18 Apr. 1956.

'A.E. Aldis: Painter & Linguist', typescript Museum legend dated 24 Apr. 1956.

'Thomas A. Sisley: Author, Painter, Poet & Elocution Teacher', typescript Museum legend dated 24 Apr. 1956.

'Karl Klimsch: Percy Grainger's only Composition-Teacher', typescript Museum legend dated 25 Apr. 1956.

'James Mackinnon Fowler: Legislator and Historian', typescript Museum legend, 1 May 1956.

'To Whoever Opens the Package marked "DO NOT OPEN UNTIL 10 YEARS AFTER MY DEATH"', manuscript dated 10 May 1956.

'Ernest John Moeran: "Back to the Land" in Music', typescript Museum legend dated 12 May 1956.

'Sir William Walton: Cosmic Composer', typescript Museum legend dated 13 May 1956.

'Robert Atkinson: Language-Reformer, Poet, Musician, Humanitarian', typescript Museum legend dated 21 May 1956.

'Edvard Grieg: A Tribute', *Musical Times*, 98 (1957), 482–3.

'Some Memories of Ralph Vaughan Williams', typescript dated 16 July 1959.

'Notes on Grainger's *Hill-Song* No. 2, by the Composer', typescript dated 16 Jan. 1960.

Index

00/133